W9-DCX-565

Lenore Sullivan

what to cook for company

what to cook

Illustrated by PAULINE CRANDALL

Published by
The Iowa State College Press, Ames

● For Lovers of Good Cookery, by

Lenore Sullivan

Professor of Institution Management
Iowa State College

for company

Copyright, 1952, by The Iowa State College Press.
All rights reserved. Composed and printed by
The Iowa State College Press, Ames, Iowa, U. S. A.

Second Printing, 1953
Third Printing, 1954
Fourth Printing, 1956
Fifth Printing, 1958

Library of Congress Catalog Card Number: 52–11248

To the students in my catering classes
who have contributed, tested, and
so cheerfully helped develop many of these recipes,
and whose enthusiasm and encouragement
have made this book a reality —
I dedicate this book

Foreword

DESIGNED for you who love the art of cookery and enjoy sharing it with your friends . . . that might well be the dedication for this book. The recipes exemplify good cookery, be the hospitality for one guest or many, the occasion afternoon tea, family barbecue picnic, buffet supper, or an elaborate dinner. The individual distinction of each recipe is born from years of testing and proving in Institution Management Catering Classes at Iowa State College.

Students enthusiastically enjoy Miss Sullivan's catering classes. Her sense of food appeal and her continuous search for unusual dishes inspire students. With her they have shared hundreds of their choice family recipes for laboratory testing. Many of them appear in this book, a delightful collection of special dishes from homes in all sections of the United States and many foreign lands.

Miss Sullivan occupies a position of national recognition among her professional associates for her Quantity Recipe File, which is used by food managers and dietitians in colleges and universities, hospitals, and other institutions. The home hostess and professional food service manager alike will welcome *What To Cook For Company* as a helpful and fascinating guide along the road to good food.

FERN W. GLEISER
Professor, School of Business,
University of Chicago

Preface

WHAT TO COOK FOR COMPANY is like Topsy — it just grew. The recipes and party suggestions represent a friendly exchange of favorite foods which students from all over have proudly contributed from their heirloom family recipes.

Indeed, the collection includes table delicacies on something of an international scale, for Iowa State College attracts students from faraway places such as the Philippines, Hawaii, England, Sweden, Finland, Panama, and India. These students, too, have brought us their cherished recipes. We have translated them into English when necessary, and have converted foreign weights and measurements into our equivalent of spoons and cups. We have experimented with the recipes to adapt them to the American food scene.

Our Catering Classes plan and serve teas, receptions, buffet suppers, after-theatre snacks, and other guest meals. A gala dessert party tops off the Catering Course. Then the buffet gleams and tantalizes with its display of fancy dishes girls like most to make, eat, and offer to their friends.

Invariably students ask for the recipes they have helped to develop. Through the years the number has multiplied until the time has come to introduce our treasures in a convenient standardized form for wider enjoyment. *What*

To Cook For Company presents the compilation. I hope you will have as much pleasure using the recipes and "treating" your guests as the girls and I experience with our cooking and hostessing adventures.

LENORE SULLIVAN

Acknowledgments

THE FIRST WORD OF APPRECIATION is for the help and inspiration of all of the students in the Catering Classes, whose enthusiasm and cooperation have made this book a reality.

I wish to express my deep appreciation to Dr. Grace M. Augustine, Head of the Institution Management Department of Iowa State College, for her encouragement in writing the book and her sympathetic understanding of the problems involved. My sincere thanks to the other members of the Staff for their interest and help.

I am especially indebted to Miss Katherine Goeppinger and Mrs. Helen Sevey of the editorial staff of the Iowa State College Press for their technical advice, helpful information, and inspiration in writing the book.

To the companies who have so generously allowed me to use their food photographs I express my sincere thanks and appreciation: American Meat Institute, General Mills, National Livestock and Meat Board, California Fruit Growers' Exchange, Poultry and Egg National Board, Wheat Flour Institute and H. J. Heinz Company.

To Pauline Crandall I am indebted for her sketches.

which so genuinely express the spirit of the book, as I am to Ruth O'Day Schonhorst for her helpful illustrative process sketches.

I wish to thank Mrs. Ruth Gaertner for her generous help in testing recipes in the laboratory and for her constructive criticism in judging them.

Additionally I am indebted to all of my other friends who, by their interest, have spurred me on to the book, *What To Cook For Company,* and who have aided me in its compilation.

Lenore Sullivan

Contents

Photographs

Appetizers, Savories, and Cocktails

APPETIZERS

Anchovy Spread
Avocado and Cheese Rounds
Bacon Cheese Puffs
Blue Cheese Cocktail Spread
Canapé Lorenzo
Caviar Spread
Cheese Cubes
Cheese Pecan Roll
Chile Con Queso
Christmas Star Canapés
Crab Meat Balls
Cucumber Cheese Rounds
Delectable Cheese Spread
Delectable Cheese with Garlic
Deviled Ham Canapés
Dill Pickle and Carrot Slices

Ham Rolls
Mexican Canapés
Mushroom Spread
Sardine Canapés
Sardine Cress Canapés
Shrimp in Cabbage
Stuffed Mushroom Caps
Stuffed Olives Wrapped in
    Broiled Bacon
Tomato and Anchovy Canapés
Tomato Appetizers
Tomato Canapés
Tomato Rings

Suggestions for Canapé Spreads
Suggestions for Garnishes

SAVORIES

Cheese Cocktail Biscuits
Cheese Mushrooms
Cheese Snacks
Cheese Straws
Cheese Twists
Chicken Biscuit Fingers
Empanadas Argentina

Empanadas Panama
English Meat Tarts
Mushroom Tarts
Shrimp Patties
Shrimp Turnovers
Walnut Cheese Pastries

COCKTAILS

Artichoke
Buffet Melon Bowl
Crab Meat
Crab Meat and Avocado
Cranberry-Ginger Ale
Fruit Ice Block for Punch Bowl
Grapefruit-Mint
Grapefruit Shrub
Hawaiian Frappé
Lime Juice
    Rainbow
Mulled Cider

Orange
    Green Crushed Ice
Orange and Banana
Orange Jellied Soup
Rhubarb
Rhubarb Juice
Shrimp
Tomato and Celery
Tomato Juice
    Accompaniments

Varied Suggestions

APPETIZERS start off a meal in grand style. They'll turn the opening party lull into an hour of easy conversation and pleasant hospitality. And the delectable tidbits whet appetites for more good things to come.

Here's the place to let your imagination go all-out. Plan a variety of tempting snacks — some hot, some cold. You may choose canapés — midget open-faced sandwiches with a well-seasoned spread, charmingly decorated, and hors d'oeuvres — highly flavored mixtures of foods to be eaten from the fingers or a wooden pick.

Serving is simple. Just load the trays with tasty finger foods and carry them to the coffee table or buffet. Pass chilled or hot beverages. Now the party will take care of itself. You can even turn the serving over to the man of the house while you sneak out to the kitchen for a last-minute look at dinner.

Or you may prefer to serve the first course at the table. Refreshing fruit, vegetable, or fish cocktails or hors d'oeuvre plates lend distinction to dinner.

You'll find the versatile appetizers will shine at many occasions other than dinner. Pass them, too, at open house, receptions, buffets, and informal parties.

In preparing canapés and hors d'oeuvres for a large party make some fancy ones, but make more of the easy varieties or you'll be spending all of your time in the kitchen and not enough with your guests. You can make up the mixtures, put them in attractive pottery and glass bowls, surround them with potato chips or crackers, and let the guests spread their own.

For canapés, cut bread in ¼-inch to ⅜-inch slices. Cut into rounds, strips, triangles, or other small shapes. In this way all of the bread may be utilized. Toast or sauté bread on one side, spread untoasted side with the mixture and garnish canapés attractively.

As a center of interest for the hors d'oeuvre tray, place olives, little cocktail sausages, vegetable cutouts, balls of cream cheese rolled in nuts, or any other tidbit you desire to use, on colored wooden picks. Stick these into a grapefruit, tomato, eggplant, or cucumber. Arrange canapés around this.

Appetizers

ANCHOVY SPREAD
About ¾ cup

¼ cup anchovy paste
1 tablespoon butter, creamed
2 tablespoons finely chopped chives

1 teaspoon lemon juice
4 tablespoons cream cheese

Combine the ingredients and blend well. Use as a spread, or as a dip for potato chips.

AVOCADO AND CHEESE ROUNDS
About 2 dozen

12 slices bread, ⅜ inch thick
1 3-ounce package cream cheese
4 tablespoons mashed avocado
¼ cup mayonnaise
2 teaspoons lemon juice

¼ teaspoon Worcestershire sauce
⅛ teaspoon salt
1 teaspoon onion juice
1 small clove garlic, finely mashed
Parsley and pimento

Cut 2 circles of bread about 2 inches in diameter from each slice of bread. Blend together the cheese, mashed avocado, mayonnaise, lemon juice, and seasonings. Spread thickly on rounds of bread. Garnish each round with a tiny sprig of parsley and a small piece of pimento.

BACON CHEESE PUFFS
About 2 dozen

12 slices bread, ⅜ inch thick
¼ cup finely cubed bacon
Whites of two eggs

½ pound American cheese, grated
¼ teaspoon baking powder
¼ teaspoon salt

Cut 2 rounds of bread 2 inches in diameter from each slice. Fry bacon until crisp. Drain on absorbent paper. Beat egg whites until stiff, but not dry. Add the grated cheese, baking powder, and salt. Sauté bread rounds in butter on one side until lightly browned. Spread the other side thickly with cheese mixture. Sprinkle a bit of crisp bacon on top. Slip under broiler 2 to 3 minutes, or until cheese melts. Serve immediately.

BLUE CHEESE COCKTAIL SPREAD
About 3 cups

4 ounces Blue cheese
2 tablespoons mayonnaise
2 3-ounce packages cream cheese
1 12-ounce package cottage cheese
1 teaspoon Worcestershire sauce

1 clove garlic, finely minced
1 tablespoon lemon juice
3 tablespoons cream
½ cup chopped chives

Combine ingredients and blend thoroughly. Add chives last. Use as spread or dip for cocktail crackers or potato chips.

CANAPE LORENZO
Crab Meat and Cheese Appetizer
Makes 12

6 slices bread, ⅜ inch thick
1 teaspoon chopped onion
2 tablespoons butter
1 cup crab meat, fresh or canned
½ cup cream
1 tablespoon flour

½ teaspoon paprika
¼ teaspoon mustard
¼ teaspoon salt
5 tablespoons Parmesan cheese
2 tablespoons cream

Cut 2 rounds of bread 2 inches in diameter from each slice. Sauté on one side. Cook onion in butter. Add crab meat, cream, flour, and seasonings; cook, stirring constantly until mixture thickens. Heap the crab mixture on the unbrowned side of bread. Place on cooky sheet. Make a cheese paste by mixing the Parmesan cheese with the 2 tablespoons cream and put a heaping tablespoon on top of each canapé. Heat in very hot oven (450°) 3 to 4 minutes or until the cheese melts. Serve immediately.

These hot crab meat canapés may be served on an assorted canapé tray or may be made larger and served as a hot appetizer.

CAVIAR SPREAD
About 1¼ cups

2 3-ounce packages cream cheese
1 2-ounce can imported caviar
½ teaspoon finely grated onion

1 teaspoon lemon juice
¼ cup cream
Dash of salt and paprika

Combine the ingredients and blend well. Spread on crackers.

CHEESE CUBES

Cut 1-inch thick slices of bread from sandwich loaf. Cut into 1-inch cubes. Cut small hole in bread cube. Butter top and sides. Mix together one 3-ounce package cream cheese and ½ pound grated American cheese. Season well with Worcestershire sauce, onion juice, dash of cayenne pepper, etc. Fill hole in bread cube with cheese mixture. Place in hot oven or under broiler until a delicate brown. Serve immediately.

CHEESE PECAN ROLL
1 roll

3 3-ounce packages cream cheese
2 tablespoons cream
½ pound Blue cheese
2 teaspoons grated onion

1 clove garlic, finely minced
½ teaspoon paprika
1 cup chopped pecans

Mix cream cheese with cream. Blend with Blue cheese. Add onion, garlic, and paprika. Form into roll about 1 inch in diameter. Spread chopped pecans on waxed paper. Roll cheese in pecans. Wrap in waxed paper and chill. Slice in thin slices. Serve with crackers and assorted cheeses.

CHILE CON QUESO
Peppery Cheese Appetizer
6 servings

1 tablespoon butter
1 tablespoon flour
½ teaspoon salt
¾ cup tomato juice

½ cup grated American cheese
⅛ teaspoon cayenne pepper
6 slices bread, ⅜ inch thick

Melt butter in double boiler; add flour and salt. Add tomato juice slowly, stirring constantly. Add cheese and cayenne pepper. Cook until mixture is smooth and thick. Cut 3-inch round of bread from each slice. Sauté lightly on one side. Heap tomato mixture on unbrowned side of bread round. **Serve hot.**

CHRISTMAS STAR CANAPES
1 dozen

12 slices white bread, ⅜ inch thick
1 tablespoon anchovy paste
4 tablespoons butter
3 tablespoons finely chopped truffles
3 tablespoons finely chopped green olives
3 tablespoons finely chopped capers
2 hard-cooked eggs, whites and yolks separated
12 curled anchovy fillets
1 pimento

Cut star-shaped canapés from each slice of bread. Blend anchovy paste and 2 tablespoons of the butter until smooth. Sauté bread on one side in remaining butter until lightly browned. Spread unbrowned side with anchovy butter. On the points of the stars carefully heap the finely chopped truffles, olives, capers, hard-cooked egg whites, and sieved egg yolk — a different color on each point. In the center, place a curled anchovy; then, in the center of the anchovy, a tiny star cut from the pimento.

CRAB MEAT BALLS
About 2 dozen

½ cup tomato juice
1 egg, beaten
1 cup dry bread crumbs
½ teaspoon salt
Dash of pepper
1 teaspoon finely chopped parsley
1 teaspoon finely chopped celery leaves
1 teaspoon finely chopped chives
1 6½-ounce can crab meat, flaked
1 teaspoon lemon juice
1 egg, beaten (for dipping)
Fine dry bread crumbs (for dipping)

Add tomato juice to beaten egg. Add remaining ingredients and mix thoroughly. Roll into balls about ¾ inch in diameter. Dip balls in egg, then in fine dry bread crumbs. Fry in deep hot fat (365°) 2 to 3 minutes or until golden in color. Serve on wooden picks on hors d'oeuvre tray.

CUCUMBER CHEESE ROUNDS
1 dozen

1 clove of garlic
1 3-ounce package cream cheese
⅓ cup finely diced peeled cucumber
½ teaspoon grated onion
2 teaspoons vinegar
Dash of salt
¼ teaspoon paprika
12 slices rye bread
2 tablespoons softened butter

Cut garlic clove in half. Rub bowl, in which spread is to be mixed, with cut clove. Combine cheese, cucumber, onion, vinegar, salt, and paprika, and mix together in garlic-rubbed bowl. Blend until of good spreading consistency. Cut circles of rye bread, 2 inches in diameter. Spread each round with the softened butter; then spread with cucumber cheese mixture.

DELECTABLE CHEESE SPREAD
About 2½ cups

3 3-ounce packages cream cheese	½ cup stuffed olives, sliced thin
½ cup mayonnaise	Onion juice
¼ cup cream	Salt and pepper

Mix cream cheese, mayonnaise, and cream. Add sliced olives, onion juice, salt, and pepper. Chill. Serve on crackers or potato chips.

If you prefer, this spread may be heaped in a bowl, sprinkled with paprika, and placed in the center of a tray. Surround bowl with crackers or potato chips and let each guest help himself.

DELECTABLE CHEESE WITH GARLIC

For a variation of Delectable Cheese Spread, omit the stuffed olives and use ¼ pound of Blue cheese instead. Add a very small amount of mashed garlic. Mix well.

DEVILED HAM CANAPES
Makes 10

5 slices white bread, ⅜ inch thick	2 hard-cooked eggs, whites and
1 3-ounce can deviled ham	yolks chopped separately
1 tablespoon mayonnaise	1 tablespoon mayonnaise
¼ cup finely chopped water cress or parsley	

Cut bread into rounds 2 inches in diameter, 2 per slice. Sauté one side of bread rounds in butter until lightly browned. Combine deviled ham, 1 tablespoon of mayonnaise, and the water cress. Spread the unbrowned side of bread round with this mixture. Arrange a border of finely chopped egg white around the outer edge. Fill centers with the chopped egg yolk combined with the remaining tablespoon of mayonnaise.

DILL PICKLE AND CARROT SLICES

Select dill pickles and carrots which are about 1 inch in diameter. Hollow out the centers with a sharp knife or apple corer. Stuff centers with cream cheese to which has been added a few drops of onion juice and Worcestershire sauce. Slice about ¼ inch thick and use on assorted hors d'oeuvre tray.

HAM ROLLS
6 rolls

1 3-ounce package cream cheese	Dash of white pepper
6 stuffed olives, chopped fine	Dash of cayenne pepper
1 teaspoon prepared horse-radish	¼ teaspoon paprika
2 tablespoons cream	6 thin slices boiled ham
¼ teaspoon salt	

Soften cream cheese. Add olives, horse-radish, cream, and seasonings. Mix well. Spread mixture on slices of boiled ham. Roll each slice. Place in refrigerator to chill. Cut into 1-inch lengths. Stick wooden pick in each to keep them rolled.

These ham rolls make attractive tidbits to stick into a grapefruit, egg-plant, or other holder in the center of an hors d'oeuvre tray.

MEXICAN CANAPES
Savory Fish Appetizers
Makes 9

1 cup finely minced cooked white-fish	¼ cup chopped nuts
	¼ cup mayonnaise
3 tablespoons chopped sweet pickles	9 3-inch rounds buttered toast
	2 tablespoons Parmesan cheese
2 tablespoons chutney	Parsley or water cress

Combine fish, chopped pickles, chutney, nuts, and mayonnaise. Spread on toast rounds and sprinkle with Parmesan cheese. Brown in hot oven (400°) about 5 minutes. Garnish with parsley or water cress. Serve as an appetizer.

These may be made smaller and served on an assorted canapé tray.

MUSHROOM SPREAD
About 1 cup

2 tablespoons finely chopped mushrooms, canned or fresh	1 tablespoon finely minced chives
	4 drops Tabasco sauce
1 teaspoon butter	1 teaspoon paprika
1 3-ounce package cream cheese	2 tablespoons mayonnaise
½ teaspoon onion juice	

Sauté mushrooms in butter. Cream the cheese and add mushrooms and other ingredients. Blend well.

Use as a spread for canapés or serve in a bowl in the center of a tray, surrounded by crackers and potato chips.

SARDINE CANAPES
2 dozen

24 slices whole wheat or white bread, ⅜ inch thick
1 3¾-ounce can sardines
¼ cup butter, creamed
¼ cup lemon juice
Dash of Tabasco sauce

Dash of cayenne pepper
2 hard-cooked eggs, whites and yolks separated
1 pimento, cut into tiny shreds
½ green pepper, cut into tiny shreds

Cut diamond-shaped piece of bread from each slice. Sauté bread in butter on one side until lightly browned. Mash sardines and add creamed butter, lemon juice, Tabasco sauce, and pepper. Spread unbrowned side of bread with sardine butter. Chop egg whites very fine and put egg yolks through wire sieve. Border half of canapés with finely chopped egg white and at intervals garnish with shreds of pimento.

Vary canapés by decorating every other one with a border of the sieved egg yolk, topped with shreds of green pepper.

SARDINE CRESS CANAPES
1 dozen

6 slices white bread, ⅜ inch thick
¼ cup mashed sardines
2 tablespoons mayonnaise
1 teaspoon lemon juice
Dash of Tabasco sauce

1 bunch water cress
2 hard-cooked eggs, whites and yolks separated
Paprika

Cut bread into 2-inch circles and into crescents. Grease skillet lightly with butter. Sauté bread in butter on one side until lightly browned. Combine sardines, mayonnaise, lemon juice, and Tabasco sauce. Spread the sardine mixture on unbrowned side of bread. Remove the small leaves from a bunch of water cress and with a small skewer or wooden pick press the tiny leaves into the topping near the edge. This makes a wreath around the canapé. Parsley may be used instead of the cress. Sprinkle the center of every other canapé with finely chopped egg white and a dash of paprika, and sprinkle the others with sieved egg yolk. Serve on tray of assorted canapés.

SHRIMP IN CABBAGE

1 pound fresh shrimp   Sea Food Cocktail Sauce (page 213)
1 medium head of cabbage

Cook fresh shrimp by dropping into boiling salted water (1 teaspoon salt to 1 quart) and allow to simmer, tightly covered, until shells turn pink, about 5 minutes. Drain, and rinse in cold water. Remove shells, leaving tails on shrimp. Remove black vein and rinse. Dry on absorbent paper.

Loosen outside leaves of cabbage; fold back like petals of a flower. Place shrimp on wooden picks and stick into cabbage. Let guests help themselves by dipping the shrimp into the cocktail sauce.

STUFFED MUSHROOM CAPS
Makes 12

1 dozen large mushroom caps   1 teaspoon lemon juice
½ cup flaked crab meat   Dash of salt
¼ cup finely chopped celery   2 tablespoons Parmesan cheese
1 tablespoon mayonnaise

Wash mushrooms and remove stems. Combine crab meat, celery, mayonnaise, lemon juice, and salt. Fill mushroom caps with this mixture. Arrange mushrooms on cooky sheet; sprinkle lightly with Parmesan cheese. Broil mushrooms or place in hot oven (400°) about 5 to 8 minutes. Insert wooden pick into each mushroom before serving. Serve as a hot hors d'oeuvre.

STUFFED OLIVES WRAPPED IN BROILED BACON
Makes 18

9 slices bacon   1½ dozen large stuffed olives

Cut each slice of bacon in half. Broil or fry bacon for a few minutes. Remove bacon from fat and drain on absorbent paper. Wrap each stuffed olive in ½ slice of bacon and secure ends with wooden pick. When ready to serve, place bacon-wrapped olives in hot oven (400°) or under broiler until bacon is crisp. Drain.

Stick olives into a grapefruit and place in center of hors d'oeuvre tray.

TOMATO AND ANCHOVY CANAPES
1 dozen

6 slices white bread, ⅜ inch thick
¼ cup butter, softened
¼ teaspoon curry powder
⅛ teaspoon salt
Dash of pepper

3 tomatoes, 2 inches in diameter
24 anchovy fillets
2 hard-cooked eggs, whites and
    yolks separated
Parsley

Cut bread into circles 2 inches in diameter, 2 per slice. Sauté one side in a small amount of butter until lightly browned. Blend softened butter with seasonings. Spread unbrowned side of bread circles with creamed butter mixture. Peel tomatoes, cut into ¼-inch slices, and place slice on top of bread. Lay two anchovy fillets crosswise on the tomato. Place alternately in open spaces finely chopped egg white and sieved egg yolk. Garnish with a small sprig of parsley in center of each.

TOMATO APPETIZERS
4 servings

1 large tomato, peeled
¼ cup French dressing

1 tablespoon mayonnaise
½ cup antipasto or crab meat

Cut tomato into 4 slices. Marinate tomato slices in French dressing. Drain. Mix mayonnaise with antipasto or crab meat and heap mixture on tomato slices. Serve as an appetizer for luncheon or dinner.

TOMATO CANAPES
Makes 8

8 slices white bread, ⅜ inch thick
1 Bermuda onion, sliced very thin
Salt and pepper

2 tomatoes, peeled
1 cup grated American cheese

Cut bread into circles 2½ inches in diameter. Sauté lightly on one side. Place a very thin slice of onion on unbrowned side of bread and season with salt and pepper. Cover the onion with a ¼-inch slice of tomato. Sprinkle a heaping tablespoon of grated cheese on top of tomato. Set in hot oven (400°) or under broiler until cheese melts. Serve at once.

TOMATO RINGS
Makes 8

4 slices white bread, ⅜ inch thick
1 tablespoon butter
¼ teaspoon curry powder
2 tomatoes, 2 inches in diameter

½ cup French Dressing (page 249)
2 tablespoons finely chopped parsley
Pâté de foie gras or cream cheese

Cut bread into circles 2 inches in diameter, 2 per slice. Sauté one side of bread until lightly browned. Blend butter and curry powder. Spread unbrowned side of bread circle with curry butter. Peel tomatoes and cut into slices ¼ inch thick. Marinate in French dressing. Place 1 slice of marinated tomato on buttered round of bread. Sprinkle tomato slices with finely chopped parsley. Place small ball of pâté de foie gras or cream cheese in center of each.

SUGGESTIONS FOR CANAPE SPREADS

Chopped egg, pickle relish, mayonnaise
Cream cheese with:
Blue cheese
Capers and horse-radish
Chives
Green pepper, onion juice, mayonnaise
Mayonnaise, onion juice
Pickle relish
Worcestershire sauce

Deviled ham, mayonnaise, pickle relish
Flaked fish (as shrimp, lobster, tuna, crab meat), French dressing, mayonnaise
Liver sausage, mashed, and mayonnaise
Sardine or anchovy butter

SUGGESTIONS FOR GARNISHES

Black caviar
Capers
Green pepper
Parsley
Pimento
Red caviar

Rolled anchovy fillets
Stuffed olive slices
Truffles, finely chopped
Water cress
White of egg, chopped
Yolk of egg, sieved

Savories

CHEESE COCKTAIL BISCUITS
About 3 dozen

1 cup grated sharp Cheddar cheese
½ cup butter
½ teaspoon Worcestershire sauce
1½ cups flour
½ teaspoon salt
Dash of cayenne pepper
½ cup mango chutney

Blend cheese and butter together and mix until light. Add Worcestershire sauce, flour, salt, and cayenne pepper. Mix thoroughly. Form into 1-inch roll, wrap in waxed paper and refrigerate for several hours. Slice in ¼-inch slices. Place on ungreased cooky sheet, 15½ x 12 inches. Put about ¼ teaspoon chutney in center of each slice. Bake in moderate oven (375°) 12 to 15 minutes. Remove with spatula to cooling rack.

These crisp, flavorful cheese cocktail biscuits may be used as a salad accompaniment or on a tray of assorted savories.

CHEESE MUSHROOMS
About 2 dozen

1 recipe Plain Pastry (page 433)
1 3-ounce package cream cheese
3 tablespoons cream
Few drops Tabasco sauce
¼ teaspoon grated onion
Paprika

Roll pastry ⅛ inch thick. Cut into 2½-inch rounds and fit into 2-inch muffin pans to make shallow cups. Prick and bake in hot oven (425°) 8 to 10 minutes. For stems, roll pastry ⅛ inch thick; cut into 1-inch squares, roll up and bake.

Blend cream cheese, cream, Tabasco sauce, and grated onion together until soft and creamy. Put about 1 teaspoon of mixture into baked pastry shell, sprinkle with paprika and press stem into center of cup to make mushroom.

Bake the "caps" until only a delicate brown.

CHEESE SNACKS
About 4 dozen

1 cup butter	2 cups flour
1 6½-ounce package process cheese, grated	½ teaspoon salt
	½ teaspoon paprika

Cream butter until light; add cheese and blend. Sift flour, salt, and paprika together. Add to creamed mixture and mix well. Form into a roll about 2 inches in diameter. Chill in refrigerator 3 hours or overnight. Cut into slices ⅛ inch thick. Place on ungreased cooky sheet, 15½ x 12 inches. Bake in slow oven (325°) 10 to 12 minutes. Remove from pan while hot.

Serve as an accompaniment with soup or salad.

CHEESE STRAWS
About 3 dozen

4 ounces sharp American cheese	Dash of pepper
1½ cups flour	Dash of cayenne pepper
¾ teaspoon salt	½ cup butter, softened

Rub cheese through a wire sieve. Sift flour and seasonings together. Cream butter until light and fluffy; add seasoned flour and cheese. Blend thoroughly with hands. Let stand in refrigerator 1 hour. Roll pastry ⅛ inch thick. Cut into 4-inch squares. Cut each square into straws 4 inches long and ⅛ inch wide. Lift carefully with spatula and place on ungreased cooky sheet, 15½ x 12 inches. Bake in hot oven (400°) 8 to 10 minutes. Watch closely as this rich cheese pastry burns easily. When done, the cheese straws should be a light golden color.

These zippy cheese straws are just the right accompaniment to serve with a salad course or they may be used on a tray of savories for afternoon tea.

CHEESE TWISTS
About 4 dozen

1 recipe Plain Pastry (page 433)	2 tablespoons caraway seeds
1 cup grated Swiss or sharp American cheese	1 egg, beaten
	2 teaspoons coarse salt

To pastry, add the grated cheese and caraway seeds. Mix well. Roll pastry into rectangle. Cut strips about ½ inch wide and 5 inches long. Brush lightly with egg. Sprinkle with coarse salt. Twist. Bake on ungreased cooky sheet, 15½ x 12 inches, in moderate oven (375°) 8 to 10 minutes or until nicely browned.

The most versatile trick of all — superb for salad, soup, or afternoon tea.

CHICKEN BISCUIT FINGERS
About 1 dozen

1 cup chopped cooked chicken
½ teaspoon salt
1 tablespoon finely chopped parsley
2 tablespoons mayonnaise

1 teaspoon lemon juice
½ recipe Plain Pastry (page 433)
1 egg, beaten
1 tablespoon milk

Combine chicken, salt, parsley, mayonnaise, and lemon juice. Make rolls of the mixture about the size of a small pickle. Roll pastry ¼ inch thick. Cut into 2-inch squares. Wrap chicken mixture in pastry, pressing the ends tightly. Prick top. Brush with egg and milk mixture and bake in hot oven (400°) 8 to 10 minutes.

EMPANADAS ARGENTINA
Argentine Mince Meat Tarts
About 2 dozen

Filling:

½ cup finely chopped pear
½ cup finely chopped peaches
1 teaspoon finely chopped chives
1 teaspoon butter
2 tablespoons finely chopped onion
½ cup chopped tomatoes

2 tablespoons chopped green pepper
¼ pound ground beef
1 teaspoon sugar
¼ teaspoon salt

Mix fruit and chives. Heat butter in pan and fry onion until light yellow. Add tomatoes, peppers, and mixed fruit. Add meat, sugar, and salt. Stir; cover, and simmer until vegetables are tender. Allow to cool.

Crust:

1½ cups sifted flour
¼ teaspoon salt
¼ teaspoon cinnamon
1 tablespoon sugar
½ cup shortening

1 egg yolk, beaten
4 tablespoons milk
1 egg, beaten
¼ cup sugar
½ teaspoon cinnamon

Sift together flour, salt, cinnamon, and sugar. Cut in shortening. Add egg yolk and milk; mix. Turn out on board and knead. Roll thin and cut in 2½-inch rounds. Place filling on one side of dough round; moisten edge. Turn ½ of round over the filling and pinch together. Prick top. Place on lightly greased cooky sheet, 15½ x 12 inches. Brush with beaten egg. Sprinkle with mixture of sugar and cinnamon. Bake in hot oven (400°) 12 to 15 minutes.

This combination of fruit and ground meat with just a touch of onion is typical of some of the food of our South American neighbors.

EMPANADAS PANAMA
About 3 dozen

¼ pound ground pork
2 tablespoons chopped onion
¼ cup raisins
Salt and pepper to taste
¼ cup sweet pickles, chopped

¼ cup stuffed olives, chopped
1 hard-cooked egg, chopped
2 tablespoons butter
½ recipe Plain Pastry (page 433)

Mix all ingredients but pastry and sauté in butter until pork is cooked. Roll pastry ⅛ inch thick and cut into 2-inch rounds. Place a teaspoon of filling near the edge of the circle and fold over the pastry, forming small semicircles. Moisten and seal edges; prick top with fork. Bake the empanadas in moderate oven (350°) 15 to 20 minutes.

Each South American country has its own version of empanadas, or fried pies, as we would call them. These come from Panama. They may be made larger and served as the entree at luncheon.

ENGLISH MEAT TARTS
About 2 dozen, small

2-pound veal shank
½ pound round of veal or pork
Salt and pepper
½ cup carrots, sliced
½ cup celery, diced

1 medium onion, sliced
¼ cup apple chutney
1 cup Jellied Meat Stock (page 46)
1 recipe Plain Pastry (page 433)

Cover meat and bone with warm water. Bring to boil. Skim. Add salt, pepper, carrots, celery, and onion. Cook until meat is well done. Remove meat from bones. Strain stock. Put meat through food chopper. Season with salt and pepper. Add apple chutney and about a cup of Jellied Meat Stock, and mix well.

Roll pastry ⅛ inch thick. Cut into 3-inch rounds and line 2-inch muffin pans. Prick pastry. Bake in hot oven (425°) 6 to 8 minutes. Pile mixture into baked pastry shells.

MUSHROOM TARTS
About 2 dozen, small

1 recipe Plain Pastry (page 433)
2 cups canned or 1 pint fresh
   mushrooms
4 tablespoons butter
2 tablespoons chopped chives

2 tablespoons chopped parsley
2 tablespoons lemon juice
1 cup cream
1 tablespoon paprika

Roll pastry ⅛ inch thick. Cut into 3-inch circles and line 2-inch muffin pans with pastry. Slice mushrooms, fresh or canned, and sauté in butter. Add chives and parsley; then add lemon juice and simmer for 5 minutes. Add cream and paprika. The mixture is thin; but don't worry — the filling will be the right consistency when baked. Fill pastry shells about ⅔ full and top each tart with two twisted strips of pastry. Bake in hot oven (425°) 20 to 25 minutes or until pastry is golden brown in color.

SHRIMP PATTIES
About 3 dozen

¼ cup butter
¼ cup flour
1 cup milk
1 cup cooked shrimp, chopped
2 teaspoons chopped parsley
1 tablespoon vinegar

⅛ teaspoon salt
Dash of pepper
1 recipe Plain Pastry (page 433)
   with ¾ cup grated American
   cheese added
1 egg, beaten

Melt butter, add flour and gradually add milk, stirring well. Cook 3 to 5 minutes. Remove from heat and add shrimp, parsley, vinegar, salt, and pepper. Roll pastry ⅛ inch thick. Cut into 3-inch circles and line 2-inch muffin pans with pastry. Put a teaspoon of the mixture into each one. Dampen the edges. Put narrow crisscross strips of pastry over filling. Brush with beaten egg. Bake in hot oven (425°) 15 to 20 minutes.

SHRIMP TURNOVERS
About 2 dozen

1 recipe Plain Pastry (page 433)

Roll pastry thin and cut into 2½-inch circles.

Filling:

1 7-ounce can shrimp
2 teaspoons lemon juice
2 tablespoons mayonnaise
1 tablespoon softened butter
Few drops Tabasco sauce

Few drops Worcestershire sauce
1 tablespoon chopped parsley
1 egg, beaten
2 tablespoons milk

Clean shrimp. Mash into a paste; add other ingredients, except egg and milk, and blend well. Add more seasonings, if necessary. Put a small amount of mixture in center of each pastry round. Fold over and press edges together with a fork. Brush with egg and milk mixture. Prick top. Bake in hot oven (425°) about 10 to 12 minutes.

WALNUT CHEESE PASTRIES
About 3 dozen

1½ cups flour
1 teaspoon baking powder
1 teaspoon salt
1 teaspoon paprika
¾ teaspoon dry mustard
Dash of cayenne pepper
½ cup shortening

4 to 5 tablespoons cold water
6 ounces (1½ cups) American cheese rubbed through a wire sieve
1 egg white, slightly beaten
½ cup chopped walnuts

Sift flour, baking powder, salt, paprika, mustard, and cayenne together. Cut in the shortening until size of peas; then add cold water gradually to make a stiff dough. It should be about the consistency of pie dough. Add grated cheese and mix well. Roll dough ⅛ inch thick. Cut into fancy shapes with cooky cutters, brush with egg white and sprinkle with chopped walnuts. Bake on an ungreased cooky sheet, 15½ x 12 inches, in hot oven (400°) 8 to 10 minutes.

NOTE: Be very careful when baking these pastries — they brown easily.

Cocktails

ARTICHOKE COCKTAIL
8 to 10 servings

1 No. 2 can artichoke hearts
1 small head lettuce
¼ cup mayonnaise
¼ cup catsup

1 tablespoon lemon juice
¼ teaspoon grated onion
Dash of salt

Drain liquid from canned artichoke hearts. Rinse with cold water. Drain. Cut leafy section of artichoke heart in quarters, almost to end. Arrange small piece of lettuce in each cocktail glass. Put one artichoke heart in each glass. Blend mayonnaise, catsup, lemon juice, onion, and salt. Pour a generous tablespoon of sauce over each artichoke heart. Chill.

BUFFET MELON BOWL
(With Watermelon Ice)

1 watermelon	¾ cup sugar
Juice 2 lemons	½ teaspoon salt
2 teaspoons grated lemon peel	1 teaspoon vinegar

Cut off top third of watermelon. Remove all watermelon meat from shells. Reduce to pulp by putting through food chopper. Add juice of lemons, grated peel, sugar, salt, and vinegar. Stir thoroughly and freeze. Pack and let stand 2 to 3 hours. Cut 1-inch deep saw-tooth edge on bottom shell. Chill. When ready to serve, put melon ice in watermelon bowl. Place grape leaves or other green leaves on a large silver tray; put melon bowl on this and decorate tray with bunches of white grapes, bananas, limes, lemons, or other pleasing combination of fruit.

This combination of fruit is suggested to serve with watermelon ice for first course:

Balls of cantaloupe

Cubes of honeydew melon

Fresh pineapple fingers

Strips of banana dipped in lemon juice and then in chopped nuts or browned coconut

Small bunches of seedless grapes

These may be put in crystal bowls around the melon.

When serving the watermelon ice with fruits as a first course, use crystal plates and a grape leaf on each plate. Serve the watermelon ice in crystal sherbet cups and let guests help themselves to the assorted fresh fruits. Serve tray of Cheese Straws (page 16) with this.

CRAB MEAT COCKTAIL
6 to 8 servings

1 6½-ounce can (1 cup) crab meat, drained	½ cup Sea Food Cocktail Sauce (page 213)
½ cup finely diced celery	Parsley for garnish

Fill cocktail glasses with alternate layers of crab meat, celery, and cocktail sauce. Garnish with a tiny sprig of parsley.

CRAB MEAT AND AVOCADO

Use diced avocado instead of celery with crab meat.

NOTE: Tuna or lobster may be used instead of crab meat.

CRANBERRY-GINGER ALE COCKTAIL
10 to 12 servings

2½ cups cranberries	1 tablespoon lemon juice
2 cups water	Crushed ice
½ cup sugar	1½ cups pale dry ginger ale

Cook cranberries and water until the skins pop open, about 5 minutes. Put through wire sieve to obtain juice. Bring juice to boiling point. Add sugar and cook about 2 minutes. Chill. Add lemon juice. Put a teaspoon of crushed ice into each parfait or cocktail glass; half fill with cranberry juice, and then add ginger ale, to fill glass, just before serving.

Serve crisp crackers, cheese sticks, and Cheese Straws (page 16) with this.

FRUIT ICE BLOCK FOR PUNCH BOWL

Use round pan about 7 to 8 inches in diameter and 3 inches deep. Place pineapple rings in bottom; fill centers with maraschino cherries. Fill pan with pineapple juice to which water has been added. Put in freezer. Remove fruit ice block when ready to serve; place in punch bowl. Pour punch into bowl.

If desired, you may use plain block of ice and put fancy lemon slices and whole strawberries on top.

GRAPEFRUIT-MINT COCKTAIL
10 to 12 servings

½ of 6-ounce glass mint jelly	½ cup sugar
1 cup water	4 medium grapefruit, sectioned

Melt mint jelly in double boiler. Beat with rotary beater until smooth. Boil water and sugar about 5 minutes to make a thin syrup. Add to mint jelly. Chill. Arrange grapefruit sections in cocktail glasses, 3 to 4 sections in each glass. Pour the chilled syrup into the glasses. Fill about ¾ full.

Try grapefruit-mint cocktail for a spring luncheon party. It is as refreshing as spring itself.

GRAPEFRUIT SHRUB
8 to 10 servings

1½ cups apple juice or cider
Red food coloring

2 No. 2 cans (5 cups)
grapefruit sections, chilled

Tint apple juice or cider a delicate pink and pour into refrigerator freezing tray; freeze to a thick mush. Put 3 to 4 grapefruit sections, with some of the grapefruit juice, into sherbet glasses; top with 2 to 3 tablespoons of frozen apple juice or cider.

HAWAIIAN FRAPPE
8 servings

½ cup sugar
1 cup water
1 teaspoon grated orange peel
1 teaspoon grated lemon peel
1 cup strained orange juice

1½ cups unsweetened pineapple juice
¼ cup lemon juice
Mint leaves

Cook sugar, water, and orange and lemon peel together for 5 minutes. Add orange, pineapple, and lemon juice. Cool and freeze to a mush. Serve in sherbet glasses garnished with mint leaves.

LIME JUICE COCKTAIL
8 to 10 servings

¼ cup sugar
¼ cup boiling water
½ cup lime juice

½ cup orange juice
2 cups pale dry ginger ale
Crushed ice

Dissolve sugar in boiling water. Boil 2 minutes to make syrup, and cool. Mix syrup, juices, and ginger ale, and pour over crushed ice in cocktail or parfait glasses. Serve at once. For a change, instead of using crushed ice, place a small float of orange or mint ice on top just before serving.

RAINBOW COCKTAIL

Make colored ice cubes: red, yellow, and green. Crush ice cubes and put a teaspoon or two of one color in a tall parfait glass. Fill with Lime Juice Cocktail. Place on the table alternately red, yellow, and green to give a rainbow effect.

MULLED CIDER
6 to 8 servings

1 quart cider
½ cup brown sugar
2 sticks cinnamon bark
½ teaspoon whole cloves

¼ teaspoon nutmeg
Dash of allspice
Dash of mace

Combine and heat. Strain through cheesecloth. Serve hot.

ORANGE COCKTAIL
4 servings

2 large oranges
1 tablespoon orange shreds
1½ cups sugar

1 cup water
½ cup orange juice
Green Crushed Ice

Wash oranges. Cut enough of outside skin into tiny shreds ½ inch long to make 1 tablespoon. Do not remove any of white portion. Combine sugar and water; add orange shreds. Cook 5 to 6 minutes. Peel and section oranges; chill thoroughly. Cool syrup and add orange juice. When ready to serve, place sections in small fruit glasses; pour 1 tablespoon orange syrup over fruit. Place in glass bowls. Surround with Green Crushed Ice. Serve as beginning course for luncheon.

GREEN CRUSHED ICE

Add green food coloring to water to give desired green shade. Pour into freezing tray and freeze. Put the ice cubes into towel or paper sack and crush with mallet or wooden handle of knife. Use to surround Orange Cocktail.

Red, blue, or yellow ice may be made in the same way.

tempters to look at and to nibble on . . .

Suggestions for Canapé Spreads, page 14.

fruit ice in a natural setting . . .

Buffet Melon Bowl, page 21.

ORANGE AND BANANA COCKTAIL
6 to 8 servings

6 ripe bananas
4 medium oranges
1 cup orange juice

6 tablespoons confectioners' sugar
4 red maraschino cherries

Peel bananas and shape into tiny balls with a ball cutter. Section oranges and add to banana balls. Pour orange juice over fruit. Sprinkle with confectioners' sugar and let mixture stand until well chilled. Serve in sherbet glasses, garnished with halves of maraschino cherries.

ORANGE JELLIED SOUP
4 to 6 servings

½ tablespoon gelatin
2 tablespoons cold water
⅓ cup boiling water
¼ cup sugar

1 cup orange juice (about 2 oranges)
⅛ teaspoon salt
2 teaspoons lemon juice
2 whole oranges

Soften gelatin in cold water for 5 minutes and dissolve in boiling water. Add sugar, orange juice, salt, and lemon juice. Section oranges and add to gelatin mixture. Fill bouillon cups about half full and place in refrigerator to chill.

Use as a beginning course for luncheon and serve with crisp crackers.

RHUBARB COCKTAIL
4 to 6 servings

1 cup Rhubarb Juice (page 26)
½ cup pineapple juice
¼ cup lemon juice

Crushed ice
1½ cups pale dry ginger ale

Combine juices. Chill. Put 1 tablespoon crushed ice in parfait glass; half fill glass with juice mixture. Just before serving, add ginger ale to fill glass.

RHUBARB JUICE

1 pound rhubarb
½ cup water

1 cup sugar

Cut rhubarb into ½-inch pieces. Cook with water and sugar until rhubarb is tender. Put into cloth bag and drain to obtain juice.

If rhubarb lacks color, add enough red food coloring to tint a delicate pink.

SHRIMP COCKTAIL
6 servings

1 pound fresh shrimp
2 lettuce leaves

Sea Food Cocktail Sauce

Cook and shell shrimp (page 155). Chill thoroughly. Line cocktail glass with small pieces of lettuce. Arrange 3 or 4 shrimp in each glass. Serve with 1 tablespoon Sea Food Cocktail Sauce.

Sea Food Cocktail Sauce:

1 cup chili sauce
1 teaspoon Worcestershire sauce
1 teaspoon grated horse-radish

Dash of Tabasco sauce
⅛ teaspoon white pepper
2 tablespoons lemon juice

Mix ingredients and chill thoroughly.

TOMATO AND CELERY COCKTAIL
10 to 12 servings

1 cup Mayonnaise (page 251)
1 cup tomato catsup
Onion juice
Few drops Tabasco sauce

1 tablespoon lemon juice
4 to 5 medium tomatoes
1 cup finely diced celery
¼ cup finely chopped green pepper

Combine Mayonnaise, catsup, and onion juice. Add Tabasco sauce and lemon juice to make a piquant sauce. Peel tomatoes and dice into ⅓-inch cubes. Put 1 teaspoon diced tomatoes in small cocktail glass; add a little diced celery and continue until glass is filled. Top with a generous teaspoon of sauce and garnish with finely chopped green pepper.

TOMATO JUICE COCKTAIL
5 to 6 servings

2 cups tomato juice
2 teaspoons vinegar
1 tablespoon sugar
½ bay leaf

2 teaspoons finely minced onion
2 tablespoons lemon juice
½ cup diced celery

Mix ingredients. Let stand in refrigerator 30 minutes. Strain. Serve cold in tall cocktail or parfait glasses. For variation, the juice may be frozen to a mush and served in sherbet glasses.

ACCOMPANIMENTS

Fingers of toast
Potato chips with cheese paste
Wafers, buttered and toasted
Wafers, spread with pimento butter and toasted
Wafers, buttered, and sprinkled with paprika

SUGGESTIONS FOR FISH COCKTAILS

Crab meat, celery
Crab meat and shrimp meat
Lobster (*sauce*: catsup, lemon juice, Tabasco, chives)
Oyster (*sauce*: lemon juice, catsup, Worcestershire, Tabasco, salt)
Oyster and grapefruit, Tabasco, lemon juice, salt
Sardines (*sauce*: catsup, Worcestershire, Tabasco, lemon juice)
Scallops (*sauce*: catsup, vinegar, olive oil, horse-radish, Tabasco, Worcestershire, salt, pepper, dry mustard, parsley, chives, shallot)

SUGGESTIONS FOR FRUIT COCKTAILS

Apples, white cherries, green cherries, lemon juice
Apricots, pineapple, maraschino cherries, pineapple juice, cherry juice, lemon juice, fresh mint leaves
Grapefruit, crab meat, tomato catsup, grapefruit juice, Worcestershire
Grapefruit, maraschino cherries, kumquats, honey, lemon juice
Grapefruit, strawberries, honey, lemon juice
Grapefruit, strawberries, pineapple, banana, lemon juice
Peaches, cantaloupe, fresh mint leaves, lemon juice

Peaches, honeydew melon, mint, lemon juice
Peaches, pineapple, strawberries
Pineapple, strawberries, candied ginger, pale dry ginger ale, lemon juice
Strawberries, orange juice, sugar
Watermelon balls, peach syrup, lemon juice, fresh mint leaves
White cherries, pineapple, grapefruit, maraschino syrup, pineapple syrup, lemon juice

SUGGESTIONS FOR FRUIT HORS D'OEUVRE PLATES

Fruit hors d'oeuvre plates may be used as a beginning course. They are especially suitable for a luncheon. Arrange fruit on a grape leaf, curly endive, water cress, or other salad green.

Suggestions for complementary fruits are:

Alternate sections of orange and grapefruit; mint leaves between sections; maraschino cherry garnish

Alternate slices of apple and fresh pineapple served in pineapple shell that has been cut lengthwise into eighths

Canned or fresh peaches cut into eighths and dipped in chopped pistachio nuts; fresh raspberries and a small bunch of grapes

Canned or fresh pineapple cut in segments and dipped in chopped fresh mint leaves; fresh strawberries and wedges of lime

Fresh or canned pear half filled with fresh red raspberries; orange sections; banana fingers rolled in toasted coconut

Fresh or canned pears brushed with a bit of red coloring to give a "blush"; fresh strawberries and a small bunch of grapes

Fresh whole strawberries; blackberries; raspberries or loganberries dusted with powdered sugar

Pineapple chunks; fresh blueberries; banana slices cut diagonally

Slices of orange; fingers of banana rolled in chopped pecans; fresh strawberries

Watermelon balls in cantaloupe ring; bing cherries

Soups and
Accompaniments

SOUPS

Barszcz
Borsch
Boston Clam Chowder
Burgonyaleves
Canadian Cheese
Chicken Rice
Chicken Velvet
Chinese Chicken Tomato
Consommé Julienne
Consommé à la Royale
Crab Chowder
Crab-Flake
Creole Gumbo
English Mulligatawny
Essence of Tomato
Garbacho
Green Onion
Minestrone
New England Fish Chowder
New England Lobster
    Chowder

Parisian Onion
Sopa de Arroz
Southern Crab Bisque
Swedish Fish
Swedish Fruit
Tortellini en Brodo di Pollo
Vichyssoise
Vienna
Won Ton Noodle

STOCK

Beef or Brown
Chicken
Fish
Jellied Meat
Veal or White
To Clarify
Bouillon
    Tomato
Consommé

ACCOMPANIMENTS

Croutons
Deviled Crackers
Imperial Sticks in Rings

Mock Almonds
Parmesan Cheese Sticks
Parsley Crescents

Soup belongs to a party — whether an elaborate dinner or an informal get-together. Bowls of savory consommé or bouillon are a delightful, stimulating opening to an hour of good eating, while a tureen of rich, hearty soup can make an intimate, highly informal supper in itself.

You'll find a wealth of cooking lore for inspiration in this chapter — the chowders of New England, English Mulligatawny, Swedish Fruit Soup, Polish Barszcz, Minestrone of Italy, and the excellent soups for which the French are famous. The secrets of their delicious flavors are simple but vital — long gentle cooking and careful seasoning. Good soup cannot be hurried. With such a variety of time-tested recipes to choose from, your soup service can be a memorable one.

Both the thick chowders and the delicate bouillons call for a crisp accompaniment. So pass a plate of oven-hot crackers or toast strips or a tray of crunchy relishes.

Soups

BARSZCZ
Polish Beet Soup
6 to 8 servings

1 pound beef soup bone
1 quart water
1 teaspoon salt
1 medium onion, chopped
½ cup diced mushrooms,
    fresh or canned
1 teaspoon sugar

1½ cups diced fresh beets
½ cup diced carrots
1 tablespoon chopped parsley
1 cup shredded cabbage
¾ cup sour cream
1 tablespoon flour
1 teaspoon lemon juice

Put soup bone in kettle and add water and salt. Add onion, and simmer for an hour or more. Strain stock, chill, and remove fat. Heat stock and add mushrooms. Sprinkle sugar over other vegetables and add to soup stock. Simmer 20 to 25 minutes or until vegetables are tender. Put soup through strainer and force vegetables through. Combine sour cream with flour and lemon juice. Add to the puréed stock and add a little more salt, if needed. Bring to a boil and serve hot.

There are various dialect spellings for Polish barszcz. This spelling is High Polish — the official language.

BORSCH
Russian Beet Soup
8 to 10 servings

2 tablespoons fat
1 medium onion, chopped
¾ cup diced potatoes
¾ cup diced carrots
¾ cup finely shredded cabbage
¾ cup chopped celery
2 quarts Beef Stock (page 45)
    or canned bouillon

1 cup canned tomatoes
¾ cup beet juice
1 cup diced cooked beets
1 tablespoon lemon juice
1 teaspoon salt
⅛ teaspoon pepper
¾ cup sour cream

Put fat into skillet; add onion, and sauté until golden in color. Combine with remaining vegetables and add to Beef Stock. Simmer for 30 minutes. Put tomatoes through a wire sieve and add to soup. Add beet juice. Simmer until vegetables are tender. Add beets and lemon juice. Season with salt and pepper. Remove from heat before beets lose color. Serve hot with a tablespoon of sour cream on each portion.

BOSTON CLAM CHOWDER
8 to 10 servings

3 slices salt pork
2 cups clams, diced
2 medium potatoes, diced
2 medium onions, diced
½ cup diced celery
2 cups hot water

2 tablespoons flour
2 tablespoons cold water
2 cups milk
1 cup cream
Salt and pepper to taste

Dice salt pork in small cubes and fry until crisp. Combine diced clams and vegetables, and add hot water. Then add crisp salt pork and drippings. Cook until vegetables are tender, adding a little more hot water if necessary. Add flour, mixed with cold water, and cook until thickened. Scald milk and cream. Just before serving, blend the two mixtures. Season to taste. Serve hot with chowder crackers.

Yes, it's real New England chowder (without any tomatoes), and it will hit the spot on a chilly day. Unhurried simmering of the vegetables brings out the best in flavor and allows for the intermingling and blending of vegetable and salt pork flavors. Taste often, for proper seasoning is all-important with this dish. If you prefer a pronounced clam flavor, lessen the amount of milk. A light sprinkling of chopped parsley will perk up the color as well as the flavor.

BURGONYALEVES
Hungarian Potato Soup
4 to 6 servings

4 tablespoons fat
3 medium potatoes, diced
1 medium onion, chopped fine
1 tablespoon paprika
1 pimento, diced

1 tablespoon chopped parsley
1 quart hot Beef Stock (page 45)
  or canned bouillon
Salt
¼ cup sour cream

Melt fat in soup kettle and add potatoes, onion, paprika, and pimento. Simmer gently without browning until the onions are a light golden color. Sprinkle with a little chopped parsley. Add the hot Beef Stock; season with salt, and bring to boil. Simmer ½ hour or until the potatoes are cooked. Stir in 2 tablespoons of the sour cream, and add remaining sour cream when soup has been removed from the heat. Serve hot.

CANADIAN CHEESE SOUP
6 to 8 servings

2 tablespoons butter
¼ cup chopped onion
2 tablespoons flour
1 tablespoon cornstarch
⅛ teaspoon paprika
½ teaspoon salt
Dash of white pepper

2 cups milk
2 cups Chicken Stock (page 45)
   or canned consommé
¼ cup cooked diced carrots
¼ cup cooked diced celery
½ cup diced sharp Cheddar cheese
2 tablespoons chopped parsley

Melt butter in double boiler. Add onion, and sauté until golden in color. Add flour and cornstarch, and blend into butter. Add seasonings. Stir in milk and Chicken Stock; cook until thickened. Add vegetables; add more seasoning, if desired. Cook in double boiler for 15 minutes. Just before serving, add cheese cubes and blend into soup. Add chopped parsley last. Serve hot.

This Canadian cheese soup is very popular at Ayres Tea Room in Indianapolis.

CHICKEN RICE SOUP
4 to 6 servings

1 quart Chicken Stock (page 45)
½ cup rice

Salt and pepper
1 tablespoon chopped parsley

Heat Chicken Stock; add rice and simmer until rice is cooked. Add salt and pepper, to taste. Serve hot, garnished with a sprinkle of chopped parsley.

CHICKEN VELVET SOUP
6 to 8 servings

½ cup butter
½ cup flour
1 cup warm milk
4 cups hot Chicken Stock (page 45)

1 cup warm cream
1 cup chopped cooked chicken
½ teaspoon salt
Dash of pepper

Blend butter and flour in double boiler. Add warm milk and 2 cups of the Chicken Stock. Stir until smooth. Add cream and cook 15 minutes. Add remaining 2 cups Chicken Stock. Just before serving, stir in chicken and seasoning. Add more seasoning, if desired. Serve hot with a sprinkle of chopped parsley.

This smooth, well-blended chicken soup is a favorite recipe from Ayres Tea Room, in Indianapolis. Miss Veronica Morrissey, who has been connected with the food service at Ayres, sent it to me.

CHINESE CHICKEN TOMATO SOUP
5 to 6 servings

3 small peeled tomatoes
4 cups chicken broth
1½ cups chopped cooked chicken
1 teaspoon monosodium glutamate*

Salt and pepper
1 egg, beaten slightly
2 teaspoons cornstarch
2 tablespoons cold water

Chop tomatoes; heat broth, add tomatoes, chicken, and seasoning. Bring to boil and add egg. Then add cornstarch blended with cold water. Stir well and cook 2 minutes. Serve hot.

* Sold under various trade names such as Accent, Zest, etc.

CONSOMME JULIENNE
6 to 8 servings

1 quart Consommé (page 47)
1 carrot
1 small turnip

1 piece celery
¼ cup cooked peas

Cut carrot, turnip, and celery in thin strips 1½ inches long and ⅛ inch wide, and cook in boiling salted water. Drain. Add all of the vegetables to Consommé and heat. When ready to serve, put some of vegetable mixture in each bouillon cup and fill cups ¾ full of hot Consommé.

Serve with Parsley Crescents (page 48) and Imperial Sticks In Rings (page 47).

CONSOMME À LA ROYALE
Consommé with Royal Custard
4 to 6 servings

1 quart hot Consommé (page 47)

Royal Custard:

3 egg yolks
1 egg
½ cup consommé

⅛ teaspoon salt
Dash of grated nutmeg
Dash of cayenne pepper

Beat egg yolks and egg slightly, add consommé and seasonings. Pour into buttered pan, 8 x 8 x 2 inches, place in pan of hot water and bake in slow oven (300°) 12 to 15 minutes or until firm. Cool; cut in small fancy shapes. Put a few custard cutouts in each cup; add hot Consommé.

NOTE: Custard should not be more than ⅓ inch thick in pan.

CRAB CHOWDER
6 to 8 servings

3 tablespoons butter
1 small onion, chopped
1 No. 2 can tomatoes
2 medium potatoes, cut into
    small cubes

2 cups water
Salt and pepper
1 6½-ounce can crab meat, flaked

Melt butter; stir in onion, and cook until golden brown. Add tomatoes and potatoes. Add water, salt and pepper to taste. Cover the kettle and cook without stirring over moderate heat for 20 minutes. Then add crab meat, and cook slowly 2 to 3 minutes longer. Serve hot in bowls.

CRAB-FLAKE SOUP
6 to 8 servings

1 6½-ounce can crab meat
1 quart Chicken Stock (page 45)
    or canned consommé
1 small onion, chopped
2 cups light cream

1 tablespoon butter
½ cup fine bread crumbs
Salt and pepper
Dash of cayenne pepper

Flake crab meat, removing any bits of shell; add to the stock, and bring to a boil. Add onion and cook 5 minutes longer. Put cream in double boiler with butter; add bread crumbs and heat. Twenty minutes before serving combine the two mixtures. Season with salt, pepper, and cayenne pepper. Serve very hot.

This is a very rich soup — almost a meal in itself.

CREOLE GUMBO
8 to 10 servings

¼ pound salt pork
½ pound ham
2 medium onions, chopped fine
1 clove garlic, minced
2 tablespoons flour
1 quart canned tomatoes
1 No. 2 can okra
2 7-ounce cans shrimp, diced

1 quart Chicken Stock (page 45)
    or canned consommé
2 teaspoons salt
⅛ teaspoon pepper
4 sprigs parsley
½ teaspoon powdered thyme
2 bay leaves

Dice salt pork and ham. Put into large saucepan and fry lightly. Add onions and fry until golden in color. Add garlic; blend in flour. Add remaining ingredients and simmer for 2 hours. Serve hot over cooked rice.

ENGLISH MULLIGATAWNY
8 to 10 servings

1 chicken, 3 to 4 pounds
¼ cup fat
½ cup chopped carrots
½ cup chopped celery
¼ cup chopped green pepper
2 green apples, pared and chopped
1 small onion, chopped fine
1 tablespoon flour
1½ teaspoons curry powder
2 quarts hot Chicken Stock
 (page 45) or hot water

4 whole cloves
Dash of mace
Dash of black pepper
1 tablespoon finely chopped parsley
1 tablespoon sugar
1 teaspoon salt
1 cup canned tomatoes
1 tablespoon lemon juice

Disjoint chicken. Melt fat in soup kettle; add chicken and brown each piece. Add carrots, celery, green pepper, apples, and onion. Cook for about 5 minutes, stirring carefully, until vegetables are nicely browned. Mix flour and curry powder, and sprinkle over meat. Add Chicken Stock or hot water to soup kettle and add remaining seasonings. Cook over low heat until chicken is tender. Add tomatoes and cook about 15 minutes longer. Remove pieces of chicken from soup kettle, take off skin and remove meat from the bones. Dice chicken meat. Strain soup, forcing vegetables through sieve. Return the sieved soup to kettle; add diced chicken, lemon juice, and more seasoning if desired. Heat soup and serve very hot with fluffy boiled rice.

This is a favorite soup in England.

ESSENCE OF TOMATO
6 to 8 servings

1 quart canned tomatoes
¾ cup diced celery
½ cup diced carrots
1 small onion, diced
Parsley
1 green pepper, diced

3 whole cloves
1 teaspoon peppercorns
1 teaspoon salt
Dash of cayenne
Dash of mace
¾ cup heavy cream, whipped

Put tomatoes in saucepan and add vegetables and seasonings. Simmer 45 minutes to 1 hour or until vegetables are cooked. Strain but do not force vegetables through sieve, as the tomato essence should be clear. Reheat and serve hot in bouillon cups. Top with teaspoon of whipped cream.

GARBACHO
Spanish Summer Soup
6 to 8 servings

2 cups water
1 quart fresh tomatoes peeled and
    sliced or 1 quart canned whole
    tomatoes
1 medium cucumber, diced (skin
    left on)

1 clove garlic, crushed
2 tablespoons sugar
Salt and pepper
⅓ cup vinegar
1 cup peeled and thinly sliced
    cucumber

Combine water, tomatoes, cucumber, garlic, and sugar. Cook slowly for 45 minutes to one hour. Add salt and pepper to taste. Strain and put soup in refrigerator to chill. Add vinegar to peeled cucumber and let stand until soup is ready to serve. Just before serving put a small block of ice in soup bowl or tureen and pour soup over this. Add sliced cucumber and vinegar. Serve cold with crisp crackers or Parmesan Cheese Sticks (page 48) and Parsley Crescents (page 48).

This is a delicious soup for a luncheon party on a hot summer day.

GREEN ONION SOUP
6 to 8 servings

6 cups Beef Stock (page 45)
    or canned bouillon
3 tablespoons soy sauce
1 tablespoon sesame seed, browned
    and pulverized

1 teaspoon salt
3 cups green onions (with tops)
    cut in 2-inch lengths
Dash of pepper

Add to Beef Stock the soy sauce, sesame seed, and salt. Simmer for ½ hour. Add onions and cook for 10 minutes longer. Add pepper just before serving. Serve hot.

MINESTRONE
8 to 10 servings

¼ pound bacon, diced
¼ pound ham, diced
1 medium onion, diced
2 tablespoons fat
2 quarts Beef Stock (page 45)
　　or canned bouillon
1 No. 2 can tomatoes, chopped
2 pieces celery, sliced thin

½ cup rice
½ cup cooked navy beans
½ cup chopped cabbage
½ cup green vegetables
　　(peas or green beans)
Salt and pepper
Parmesan cheese

Fry bacon, ham, and onion slowly in fat until onion is lightly browned. Add remaining ingredients to Beef Stock except cabbage, green vegetables, and Parmesan cheese. Simmer until vegetables are tender. Add cabbage and green vegetables. Add salt and pepper to taste. Simmer 10 to 15 minutes longer. Serve hot in bowls. Garnish with Parmesan cheese.

Minestrone is a thick hearty Italian soup and is almost a meal in itself.

NEW ENGLAND FISH CHOWDER
8 to 10 servings

1 pound haddock or halibut
4 cups cold water
1 bay leaf
Parsley
½ cup chopped celery
¼ pound salt pork, diced

1 medium onion, chopped fine
2 tablespoons flour
2 medium potatoes, diced
1 cup rich milk
1 teaspoon salt
¼ teaspoon pepper

Cut fish in ½-inch cubes. To one half of the cubed fish add the water, bay leaf, parsley, and celery. Simmer 20 to 30 minutes. Strain and use liquid for fish bouillon. Fry the salt pork, add onion and cook until onion is golden in color, then add flour and blend thoroughly. Add the diced potatoes and the fish bouillon. Simmer 15 to 20 minutes; then add remainder of fish. Simmer until fish and potatoes are done, about 10 to 15 minutes. Add the milk, reheat. Then add salt and pepper to taste. Serve hot.

This is fish chowder with an added tantalizing bay leaf aroma. It's amazing how just the right seasoning points up the flavor of this otherwise bland chowder.

NEW ENGLAND LOBSTER CHOWDER
2 quarts

1 small onion
½ cup diced salt pork
3 soda crackers, rolled fine
1 quart milk, scalded

2 6-ounce cans lobster or 2½ cups
    fresh, cooked lobster
Salt, pepper, and cayenne pepper
¼ cup butter
1½ cups hot cream

Chop onion and cook with salt pork until golden in color. Strain and discard onion and pork. To 4 tablespoons of the fat, add soda cracker crumbs. Pour in hot milk gradually, stirring constantly until smooth; add lobster and heat in double boiler for 15 minutes. Season to taste, then add butter and hot cream. Serve with crisp crackers.

The cracker crumbs (in case you're wondering) are a good way to prevent fat separation. In this rich, creamy chowder the onion is only a hint, with the delicate lobster flavor predominating.

Better plan on small servings because this chowder allows no room for seconds. You'll probably enjoy a spicy pickle as an accompaniment.

PARISIAN ONION SOUP
6 to 8 servings

1 pound (3 to 4) Bermuda onions
¼ cup butter
6 cups Chicken Stock (page 45)
    or canned consommé

Salt and pepper
1 hard roll
Parmesan cheese

Slice onions thinly. Melt butter in heavy kettle; add onions; sauté until golden in color. Add Chicken Stock, season, and bring to boil. Pour soup into earthenware soup tureen or individual bowls. Slice roll crosswise ¼ inch thick and toast the slices. Put slice of toasted roll on top of soup; sprinkle generously with Parmesan cheese. Serve at once.

SOPA DE ARROZ
Rice Soup
6 servings

1 cup rice
4 tablespoons fat
1 small onion, chopped fine
1 small clove garlic, minced
½ green pepper, diced

2 cups canned tomatoes
2 cups hot water
1 teaspoon salt
Dash of pepper

Wash rice thoroughly. Put fat in skillet; add rice and stir constantly so each grain will brown. Add onion, garlic, and green pepper. Sauté until onion is golden in color. Add tomatoes, hot water, salt and pepper. Simmer slowly until rice is thoroughly cooked. Add more water if necessary.

Sopa de arroz is a thick soup.

SOUTHERN CRAB BISQUE
4 to 6 servings

1 6½-ounce can crab meat	1 cup cream
2 tablespoons butter	Salt and pepper
2 tablespoons flour	Dash of cayenne pepper
3 cups milk	

Cut crab meat into small pieces. Melt butter in double boiler and gradually add flour. Cook until mixture begins to bubble, then add milk and cream, stirring constantly. Cook until slightly thickened, add crab meat and heat in double boiler 15 minutes. Season and serve very hot with buttered crackers.

SWEDISH FISH SOUP
6 to 8 servings

¾ pound haddock	4 tablespoons flour
2 slices onion	1 cup cream
2 carrots, sliced	1 cup diced cooked carrots
2 sprigs parsley	1 cup cooked peas
1¼ quarts cold water	Salt
¼ teaspoon peppercorns	Dash of white pepper
1 bay leaf	Dash of paprika
1 teaspoon salt	1 teaspoon onion juice
2 tablespoons butter	1 tablespoon finely chopped parsley

Break fish into small pieces and put into saucepan. Add onion, carrots, parsley, water, peppercorns, bay leaf, and salt. Simmer for 1 hour. Strain fish stock. Discard fish and seasonings. Blend butter and flour and add to fish stock. Cook over low heat until slightly thickened. Add the cream, diced cooked carrots, and peas. Season to taste with salt, pepper and paprika. Add onion juice. Just before serving, add chopped parsley.

SWEDISH FRUIT SOUP
18 to 20 servings

1 cup dried prunes
1 cup raisins
1 cup dried apricots
2 quarts water
½ cup pearl tapioca (soaked)
1 quart water
1 cup sliced apples

1 cup pitted red sour cherries
1 cup grape juice
½ cup orange juice
¼ cup lemon juice
1 tablespoon grated orange peel
1 cup sugar

Soak prunes, raisins, and apricots in 2 quarts of water overnight or 6 to 8 hours. Cook dried fruit slowly in water in which it was soaked. Cook tapioca in remaining quart of water until tapioca is almost clear. Add to cooked fruits, then add apples, cherries, and grape juice. Cook until tapioca is clear. Add orange and lemon juice, orange peel, and sugar. Serve hot or cold as soup or dessert. Canned fruits, such as pears, peaches, cherries, or plums, may be added at end of cooking period. Serve plain or with whipped cream.

NOTE: Fruit should be quite firm and distinct and not mushy. Liquid should be clear.

This is the traditional fruit soup for the Smörgåsbord (page 460).

TORTELLINI EN BRODO DI POLLO
Chicken Broth with Filled Dough

Broth:

1½ quarts chicken broth

Dough:

2 cups flour
1 egg
1 egg yolk

1 tablespoon oil
½ teaspoon salt
2 to 3 tablespoons water

Put flour in bowl. Beat egg and egg yolk; add oil and salt, and pour into flour. Add water and mix until a smooth, stiff dough is formed. Turn out on lightly floured board and knead until smooth. This resembles noodle dough. Roll dough into rectangular shape ⅛ inch thick. Cut in 3-inch squares.

Filling:

1 cup finely chopped cooked
   chicken
1 tablespoon Parmesan cheese
1 egg, beaten

¼ cup fine bread crumbs
½ teaspoon salt
Dash of pepper

Mix chicken, Parmesan cheese, egg, bread crumbs, salt, and pepper together. Put 1 teaspoon of filling on dough square, fold over and press edges together to seal. Dry for a few hours. Add to boiling chicken broth. Cook 10 to 12 minutes or until dough is tender. Serve soup with a dash of Parmesan cheese on top.

Carolyn De Bartolo brought this recipe with her from Chicago. It belonged to her Italian grandmother. Carolyn prepared the tortellini for an Italian dinner served by the Catering Class.

VICHYSSOISE
6 to 8 servings

3 small onions, sliced thin
3 tablespoons butter
4 small potatoes, diced
3 cups Chicken Stock (page 45)
    or canned consommé

2 cups cream
½ teaspoon salt
Dash of pepper
2 tablespoons finely cut chives or
    parsley

Cook onions in butter until soft and golden in color. Add potatoes. Combine Chicken Stock with potatoes and onions. Cook 40 minutes or until vegetables are tender; put through a fine wire sieve. Return to heat; add cream. Add salt and pepper to taste. Reheat.

When weather is cold, serve soup hot with chopped chives or chopped parsley. In summertime the vichyssoise may be chilled and served cold.

VIENNA SOUP
6 to 8 servings

¼ cup barley
1 onion, sliced thin
1 small carrot, diced
¼ cup peas
1 bay leaf
1 sprig parsley

1 quart White Stock (page 46)
    or canned chicken consommé
¾ cup cream
1 egg yolk
½ cup cooked asparagus tips
Salt and pepper
⅛ teaspoon paprika

Add barley, onion, carrot, peas, bay leaf, and parsley to White Stock, and simmer for 1 to 1½ hours. Stir cream into egg yolk and add to the soup. Put through a sieve. Reheat in double boiler. Add asparagus tips, salt and pepper to taste, and paprika. Serve hot.

A few crisp croutons may be added to each cup of soup when it is served.

WON TON NOODLE SOUP
6 to 8 servings

1 recipe Pincit Frito (page 110)   ¾ cup shredded Chinese cabbage
1½ quarts hot chicken broth   ½ cup diced water chestnuts
½ cup diced ham   Salt and pepper

Prepare Pincit Frito and drop into hot chicken broth. Cook 15 to 20 minutes. Add ham, Chinese cabbage, and water chestnuts. Cook 10 minutes longer. Season with salt and pepper.

Serve this soup as the beginning course for the Chinese Filipino Dinner (page 454).

Stock

BEEF OR BROWN STOCK
About 2 quarts

5 pounds beef knuckle
3 quarts cold water
1 medium onion, sliced
2 carrots, sliced
1 medium turnip, diced
4 pieces celery (with leaves), cut
    into ½-inch pieces

½ teaspoon peppercorns
5 whole cloves
1 small bay leaf
3 sprigs parsley
1 tablespoon salt

Have beef knuckle cut in several pieces. Cut meat from bone and cut in cubes. Brown meat cubes. Combine beef bone and browned meat cubes. Put meat and bone into soup kettle; add water and let stand 1 hour to draw out juices. Bring to boil; skim and reduce heat to simmering; cook slowly 4 to 5 hours Add vegetables and seasonings during last hour of cooking. Strain stock. Chill. Remove layer of fat when stock is chilled.

CHICKEN STOCK
About 1 quart

1 4- to 4½-pound hen
6 cups cold water
2 small onions, sliced
2 pieces celery, diced
1 carrot, sliced

3 sprigs parsley
1 teaspoon salt
Dash of pepper
4 peppercorns

Disjoint chicken. Put in soup kettle and cover with cold water. Bring to boiling point and skim. Add vegetables and seasonings, and simmer until meat is tender. Remove chicken and strain stock. Cool. Place in refrigerator until needed. Before using chicken stock, remove fat film from top. The chicken stock may be used for sauces or as a soup base.

Use the chicken meat in chicken salad, chicken loaf, or soufflé.

FISH STOCK
About 1 quart

2 pounds whitefish	½ teaspoon salt
5 cups cold water	1 piece celery, diced
2 peppercorns	1 small carrot, sliced
3 sprigs parsley	1 small onion, sliced

Cut fish into small pieces. Combine with other ingredients and simmer for 1 hour. Strain through cheesecloth. Use stock for fish sauces or as stock in which to cook fish.

JELLIED MEAT STOCK

1 tablespoon (1 envelope) unflavored gelatin	1½ cups well-seasoned hot Chicken Stock (page 45) or
¼ cup cold water	Veal Stock (below)

Soften gelatin in cold water. Add to hot meat stock and stir until dissolved. Cool and let stand until jelly-like in consistency.

VEAL OR WHITE STOCK
About 2 quarts

1 4-pound hen	½ teaspoon peppercorns
3 pounds veal knuckle	5 whole cloves
3 quarts cold water	¼ teaspoon thyme
1 medium onion, sliced	¼ teaspoon marjoram
2 carrots, sliced	1 tablespoon salt
4 pieces celery (with leaves), cut into ½-inch pieces	

Disjoint chicken. Have veal knuckle cut in several pieces. Cut veal in 1-inch cubes. Put chicken and veal (bone and meat) into soup kettle; add water and let stand 1 hour to draw out juices. Bring to boil, skim stock and reduce heat to simmering; cook slowly 4 to 5 hours. Add vegetables and seasonings the last hour of cooking. Strain stock. Remove fat after stock has been chilled.

TO CLARIFY STOCK

For one quart of stock, combine 2 tablespoons water with 1 egg white and shell. Add to cold stock. Heat stock and stir constantly until it boils. Boil 5 to 10 minutes without stirring. Let stand 15 to 20 minutes at back of range for stock to settle. Strain through two thicknesses of cheesecloth.

BOUILLON

Clarify Brown Stock (page 45) and use as bouillon.

TOMATO BOUILLON

Use equal parts of Bouillon and tomato juice. Season with dash of Tabasco sauce and additional salt and pepper, if desired.

CONSOMME

Clarify White Stock (page 46) and use as consommé.

Soup Accompaniments

CROUTONS

Cut stale bread into ½-inch cubes or cubes of any desired size. Toast in slow oven (300°) until crisp and delicately browned. Sauté cubes in a small amount of butter. Serve as a soup accompaniment.

DEVILED CRACKERS

Mix 1 teaspoon each of prepared mustard and curry powder to a paste by adding a little Worcestershire sauce and a few drops of Tabasco sauce. Stir the paste into 4 tablespoons of softened butter. Spread mixture on the upper side of thin crackers and place in hot oven (400°) 3 to 4 minutes. Be careful that the crackers do not become too brown, as this detracts from their appearance. Before serving, sprinkle lightly with paprika.

IMPERIAL STICKS IN RINGS

Cut day-old bread in ⅓-inch slices; remove crusts, spread thinly with butter. Cut slices in ⅓-inch strips and rings about 2½ inches in diameter; put on cooky sheet and place in hot oven (425°) or under broiler flame until delicately browned. Arrange three strips in each ring. Attractive to use in center of plate of soup accompaniments.

MOCK ALMONDS

Cut stale bread into ⅓-inch slices. Cut slices with round cutter 2 inches in diameter, then cut in almond-shaped pieces. Brush with melted butter, put on cooky sheet; place in hot oven (425°) or under broiler until lightly browned.

PARMESAN CHEESE STICKS

Use day-old bread and slice ⅓ inch thick. Cut slices into strips about 1½ inches wide and 3 inches long. Have ready ½ cup melted butter, into which to dip the strips. Pick them up with a fork, dip in butter; drain and hold until butter ceases to drip, then drop into a dish of grated Parmesan cheese; coat entirely with cheese and place on a cooky sheet. Put in hot oven (425°) and brown lightly. Turn with spatula and brown on other side. Drain on absorbent paper. These sticks may be prepared 2 or 3 hours in advance, if desired. Serve as an accompaniment with soup or salad.

PARSLEY CRESCENTS

Cut day-old bread in ¼-inch slices and cut with a crescent cutter. Place on cooky sheet. Put in hot oven (425°) and brown lightly. Brush upper side with melted butter and then dip in parsley which has been chopped fine. Parsley should be dry when chopped. Serve as soup accompaniment.

Breads

A BASKET of fragrant hot rolls or muffins can add an extra flourish to your already wonderful dinner, or it can be the star at a friendly morning coffee, an afternoon tea, or a leisurely Sunday brunch.

Breads are festive. Even the simplest biscuit, freshly baked and served with butter and your best jam or jelly, is an adventure in delightful eating.

Every nation has its favorite breads, with different flavorings and traditions. America is rich in this heritage. So by combining the secrets of foreign cooks with our best native culinary ability, we have an array of tempting breads for all occasions.

The quick breads — muffins, biscuits, nut loaves, popovers, waffles, and their variations — are what their name implies, speedy to make. They're leavened with baking powder, steam, or soda. The yeast breads take longer but are rewarding in their tantalizing aroma and satisfying flavor.

We can have a different bread for every day in the week. Any meal is made more memorable and distinctive by the addition of a fragrant, light-as-a-feather roll or hot bread.

Compressed yeast cakes are designated in these recipes, but the dry granular yeast may be used if preferred, by following directions on package.

The combination or double-acting type of baking powder has been used in these recipes. About one-third of the leavening gas is released in the mixing, the remainder when heated. To adjust the baking powder to another type, follow the manufacturer's directions.

ANADAMA BREAD
2 loaves

½ cup water-ground corn meal	3 teaspoons salt
2 cups boiling water	2 cakes compressed yeast
2 tablespoons shortening	½ cup lukewarm water
½ cup molasses	5 to 6 cups sifted flour

Add corn meal gradually to boiling water while stirring constantly. Then add shortening, molasses, and salt, and cool to lukewarm (about 85°). Soften yeast cakes in the lukewarm water and stir into corn-meal mixture. Add enough flour to make a stiff dough and knead well. Place in a greased bowl, cover with a towel, and let rise in a warm place (75° to 85°) until double. Punch dough down with the finger tips, cover, and let rise again for 45 minutes. Toss onto a lightly floured board and knead well, adding more flour if necessary.

Shape into two loaves and place in two greased loaf pans, 9½ by 5¼ by 2¾ inches. Cover with a towel, put in a warm place, and let rise until double. Bake in moderate oven (375°) 15 minutes, then reduce heat 25 degrees and finish baking, allowing about 1 hour in all for the bread. Brush the crust with melted fat, remove the bread from the pans at once and place on a cooling rack.

Tradition has it that once upon a time there was a New England fisherman who had a lazy wife named Anna. He fished all day, but when he came home his wife was too lazy to prepare his food, so he had to do the cooking himself. He experimented with bread with corn meal added to it and became very well known for his bread. One day someone asked him what he called the bread. He answered that Anna, "damn her," was too lazy to bake the bread, so he had to make it himself. So, he guessed he'd call it "Anadama Bread."

BABA CAKES
About 12 small cakes

⅓ cup seeded raisins
⅓ cup thinly sliced citron
⅓ cup currants

⅓ cup maraschino syrup
½ recipe Brioche Dough (page 59)

Soak fruit in maraschino syrup for one hour. Drain, add fruit to dough. Drop from teaspoon into greased 2-inch muffin pans. Cover and let rise until double in bulk. Bake in moderate oven (350°) 25 minutes.

BAKING POWDER BISCUITS
About 16, medium size

2 cups flour
3 teaspoons baking powder
¾ teaspoon salt

⅓ cup shortening
⅔ cup milk

Sift flour, baking powder, and salt together; cut in shortening until mixture resembles coarse corn meal. Add all of milk and mix to smooth dough (about 25 strokes). Turn out on lightly floured board. Knead lightly about 25 to 30 times. Roll or pat ½ inch thick. Cut with biscuit cutter 2 inches in diameter. Place on ungreased cooky sheet, 15½ x 12 inches. Bake in very hot oven (450°) 12 to 15 minutes.

Whenever I eat hot biscuits I think of my undergraduate days at Montana State College and our wonderful dean of women, Dean Una B. Herrick. Mrs. Herrick always described her coming to Montana with a wide gesture, as she called it — the big pioneer state of Montana. She came from the more settled and more densely populated state of Tennessee and brought her own servants with her. Her beloved Molly was our cook at the freshman dormitory and she baked the tender, thin, crusty hot biscuits that Dean Herrick liked so well. When we sat at the Dean's table and there were hot biscuits on the table she would look around at us and say in her rich southern drawl, "Butter your biscuits, you little Yankees, butter 'em while they're hot." It was sacrilege, in her opinion, to let the biscuit cool one minute without popping the butter into it. And all of us little Yankees did "butter 'em while they're hot" from that time on!

BUTTERSCOTCH BISCUITS — About 12

1 recipe Baking Powder Biscuits
   (page 53)
½ cup brown sugar

½ teaspoon cinnamon
¼ cup butter, softened
½ cup brown sugar

Roll dough ¼ inch thick. Mix ½ cup brown sugar with the cinnamon. Spread dough with 2 tablespoons of the butter, sprinkle with sugar-cinnamon mixture. Roll, and cut in ½-inch slices. Sprinkle remaining ½ cup sugar in 9-inch round pan, dot with remaining butter. Place biscuits on brown sugar mixture. Bake in very hot oven (450°) 12 to 15 minutes.

CHEESE BISCUITS — About 16

1 recipe Baking Powder Biscuits
   (page 53)

½ cup grated American cheese

Add cheese to shortening and flour mixture before liquid is added. Proceed as for Baking Powder Biscuits. Place on ungreased cooky sheet, 15½ x 12 inches. Bake in very hot oven (450°) 12 to 15 minutes.

COCONUT TWISTS — About 16

1 recipe Baking Powder Biscuits
   (page 53)
2 tablespoons butter, softened

¾ cup brown sugar
¾ cup coconut

Roll dough ¼ inch thick. Spread with softened butter. Sprinkle lightly with brown sugar and coconut. Cut into strips 1 x 6 inches. Bring the two ends of the strips together and twist. Place on ungreased cooky sheet, 15½ x 12 inches. Bake in very hot oven (450°) 12 to 15 minutes.

CURRANT SCONES — About 18

1 recipe Baking Powder Biscuits
   (page 53)
1 tablespoon sugar
½ cup currants

1 egg, slightly beaten
2 tablespoons milk

Add sugar and currants to flour mixture. After dough has been rolled out, cut in 2½-inch squares. Cut each square diagonally in two so as to make triangles. Combine egg and milk, and brush scones with mixture. Place on ungreased cooky sheet, 15½ x 12 inches. Bake in very hot oven (450°) 12 to 15 minutes.

BANANA NUT BREAD
2 loaves

¾ cup butter
1½ cups sugar
2 eggs, beaten
3 cups sifted flour
2 teaspoons baking powder

½ teaspoon salt
½ teaspoon soda
¼ cup milk
¾ cup mashed banana pulp
1 cup pecans, chopped

Cream butter; add sugar and mix until light and fluffy. Add beaten eggs and blend well. Sift flour, baking powder, salt, and soda together. Add milk to banana pulp. Add alternately with dry ingredients to creamed fat and sugar mixture. Fold in chopped pecans. Pour into two greased loaf pans, 9½ x 5¼ x 2¾ inches. Bake in moderate oven (350°) 40 to 45 minutes.

BASIC SWEET DOUGH
24 medium-size rolls

This dough may be used as plain rolls, coffee cake dough, or as basic dough for variations.

1 cake compressed yeast
½ cup sugar
1 teaspoon salt
1 cup scalded milk, cooled to lukewarm

2 eggs, beaten
2½ cups flour
½ cup butter or shortening, melted
2½ cups flour

Crumble yeast into bowl, add sugar, salt, milk, and eggs. Mix well. Add 2½ cups flour and beat until bubbles form on surface. Add shortening and remaining 2½ cups flour. Let rise in a warm place until double. Punch down. Roll into desired shapes. Allow to double in bulk again and then bake in hot oven (400°) 15 minutes.

This dough may also be used for any of the following forms of rolls: Bowknots, Crescents, Clover Leaf, Butterhorns, Layer, Coffee Cakes, Braids, and Parker House.

CINNAMON ROLLS — About 12

Make ½ recipe Basic Sweet Dough. Roll dough into rectangle 9 x 18 inches and about ¼ inch thick. Spread with 2½ tablespoons softened butter, and sprinkle with mixture of ¾ cup brown sugar and 2½ teaspoons cinnamon. Roll up jelly-roll fashion, beginning on long side. Cut quickly with a sharp knife into 1-inch slices. Place portions, cut side down, in well-greased muffin pans. Cover and let rise until double in bulk. Bake in hot oven (400°) 15 minutes.

CINNAMON PECAN ROLLS — About 30

Make Basic Sweet Dough (page 55). Divide dough in half. Roll out each half into a rectangle ¼ inch thick. Brush dough with melted butter. Sprinkle each half with mixture of ½ cup white sugar, ½ cup brown sugar, and 2 teaspoons cinnamon. Roll like a jelly roll, cut with a sharp knife, and place portions, cut side down, in well-greased muffin pans which contain 1 tablespoon Butterscotch Syrup and a few pecans. Allow to double in bulk. Bake in hot oven (400°) 15 minutes.

BUTTERSCOTCH SYRUP:

1 cup light corn syrup	3 tablespoons butter
1 cup brown sugar	1½ cups pecans

Mix corn syrup, brown sugar, and butter together. Heat in double boiler.

HONEY-BUTTER ROLLS — About 24

Make Basic Sweet Dough (page 55). Divide dough in half. Roll out each half into a rectangle ¼ inch thick. Brush dough with Honey-Butter Mixture. Roll like a jelly roll. Cut quickly with a sharp knife and place portions, cut side down, in well-greased muffin pans. Allow to double in bulk. Bake in hot oven (400°) 15 minutes.

HONEY-BUTTER MIXTURE:

½ cup strained honey	1 egg white
2 tablespoons butter, softened	Confectioners' sugar

Combine honey, butter, and egg white. Add confectioners' sugar to make mixture of icing consistency.

MARMALADE ROLLS — About 24

Make Basic Sweet Dough (page 55). Divide dough in half. Roll each half into a rectangle ¼ inch thick. Spread with your favorite marmalade and roll like a jelly roll. Cut with a sharp knife, place portions, cut side down, in well-greased muffin pans. Brush with beaten egg, allow rolls to double in bulk, and bake in hot oven (400°) until brown, about 15 minutes. Remove from pan immediately.

a most-requested treat . . .

Kolacky, page 72.

glamourized from basic dough . . .

Bohemian Christmas Braid, page 58.

ORANGE BOWKNOT ROLLS — About 24

In Basic Sweet Dough (page 55) use ¼ cup orange juice and ¾ cup milk as liquid. Add two tablespoons grated orange peel. Proceed as for Basic Sweet Dough. After dough has doubled in bulk, punch down. Roll dough ½ inch thick. Cut into strips about 9 inches long and ½ inch wide. Tie each in a knot. Place on greased cooky sheet. Cover. Let rise until double in bulk. Bake in hot oven (400°) 15 minutes. Spread while still warm with thin frosting made with 3 tablespoons orange juice, 1½ teaspoons grated orange peel, and 1½ cups sifted confectioners' sugar.

These delicately flavored orange rolls will be welcome at any luncheon.

POPPY-SEED LEMON ROLLS — About 24

Make Basic Sweet Dough (page 55). Divide dough in half. Roll each half into a rectangle ¼ inch thick. Brush with Poppy-Seed Syrup and roll like a jelly roll. Cut with a sharp knife and place portions, cut side down, in well-greased muffin pans. Allow to double in bulk. Bake in hot oven (400°) 15 minutes. Remove from pan immediately.

POPPY-SEED SYRUP:

1 cup sugar	3 tablespoons lemon juice
½ cup water	½ cup poppy seed
1 lemon, grated peel	

Cook together for 3 minutes the sugar and water; cool. Add the grated lemon peel, lemon juice, and poppy seed.

RUM ROLLS — About 24

To Basic Sweet Dough (page 55) add 2 teaspoons rum flavoring. Divide into 2 parts. Roll each part into rectangle ¼ inch thick. Brush with 2 tablespoons melted butter. Combine 1 cup seedless raisins and 1 cup brown sugar and sprinkle over dough. Roll up like jelly roll. Cut into ¾-inch slices. Place portions, cut side down, in greased muffin pans. Cover and let rise in a warm place until double in bulk. Bake in moderately hot oven (400°) 15 to 20 minutes. Remove rolls from muffin pans and brush with thin frosting made of 1 cup confectioners' sugar, 2 tablespoons hot water, and 1 teaspoon rum flavoring.

BOHEMIAN CHRISTMAS BRAID

Add to flour in Basic Sweet Dough (page 55):

2 teaspoons grated lemon peel	½ cup raisins
⅛ teaspoon mace	½ cup mixed glacé fruit
¼ teaspoon nutmeg	½ cup glacé cherries
1 teaspoon lemon extract	¾ cup coarsely chopped pecans

Add lemon peel and dry ingredients to flour, pour lemon extract over the raisins and mixed glacé fruit before adding to flour, and proceed as for Basic Sweet Dough. To make braid, divide dough into 4 equal parts. Shape 3 of the parts into strands 14 inches long. Place about 1 inch apart on lightly greased cooky sheet. Braid loosely. Seal ends well.

Divide remaining portion of dough into 3 parts and shape into 3 strands each 12 inches long. Make another braid as before and place small braid on top of large braid, pinching ends of small braid into large braid.

Cover and let rise in warm place until double in bulk (about 1 hour). Bake in moderate oven (350°) 40 to 50 minutes. Ice while warm with Confectioners' Frosting (page 413). Decorate with glacé cherries and pecan halves.

BOSTON BROWN BREAD
3 pans

1 cup sifted flour	1 cup graham flour
1 cup corn meal	½ cup molasses
2 teaspoons soda	2 cups sour milk
1 teaspoon salt	¾ cup raisins

Sift together flour, corn meal, soda, and salt. Add graham flour and molasses. Add sour milk and raisins, and stir until mixed. Fill well-greased brown-bread pans ⅔ full. (Use brown-bread pans, 4 inches in diameter, 5½ inches in depth, or baking powder cans.) Cover closely and steam 2½ to 3 hours.

Serve with Boston Baked Beans (page 165) for a typical New England Saturday night supper.

BRIOCHE
3 dozen

1 cup milk
⅔ cup butter
2 cakes compressed yeast
3 eggs
4 egg yolks
½ cup sugar
4⅔ cups sifted flour

½ teaspoon lemon juice or
   2 pounded cardamom seeds
2 teaspoons salt
⅓ cup butter
1 cup confectioners' sugar
2 tablespoons hot water
½ teaspoon vanilla

Scald milk and add the ⅔ cup of butter; cool to lukewarm. Add yeast cakes to lukewarm milk to soften. Add eggs and egg yolks, sugar, flour, lemon juice or cardamom seeds, and salt, and beat for 10 minutes. Let rise until double in bulk. Knead down and chill overnight in the refrigerator. Turn out on a floured board, roll into rectangle about ½ inch thick. Spread with remaining ⅓ cup of butter, fold sides to the center to make three layers. Cut off pieces ¾ inch wide, cover and let rise until double. Take each piece separately in the hands and twist from ends in opposite directions. Coil and bring ends together. Twist again. Let rise in pan until light and bake 20 minutes in moderate over (375°). Make a thin vanilla frosting of the confectioners' sugar moistened with hot water and vanilla. Brush over the brioches while still warm.

    This is a very soft dough. A little flour may have to be used on the board to handle it, but don't add any more than necessary.

The brioches are light, feathery twisted rolls — perfect accompaniment with hot chocolate or coffee.

BUTTERHORN ROLLS
3 to 4 dozen

2 cakes compressed yeast	½ cup sugar
1 tablespoon sugar	1½ teaspoons salt
1 cup milk	3 eggs, well beaten
½ cup butter	5 cups sifted flour

Crumble yeast cakes. Add the tablespoon sugar and stir until liquid. Scald milk; add butter, sugar, and salt; cool to luke-warm. Add yeast, eggs, and ⅓ of the flour. Beat vigorously until bubbles form on surface. Cover and let stand in warm place 25 to 30 minutes or until sponge is light. Add remaining flour to make a smooth dough. Turn out on floured board and knead until smooth and elastic. Place dough in greased bowl and brush with melted butter. Cover and let rise until double in bulk. Knead down; turn out on lightly floured board. Divide dough into thirds; roll each third into 9-inch circle. Brush with melted butter. Cut each circle into 12 or 16 wedge-shaped pieces. Pull out ends of each wedge and, beginning at broad end, roll toward point. Place on greased cooky sheets with point downward to prevent unrolling. Brush with melted butter. Cover and let rise until very light. Bake in hot oven (400°) 12 to 15 minutes. Brush with melted butter when taken from oven.

CRESCENTS
Shape Butterhorn Rolls into crescent shape and bake.

CHRISTMAS BREAD
1 loaf

1 cup milk, scalded	1 cup sugar
1 cake compressed yeast	1 cup sifted flour
1 cup sifted flour	1 teaspoon salt
½ cup shortening, softened	1 teaspoon baking powder
½ teaspoon vanilla	½ teaspoon nutmeg
½ teaspoon lemon extract	1 cup raisins
1 egg, beaten	¼ pound finely sliced citron

Cool milk to lukewarm. Crumble yeast in lukewarm milk and add the 1 cup of flour. Beat well, cover and let rise an hour or until light. Add softened shortening, vanilla and lemon extract, beaten egg, and sugar. Combine the remaining cup of flour, the salt, baking powder, and nutmeg. Add to sponge mixture. Beat well and add raisins and citron. Turn into greased loaf pan, 9½ x 5¼ x 2¾ inches, and bake in moderate oven (375°) 25 minutes.

This is a good fruit bread to serve at Christmastime.

CINNAMON ROLL LOAF OR FRUIT RING

Basic Dough:

½ cup melted butter
½ cup sugar
2 teaspoons salt
2 eggs, beaten
1 cake compressed yeast

½ cup lukewarm water
2 cups milk, scalded
7 cups sifted flour
2 tablespoons melted butter

Combine shortening, sugar, salt, and eggs. Soften yeast in lukewarm water, and add to above mixture. Add lukewarm milk alternately with flour to make a stiff dough. Knead lightly, let double in bulk, punch down. Divide in half, roll into rectangles; brush with melted butter.

Cinnamon Roll Loaf:

Sprinkle ½ Basic Dough with mixture of ½ cup brown sugar and 1 teaspoon cinnamon; roll as for jelly roll. Put in loaf pan, 9½ x 5¼ x 2¾ inches; let rise until double in bulk. Bake in moderate oven (350°) 45 minutes.

Fruit Ring:

Spread ½ Basic Dough with 1 cup mixed candied fruits; join ends to make ring. Place on cooky sheet and snip at 2-inch intervals. Let rise until light. Bake in moderate oven (350°) 30 to 35 minutes. Frost with Thin Confectioners' Frosting made by adding ¼ cup hot water to 1 cup confectioners' sugar. Sprinkle with chopped nuts.

CINNAMON TOAST SQUARES
16 squares

4 slices bread, cut ¼ inch thick
2 tablespoons butter, softened

6 tablespoons sugar
1 tablespoon cinnamon

Remove crusts from bread. Cut each slice of bread in half and each half into 2 squares. Toast squares in oven. Combine butter, sugar, and cinnamon. Spread toast squares with creamed sugar-cinnamon mixture. Place in hot oven (400°) or under broiler until mixture is melted.

CINNAMON TULIPS
1½ dozen rolls

1 cake compressed yeast
¼ cup lukewarm water
½ cup milk, scalded
¼ cup sugar
1 teaspoon salt
1 cup sifted flour

1 egg, beaten
2 tablespoons melted shortening
1½ cups sifted flour
2 tablespoons melted butter
4 tablespoons sugar
¼ teaspoon cinnamon

Soften yeast in lukewarm water. Add sugar and salt to milk; cool to lukewarm. Add the 1 cup of flour. Mix well. Add softened yeast and egg. Beat well. Add shortening and blend in. Add remaining 1½ cups flour or enough for a soft dough. Turn out on lightly floured board and knead until smooth and satiny. Place in greased bowl; cover and let rise until double. Knead down. Roll to long narrow sheet ¼ inch thick. Brush with melted butter. Sprinkle with mixed sugar and cinnamon. Roll up like jelly roll and seal edge. Cut slices two inches long and, with scissors, make two cuts almost through to edge of each slice. Separate the three strips to form tulip-shaped rolls. Place on greased cooky sheet. Let rise until double in bulk. Bake in moderate oven (375°) 15 to 20 minutes.

COFFEE RING
Makes two 9-inch rings

1 cake compressed yeast
¼ cup lukewarm water
1 cup milk, scalded
¼ cup sugar
1 teaspoon salt
½ cup melted shortening

1 cup sifted flour
2 eggs, beaten until light
2¼ cups sifted flour
½ teaspoon vanilla
1 cup seedless raisins
Confectioners' Frosting (page 413)

Soften yeast in lukewarm water. Add sugar, salt, and shortening to milk, and cool to lukewarm. Add the 1 cup of flour and beat well, then beat in the eggs. Mix in thoroughly the softened yeast. Add remaining 2¼ cups flour to make a stiff batter. Add vanilla and beat thoroughly until smooth. Cover and let rise until bubbly, about one hour. When batter is light, stir in raisins. Turn batter into 2 greased 9-inch ring molds. Sprinkle with ½ of the Topping. Let rise until light, about 20 minutes. Bake in moderate oven (375°) about 35 minutes. Frost with Confectioners' Frosting; sprinkle with remaining topping.

Topping:

½ cup flour
½ cup fine bread crumbs
½ cup sugar

2 teaspoons cinnamon
½ cup butter

Mix together until crumbly.

CORN BREAD
8 servings

¾ cup yellow corn meal
¼ cup sifted flour
1 teaspoon baking powder
1 tablespoon sugar
½ teaspoon salt

¼ teaspoon soda
¾ cup sour milk
1 egg, beaten
2 tablespoons melted shortening

Combine corn meal with remaining dry ingredients which have been sifted together. Add sour milk and egg; blend. Stir in shortening. Pour into greased 8-inch square pan. Bake in hot oven (400°) 20 minutes. Cut into 16 squares.

CORN STICKS
1 dozen

1 egg
1 cup milk
2 tablespoons melted butter
2 cups white or yellow corn meal

¼ cup sifted flour
1 tablespoon sugar
2 teaspoons baking powder
½ teaspoon salt

Beat egg; add milk and melted butter. Sift together dry ingredients. Add liquid ingredients and beat well. Preheat corn-stick pans in oven and grease thoroughly. Pour batter into hot corn-stick pans. Bake in very hot oven (450°) 12 to 15 minutes.

These crunchy corn sticks are excellent with luncheon dishes.

CRANBERRY NUT MUFFINS
About 2 dozen

¼ cup shortening
¼ cup sugar
1 egg, beaten
2 cups sifted flour
½ teaspoon salt
¾ teaspoon soda
1 cup cranberries

½ cup sugar
¾ cup sour milk
½ cup chopped nuts
1 teaspoon grated orange peel
½ teaspoon cinnamon
½ cup sugar

Cream shortening; add the ¼ cup of sugar and continue cream-ing until light. Blend in beaten egg. Sift flour, salt, and soda together. Grind cranberries and add remaining ½ cup of sugar. To creamed mixture add flour mixture, cranberries, sour milk, nuts, and orange peel. Mix just enough to blend. Fill greased 2-inch muffin pans ¾ full. For topping, combine cinnamon and sugar, and sprinkle ½ teaspoon over each muffin before baking. Bake in hot oven (400°) 20 to 25 minutes or until light brown. Remove from pans at once and serve hot.

DATE NUT BREAD
1 loaf

¼ cup shortening
¾ cup sugar
1 teaspoon vanilla
2 eggs, beaten
2¼ cups sifted flour
1 teaspoon salt

4 teaspoons baking powder
¾ cup milk
1 cup (7¼-ounce package) chopped pitted dates
1 cup coarsely chopped pecans

Cream shortening; add sugar and continue creaming until light and fluffy. Blend in vanilla. Add beaten eggs and mix well. Sift together flour, salt, and baking powder. Add alternately with milk to creamed mixture. Stir in dates and pecans. Pour batter into greased loaf pan, 9½ x 5¼ x 2¾ inches. Bake in moderate oven (350°) 45 to 50 minutes. Put paper towel-ing over top of pan last 20 minutes of baking to prevent loaf from becoming too brown. Cool in pan 5 minutes, then remove from pan and cool on cake rack.

DROP DOUGHNUTS
About 2½ dozen

2 eggs, well beaten
¾ cup sugar
1 tablespoon melted shortening
1 teaspoon vanilla
½ cup milk
2 cups sifted flour

½ teaspoon salt
2½ teaspoons baking powder
½ teaspoon nutmeg
1 teaspoon cinnamon
1 cup sugar to coat doughnuts

Combine eggs, sugar, shortening, and milk, and beat together for about one minute. Sift together flour, salt, baking powder, and spices. Add to egg mixture and blend until smooth. Drop from teaspoon into deep hot fat (365°) 3 to 5 minutes or until golden brown. Roll doughnuts in sugar while still warm.

The recipe for these drop doughnuts was developed in Experimental Class by Jacqueline Morrison and Loraine Miller. They wanted to work out a recipe for doughnuts that didn't have to be rolled and cut out. These easy-to-make drop doughnuts are the result. The spicy fragrance of the doughnuts brought so many students to our kitchen to sample the product that the doughnuts didn't even have time to cool.

FARITELLI
Italian Fried Bread
3 dozen

1 egg
⅓ cup water
1½ cups sifted flour

½ teaspoon baking powder
⅓ teaspoon salt

Beat egg and add water; then add dry ingredients. Knead until dough is springy. Roll ¼ inch thick; cut in diamond shapes 1½ inches in width. Fry in deep hot fat (375°). Serve bread hot, as it becomes rather tough when allowed to cool.

This fried bread is especially good with Italian food.

FIG SQUARE
8-inch square

1 cake compressed yeast
¼ cup lukewarm water
½ cup milk, scalded
¼ cup sugar
1 teaspoon salt
2 tablespoons melted shortening

1 cup sifted flour
1 egg, beaten
½ teaspoon grated lemon peel
1½ cups sifted flour
Melted butter

Soften yeast in lukewarm water. Add sugar, salt, and shortening to milk, and cool to lukewarm. Stir in 1 cup flour to make a thick batter and mix well. Add softened yeast, egg, lemon peel. Beat well. Add remaining 1½ cups flour or enough to make a soft dough. Turn out on lightly floured board and knead until smooth and satiny. Place in greased bowl. Cover and let rise in warm place until double in bulk, about 1½ hours. When light, punch down. Let rest 10 minutes. Pat or roll into a rectangular sheet about ½ inch thick and 8 inches wide. Brush with melted butter. Spread with Fig Filling. Roll up like jelly roll, sealing edge. Shape in an 8-inch square pan (*see* page 472). At each corner, with scissors, cut through the roll almost to the bottom. Then cut slantwise through the roll in three places on each side of the square. Let rise until double, about 1 hour. Bake in moderate oven (350°) 20 to 25 minutes.

Fig Filling:

⅔ cup dried figs
½ cup cold water
4 tablespoons sugar

1 tablespoon flour
Dash of salt
1 tablespoon lemon juice

Cover figs with boiling water and let stand about 10 minutes. Drain, clip off stems, and snip figs into small pieces with scissors. Add cold water, sugar mixed with flour, and salt. Cook slowly 10 minutes or until thickened. Add lemon juice and cool.

FINSKA KAFFEBROD
Finnish Coffee Cake Strips
3 dozen

Dough:

1 cup butter
2½ cups sifted flour
3 tablespoons sugar

1 teaspoon almond extract
½ cup finely chopped blanched
    almonds

Topping:

1 egg white, beaten until frothy
½ cup finely chopped almonds

2 tablespoons sugar

Cream butter, add flour and sugar, and mix thoroughly to a smooth dough. Add almond extract and chopped blanched almonds, and mix. Pinch off pieces the size of a walnut. Roll each piece into finger-sized strip ½ inch wide and 5 inches long. Place on lightly greased cooky sheet, 15½ x 12 inches. Brush each with beaten egg white and dip into chopped almonds. Sprinkle a little sugar on top. Bake in moderate oven (350°) 12 to 15 minutes or until a light golden brown.

These delicate crispy strips are more like a cooky than a bread and are delicious with midmorning coffee.

FRESH BLUEBERRY PANCAKES
6 to 8, small

1 egg, beaten
1 cup buttermilk
1 tablespoon butter, melted
1 cup sifted flour, less two tablespoons

½ teaspoon salt
½ teaspoon soda
¾ teaspoon baking powder
½ cup fresh blueberries, washed
and drained

Combine beaten egg, buttermilk, and melted butter. Sift flour, salt, soda, and baking powder together. Add liquid to dry ingredients and add blueberries. Mix just enough to dampen dry ingredients (leave lumpy). Drop from spoon onto lightly greased griddle and bake until top is bubbly and underside nicely browned. Turn *only* once. Serve immediately.

Pancakes should be small — 3 to 4 inches in diameter.

FRUIT BREAD
1 loaf

2 cups sifted flour
¾ cup sugar
3 teaspoons baking powder
¼ teaspoon salt
¼ cup chopped citron
¼ cup currants
2 tablespoons chopped candied
lemon peel

2 tablespoons chopped glacé
cherries
½ cup chopped nuts
2 eggs, beaten
1 cup milk
3 tablespoons melted shortening

Sift dry ingredients together. Add fruit and nuts. Combine eggs, milk, and shortening. Mix with dry ingredients, then pour into well-greased loaf pan, 9½ x 5¼ x 2¾ inches. Let stand 30 minutes. Bake in moderate oven (350°) 45 to 50 minutes.

GARLIC-BUTTERED FRENCH BREAD

1 loaf French bread	2 cloves garlic, peeled
¼ pound butter, softened	1 tablespoon finely minced parsley
⅛ teaspoon salt	

Cream butter. Add salt. Place peeled garlic between folds of waxed paper and pound fine with wooden handle of knife or wooden mallet. Blend finely pounded garlic and minced parsley into butter. Slice French bread diagonally into ½-inch slices, not quite through loaf. Spread slices slightly apart and spread generously with garlic butter. Heat in moderate oven (350°) 15 to 20 minutes, or until bread is crisp and heated through.

GERMAN CHRISTMAS STOLLEN
2 large loaves

1 cup milk	½ cup glacé cherries
½ cup sugar	1½ teaspoons grated lemon peel
1 teaspoon salt	¼ teaspoon nutmeg
2 cakes compressed yeast	4 cups sifted flour
1 cup sifted flour	¼ cup butter, melted
2 eggs, beaten	¼ cup sugar
¾ cup butter, softened	½ teaspoon cinnamon
1 cup seedless raisins	Confectioners' Frosting (page 413)
½ cup citron	Walnuts or candied fruit

Scald milk, add ½ cup sugar and the salt. Cool to lukewarm. Add crumbled yeast and mix thoroughly. Add the 1 cup of

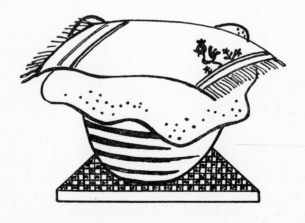

flour and stir until smooth, cover and let rise until double in bulk. Add the beaten eggs, softened butter, fruit, and nutmeg, and mix thoroughly. Add remaining 4 cups flour to make a dough stiff enough to knead. Knead until smooth and elastic. Allow to rise until double. Knead down and divide in two. Roll each half into an 8-inch circle. Brush with melted butter, sprinkle with combined sugar and cinnamon. Make a crease down the center of the dough and fold over. Place in greased loaf pans, 9½ by 5¼ by 2¾ inches, and let rise until double in bulk. Bake in moderate oven (350°) 30 to 40 minutes. Frost with Confectioners' Frosting and sprinkle with chopped walnuts or candied fruit.

The stollen will keep for a week, at least. It may be cut in thin slices and toasted, or buttered and placed under the broiler until lightly browned.

Try this fruit-filled fragrant bread for your Christmas breakfast, or give it to friends for an edible gift.

GINGERBREAD
24 servings

1 cup melted shortening	2 teaspoons ginger
1 cup molasses	2 teaspoons soda
1 cup brown sugar	¼ teaspoon salt
3 cups sifted flour	1⅓ cups boiling water
2 teaspoons cinnamon	2 eggs, beaten

Mix melted shortening, molasses, and brown sugar. Add sifted dry ingredients and mix well. Stir in boiling water; fold in beaten eggs. Pour into greased pan, 13 x 9½ x 2 inches. Bake in moderate oven (375°) 40 to 45 minutes.

If you want something quick and easy to make for a gang of teen-agers, just toss this gingerbread together and serve large fluffy pieces of it while still warm. You won't have to worry about any leftovers. This is a favorite recipe of Mrs. Vera Swearingen, of our Institution Management Staff, whom all of the students in the Catering Classes know as one of the best cooks in town.

HUSH PUPPIES
About 1½ dozen

2 cups corn meal
3 tablespoons flour
1 tablespoon baking powder
1 teaspoon soda

1 teaspoon salt
½ cup finely chopped onion
2 eggs, beaten
1½ cups buttermilk

Mix together dry ingredients; add chopped onion. Combine eggs and milk; add to dry ingredients. Stir just enough to combine. Drop by teaspoonfuls into deep hot fat (375°) and cook about 5 minutes or until nicely browned. Drain on absorbent paper.

Serve with fried fish.

And how did hush puppies get their droll name? According to legends fish fries were popular in the deep South. And as the fragrant odor of the frying fish was wafted on the evening breeze it would set the hound dogs to howling. One night, to quiet them, one of the fishermen added bits of onion to the corn-meal mixture that the fish had been rolled in, fried it in the same fat, then threw it to the hungry hounds with the admonition, "Hush, puppies." And so, hush puppies were born!

JULE KAGE
Scandinavian Christmas Bread
2 loaves

2 cups milk, scalded
1 cup sugar
1½ teaspoons salt
1½ teaspoons cardamom seed, crushed
½ cup butter

1 cake compressed yeast
2 eggs, well beaten
6 cups sifted flour, or more if necessary
1½ cups seedless raisins
½ cup chopped citron

To scalded milk add sugar, salt, cardamom seed, and butter. Cool to lukewarm; add crumbled yeast and mix well. Stir in eggs and 3 cups of the flour, and beat until smooth. Combine raisins and citron with remainder of flour and add to yeast mixture. If necessary add more flour to make a smooth elastic dough which can be kneaded on a bread board. Place in greased bowl; cover. Let rise until double in bulk. Knead down; shape into 2 loaves and put into greased loaf pans, 9½ x 5¼ x 2¾ inches. Let rise again until double. Bake in moderate oven (375°) 45 to 60 minutes or until done. Brush top of loaves with butter when they come from the oven. Remove from pans and place on cooling racks.

KARJALAN PIIRAKAT
Finnish Bread with Egg Butter
12 servings

½ **cup rice**
1½ **cups milk**
½ **teaspoon salt**
⅔ **cup water**

2 **cups rye flour**
1 **teaspoon salt**
2 **hard-cooked eggs**
¼ **cup butter, softened**

In double boiler, cook rice in milk to which the ½ teaspoon of salt has been added. Make a stiff dough of the water, rye flour, and remaining teaspoon of salt. Shape into roll about one inch thick. Cut into twelve 1-inch pieces. Roll each piece of dough into a *very* thin circle 6 inches in diameter. Place 1 tablespoon cooked rice in center of circle of dough. Pleat dough up around rice so some of the rice shows through. Place on ungreased cooky sheet. Bake in hot oven (425°) 5 minutes. Serve the piirakat hot with egg butter.

Make egg butter by dicing the hard-cooked eggs and blending with the softened butter.

Lea Juvonen, a graduate student from Finland, made karjalan piirakat whenever she became homesick for her native land. This is one of the most intriguing kinds of bread that I have ever encountered. The finished product resembles a baked potato in color. The piirakat should be spread generously with the egg butter and eaten while hot. I heartily recommend the karjalan piirakat and hope you'll try it sometime with its crisp brown crust enclosing the mound of flaky rice.

Just as this book was going to press, a long narrow package with many gay, colorful, red and white stamps and foreign-looking labels arrived from Helsinki. I knew, even before I opened it, that it was the rolling pin Lea Juvonen had promised to send when she went back to Finland. To Lea, our rather large bulky rolling pins were quite unmanageable and difficult to handle. Each time she used one she wished for the kind she used at home. Now, thanks to Lea, I am the proud possessor of a long, slender, tapered, well-balanced Finnish rolling pin that is about one inch thick in the middle and one-half inch at the ends. We will have no trouble rolling the karjalan piirakat as thin as paper.

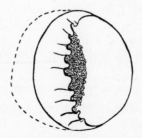

KOLACKY
Bohemian Fruit-Filled Buns
About 2½ dozen

¼ cup milk
1 cake compressed yeast
1 teaspoon sugar
1 tablespoon flour
½ cup butter
2 tablespoons sugar

1 teaspoon salt
3 egg yolks
1½ teaspoons grated lemon peel
1 cup milk
4 cups sifted flour
1 egg white

Heat the ¼ cup milk to lukewarm; soften yeast cake in milk. Add the teaspoon sugar and tablespoon flour. Mix together to make sponge; cover and let rise. Soften butter; add sugar and salt and blend well. Add egg yolks one at a time to creamed butter and sugar mixture; stir well after each addition. Add grated lemon peel. Scald the cup of milk; then cool to lukewarm. Add sponge and 1 cup of the flour. Add to creamed butter and sugar mixture; stir in remainder of flour to make a soft dough. Beat egg white to soft peak stage and fold into dough. This will be a soft dough; add a little more flour if necessary, so dough will not be too sticky. Knead lightly on floured board. Place dough in greased bowl. Cover and let rise until double in bulk; knead down. Pinch off balls about the size of a walnut; place on lightly greased cooky sheet. Let rise until light.

Press down the centers with thumb to make a cavity for the fruit filling. Fill center cavity with 1 teaspoon Fruit Filling or jam. Brush with melted butter and sprinkle with chopped nuts. Bake in hot oven (400°) 12 to 15 minutes. When cool, sprinkle with powdered sugar.

Fruit Filling:

1½ cups prunes	½ teaspoon cinnamon
1 cup dried apricots	¼ teaspoon cloves
½ cup sugar	¼ teaspoon salt

Cook prunes and apricots separately until tender. Drain, and remove pits from prunes. Chop fruits fine. Combine prunes, apricots, sugar, spices, and salt, and mix well. Fill cavity of kolacky with this mixture.

This is the history of these Bohemian kolacky (pronounced ko-lahch'-kee): When I first came to Iowa State College one of my students, Rose Simanek, brought me some delicate kolacky that her mother had sent to her. I was so impressed with her good recipe that I asked for it. And of course, Mrs. Simanek had made her kolacky so often that she didn't measure by cups and spoons — she just made them! So the next time Rose went home, she measured the ingredients as her mother stirred up the kolacky. Afterward we worked out the recipe. The kolacky have attained great popularity in our Institution Tea Room and are frequently requested by our guests.

KROPBROOD
Dutch Graham Bread
3 loaves

1 cake compressed yeast	2 tablespoons butter or other
1 cup lukewarm water	shortening
1 cup milk, scalded	3 teaspoons salt
1 cup chopped nuts	4 cups graham or whole-wheat
¼ cup brown sugar	flour
4 tablespoons molasses	7 cups sifted white flour

Soften yeast in lukewarm water. Cool milk to lukewarm. Add nuts, brown sugar, molasses, butter, salt, softened yeast, and graham or whole-wheat flour. Beat well. Add enough white flour to knead to a stiff dough. Cover, let rise in a warm place until double in bulk. Divide into 3 pieces. Shape into loaves, place in greased loaf pans, 9½ x 5¼ x 2¾ inches. Let rise again until double. Bake in hot oven (400°) 20 minutes; reduce heat to moderate (350°) and continue baking 40 to 50 minutes. Brush with butter when loaves come from oven; remove from pan and place on cooling racks.

LEFSE
Norwegian Bread

2 cups milk	½ cup mashed potatoes
¾ cup boiling water	6 cups sifted flour
¼ cup shortening	½ teaspoon salt

Scald milk; add boiling water, shortening, and mashed potatoes. Mix thoroughly. Combine flour and salt, and stir milk-and-potato mixture into flour. Mix well. If necessary, add a little more flour to make a smooth dough. Pinch off portions of the dough into pieces about the size of an egg. Knead lightly. Roll each portion into a 12-inch circle about ⅛ inch thick. Use the corrugated rolling pin that is used to roll lefse, if you have one. Place circle of lefse over a wooden stick and transfer to moderately hot griddle, rotating the dough with a spatula as it browns. Turn dough when it is puffy in spots. Cook on reverse side until lightly browned. Cool between pieces of paper toweling.

When ready to serve, dip the crisp dough into a large kettle of boiling water. Place dough between folds of a cloth towel to absorb excess moisture and steam. Let stand 5 minutes, then remove from towel. The lefse may be spread with softened butter and made into a roll about 1 to 1½ inches in diameter, or it may be buttered and spread lightly with a sugar and cinnamon mixture. Cut roll into 5- to 6-inch lengths. Serve immediately.

This is a cherished family recipe from the great-grandmother of Gay Wood of Kiron, Iowa. The family tradition calls for lefse on Christmas eve when it is served with creamed lutefisk and potatoes cooked in their jackets. Lingonberries are a traditional dessert with this meal. A favorite method of serving the lingonberries is to drain them well, fold into whipped cream, and serve over thin pancakes.

LIMPA
Swedish Rye Bread

1 cup milk, scalded	1 teaspoon caraway seed
1 cake compressed yeast	1 tablespoon grated orange peel
¼ cup lukewarm water	1 teaspoon salt
½ cup brown sugar	1 cup sifted white flour
¼ cup shortening	3 cups sifted rye flour

Cool milk to lukewarm. Soften yeast in lukewarm water; add to milk. Stir in brown sugar, shortening, caraway seed, orange

peel, salt, and white flour. Beat thoroughly to make sponge.
Let rise until light, about 1½ hours. Add rye flour to make
a stiff dough. Turn onto floured board and knead until smooth.
Put into greased bowl. Cover, let rise until double in bulk.
Shape into a loaf and put into a greased loaf pan, 9½ x 5¼
x 2¾ inches. Let rise until double. Bake in hot oven (400°)
15 minutes; then reduce heat to moderate (350°) and bake 45
minutes longer.

NEW ENGLAND FLANNEL CAKES
Makes 24

2 cups sifted flour	2 egg yolks
3 teaspoons baking powder	1½ cups milk
1 tablespoon sugar	2 tablespoons butter
¼ teaspoon salt	2 stiffly beaten egg whites

Sift dry ingredients together. Separate eggs and beat egg yolks.
Combine beaten yolks, milk, and butter, and add gradually
to the dry ingredients, beating to form a smooth batter. Fold
in stiffly beaten egg whites. Pour the mixture onto a hot
greased griddle to make small pancakes. Brown on both sides.
Serve hot with syrup and butter.

ORANGE MARMALADE SWIRL
Makes two 8-inch coffee cakes

1 cake compressed yeast	1 teaspoon salt
¼ cup lukewarm water	1 cup sifted flour
1 cup milk	2 eggs
¼ cup sugar	2¼ cups sifted flour
½ cup melted shortening	½ teaspoon vanilla
	½ cup orange marmalade

Soften yeast in lukewarm water. Scald milk; add sugar, shortening, and salt. Cool to lukewarm. Stir in the 1 cup of flour
and beat well. Add eggs and beat well. Add softened yeast
and mix thoroughly. Stir in the 2¼ cups flour to make a stiff
batter. Add vanilla and beat until smooth. Cover and let rise
until light, about 1 hour. Stir down. Spread in 2 greased 8-inch
layer pans. With floured fingers make indentations in batter
in shape of a round swirl. Fill with orange marmalade. Let
rise until light, about 20 minutes. Bake in moderate oven (375°)
about 30 minutes.

ORANGE NUT BREAD
1 loaf

1 orange
½ cup boiling water
¾ cup raisins or dates
1 cup sugar
2 tablespoons melted butter
1 egg, beaten

2 cups sifted flour
1 teaspoon baking powder
¼ teaspoon salt
1 teaspoon soda
½ cup chopped nuts

Squeeze juice from orange (should be about ½ cup). Add the boiling water to make 1 cup liquid. Remove pulp from orange and put peel through food chopper. Combine with raisins or dates. Combine liquid, fruit, sugar, butter, and egg. Sift flour, baking powder, salt, and soda together, and add liquid and fruit. Mix and add chopped nuts. Bake in greased loaf pan, 9½ x 5¼ x 2¾ inches, in moderate oven (350°) about 50 minutes. Cool in pan.

PANE BASTONE
Bread Sticks
About 3 dozen

1 cup milk, scalded
¼ cup shortening
1½ tablespoons sugar
1 teaspoon salt
1 cake compressed yeast
¼ cup lukewarm water

2 cups sifted flour
1 egg white, stiffly beaten
1½ to 2 cups sifted flour
1 egg, beaten
1 tablespoon milk
Coarse salt

Add shortening, sugar, and salt to milk; cool to lukewarm. Soften yeast cake in lukewarm water and stir into milk. Add 2 cups of flour, fold in egg white. Add remaining 1½ to 2 cups flour to make a soft dough. Turn out on lightly floured board and knead until smooth and satiny. Place in greased bowl. Grease surface of dough; cover and let rise until double in bulk. Knead down; pinch off pieces of dough about the size of a small egg; roll about 8 inches long and ½ inch thick on unfloured board. Keep uniform in size and rounded at the ends. Place on lightly greased cooky sheet, 15½ x 12 inches. Brush with egg and milk mixture. Sprinkle with coarse salt. Let rise. Bake in hot oven (425°) 5 minutes; reduce heat to moderate (350°) and bake 10 to 12 minutes longer, so that sticks will be crisp and dry.

PIZZA
About 36 pieces

8 cups sifted flour
1 cake compressed yeast
2 cups warm water
1 tablespoon sugar

1 teaspoon salt
½ cup salad oil
Salt and pepper

Put flour into large bowl. Crumble yeast into warm water. Add sugar and salt, and stir to a froth; pour liquid into flour. Mix until dough is smooth and elastic. Add more flour if dough is not stiff enough. This should be a stiff dough. Turn onto board and knead until smooth and satiny. Put into greased bowl. Cover and let rise until double, about 2 hours. Knead down. Divide dough into 4 pieces. Roll each piece of dough ¼ inch thick and place in greased 9-inch square pan, letting the edges extend up so that the topping will not run off. Brush dough generously with oil. Sprinkle with salt and pepper. Pour Topping on dough to depth of ½ inch. Sprinkle generously with grated cheese and dot with bits of anchovy fillet or ham. Let rise 15 minutes. Bake in very hot oven (450°) 15 minutes. Cut into 3-inch squares. Serve while hot and bubbly. Pizza might be called a tomato pie with cheese topping.

The dough may be rolled to fit 9-inch pie pans, the topping poured on, and the pizza baked in the same way. The pizza should be cut into wedges when baked in pie pans.

Topping:

2 medium onions, finely chopped
6 cloves garlic, finely minced
¼ cup olive or salad oil
2 No. 2½ cans tomatoes
3 6-ounce cans tomato paste
2 teaspoons salt

½ teaspoon pepper
½ teaspoon orégano
1½ pounds grated American cheese
2 2-ounce cans anchovy fillet or
  ½ cup chopped ham

Sauté onions and garlic in oil until onions are golden in color. Drain tomatoes and add tomato pulp to onions; stir in tomato paste, salt, pepper, and orégano. Simmer 15 to 20 minutes or until sauce has thickened.

There are numerous versions of the pizza, but this particular recipe was brought by Annetta Paranti when she was in the Catering Class. Annetta made pizza for the class and the girls were very curious about it. There were delighted oh's and ah's when the pizza came from the oven and it disappeared like magic. The classes have made pizza for picnics and informal parties ever since and they always enjoy it.

Pizza is served in most Italian restaurants and can be bought at pizzerias — shops where nothing but pizza is made or sold.

PLAIN ROLL DOUGH

1 cup milk, scalded	1 cake compressed yeast
3 tablespoons sugar	¼ cup lukewarm water
3 tablespoons butter	1 egg, well beaten
1 teaspoon salt	3½ to 4 cups sifted flour

Combine milk, sugar, butter, and salt; cool to lukewarm. Soften yeast in lukewarm water; add egg and stir into milk mixture. Stir in ½ of flour; beat vigorously. Add remaining flour to make a soft dough. Turn onto floured board and knead until smooth and satiny. Put in greased bowl; grease surface of dough. Cover and let rise in warm place until double. Knead down; turn out on board and make up into desired shapes.

FINGER ROLLS — About 2½ dozen

Pinch off pieces of Plain Roll Dough (above) about the size of a walnut. Roll into finger-shaped rolls about 4½ inches long. Place on greased cooky sheet, 15½ x 12 inches. Cover and let rise in warm place until double in bulk. Brush lightly with mixture made by combining 1 beaten egg with 1 tablespoon milk. Bake in hot oven (400°) 12 to 15 minutes.

POPPY-SEED OR SESAME-SEED ROLLS

After Finger Rolls have been brushed with mixture of egg and milk, sprinkle each roll with poppy- or sesame-seeds. Bake as for Finger Rolls.

LAYER ROLLS — About 2 dozen

Roll Plain Roll Dough (above) ¼ inch thick. Brush with melted butter; cut into strips 1½ inches wide and lay 4 or 5 strips together, one on top of the other. Cut strips into 1½-inch squares and stand each square with edges upright in greased muffin pans. Let rise until double in bulk. Bake in hot oven (400°) 15 to 20 minutes.

PARKER HOUSE ROLLS — About 2½ dozen

Roll Plain Roll Dough (page 78) ½ inch thick. Cut with 2½-inch biscuit cutter; brush surface with melted butter. Press handle of knife in center to make crease and fold over; press edges together. Place on lightly greased cooky sheet, 15½ x 12 inches. Brush with melted butter and let rise until double in bulk. Bake in hot oven (400°) 12 to 15 minutes.

POPCORN ROLLS — About 2½ dozen

Roll Plain Roll Dough (page 78) ¼ inch thick. Brush surface of dough with melted butter; cut into ½-inch squares. Half-fill greased muffin pans with squares of dough. Let rise until double in bulk. Bake in hot oven (400°) 15 to 20 minutes. Remove carefully from pans, so rolls will not fall apart.

This makes a roll that looks a little like a popcorn ball.

SALLY LUNN
24 servings

2 cups sifted flour	2 eggs
4 teaspoons baking powder	1 cup milk
½ teaspoon salt	3 tablespoons butter, softened
⅓ cup sugar	

Sift together flour, baking powder, salt, and sugar. Beat eggs until light and add the milk. Add to flour mixture and stir until flour is dampened. Add softened butter and stir until mixture is smooth. Pour batter into greased 9-inch square pan. Bake in moderate oven (350°) about 20 to 25 minutes. Cut in small squares, break open one side and slip in a thin piece of butter. Serve piping hot.

These light golden squares of Sally Lunn are a favorite in the South.

SOUTHERN SPOON BREAD
6 servings

2 cups milk	3 egg yolks
½ cup corn meal	2 tablespoons butter
1 teaspoon salt	3 egg whites
¼ teaspoon baking powder	

Scald milk, add corn meal, and cook until mixture is very thick. Add salt and baking powder. Beat egg yolks until light and add a small amount of the corn-meal mixture and then combine both mixtures. Add butter and fold in egg whites beaten to soft peak stage. Turn into buttered 1½-quart casserole and bake uncovered in moderate oven (350°) 25 to 30 minutes or until well puffed. Serve immediately in casserole.

This fluffy, light spoon bread has a moist texture like a soufflé. It is often served with meat instead of potatoes in the South. It is especially good with lots of butter. Just try creamed chicken or creamed dried beef over spoon bread for breakfast or luncheon. The family should be at the table when the spoon bread makes its appearance so it can be served while still light and fluffy.

SPANISH COFFEE CAKE PUFFS
6 servings

1 cake compressed yeast	¼ cup sugar
⅓ cup lukewarm milk	4 egg yolks
1 teaspoon sugar	1½ cups sifted flour
½ cup flour	¼ cup soft butter to brush rolls
¼ cup butter	Confectioners' sugar

Make a sponge by softening yeast cake in lukewarm milk and adding sugar and the ½ cup flour. Beat well. Cover and let rise until double. Cream together butter and sugar. Add egg yolks one at a time, beating well after each addition. When sponge is light, add creamed mixture and mix well. Add the 1½ cups flour and mix until a smooth dough is formed. Turn out on board floured with ⅓ cup flour. Knead until all of flour has been blended in. Finish kneading by using 1 tablespoon butter on board. Divide dough in 6 parts. Knead each ball of dough by covering with hand and rolling on board with circular motion until surface of dough is slightly blistered in appearance.

Roll each portion of dough into rectangular shape 12 x 9 inches and about ⅛ inch thick. It should be as thin as possible

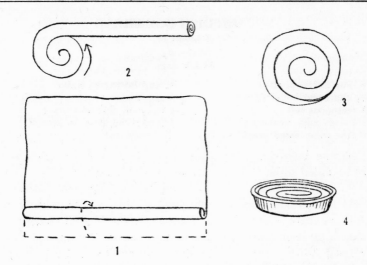

without tearing dough. Spread with softened butter. Roll up jelly-roll fashion and coil around so it looks like a snail. Use individual 5-inch pie pans if you have them or use 2 greased 9-inch pie pans to bake puffs and allow 3 per pan as they will be quite large and should not be crowded. Set in warm place and let double or more in bulk, about 2½ hours. They should be very light and puffy. Bake in moderate oven (350°) 15 to 20 minutes. Cover tops of puffs with paper toweling for last part of baking period, as this is a rich dough and browns easily. To be authentic they should be just a light golden brown in color. As soon as puffs are removed from the oven, brush surface with melted butter and roll in confectioners' sugar. Serve warm with coffee.

The recipe for these delectable Spanish coffee cake puffs came from Manila with Maria Caminog, when she came to Iowa State College to study. She is a teacher at the Philippine Women's University. Many times Maria and I spent an entire Saturday afternoon making the rolls, as each ball of dough had to be rolled round and round with a slight pressure from the palm of the hand so that the surface of the dough would be well blistered and each roll have an air space in the bottom. This is called the Chinese method of kneading dough — though we were applying it to Spanish rolls. The dough is a rich yellow color, because of the amount of butter and egg yolks used. They are really a first cousin of the French brioche. These light, golden-brown, puffy rolls in snail shape are fine-textured and even-grained and are wonderful for a Sunday morning breakfast treat.

SWEDISH DOUGH
3 braids or
4 coffee rings or
4 tea rings

½ cup butter, melted
⅔ cup sugar
2 teaspoons salt
2½ cups milk, scalded
1 cake compressed yeast

¼ cup lukewarm water
1 egg, beaten
1 teaspoon almond extract
7 cups sifted flour, or more if
    necessary

Combine melted butter, sugar, and salt in a large bowl, and
add scalded milk. Cool to lukewarm, add yeast which has been
softened in lukewarm water. Add beaten egg and flavoring.
Add 3 cups flour and mix thoroughly, then add enough more
flour to make a soft dough. Turn out on a floured board and
knead until mixture is smooth and elastic. Put in a lightly
greased bowl, cover and let rise until double in bulk. Shape
into braids, coffee rings, or tea rings.

SWEDISH COFFEE RING — 4 rings

1 recipe Swedish Dough
¼ cup butter, softened
2 cups brown sugar
¾ cup chopped nuts

To decorate rings:
½ cup seedless raisins
½ cup chopped nuts
¼ cup maraschino cherries

Divide dough into fourths. Roll each fourth into a rectangle
10 x 20 inches and about ⅓ inch thick. Brush with softened
butter. Sprinkle each rectangle with brown sugar and nuts.
Roll up like a jelly roll. Shape into a ring. Place on greased
cooky sheet. Let rise until double in bulk. Bake in moderate
oven (350°) 20 to 25 minutes. Frost top of coffee ring with
Thin Confectioners' Frosting made by mixing 1 cup confectioners' sugar with ¼ cup hot water. Decorate with raisins,
nuts, and cherries.

SWEDISH TEA BRAID — 3 braids

1 recipe Swedish Dough
1 egg yolk
1 tablespoon cold water

½ cup chopped blanched almonds,
    cut diagonally

Divide dough into thirds. Cut each third into 3 equal pieces.
Roll each piece on board with both hands into a roll about
1 inch wide and 24 inches long. Make into braid 18 inches

long. Place on greased cooky sheet, brush with melted butter. Cover and let rise. Brush with beaten egg yolk diluted with the cold water; sprinkle with cut almonds. Bake in moderate oven (350°) 20 minutes.

To make a braided tea ring, bring ends of braid togther, place tea braid in a 9-inch greased pie pan. Brush with mixture of beaten egg yolk and cold water, and sprinkle with cut almonds. Let double in bulk. Bake as for Tea Braid.

SWEDISH TEA RING — 4 rings

1 recipe Swedish Dough (page 82)	2 teaspoons cinnamon
¼ cup melted butter	½ cup chopped almonds
2 cups brown sugar	½ cup chopped nuts for frosting

Divide dough into fourths. Roll each fourth into a rectangle 10 x 20 inches and about ⅓ inch thick. Brush with melted butter. Mix sugar, cinnamon, and almonds. Sprinkle on dough. Roll like a jelly roll and join ends to form a ring. Trim the ends if necessary. Place on a greased cooky sheet; snip with scissors every inch. Pull sections apart and twist slightly. Brush with melted butter. Let rise until double in bulk. Bake in moderate oven (350°) 20 to 25 minutes. Frost with Thin Confectioners' Frosting made by mixing 1 cup confectioners' sugar with ¼ cup hot water. Add ½ teaspoon cinnamon. Sprinkle with nuts.

TORTILLAS
2½ dozen

1 cup sifted flour	1 egg, beaten
½ cup corn meal	1½ cups water or enough to make
¼ teaspoon salt	a very thin batter

Combine all ingredients and mix well. Pour batter onto ungreased griddle to make a very thin pancake about six inches in diameter. When brown on one side turn on other side and brown. In the Southwest the tortillas may be bought in most grocery stores, fresh or canned. They are used as the basis for Tacos (page 99) and Enchiladas (page 274).

For soft tortillas serve plain tortillas as such, cut into triangles.

TOSTADAS

For tostadas, cut Tortillas (page 83) in triangles; drop into deep hot fat (375°) 1 minute or until crisp. Drain on absorbent paper. Sprinkle lightly with salt. Serve as bread for the Mexican Dinner (page 458).

WAFFLES BY JANE
6 waffles

2 cups sifted cake flour	2 eggs, separated
4 teaspoons baking powder	1½ cups milk
½ teaspoon salt	6 tablespoons butter, melted

Sift flour, baking powder, and salt together. Separate eggs. Beat whites to soft peak. Beat yolks; add milk and combine with melted shortening that has been cooled a little. Stir liquid into dry ingredients. Mix until smooth. Fold in egg whites. This will be rather a thin batter. Bake in hot waffle baker. When steam no longer appears, waffle is done. Don't raise cover during baking. Let waffle remain in baker long enough to become crisp.

This recipe for light, golden, crisp waffles comes from Mrs. Jane Stebbins, graduate student from Montana. They're favorites of her two sons, Bob and Bruce. The boys like them with lots of butter and plenty of luscious maple syrup.

BACON WAFFLES

Add ½ cup crisp diced bacon to batter.

COCONUT WAFFLES

Add ¾ cup shredded coconut to batter.

DATE WAFFLES

Add ¾ cup pitted chopped dates to batter.

PECAN WAFFLES

Add ¾ cup coarsely chopped pecans to batter.

ZITNY CHLEB
Russian Rye Bread
2 loaves

2 cups sifted rye flour
2 cups warm water
½ cup shortening
½ cup sugar
1½ teaspoons salt
½ teaspoon anise seed

2 teaspoons grated orange peel
¼ cup molasses
1 cake compressed yeast
¼ cup warm water
4 cups sifted flour

Mix rye flour and water; add shortening, sugar, salt, anise seed, orange peel, molasses, and yeast which has been softened in warm water. Add 2 cups of the flour to make a soft dough. Let rise in a warm place until double. Then add remaining 2 cups flour or enough to make a stiff dough. Put into greased bowl; cover. Let dough rise until double; knead down. Shape into 2 loaves, place in greased pans, 9½ x 5¼ x 2¾ inches. When loaves have risen to nearly double in bulk, bake in moderate oven (350°) about 1 hour.

ZOETE BROODJES
Dutch Sweet Rolls
3 dozen, medium size

2 cups milk
¼ cup shortening
¼ cup sugar
1 teaspoon salt
1 cake compressed yeast

6 cups sifted flour, more if
   necessary
¼ cup melted butter
½ cup brown sugar
½ cup granulated sugar

Scald milk; add shortening, sugar, and salt. Cool to lukewarm and add crumbled yeast. Let stand ten minutes, mix well and add flour. Knead until smooth and satiny. Cover and let rise in a warm place until double. Roll dough ¼ inch thick, cut into rectangles 4 x 3 inches, spread with melted butter, and sprinkle with brown and granulated sugar. Roll; place close together in greased 9-inch square pan. Let rise until double and bake in hot oven (400°) 15 to 20 minutes.

Meats

BEEF

Barbecued Hamburgers
    Barbecue Sauce
Beef à la Mode
Beef Stroganoff
Belgian Roast Beef
Carne con Chile
Cornish Pasties
Frikadeller Med Lög Saus
Hungarian Steak
Italian Spaghetti — Meat Balls
    Sauce
Köttbullar
New England Corned Beef
    Hash
Planked Steak
Red Flannel Hash
Rolled Rib Roast of Beef
    Yorkshire Pudding
Russian Beefsteak in Sour
    Cream
Russian Meat Turnovers
Sauerbraten
Tacos
Tereyaki Steak

LAMB

Barbecued Lamb
Caucasian Shashlik
English Mixed Grill
Planked Broiled Lamb Chops

HOW TO PLANK

PLANK GARNISHES

PORK

Bola-Bola Special
Ch'A Hsiao
Crisp Fried Won Ton
    Noodle Paste Wrapper
Egg Roll

English Pork Pie
French Pork Chops with
    Capers
French Pork Chops with
    Onion Sauce
Hang-Yen-Yok-Ding
Hawaiian Spareribs with Pine-
    apple
Hungarian Pork with Sauer-
    kraut
Lumpia Macao
    Pincit Frito
Niw-Goo-Yok
Ponhaus
Potatis Korf
Sausage Rolls

HAM

Baked Ham
    Glazes
Individual Baked Ham Loaves
Individual Glazed Ham
    Loaves
Planked Ham Puff
Plantation Style Ham Slice
Schnitz un Knepp
Sweetbreads and Broiled Ham

VEAL

Planked Veal Cutlets
Ravioli
Russian Meat Balls
Sylta
Veal Chops with Paprika Sauce
Veal Cutlets à la Française
Veal Marengo
Veal Steak Paprika
Veau Roulu
Wiener Schnitzel

D INNER'S SUCCESS can depend upon what you put on the meat platter. It sets the pace for the meal — all the other foods are planned to complement it. You're wise to choose the meat carefully and thoughtfully.

Chances are, too, that meat will be your largest investment. It deserves expert cooking.

Often the most outstanding meals are those in which you use your ingenuity with the meat course. You might try only one new seasoning or go all-out with a foreign meat dish. Check the following pages for something extra-special for your next party or a surprise for the family.

Beef

BARBECUED HAMBURGERS
4 servings

1 pound ground beef
Salt

Pepper
¼ cup cream

Combine meat, salt, pepper, and cream. Mix well and form into four patties. Broil or pan broil until nicely browned on both sides, about 3 to 4 minutes. Add sauce to meat patties and cook 20 to 25 minutes longer.

BARBECUE SAUCE

3 tablespoons salad oil
1 tablespoon Worcestershire sauce
1 tablespoon prepared meat sauce
1 tablespoon vinegar
1 teaspoon sugar

½ cup catsup
1½ cups water
Few drops Tabasco sauce
1 clove garlic, chopped
1 tablespoon chopped onion

Mix together salad oil and other ingredients to make sauce. Simmer 25 to 30 minutes.

This is an easy and delicious way to precook hamburgers for a picnic with no last-minute fuss. The highly seasoned sauce blends with the meat during cooking and the hamburger is ready with everything on it.

BEEF À LA MODE
6 to 8 servings

4 pounds beef round or chuck
½ pound salt pork, cut in thin
    strips
2 teaspoons salt
⅛ teaspoon pepper
½ cup flour

½ cup fat
1 cup peas
½ cup diced carrots
½ cup diced celery
½ cup diced onions

Lard beef with salt pork, using a larding needle to insert ¼-inch strips of salt pork into meat. Season with salt and pepper. Coat with flour and brown in fat. Add cup of hot water, cover and cook slowly about 2½ to 3 hours or until meat is tender. Add peas, carrots, celery, and onions ½ hour before meat is done, adding more water if necessary, to cover the vegetables. When meat is done, place on hot platter with vegetables arranged around it and serve with brown gravy.

BEEF STROGANOFF
3 to 4 servings

1 pound lean beef, cut in thin strips about 3 inches long and ½ inch wide
¼ cup flour
½ teaspoon salt
⅛ teaspoon pepper
¼ cup fat

1 cup hot Beef Stock (page 45) or canned bouillon
3 tablespoons tomato juice
1 tablespoon prepared mustard
1 teaspoon Worcestershire sauce
¾ cup sour cream
Salt and pepper

Roll strips of beef in flour which has been mixed with salt and pepper. Brown in fat and remove meat from skillet. Add hot Beef Stock and bring to a boil. Add tomato juice, mustard, Worcestershire sauce, sour cream, salt and pepper to taste. Bring to a boil again; add the meat. Simmer for about 20 to 25 minutes or until meat is tender. For the last part of cooking, turn up heat and cook a little faster so liquid will be reduced and thickened. Serve the meat with the sauce in which it has been cooked. This Russian beef dish should be served with rice. The beef for the Stroganoff should preferably be fillet.

The sour cream and other seasonings give this dish a flavor long to be remembered. In the past the Stroganoff has been a great favorite in Russia, and it is served today in many of the Russian restaurants in this country.

BELGIAN ROAST BEEF
6 to 8 servings

3 to 4 pounds boneless rump of beef
½ pound salt pork
2 teaspoons salt
Dash of pepper
2 tablespoons dry mustard

½ cup fat
4 large onions, sliced thin
1 cup (or more) Beef Stock (page 45) or canned bouillon
3 medium tomatoes, peeled
2 tablespoons red wine vinegar

Lard beef, using thin strips of salt pork in larding needle. Combine salt, pepper, and mustard, and rub into meat on both sides. Melt fat in skillet or Dutch oven. Brown meat on both sides, remove from skillet. Add onions and cook until a golden brown. Then put meat on bed of onions and add Beef Stock. Cook covered 2½ to 3 hours in slow oven (325°). During last half hour of cooking add tomatoes cut in half and red wine vinegar. Continue cooking until meat is tender. Serve on platter, surrounded by onions. Garnish with parsley or water cress.

CARNE CON CHILE
Meat with Chili
4 to 6 servings

1½ pounds beef round	1 teaspoon salt
2 tablespoons fat	1 teaspoon orégano
½ cup finely chopped onions	1 teaspoon paprika
1 clove garlic, chopped fine	1 cup Beef Stock (page 45)
1 tablespoon chili powder	1 cup canned tomatoes
1 cup chili sauce	

Cut meat into ¾-inch cubes. Sauté in the fat until brown. Add onions and garlic and cook about 5 minutes, stirring constantly. Add chili powder and chili sauce. Season with salt, orégano, and paprika. Add Beef Stock and tomatoes. Cook 45 minutes to 1 hour or until meat is tender and liquid has thickened. Add more meat stock or tomatoes if necessary. Serve with rice or frijoles.

Don't ever ask a Mexican to put beans in his chili, for that just isn't done. But what is lacking in the beans is more than made up in the spicy flavor. If you like chili with beans, add 2 cups cooked kidney beans or 2 cups cooked pinto beans just before serving and add a little more liquid.

CORNISH PASTIES
10 to 12 servings

2½ pounds round steak	1 cup butter
3 pounds potatoes	Water
1 recipe Plain Pastry (page 433)	Salt and pepper
1 large onion, sliced thin	1 egg, beaten
½ cup chopped parsley	

Cut round steak into ½-inch cubes. Pare potatoes and slice thin. Roll pastry and cut into 6-inch rounds. Put layer of meat, potatoes, onion, and chopped parsley on each round of pastry. Dot with butter. Put a tablespoon of water over meat and potatoes; salt and pepper each. Dampen edges of pastry, fold over, press edges together, and crimp edge with finger and thumb. Brush with beaten egg. Make two small slits in top of each pasty. Bake in hot oven (400°) 45 minutes to 1 hour or until meat is done. Serve hot or cold.

These hearty meat pasties in their flaky crust are a favorite dish among the Cornish. I grew up in a community where there were many

Cornish people and I was introduced to pasties at an early age. We served them for lunch or dinner and took them on picnics just as we do hamburgers today. They are good hot or cold and can be picked up and eaten in the fingers. The pasties can be made larger or smaller, just as you wish. In the days when we lived in Butte, Montana, a nice big pasty in a lunch bucket made a good meal for a man working in the mines.

FRIKADELLER MED LOG SAUS
Danish Meat Balls with Onion Sauce
5 to 6 servings

½ cup dry bread crumbs
1 cup milk
1 egg, beaten
1 medium onion, chopped
1¼ pounds ground beef
½ pound ground pork

1½ teaspoons salt
⅛ teaspoon nutmeg
Dash of pepper
4 tablespoons fat
Onion Sauce (page 210)

Soak crumbs in milk for about 10 minutes. Add egg, onion, meat, and seasonings. Shape into balls about 2 inches in diameter. Heat fat in skillet. Drop meat balls into hot fat and flatten slightly. When meat balls are browned nicely on both sides, cover pan and simmer about 30 minutes or until done. Serve with Onion Sauce.

HUNGARIAN STEAK
5 to 6 servings

½ cup fat
2 onions, sliced thin
2 pounds chuck or round steak
1 teaspoon salt
⅛ teaspoon pepper

1 clove garlic, mashed
½ pound fresh mushrooms, sliced
1 green pepper, sliced thin
1 8-ounce can tomato sauce
1 cup water

Melt fat in heavy skillet. Add onions and cook until golden brown; remove onions. Rub meat with salt, pepper, and mashed garlic; place in hot skillet and sear quickly on both sides. Add browned onions, sliced mushrooms, green pepper, and tomato sauce. Cook 15 minutes, then add water. Simmer over slow heat about 1½ hours or until meat is tender and sauce has thickened. Remove to hot platter. Serve hot with parsley buttered potato balls.

ITALIAN SPAGHETTI WITH MEAT BALLS
6 to 8 servings

1½ pounds ground beef
½ pound ground pork
½ cup bread crumbs
1 clove garlic, crushed
1 egg, beaten

¼ cup grated cheese
1 teaspoon salt
⅛ teaspoon pepper
½ cup fat

Mix all ingredients except fat, roll into tiny balls about ¾ inch in diameter. Brown in fat. Be careful not to burn meat balls.

Sauce:

4 tablespoons fat
1 onion, chopped
1 green pepper, chopped
1 tablespoon chopped parsley
1 No. 2½ can tomatoes

1 6-ounce can tomato paste
½ teaspoon salt
⅛ teaspoon pepper
Dash of orégano
Parmesan cheese

Sauté onion and green pepper in the fat. Add parsley, tomatoes, tomato paste, and seasonings. Simmer for 2 hours over very low heat. Add more seasoning if necessary. Add the meat balls and cook for 15 minutes longer.

Cook one 1-pound package long Italian spaghetti in boiling salted water for about 20 to 25 minutes. Don't break up the spaghetti — it should be left long. Remove to serving platter. Serve meat sauce over spaghetti or, if desired, put spaghetti in baking pan and pour the sauce over it and bake in slow oven (325°) 20 to 30 minutes. Serve with plenty of Parmesan cheese.
NOTE: To cook long Italian spaghetti successfully, you'll need a large kettle and plenty of boiling water. Put about three quarts of water into a 12-inch kettle. Let water come to a boil. Add 3 teaspoons salt. Now you are ready to cook the spaghetti. Remove spaghetti from wrapper and hold it all with one hand. Put one end of spaghetti into the boiling water, and as it softens force more of it in and coil spaghetti around bottom of pan until all of it is in the water. Lift gently with a fork from bottom of pan several times during cooking period so it will not stick. Cook 15 to 20 minutes, or long enough to just cook through. The spaghetti should be rather firm and not soft or mushy.

This is a choice recipe from Carolyn De Bartolo's Italian grand-mother. Try it the next time you are having an Italian dinner. Be sure to have lots of Parmesan cheese for generous sprinkling. Serve with crisp bread sticks and a green salad that has been dressed with a tangy garlic salad dressing — just enough to make each leaf glisten. For dessert, a cool lime sherbet.

Of course, you may have to teach your guests how to eat this long spaghetti by using a spoon in the left hand and twisting a forkful against the inside of the spoon to get it coiled around the fork. It may take a little practice, but it's an accomplishment.

KOTTBULLAR
Swedish Meat Balls
10 to 12 servings

1½ pounds beef round
1 pound pork
2 eggs, beaten
1 medium onion, chopped fine
1½ teaspoons salt
¼ teaspoon pepper

1 teaspoon ginger
½ teaspoon nutmeg
1 tablespoon cornstarch
1 pint milk, or more if necessary
1 cup bread crumbs
½ cup fat

Have meat ground together three times. Mix all ingredients except fat. Form meat mixture into small balls about the size of a walnut. Melt fat in skillet, add meat balls a few at a time and fry until brown. Add 2 cups boiling water or Beef Stock (page 45) and cook 20 to 30 minutes. Thicken liquid with a paste of 2 tablespoons flour and ¼ cup cold water and cook 5 minutes longer. Sauce should not be too thick.

These are typical Swedish meat balls and may be served at the Smörgåsbord (page 460). This recipe makes 35 to 40 small meat balls.

NEW ENGLAND CORNED BEEF HASH
6 to 8 servings

2 cups chopped corned beef
2 medium potatoes, cooked and
   diced
¼ cup butter

1 small onion, chopped fine
½ cup cream
½ teaspoon salt
Pepper

Combine corned beef and potatoes. Melt butter in heavy skillet, add onion and sauté until golden brown. Add corned beef and potatoes, cream, salt, and pepper to taste. Cook in skillet over low heat for about 15 minutes, or until a brown crust has formed. Then fold over as omelet is folded. Remove to hot serving platter.

This fragrant corned beef hash, delicately browned, is a favorite New England dish on a cold winter night, and makes a hearty supper dish any time.

PLANKED STEAK
2 to 3 servings

1 porterhouse steak, 2 inches thick
Duchess Potatoes (page 185)
2 tablespoons softened butter
Salt and pepper

2 tablespoons finely chopped
   parsley
1 12-ounce package frozen peas,
   cooked
6 or 8 broiled mushroom caps

Broil or pan broil steak on each side 8 to 10 minutes. Force
Duchess Potatoes through pastry bag with rose tube to make
a border of potatoes around edge of plank. Place steak in
center of plank, and put in hot oven (400°) or under broiler
until potatoes are brown and steak is done, as desired. Spread
steak with softened butter, sprinkle lightly with salt, pepper,
and finely chopped parsley. Arrange peas in border around
steak. Garnish steak with broiled mushroom caps.

RED FLANNEL HASH
4 to 6 servings

4 medium beets, cooked
3 medium potatoes, cooked
2 cups chopped cooked beef
1 teaspoon salt

¼ teaspoon pepper
¼ cup butter
¼ cup chopped onion
½ cup cream

Chop beets and potatoes and mix with the chopped beef;
season with salt and pepper. Melt butter in a heavy skillet;
add onion and sauté until golden brown. Add the meat mixture
and pour cream over top. Cook slowly for about 15 to 20
minutes until brown crust has formed, or bake in moderate
oven (350°) 35 minutes. Turn onto hot platter and serve at once.

*This red flannel hash is an excellent way to use up leftover meat or
vegetables from a New England boiled dinner. Almost any combination of meat and vegetables may be used. Remember to season well.*

ROLLED RIB ROAST OF BEEF
6 to 8 servings

3 to 4 pounds rib of beef

Have beef boned, rolled, and tied. Wipe meat with damp cloth.
Insert meat thermometer into thickest part of roll. Put fat side
up in roasting pan and roast uncovered in slow oven (325°) to
an inner temperature of 140° for rare roast beef, 160° for medium, and 170° for well done. Allow 20 to 35 minutes per pound,

depending upon desired doneness. Remove fat and use drippings to make roast beef gravy, or serve beef with Brown or Espagnole Sauce with Mushrooms (page 205) or with Yorkshire Pudding.

YORKSHIRE PUDDING — 6 to 8 servings

1 cup flour	1 cup milk
½ teaspoon salt	½ cup beef drippings
2 eggs	

Sift flour and salt into a bowl. Beat eggs until light; add milk. Add to dry ingredients gradually and beat for two minutes with rotary beater. Have drippings very hot in a baking pan. Pour in batter and bake in hot oven (425°) 30 to 35 minutes. This may be made in individual portions by baking in popover pans. Serve with Rolled Rib Roast of Beef.

An easier way to make Yorkshire pudding is to remove the roast beef from the pan about 30 minutes before it is done, and put it in another pan to finish roasting. Pour off the excess fat from the roast beef pan, leaving about half a cup. While the pan is still hot, pour in the Yorkshire pudding batter to the depth of about ½ inch. Bake in hot oven (425°) 30 to 35 minutes. Cut in squares and serve at once with roast beef.

The Yorkshire pudding batter resembles popover batter, and puffs way up as it bakes. When done, it settles down a little, but should be soft and fluffy in the center, crisp and crusty on the sides and bottom, and a delicate brown on top.

RUSSIAN BEEF STEAK IN SOUR CREAM
8 to 10 servings

2 pounds round steak, cut in 1-inch cubes	1 8-ounce can tomato sauce
1 large onion, chopped fine	¾ cup beef bouillon
1 clove garlic, chopped fine	1 tablespoon Worcestershire sauce
¼ cup bacon fat	1 teaspoon salt
1 4-ounce can sliced mushrooms	⅛ teaspoon pepper
1½ cups sour cream	2 tablespoons flour
	2 tablespoons water

Sauté onion and garlic in bacon fat. Remove from fat; add diced round steak and brown. Add mushrooms and juice, sour cream, tomato sauce, bouillon, Worcestershire sauce, salt and pepper. Cook slowly for 1½ to 2 hours, or until meat is tender. Make a paste of flour and water and add to gravy to thicken it. Cook 10 to 15 minutes longer. Serve hot.

RUSSIAN MEAT TURNOVERS
About 4 dozen

Pastry:

2 cups flour
½ teaspoon salt
⅔ cup shortening

1 egg yolk, beaten
5 tablespoons milk

Sift flour and salt together. Cut shortening into flour until mixture resembles coarse corn meal. Combine beaten egg yolk and milk. Add to flour mixture. Mix lightly until all of liquid is blended into dry ingredients. Turn out on board and knead six or eight times. Roll pastry to ⅛-inch thickness and cut into 2½-inch rounds. Put a scant teaspoon of filling on half of circle. Moisten edges, fold other half over meat filling and pinch edges together. Prick top. Put on greased cooky sheet, 14 x 10 inches. Brush with beaten egg to which 1 tablespoon of milk has been added. Bake in hot oven (400°) 12 to 15 minutes.

Filling:

½ pound ground beef
½ pound ground pork
1 tablespoon finely chopped onion
1 teaspoon salt

⅛ teaspoon pepper
2 tablespoons fat
1 hard-cooked egg, diced

Combine meat, onion, salt and pepper. Heat fat in skillet and add meat mixture. Sauté until meat is cooked. Add diced hard-cooked eggs. Use as filling for pastry.

Serve as an accompaniment with Borsch (page 32).

SAUERBRATEN
Pennsylvania Dutch Pot Roast
4 to 6 servings

2 pounds beef, chuck or rump
Salt and pepper
1 cup vinegar
Water
3 bay leaves
3 cloves

8 peppercorns
¼ cup fat
6 medium carrots, cut in strips
4 medium onions, sliced thin
1 tablespoon sugar
8 gingersnaps

Wipe meat with damp cloth and then sprinkle thoroughly with salt and pepper. Place meat in earthen dish or crock and add vinegar and enough water to cover. Add the bay leaves, cloves, and peppercorns, and let stand tightly covered in a cool place for 5 days. Put fat in Dutch oven, add meat and brown well on all sides. Add the carrots and onions and 1½ cups of the spiced vinegar in which meat was marinated. Cover tightly and cook over low heat for about 3 hours or until meat is tender. Add more of the spiced vinegar, if necessary. When the meat is cooked, add the sugar and crumbled gingersnaps and cook for 10 minutes longer. This Pennsylvania Dutch meat dish should be served with the gingersnap gravy.

This is an excellent way to tenderize less tender cuts of meat and at the same time introduce an interesting and pleasing sweet-and-sour taste. If you prefer, more spiced vinegar may be added to make extra sauce. An old stone crock or pickling jar is excellent for marinating but be sure to keep it well covered and in a cool place.

TACOS
Mexican Sandwich
6 to 7 servings

1 No. 2½ can tomatoes
12 to 14 Tortillas (page 83)
1 pound hot fat
1 pound ground beef
Salt and pepper

2 bunches green onions, chopped
1 head lettuce, shredded
½ pound grated American cheese
1 tablespoon red hot sauce

Cook tomatoes (well seasoned) until juice of tomatoes has been reduced to consistency of a thick sauce. Fold each Tortilla in half, and fasten with wooden pick. Drop into hot fat and let remain a few minutes or until crisp. Remove from fat and drain. Take out pick. Season meat with salt and pepper, and cook until done. Place generous tablespoon of cooked meat on inside of folded Tortilla, add a little chopped green onion and some of the tomato sauce. Sprinkle with shredded lettuce and grated cheese. Add red hot sauce, and salt to taste. Place tacos on individual plate or pile on platter. Serve hot.

TEREYAKI STEAK
3 to 4 servings

1 pound sirloin steak, ½ inch thick
1 clove garlic, mashed
1 tablespoon chopped fresh
    ginger root

½ cup soy sauce
1 tablespoon vinegar
1 teaspoon sugar
1 small onion, sliced

Cut steak into 3 or 4 servings. Combine garlic, ginger root, soy sauce, vinegar, sugar, and onion. Pour over steak and let stand 2 hours. Turn steak several times during this period. Broil in a charcoal broiler, preferably, or pan broil if desired.

This is a Japanese method of preparing steak that is also very popular in Hawaii. Mrs. Elsie Boatman, food director of the University of Hawaii Cafeteria, contributed this recipe.

Lamb

BARBECUED LAMB
8 to 10 servings

1 leg of lamb, 5 pounds	¼ cup vinegar
Salt and pepper	½ teaspoon dry mustard
Flour	½ cup catsup
2 onions, chopped	2 tablespoons sugar
1 cup water	2 tablespoons Worcestershire sauce

Salt and pepper lamb and roll in flour. Put in roaster; add chopped onions. Mix remaining ingredients and pour over meat. Cover roaster and roast in slow oven (325°) 2½ to 3 hours or until meat is tender. Meat should be turned and basted with sauce in roaster every half hour. Remove lid from roaster ½ hour before meat is done to permit browning. Serve with sauce.

CAUCASIAN SHASHLIK
4 to 6 servings

2 pounds loin or leg of mutton or lamb	Coarse black pepper
1 teaspoon salt	½ cup lemon juice
2 onions, chopped fine	½ cup water

Cut the meat into 1-inch cubes, put in glass bowl or earthenware dish; sprinkle with salt, chopped onion, and a little pepper, and cover with lemon juice and water. Let stand for 4 to 6 hours, or overnight. The pieces of meat should then be well drained. Put on skewers and broil about 15 to 20 minutes, so that all sides are nicely browned. They should be removed from the skewers and served immediately. This meat should be accompanied by boiled rice.

Another version of the shashlik is to alternate the meat cubes with mushrooms and small tomatoes or cubes of tomato on the skewers.

These tender morsels of mutton or lamb, broiled to a delicate brown and served with a big helping of fluffy white rice, make a mouth-watering combination that is hard to beat.

ENGLISH MIXED GRILL
1 serving

1 lamb kidney
1 small piece beef steak—sirloin
   or fillet
1 lamb chop
2 link pork sausages

1 tomato
2 mushroom caps
2 slices bacon
Shoestring potatoes or potato chips

Wash and skin kidney, slit across and remove core. Place two
skewers through kidney to hold together. Brush steak and lamb
chop with melted fat. Prick sausages. Cut tomato in half.
Place kidney, steak, and chop under broiler and broil 5 to 6
minutes, turning so both sides will be nicely broiled. Cook
sausages. Place tomato halves (cut side up), bacon, and mushrooms on broiler rack. Brush tomato and mushrooms with
melted fat. Broil a few minutes longer. Arrange on a hot plate;
brush meat with butter to which a little lemon juice has been
added. Garnish with water cress or parsley and serve shoestring
potatoes or potato chips.

PLANKED BROILED LAMB CHOPS
2 servings

2 English lamb chops, cut 2 inches
   thick
Salt and pepper
2 tablespoons softened butter
Duchess Potatoes (page 185)

1 12-ounce package frozen peas,
   cooked
2 tomatoes, cut into wedges and
   broiled

Chops may be boned and rolled, if desired. Place chops in
broiler and broil 15 minutes on each side, turning so both sides
will be nicely browned. Pan broil if broiler is not available.
Sprinkle with salt and pepper and spread with softened butter.
Place on plank and surround with border of Duchess Potatoes.
Put plank in oven to brown potatoes; remove and add cooked
peas and broiled tomato sections to complete plank. Garnish
as desired. Serve at once.

HOW TO PLANK

Planked meals are once again in vogue. What is more appetizing than a juicy steak or chops on a plank garlanded by a border of fluffy potatoes and colorful vegetables?

Select a plank of kiln-dried oak, 1 inch thick. Common plank sizes are: 14 x 9½ inches, 16 x 10¾ inches, and 20 x 12 inches.

The plank should be a little longer and wider than the fish or meat to be arranged on it. A new plank should be brushed with oil and heated in a slow oven for an hour before being

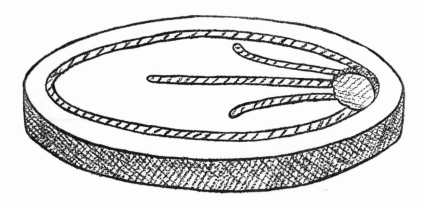

used the first time. A potato border should come well to the edge of the plank so that the wood will not scorch during the cooking. If any part of the plank is exposed it should be well oiled.

To clean the plank, wipe off thoroughly and give it a quick scrub in hot water; never soak the plank, because it may warp. Before each using, the plank should be oiled and preheated in a slow oven.

A variety of meats, fish, and vegetables may be prepared by the planked method. The tender meats that may be easily carved on the plank are best to use. Beef, such as porterhouse or sirloin steak and tenderloin, is good planked. Mutton or lamb chops, fish, lobster, and vegetables such as stuffed onions make a very attractive plank.

PLANK GARNISHES

Peas and broiled tomato slices or wedges
Mashed potato nests filled with peas and buttered carrot cubes
Stuffed tomatoes
Glazed onions, buttered carrots cut in julienne strips, mushroom caps
Broiled tomato halves, mushroom caps cooked in butter, peas
Cauliflower, peas, and diced carrots
Broccoli and broiled tomatoes
Baby lima beans and broiled tomatoes

BOLA-BOLA SPECIAL
Chinese Pork and Shrimp
8 to 10 servings

½ pound pork, ground fine	Salt
½ pound shrimp	Soy sauce
½ cup water chestnuts, chopped	½ teaspoon sugar
1 small onion, chopped fine	2 eggs

Mix pork, shrimp, water chestnuts, and onion; season with salt, soy sauce, and sugar. Add unbeaten eggs. Shape into balls and fry in deep hot fat (360°) until brown. Serve with Sweet-Sour Sauce (page 214).

These crisp balls of bola-bola are often served at a Chinese meal.

CH'A HSIAO
Chinese Roast Pork
3 to 4 servings

1 pound lean pork
½ teaspoon salt
⅓ cup soy sauce
3 tablespoons lemon juice
¼ cup sugar
⅛ teaspoon red food coloring
1 small onion, sliced

4 green onions, cut in 1-inch
　lengths
3 pieces fresh ginger, crushed, or
　¼ teaspoon ground ginger
6 cloves garlic, crushed
½ cup Chicken Stock (page 45) or
　canned consommé

Combine salt, soy sauce, lemon juice, sugar, and red coloring.
Rub onto pork. Add onion, green onions, ginger, and garlic.
Allow to stand ½ hour. Place in roasting pan. Add ½ cup
Chicken Stock. Cook in slow oven (325°) 1 hour. Slice in ¼-
inch slices. Serve hot with rice.

*This is an Oriental method of preparing roast pork. It comes from the
University of Hawaii, via Mrs. Elsia Boatman, the Cafeteria food director.*

CRISP FRIED WON TON
6 to 8 servings

½ cup finely chopped cooked lean
　pork
¼ cup finely chopped ham
3 tablespoons finely chopped green
　onions, with tops
¼ cup finely chopped water
　chestnuts

1 tablespoon soy sauce
1 egg, beaten
16 squares Won Ton Noodle Paste
　Wrapper Dough
3 cups peanut oil or other frying
　fat

Combine the meat, onions, and water chestnuts. Add soy sauce
and egg. Mix thoroughly. Place 1 teaspoon of this mixture in
each square of won ton. Dampen the two opposite corners of
the won ton and fold the won ton forming a triangle. Fold the
2 narrow ends together and press tightly. Fold the center corner
back to hold the filling inside. Fry in deep hot fat (375°) 4 to 5
minutes or until brown. Drain on unglazed paper and serve hot.
Fresh or canned shrimp may be substituted for the pork if desired.
Serve with soy sauce and lemon juice.

NOODLE PASTE WRAPPER DOUGH

3 eggs, beaten	3 cups flour
1 teaspoon salt	

Combine salt and flour and add to beaten eggs to make a stiff dough. Roll paper-thin on well-floured board. Let remain on board for ½ hour to dry. Cut into 3-inch squares. Use a teaspoon of filling in the center of the square and shape as desired.

The shape of the won ton may be varied by placing the meat mixture in the center of the square and twisting both ends until dough resembles a bow tie. They may also be cooked by boiling or steaming.

Won ton may be served with Chinese meals or boiled in chicken or meat broth and served in soup.

EGG ROLL
8 to 10 servings

2 ounces lean pork, cut in thin strips	½ pared sweet potato
¼ cup cooking oil	¼ cup chopped onion
1 piece celery	¼ cup diced shrimp
1 small green pepper	2 eggs, beaten

Cook pork in oil until well done. Cut celery, green pepper, and sweet potato into julienne strips 2 inches long and add with onion to the pork; cook for about 10 minutes. Add shrimp, and stir carefully. Put a tablespoon of beaten egg into lightly greased skillet; tilt pan so egg will spread evenly and thinly over surface like pancakes. Brown lightly on each side. Remove from pan. Put a tablespoon of vegetable mixture on each egg pancake and roll up. Serve hot with Chicken and Pork Adobo (page 128).

This recipe for egg roll was brought by Matilda Gussman from Manila when she came to do graduate work at Iowa State College. Mrs. Gussman served the egg roll with Chicken and Pork Adobo. The Adobo is a native Philippine dish, but the egg roll shows the Chinese influence.

ENGLISH PORK PIE
10 to 12 servings

Pastry:

3 cups flour
1 teaspoon salt

¾ cup milk
¾ cup lard or other shortening

Sift together flour and salt. Combine milk and lard and heat to boiling. Stir into the flour and mix well. Turn onto lightly floured board and knead until smooth.

Filling:

1½ pounds diced medium-lean
    pork (½-inch cubes)
½ cup soda cracker crumbs
3 teaspoons salt

¼ teaspoon powdered sage
¼ teaspoon pepper
4 hard-cooked eggs
1 cup Jellied Stock (page 46)

Combine pork, cracker crumbs, salt, sage, and pepper, and mix thoroughly. Roll pastry ¼ inch thick. Cut to fit loaf pan, 9½ x 5¼ x 2¾ inches. Line bottom and sides of pan with pastry. Put half of pork mixture into pan; place hard-cooked eggs end to end down center of pan on top of meat mixture. Cover with remaining meat. Cut crust a little larger than top of pan; cut several slits in crust to allow for escape of steam. Cover meat mixture with crust and press onto edges of pan. Bake in moderate oven (350°) about 1½ hours. Cover top with brown paper during last half of baking period, so crust will not become too brown. Heat Jellied Stock and pour into pie through one of the slits in crust. The pork pie may be served hot or cold. It is a hearty meal any time.

This is the typical English pork pie with its tasty filling and flaky crust that we hear so much about. Joan Smith, who brought the recipe from England, made it for us in Catering Class and the students could hardly wait for the pie to come out of the oven — it had such a tantalizing aroma!

FRENCH PORK CHOPS WITH CAPERS
6 servings

6 pork chops, ¾ inch thick
¾ cup flour
½ teaspoon salt
Dash of pepper
2 tablespoons fat
1 cup hot Beef Stock (page 45)
   or canned bouillon

1 tablespoon vinegar
1 green pepper, chopped fine
1 small onion, chopped fine
2 tablespoons capers
Parsley

Roll chops in flour which has been mixed with salt and pepper.
Melt fat in skillet; brown chops on both sides. Then add stock
and vinegar. Cover and cook slowly over moderate heat for 40
minutes. Add green pepper, onion, and capers, and cook uncovered 15 minutes longer or until thoroughly done. Garnish
with parsley.

FRENCH PORK CHOPS WITH ONION SAUCE
6 servings

6 center-cut pork chops, ¾ inch
   thick

2 tablespoons fat

Sauté chops in fat in heavy skillet. Brown on both sides.

Sauce:

1 large onion, chopped
1 tablespoon fat
1 teaspoon flour
Salt and pepper
1 teaspoon prepared mustard

1 cup Beef Stock (page 45) or
   canned bouillon
2 tablespoons chopped sweet
   pickles

Cook onion in fat until golden in color and add flour, salt,
pepper, and mustard; stir until well blended. Add stock and
cook 5 minutes. Add sweet pickles and more seasoning if necessary, to give well-seasoned sauce. Pour over meat and cook 50
minutes, or until well done and stock is reduced. Serve on platter garnished with parsley and strips of pimento.

HANG-YEN-YOK-DING

Chinese Diced Pork with Almonds and Vegetables

6 to 8 servings

½ cup chopped blanched almonds
¼ cup oil
1 pound lean pork, cut in ½-inch cubes
½ cup Chicken Stock (page 45) or canned consommé
1 teaspoon salt

1 cup diced cooked carrots
2 cups cooked peas
1½ cups diced celery
2 tablespoons cornstarch
2 teaspoons soy sauce
⅓ cup cold water

Brown almonds in 1 tablespoon of the oil. Put remainder of oil in a heavy skillet; add pork and cook until golden brown. Add Chicken Stock and salt and cook about 30 minutes or until pork is tender. Add carrots, peas, and celery; cook 10 to 15 minutes longer. Blend cornstarch, soy sauce, and water. Add to meat mixture and cook until juice thickens. Turn into serving dish. Garnish with almonds. Serve immediately with hot boiled rice. Add additional soy sauce, if desired.

HAWAIIAN SPARERIBS WITH PINEAPPLE

4 servings

2 pounds spareribs, cut in 2-inch pieces
½ teaspoon salt
¼ cup soy sauce
½ cup salad oil
2 tablespoons flour
¾ cup pineapple juice

½ teaspoon salt
2 tablespoons sugar
¼ cup vinegar
1 cup water
1 teaspoon cornstarch
½ cup chopped sweet pickles
½ cup diced pineapple

Add salt and soy sauce to spareribs. Heat oil in skillet. Brown ribs in oil. Add flour and stir into oil; then add pineapple juice, salt, sugar, vinegar, and water. Simmer for 40 minutes or until pork is tender. Make a smooth paste by combining the cornstarch with 1 tablespoon cold water. Add to the pork mixture, stirring constantly. Add pickles and pineapple to the pork. Bring mixture to boiling point and simmer 1 to 2 minutes. Serve hot.

HUNGARIAN PORK WITH SAUERKRAUT
4 servings

¼ cup fat	1 teaspoon salt
1 large onion, chopped fine	½ cup water
¼ teaspoon paprika	1 pound sauerkraut
1 pound pork, cut in ½-inch cubes	½ cup sour cream

Put fat in skillet; add onion and cook until golden brown in color. Sprinkle with paprika. Add meat and salt and cook for 5 minutes. Pour in the water and simmer until water has evaporated. Add more water, if necessary, and cook until meat is done, 35 to 40 minutes. Heat the sauerkraut and combine with the meat; add sour cream and reheat. Serve hot.

LUMPIA MACAO
Steamed Filipino Pork and Shrimp in Wrapper
10 to 12 servings

Wrapper for Lumpia:

2 cups flour	½ teaspoon salt
½ cup water	

Mix all ingredients. Knead to make a smooth dough. Use cornstarch instead of flour on the board and roll dough very thin. Cut into circles 3 inches in diameter. This will be a very stiff dough.

Filling:

¼ cup water chestnuts	2 egg yolks
½ pound lean pork	Salt
2 ounces ham	¼ cup soy sauce
½ cup shrimp	1 tablespoon lemon juice

Chop chestnuts, pork, ham, and shrimp. Bind with unbeaten egg yolks. Season with salt. Place a teaspoonful on each circle of dough and pinch dough together to enclose meat. Steam for 15 to 20 minutes. When done, serve with a generous amount of soy sauce to which lemon juice has been added.

This Chinese recipe has come to us via the Philippines from Maria Caminog of Manila. According to custom there should be something fried, something steamed, and something baked in a Chinese meal. This is the "something steamed."

NIW-GOO-YOK
Chinese Sweet and Pungent Pork
5 to 6 servings

4 green peppers
¾ cup oil
1½ teaspoons salt
1 small clove garlic, minced
2 eggs, beaten
3 tablespoons flour
Dash of pepper

1½ pounds lean pork, cut in
    ½-inch cubes
½ cup Chicken Stock (page 45)
    or canned consommé
6 slices canned pineapple, cut in
    ½-inch pieces

Wash green peppers and remove stem and seeds. Cut in strips about ½ inch wide. Cook in boiling salted water until almost tender. Pour oil into heavy skillet and add 1 teaspoon of the salt and minced garlic. Combine eggs, flour, the remaining ½ teaspoon salt, and pepper, and add to the pork. Mix lightly until every piece of pork is coated. Separate pieces with a fork, drain slightly, and drop one piece at a time into skillet. Cook over medium heat until brown on one side; turn and brown on other side. Pour out all but about 1 tablespoon of the oil. Return to heat; add Chicken Stock, pineapple, and green pepper. Cover and simmer for about 20 minutes. Add the Sweet-Sour Sauce and cook about 10 minutes longer or until juice thickens and ingredients are well blended. Serve immediately with hot boiled rice.

Sweet-Sour Sauce:

2½ tablespoons cornstarch
1 tablespoon soy sauce
½ cup vinegar
3 tablespoons lemon juice

2 tablespoons water
½ cup sugar
¼ teaspoon salt
1 cup Chicken Stock (page 45)

Combine ingredients; mix until smooth and pour over pork.

PINCIT FRITO
Crisp Filipino Pork and Shrimp in Wrapper
About 3 dozen

Use dough and filling for Lumpia Macao (page 109). Roll dough very thin. Cut into 6-inch circles. Cut each circle into 8 triangular-shaped pieces. Place ½ teaspoon filling in center of triangle. Fold edges of triangle over filling. Fry in deep hot fat (365°) 4 to 5 minutes or until the pincit are light brown in color and crisp.

PONHAUS
Pennsylvania Dutch Scrapple
10 to 12 servings

3 pounds spareribs
3 to 3½ cups Beef Stock (page 45)
   or canned bouillon
1 teaspoon salt

1 medium onion, chopped fine
2 tablespoons parsley
1 bay leaf
2½ cups corn meal

Cook meat in stock to which salt, onion, parsley, and bay leaf have been added. When done, remove meat from bones. Add enough water to stock to make a quart, then add corn meal and cook until very thick. Add meat to corn-meal mixture. Pour into greased loaf pans, 9½ x 5¼ x 2¾ inches. Let stand until cold. Slice in ½-inch slices and fry until golden brown. Serve with syrup if desired. A favorite breakfast dish in Philadelphia.

POTATIS KORF
Potato Sausage
10 to 12 servings

3 pounds pork butt, ground
2 pounds ground beef
5 pounds raw potatoes, ground
1 large onion, chopped fine

1 tablespoon salt
1 teaspoon pepper
½ teaspoon allspice
1 pound sausage casings

Mix all ingredients thoroughly. Stuff into well-cleaned sausage casings. Make each sausage about 18 to 24 inches long. Tie both ends. Do not fill casings too full or they will burst when cooked. Place sausages in mild salt brine and keep cold. Change brine every two days.

To cook: Place sausage in hot, but not boiling, salted water and boil slowly about 30 to 40 minutes. Serve hot in this manner or sliced and browned in butter.

This potato sausage is one of the varieties of sausage that may be served at the Smörgåsbord (page 460).

SAUSAGE ROLLS
About 3 dozen

1 recipe Plain Pastry (page 433)   2 pounds pork sausage

Divide pastry in half. Roll into rectangle about ¼ inch thick. Divide sausage in half. Shape into roll about 1 inch in diameter and same length as pastry. Place roll of sausage on pastry about 3 inches from edge. Fold end of pastry over sausage so as to cover it. Cut off pastry roll. Cut into 2-inch lengths. Repeat until all of sausage has been used. Place sausage rolls on ungreased cooky sheet, 15½ x 12 inches. Bake in hot oven (400°) 20 to 25 minutes. Be sure sausage is well cooked.

Ham

BAKED HAM

Purchase smoked ham. Allow ⅓ pound per person for tenderized ham and ¼ pound per person for precooked ham with bone. Cook according to the directions of the packer. Remove skin and as much fat as you desire. Score the remaining fat into diamonds and insert a whole clove in the center of each diamond. Spread with desired glaze; bake in slow oven (325°) until brown.

GLAZES

1 cup brown sugar and 3 tablespoons tart fruit juice
1 cup honey
1 cup syrup
1 cup brown sugar and 3 tablespoons prepared mustard
1 cup brown sugar and 3 tablespoons ginger ale

INDIVIDUAL BAKED HAM LOAVES
6 to 8 servings

¾ pound smoked ham, ground fine	3 tablespoons finely chopped onion
¾ pound lean pork, ground fine	½ cup fine bread crumbs
½ teaspoon salt	1 egg, beaten
Dash of pepper	¾ cup milk

Combine ingredients and mix well. Pack lightly in large muffin pans. Bake in moderate oven (350°) 45 minutes. Serve with Horse-Radish Sauce (page 209) or Mustard Sauce (page 211).

The mixture may be baked in a loaf pan, 9½ x 5¼ x 2¾ inches, if desired.

INDIVIDUAL GLAZED HAM LOAVES

1 cup brown sugar   ¼ cup vinegar
1½ teaspoons dry mustard

Mix brown sugar and mustard. Add vinegar. Boil 1 minute.
Allow Individual Baked Ham Loaves (page 112) to cook for
about 20 minutes, then remove from oven and pour a tablespoon
of brown sugar glaze over each. Return to oven to finish.

PLANKED HAM PUFF
4 servings

1 cup chopped cooked ham   1 cup grated American cheese
1 cup mashed potatoes   1 12-ounce package frozen julienne
Salt and pepper   green beans
2 egg yolks, beaten   2 tablespoons butter
2 egg whites, stiffly beaten   8 to 10 mushroom caps

Mix ham and mashed potatoes together and season to taste with
salt and pepper. Add beaten egg yolks and fold in stiffly beaten
egg whites. Pile the ham mixture on the center of a hot, well-
greased plank and sprinkle generously with grated cheese. Bake
in slow oven (325°) 30 minutes. Cook the green beans, add
butter, and surround ham puff with beans as soon as it comes
from the oven. Sauté the mushroom caps and garnish beans
with them. Serve at once.

If desired, the ham and potato mixture may be made in
individual puffs instead of one large puff. Chopped cooked
chicken or any other leftover meat may be used instead of ham.

PLANTATION STYLE HAM SLICE

1 cup brown sugar   1 2-inch center slice ham
1 teaspoon dry mustard   1¼ cups pineapple juice

Mix ¾ cup of the brown sugar with mustard and rub into ham
on both sides until it is all used. Place in a roasting pan or
heavy skillet and sprinkle with the remaining ¼ cup brown
sugar. Add pineapple juice. Bake in moderate oven (350°)
2 hours or until tender. Baste occasionally. Remove to hot
platter. Decorate with orange slices or Fried Peaches (page 326)
and serve hot.

Serve this tender, juicy slice of ham with Sweet Potato Soufflé
(page 192), green beans, and Fruit Salad (page 228) — a meal to
suit any epicure!

SCHNITZ UN KNEPP

Pennsylvania Dutch Ham and Dried Apples with Button Dumplings
8 to 10 servings

Schnitz:

1 pound dried apples (schnitz)   2 tablespoons brown sugar
3-pound end piece smoked ham

Add enough water to dried apples to cover them. Soak for 3 hours. Place ham in a large kettle that has a tight-fitting lid; a Dutch oven would do very nicely for this. Add enough water to just cover meat and simmer about 1½ hours. Change water once after 30 minutes of simmering. When ham is tender add dried apples with water in which they have been soaked. Add brown sugar; simmer for ½ hour or until the apples are tender.

Knepp:

2 cups sifted flour   1 egg, beaten
4 teaspoons baking powder   ⅔ cup milk
1 teaspoon salt   3 tablespoons melted shortening
¼ teaspoon pepper

To make the knepp, or dumplings, sift together flour, baking powder, salt, and pepper. Combine egg and milk and add to dry ingredients. Pour in the melted shortening and mix just enough to dampen dry ingredients. Remove ham and schnitz to a hot platter and keep in a warm place. Bring to a boil the liquor in which ham was simmered. Drop dumpling batter from a tablespoon into boiling liquor. Cover tightly and cook 18 to 20 minutes. Surround ham and schnitz with the knepp, or dumplings. Pour remaining liquor over ham. Serve hot.

To make good schnitz pie or schnitz un knepp one should have the real schnitz as made by the Pennsylvania Dutch. These delicious dried apple slices have a flavor all their own. Some of the authentic schnitz were sent to us by a former student, Luella Laughlin, who lives in Pennsylvania, and we made the schnitz un knepp for a Pennsylvania Dutch dinner. It is a treat to go to a quaint Pennsylvania Dutch market to buy the schnitz and to see all the tempting food displayed.

For a dinner with genuine Pennsylvania Dutch flavor, plan schnitz un knepp for the main course. The juicy ham bedecked with the feathery dumplings and the tangy schnitz make a delightful meal for any season of the year.

SWEETBREADS AND BROILED HAM
6 servings

1 pound sweetbreads
¼ cup butter
6 thin slices boiled ham
4 slices bread, cut in half
1 small onion, diced
1 clove garlic, crushed
4 tablespoons butter
2 tablespoons flour

1⅓ cups Chicken Stock (page 45) or canned consommé
1 tablespoon chopped parsley
1 tablespoon soy sauce
½ teaspoon salt
¼ teaspoon ground thyme
Dash of pepper

Precook sweetbreads by cooking in boiling water to which 1 teaspoon vinegar and salt have been added. Simmer 20 to 25 minutes, or until sweetbreads are tender. Drain. Hold under cold running water. Then separate each sweetbread into four pieces and remove membrane and thick connective tissue. Brown sweetbreads in the ¼ cup of butter. Wrap each piece in slice of boiled ham; hold in place with a wooden pick and broil on both sides. Sauté the bread on both sides in 2 tablespoons of the butter until lightly browned. Remove the picks and place each roll of sweetbread and ham on a slice of the fried bread. Make a sauce by browning onion and garlic in remaining 2 tablespoons butter. Add flour and continue to brown without burning. Pour in the Chicken Stock and add remaining ingredients. Let this simmer gently for 10 minutes and then strain sauce. Serve the sweetbreads and ham with 1 tablespoon of the sauce on each roll.

Try sweetbreads and broiled ham as an entree for a luncheon. Serve a green vegetable, crisp rolls, tossed salad, and a simple dessert, as Ginger Lemon Sherbet (page 316).

Veal

PLANKED VEAL CUTLETS
4 servings

4 veal cutlets, ½ inch thick
Salt and pepper
2 eggs, beaten with 2 tablespoons
 water
1 cup bread crumbs

1½ cups hot cooked rice
4 carrots, cut in julienne strips and
 cooked
½ cup grated cheese, if desired

Sprinkle veal cutlets with salt and pepper and dip in beaten egg, then in crumbs. Brown on both sides in a small amount of fat. Add ½ cup water; simmer for 25 minutes. Remove from pan and place overlapping slices of veal cutlets in center of the hot plank. Garnish with a border of fluffy boiled rice and buttered julienne carrots. Place under broiler 5 minutes. Garnish with parsley and serve at once.

For color and flavor, the rice border may be sprinkled with grated cheese just before plank is put under broiler.

RAVIOLI
10 to 12 servings

Dough:

3 eggs
2½ cups flour

2 teaspoons salt

Beat eggs lightly and add flour and salt. This dough will be stiff like noodle dough. Knead. Roll ⅛ inch thick.

Filling:

1½ cups ground cooked veal
⅓ cup finely chopped onion
1 piece celery, chopped fine
¼ pound cream cheese

½ cup cooked spinach, squeezed
 dry
Dash of nutmeg
2 eggs, beaten

Mix veal, onion, celery, cream cheese, spinach, and nutmeg. Thin with beaten egg until the consistency of hamburger.

Cut dough into 2½-inch squares. Place 1 teaspoon of filling in center of square. Place another square of dough over filling and press edges together to seal dough. Brush the surface with beaten egg. Place squares of filled dough in pan of boiling salted water or chicken broth. Cook 12 to 15 minutes or until dough is tender. Serve hot with Tomato Sauce and Parmesan cheese.

Tomato Sauce:

4 tablespoons butter or olive oil
2 small onions, chopped
1 clove garlic, minced

1 No. 2 can tomatoes
Salt and pepper
Parmesan cheese, grated

Put butter or olive oil in skillet. Add chopped onion and minced garlic. Sauté until onion is golden in color. Add tomatoes, salt, and pepper. Cook slowly until liquid has thickened. Add more seasoning, if desired, to make well-flavored tomato sauce. Serve over ravioli and sprinkle generously with Parmesan cheese.

This recipe is one contributed by Carolyn De Bartolo, of Chicago, whose grandmother taught her to make authentic Italian dishes.

RUSSIAN MEAT BALLS
6 to 8 servings

1½ pounds veal, ground fine
4 medium potatoes, cooked and
    chopped
1 medium onion, grated
1½ teaspoons salt

⅛ teaspoon pepper
1 egg, beaten
¼ cup butter
1¼ cups sour cream

Mix together veal, potatoes, onion, seasonings, and egg. Shape in round balls and fry in butter or other fat until well browned. Add ¾ cup sour cream and simmer 15 minutes. Just before serving, add remaining ½ cup cream; bring to boil. Serve hot.

SYLTA
Swedish Pressed Veal
12 to 15 servings

5 pounds pork shoulder
3 pounds veal
1 onion, sliced

2 bay leaves
10 whole allspice
10 whole peppercorns

Cover pork and veal with water and add onion and spices. Cook until meat is well done. Cool. Cut up meat and place on a piece of clean cheesecloth (double thickness), alternating the veal and pork, and seasoning each layer with salt and pepper. Tie ends of cloth into a bag. Place bag in a pan. Cover with a plate and a heavy weight. Let remain in press 24 hours. Remove loaf from cloth and place in mild salt brine. Slice off as needed and serve cold.

This is a favorite dish for the Smörgåsbord (page 460).

VEAL CHOPS WITH PAPRIKA SAUCE
4 servings

8 slices bacon
1 tablespoon chopped onion
4 veal chops, 1 inch thick

Salt and pepper
1 tablespoon paprika
1 cup sour cream

Fry bacon, and when done remove from pan and keep warm. Sauté onion in bacon fat; remove onion. Brown chops on both sides in hot bacon fat, add ½ cup hot water, and simmer 25 to 35 minutes, or until chops are tender. Season with salt, pepper, and paprika. Add the sour cream gradually. Cook slowly about 30 minutes until cream has thickened. Serve hot with plain boiled rice. Put rice in center of serving dish, arrange chops around it and place bacon slices over meat. Garnish platter with parsley.

VEAL CUTLETS À LA FRANÇAISE
4 servings

4 veal cutlets, ½ inch thick
3 tablespoons fat
½ pound ham, cut into thin strips
8 anchovy fillets
4 small onions, cut in halves

Small bunch parsley
½ teaspoon sweet basil
2 or 3 cloves
½ cup water or chicken broth

Sauté cutlets in fat until nicely browned. Lay strips of ham and anchovy fillets crisscross on cutlets. Place in 1½-quart casserole. Add the onions, parsley, basil, and cloves, and add water or broth. Bake in moderate oven (350°) 45 minutes or until meat and onions are done. Add a little more broth if necessary. Serve on a hot platter garnished with parsley.

Only the French could think of a combination like this! The tantalizing aroma of this dish will make you hungry before it comes from the oven.

VEAL MARENGO
6 servings

1½ pounds veal round, ½ inch thick
Flour, salt, and pepper
½ cup fat
1 small onion, chopped
1 clove garlic, minced
4 tablespoons flour

1½ cups Beef Stock (page 45) or canned bouillon
4 medium tomatoes or 2 cups canned tomatoes
½ pound fresh mushrooms or 1 cup canned mushrooms

Cut the veal into six pieces. Dip in flour, salt, and pepper. Heat fat in skillet, add onion and garlic and cook until golden brown; remove from fat. Brown meat in flavored fat; remove from skillet. Add flour to fat and stir until browned. Add stock to make brown sauce, cooking until smooth. Season well and add onion and garlic. Peel and slice tomatoes (if fresh ones are used) and arrange in greased 1½-quart casserole. Lay meat on layer of tomatoes and pour brown sauce over meat. Cover and bake in moderate oven (350°) 45 to 50 minutes. During the last 15 minutes of cooking add mushrooms, and finish cooking with cover off.

VEAL STEAK PAPRIKA
3 to 4 servings

1 bunch green onions
2 tablespoons fat
1½ pounds veal steak, cut 1 inch thick
¼ cup flour
Salt and pepper

1 teaspoon paprika
½ cup sour cream
2 tablespoons milk
1 tablespoon flour
½ cup water

Chop the green onions (including part of the tops) and brown lightly in hot fat in skillet. Skim out onions and reserve. Coat veal steak with flour and brown in hot fat. When browned, sprinkle each side well with salt, pepper, and paprika. Scatter onions over the steak. Combine sour cream and milk; pour over veal steak. Cover skillet, and cook slowly 1 hour or until very tender. Remove meat from skillet to hot serving platter; garnish with onions. Make gravy from sour cream and drippings in pan by adding the tablespoon of flour and ½ cup water. Cook 5 minutes. Pour over veal steak. Serve with buttered cauliflower.

VEAU ROULU
French Veal Rolls
6 servings

6 veal cutlets, cut 3 per pound
½ cup fine bread crumbs
¼ cup milk
¼ pound bulk pork sausage, cooked
¼ cup chopped onion
½ clove garlic, minced
2 slices bacon, cooked and diced

1 tablespoon minced parsley
1 egg yolk
2 tablespoons fat
2 cups Veal Stock (page 46) or canned consommé
1 tablespoon flour
Parsley
6 slices lemon

Pound veal until it is ¼ inch thick. Combine crumbs with milk. Mix together the sausage, crumbs, onion, garlic, bacon, parsley, and egg yolk. Lay 1 tablespoon of this filling across the center of each piece of veal; roll up, securing with wooden pick. Heat fat in iron skillet and sauté veal rolls until nicely browned. Add hot meat stock and simmer until done, 45 minutes to 1 hour. Thicken the liquid with flour to make sauce. Place veal rolls on serving platter and pour sauce over them. Garnish with parsley and lemon slices.

WIENER SCHNITZEL
Breaded Veal Cutlet
4 to 6 servings

2 pounds veal round, cut ½ inch thick
2 eggs
¼ cup milk
Flour
Salt

Fine bread crumbs
¼ cup butter
¼ cup sour cream
Parsley
6 thin slices lemon

Cut meat into pieces for serving; put on board, flatten to make cutlets. Beat eggs and add milk. Dip the veal cutlets first in flour and salt, then in the beaten egg mixture, and finally in the bread crumbs. Fry on both sides in butter until golden brown. Cover skillet; add sour cream and cook at low heat 30 minutes or until meat is tender. Serve, garnished with parsley and lemon slices.

Poultry

CHICKEN
Arroz con Pollo
Arroz à la Valenciana
Baked Chicken with Mush-
    rooms
Breast of Chicken Supreme
  Sauce Supreme
Chicken Croquettes
  Ham or Veal Croquettes
Chicken Curry
Chicken Curry (India)
Chicken Loaf
Chicken Marengo
Chicken and Pork Adobo
Chicken Soufflé
Chicken Tamale Pie
Chicken Terrapin
Creole Chicken
Csirke Paprikas
Fried Chicken
  Chicken Gravy

Polenta with Creamed Chicken
Pollo con Salsa de Almendras
Southern Fried Chicken

DUCKLING
Fried Duckling
Roast Duckling

GUINEA HEN
Guinea Hen De Luxe

TURKEY
Turkey Selection
Turkey Stuffing
Turkey Roasting
Turkey Gravy
Turkey Giblet Gravy

STUFFINGS FOR POULTRY
Apple
Celery and Chestnut
Corn Bread
Savory

WHEN you come right down to popularity, it's hard to beat a chicken dinner. You may serve the old-fashioned kind — tender, crispy fried chicken or a succulent baked chicken with fluffy whipped potatoes and smooth country gravy. Or chicken dressed with new flavors, such as Arroz con Pollo from south of the border, Chicken with Almond Sauce, or flavorful Creole Chicken. Any way you serve it, you can bank on gathering praises from your guests.

Poultry always means a special meal. There is the traditional turkey for the holidays and duck for Sunday dinner. So what could be better party fare?

ARROZ CON POLLO
Rice with Chicken
8 to 10 servings

1 5-pound hen	2 teaspoons salt
2 cups rice, washed and drained	2 teaspoons paprika
4 tablespoons fat	2 cups canned tomatoes
2 small onions, chopped fine	4 cups chicken broth
½ green pepper, chopped fine	2 cups green peas

Cook chicken until tender. Brown rice in hot fat, add onion, pepper, salt, paprika, and tomatoes; pour in broth. Cook covered until rice is tender, about 30 minutes. Remove cover from pan. Do not stir after cooking starts. Remove chicken meat from bones and dice into 1-inch pieces. Cook peas until done. Add chicken and peas to rice, and if too dry, add extra chicken broth. The rice should be moist, but not *too* moist. Serve very hot, garnished with parsley.

This is a favorite way of preparing rice and chicken in Panama.

ARROZ À LA VALENCIANA
Rice with Meat and Chicken
8 to 10 servings

1 medium onion, chopped	3 cups chicken broth
3 cloves garlic, crushed	2 cups rice
3 tablespoons fat	1 teaspoon salt
1 No. 2 can tomatoes	1 cup cooked peas
1 No. ½ can Vienna sausage	½ cup diced pimentos
1½ cups diced cooked chicken	3 hard-cooked eggs, cut into
½ pound ham, diced	quarters

Sauté the onion and garlic in hot fat until lightly browned. Add tomatoes, sausage, chicken, and ham. Cook for 10 minutes and then add chicken broth, rice, and salt. Cook until rice is done. Add peas and pimentos. Turn onto platter and garnish with hard-cooked eggs.

BAKED CHICKEN WITH MUSHROOMS
6 servings

1 roasting chicken, 3½ to 4 pounds	½ cup fat
Milk	½ pound fresh mushrooms
Flour	1 small onion, sliced thin
Salt and pepper	2 cups hot cream or top milk

Cut chicken into serving pieces. Dip the pieces of chicken in milk, then in seasoned flour. Fry in hot fat until nicely browned.

Put in 1½-quart casserole. Clean mushrooms and cut caps and stems into pieces. Fry mushrooms in fat about 2 or 3 minutes. Add mushrooms and onion slices to chicken, and add hot cream or top milk. Bake in moderate oven (350°) 1½ to 2 hours or until chicken is tender and cream is a thick sauce. Serve on a hot platter.

NOTE: If cream is used, it may curdle slightly. A little water can be added to it and stirred until sauce is smooth.

The blended flavor of the onion and mushrooms adds distinction to this baked chicken dish and gives it a flavor all its own.

BREAST OF CHICKEN SUPREME
4 to 6 servings

Select two or three broilers, 1½ to 2 pounds each. Remove breast skin and cut out the entire breast. Sprinkle lightly with salt and pepper and dip in heavy cream, then in flour. Sauté in butter until lightly browned and meat is tender. Allow one thin slice of broiled ham for each breast, cut the same size as the chicken breast. Arrange each piece of broiled ham on a piece of buttered toast and place the sautéed chicken breast on top. Make Sauce Supreme in the pan in which the chicken was cooked and pour it over the chicken breasts. Garnish with mushroom caps that have been sautéed in butter.

Sauce Supreme:

2 tablespoons butter	½ teaspoon salt
2 tablespoons flour	Dash of nutmeg
1 cup Chicken Stock (page 45)	1 egg yolk, slightly beaten
½ cup cream	

Melt butter in double boiler, add flour and stir until well blended. Add chicken stock and cream gradually and bring to the boiling point, stirring constantly. Season with salt and nutmeg. Cook over hot water 10 minutes. Add ⅓ of the mixture to egg yolk, combine both mixtures and cook for a minute or two longer. Do not allow the sauce to boil again.

For a flavor treat for your next party, try this combination of broiled ham and delicately browned chicken breast with sauce supreme.

CHICKEN CROQUETTES
6 servings

2 cups finely chopped cooked
  chicken
½ cup chopped canned mushrooms
½ teaspoon grated onion
¼ teaspoon salt
Dash of pepper

1 cup hot Thick White Sauce
  (page 215)
1 egg, slightly beaten
2 tablespoons water
1 cup fine bread crumbs

Combine chicken and mushrooms; add grated onion, season-ings, and hot white sauce. Mix well. Chill thoroughly. Mold into croquettes about 4 inches long and 1 inch thick. Add water to slightly beaten egg. Roll croquettes in bread crumbs; dip into egg and water mixture; drain, and roll again in crumbs. Fry in deep hot fat (375°) 5 to 6 minutes or until nicely browned. Drain on absorbent paper. Serve hot with Velouté Sauce (page 214).

HAM OR VEAL CROQUETTES

Substitute 2 cups of finely chopped ham or veal for chicken.

CHICKEN CURRY
6 to 8 servings

2½ cups diced cooked chicken
2 cups hot milk
2 cups grated coconut
2 cloves garlic, mashed
2 medium onions, chopped
1 tablespoon chopped fresh ginger
  root

4 tablespoons butter
1 tablespoon curry powder
1 cup milk
½ cup flour
4 tablespoons butter
1 teaspoon salt
1 tablespoon lemon juice
½ cup cream

Pour hot milk over coconut. Let stand 45 minutes. Sauté the garlic, onions, and ginger in the 4 tablespoons of butter until onions are golden in color. Add curry powder and mix thoroughly. Add the cup of milk and cook about 10 minutes; add to milk and coconut. Cook in double boiler over low heat for 1 hour, stirring frequently. Cool. Strain through double cheesecloth. Squeeze out as much liquid as possible. Discard the coconut, onion, and ginger mixture. Heat the liquid in double boiler. Blend flour with remaining butter and add to liquid; add salt and cook until thick. Add lemon juice slowly. Stir in cream and chicken. Reheat and add more seasoning, if desired. Serve with rice and Curry Accompaniments (page 157).

CHICKEN CURRY (INDIA)
4 to 6 servings

1 frying chicken, 2½ to 3 pounds	3 teaspoons salt
1 medium onion	½ pound potatoes, pared and
2 tablespoons fat	quartered
1 tablespoon curry paste or powder	1 No. 2 can butter beans
1 No. 2 can tomatoes	1 tablespoon lemon juice

Disjoint chicken into serving pieces. Cut ½ of the onion into thin strips for seasoning. Cut remaining half in bigger pieces. Heat fat in a saucepan and when hot add the fine onions and fry until a light golden brown. Add curry paste or powder and stir for one minute. Add ½ cup of the tomatoes and cook for a few minutes. Then add chicken and stir well for 5 minutes. Add another ½ cup of the tomatoes. Add salt, potatoes, remainder of the onion, and enough water to just cover the chicken. Cook until chicken is tender and the liquid has evaporated. Add remainder of the canned tomatoes, then the beans or other vegetable. If a raw vegetable is used, it may be put in just a little before the meat is cooked so that meat and vegetable will be cooked together. Cook until mixture has thickened. Add lemon juice and salt to taste and serve hot on steaming rice.

Gwendolyn Matthews brought this recipe for chicken curry to us from her home in Madras, India. And with the help of the Catering Class she prepared the food for the Buffet Featuring Foods of India (page 454).

CHICKEN LOAF
6 to 8 servings

3 eggs	¾ teaspoon salt
1 cup milk	½ teaspoon paprika
½ cup chicken broth, heated	2 cups diced cooked chicken
1 teaspoon finely chopped onion	¾ cup bread crumbs

Beat eggs, add milk, chicken broth, onion, seasonings, chicken, and bread crumbs. Mix well. Pour mixture into greased loaf pan, 9½ x 5¼ x 2¾ inches. Set in pan of hot water. Bake in moderate oven (350°) 45 to 50 minutes, or until done. Invert loaf onto hot platter. Serve with Almond Mushroom Sauce (page 203).

CHICKEN MARENGO
4 to 6 servings

1 roasting chicken, 3 to 3½ pounds
½ cup flour
Salt and pepper
3 tablespoons oil
1 small onion, diced
3 tomatoes
3 tablespoons tomato purée

¾ cup Veal Stock (page 46) or
    Chicken Stock (page 45)
1 clove garlic, mashed
12 mushroom caps
½ cup Croutons (page 47)
Parsley

Cut chicken into serving pieces. Roll in flour to which salt and pepper have been added. Put oil in a skillet and when hot add the pieces of chicken and cook to a golden brown on all sides. Add onion and sauté. Add tomatoes, tomato purée, the stock, and mashed clove of garlic. Season with salt and pepper and simmer slowly 1 to 1½ hours, or until chicken is tender. Sauté mushroom caps in butter. Serve the chicken on a hot platter, put croutons over chicken and pour sauce from the pan over this. Sprinkle with chopped parsley and garnish with mushroom caps.

According to the story, this was created by the Chef of Napoleon after the victorious battle of Marengo, June 14, 1800. Napoleon had called for a celebration for his generals. There was very little food on hand, so the chef had to scout around to see what he could procure. He found chickens on a nearby farm, also tomatoes and garlic. He had no butter, only oil to sauté the chickens in — and this he did. Then he added the tomatoes and garlic, a few onions and mushrooms, and thus provided the pièce de résistance for the celebration.

CHICKEN AND PORK ADOBO
4 servings

1 frying chicken, 2½ to 3 pounds
½ pound pork, cut in 1-inch cubes
½ cup vinegar
2 cloves garlic, crushed
3 bay leaves

3 tablespoons soy sauce
1½ teaspoons salt
⅛ teaspoon pepper
¼ cup fat or oil

Disjoint chicken and cut into serving pieces. Put chicken and pork into 3-quart saucepan. Add vinegar, garlic, bay leaves, soy sauce, and seasonings; let stand 1 hour. Then add enough boiling water to just cover the meat. Simmer over low heat until meat is tender. Remove garlic, bay leaves, and any excess liquid. Add fat; fry pork and chicken, one piece at a time, so that each piece is nicely browned. After the meat has been removed from the pan, add ½ cup of the meat stock and stir to remove any bits of chicken or pork from bottom of pan. Simmer for about 5 minutes and pour over chicken and pork. Serve hot with dry, flaky rice.

This highly regarded native dish of the Philippines was introduced to us by Maria Caminog and Matilda Gussman.

CHICKEN SOUFFLE
6 servings

2 tablespoons butter	⅛ teaspoon pepper
2 tablespoons flour	¼ teaspoon paprika
½ cup soft bread crumbs	3 egg yolks, beaten until light
1 cup milk or Chicken Stock	1 teaspoon lemon juice
(page 45)	2 cups diced cooked chicken
1 teaspoon salt	3 egg whites, stiffly beaten

Melt butter; add flour and blend. Scald soft bread crumbs in milk or stock. Add butter and flour mixture, salt, pepper, and paprika. When slightly cooled add the egg yolks and fold in. Add lemon juice and diced chicken. Fold in the stiffly beaten egg whites. Pour into buttered ring mold or custard cups. Set in pan of hot water and bake in moderate oven (350°). If custard cups are used, 15 to 20 minutes will be required; if large ring mold, 35 minutes. Serve with Béchamel Sauce (page 204) or Velouté Sauce (page 214).

CHICKEN TAMALE PIE
6 to 8 servings

3 cups Chicken Stock (page 45) or	1 No. 2 can whole kernel corn
water	1 cup canned tomatoes
1½ teaspoons salt	2 teaspoons chili powder
1 cup yellow corn meal	¼ teaspoon pepper
1 large onion, minced	½ teaspoon paprika
1 clove garlic, minced	2 cups diced cooked chicken
2 ounces diced salt pork	2 eggs, beaten
¼ cup salad oil	½ cup grated American cheese

Heat stock or water to boiling. Add salt. Stir in corn meal slowly and cook to a thick mush. Put minced onion, garlic, and diced salt pork in skillet with oil. Cook until onion is a light golden color. Add drained corn, tomatoes, and seasonings. Heat and stir until well blended. Combine with cornmeal mixture; add chicken and fold in beaten eggs. Turn into buttered 2-quart casserole. Bake in moderate oven (350°) 50 to 60 minutes. Sprinkle with grated cheese 15 minutes before tamale pie is removed from oven. Serve immediately.

CHICKEN TERRAPIN
6 servings

4 tablespoons butter
4 tablespoons flour
½ teaspoon salt
Dash of pepper
1 cup milk
1 cup Chicken Stock (page 45)
¼ cup pimentos

2 tablespoons ripe olives, cut in strips
Juice of 1 lemon
1 teaspoon prepared mustard
1½ cups diced cooked chicken
3 hard-cooked eggs

Melt butter in double boiler. Add flour, salt, and pepper, and mix until smooth. Stir in milk and stock slowly; stir until thick. Add pimentos, ripe olives, lemon juice, mustard, and chicken. Mash the egg yolks and cut the whites in strips. Add to the sauce. Cook over low heat 10 minutes longer. Serve in Patty Shells (page 427), timbale cases, or toasted bread cups.

CREOLE CHICKEN
4 to 6 servings

1 frying chicken, 3 to 3½ pounds
5 tablespoons fat
2 medium onions, sliced thin
2 raw carrots, diced
1 cup tomatoes
2 whole cloves

½ teaspoon paprika
¼ teaspoon pepper
1½ teaspoons salt
3 cups boiling water
1 cup rice, washed and drained
12 stuffed olives, sliced

Cut chicken into frying pieces and flour lightly. Put fat in heavy skillet and brown onions until golden in color, then remove from fat. Pan-fry chicken in same fat until well browned. Put chicken in center of 2-quart casserole or roasting pan with tight cover. Combine carrots, tomatoes, cloves, seasonings, and boiling water. Pour around chicken. Sprinkle rice evenly around chicken, and also slices of fried onion. Cover tightly. Bake in moderate oven (350°) 1 to 1½ hours or until rice is fluffy, chicken is tender, and water has evaporated. Uncover pan for last 5 to 10 minutes. In serving, place chicken in center of platter, pile rice and vegetables around it, and garnish with sliced olives.

CSIRKE PAPRIKAS
Hungarian Chicken Paprika
4 servings

2 medium onions, chopped	2 tablespoons lemon juice
3 tablespoons butter	1 tablespoon flour
1 frying chicken, 2½ to 3½ pounds	Salt and pepper
1 teaspoon paprika	1 cup sour cream

Sauté onions in butter until lightly browned. Cut chicken in serving pieces and brown lightly. Add paprika and lemon juice. Cover tightly and cook over low heat until tender. Remove chicken and keep hot. Add flour to saucepan, season with salt and pepper. Blend in the sour cream, stirring constantly over low heat until thick and smooth. Pour sauce over chicken. Reheat. Serve on a hot platter.

FRIED CHICKEN
4 servings

1 frying chicken, 2½ to 3 pounds	⅛ teaspoon pepper
1 cup flour	Fat for frying
1 teaspoon salt	

Cut chicken into quarters or into serving pieces. Put seasoned flour in paper bag, add pieces of chicken, one at a time, and shake in bag to coat with flour. Shake off any excess flour. Heat fat in heavy skillet to depth of about ½ inch. Place meaty pieces of chicken in hot fat, then other pieces. Do not crowd chicken in pan, but allow room to turn pieces easily. When chicken begins to brown, turn carefully so it is nicely browned on all sides. Use tongs for turning chicken. As soon as chicken has browned, reduce heat, cover, and cook slowly until tender, 40 to 60 minutes, according to size of chicken. Add 2 or 3 tablespoons of water or stock, if necessary, to keep chicken from sticking to pan. Uncover pan last 5 or 10 minutes so chicken will be crisp. Serve hot with Chicken Gravy.

CHICKEN GRAVY

3 tablespoons chicken fat	2 cups milk
3 tablespoons flour	Salt and pepper

Pour fat from skillet and scrape pan to remove any charred bits. Measure 3 tablespoons of fat and return to pan. Add flour to the fat and blend thoroughly. Pour in milk slowly, stirring constantly until gravy has thickened. Boil briskly for about 5 minutes. Season to taste with salt and pepper. Serve hot.

POLENTA WITH CREAMED CHICKEN
6 servings

2½ cups finely diced potatoes
1 quart water

2 teaspoons salt
¾ cup yellow corn meal

Put potatoes into boiling salted water in deep kettle. Bring
again to a boil. Add corn meal very gradually, stirring constantly. Continue to stir and cook over low heat for 45 minutes. This can be cooked over hot water to avoid burning.
When the polenta is stiff, turn into a buttered 2-quart ring
mold or turn out in a mound onto a hot platter. Serve with
Creamed Chicken.

CREAMED CHICKEN

¼ cup butter
1 clove garlic, cut in half
4 tablespoons flour
1 teaspoon salt

2 cups milk or Chicken Stock
    (page 45)
2 cups cubed cooked chicken
Chopped parsley or chives

Melt the butter in a saucepan and add the garlic. Stir and
cook 1 minute. Remove garlic. Add flour and salt. Stir and
cook and then add milk or chicken stock. Stir and cook 10
minutes to blend seasonings. Add cubed chicken. Serve in
bowl topped with parsley or chopped chives.

Butter-browned mushrooms or ripe olives make a good
accompaniment.

Ceremony of Making Polenta

Emma Francesia came to Iowa State College from Montana to study
Institution Management. She brought her family's recipe for Polenta,
and this is her description of this famous Italian dish:

*Polenta is a food typical of northern Italy. When my parents moved
to Montana, they brought with them the secrets and ceremonies of
making this special dish. It was always our Sunday treat — a steaming
hot base for meat and gravy. An unromantic description of our Polenta
would be a corn meal and potato mush, but to us it was a family
tradition.*

*Papa always took over the honors on Sunday. This was the only
part of Sunday dinner that he made, for it required one hour of constant stirring, if done the Italian way.*

A *10-quart kettle was used. Mama would pare potatoes and boil them until they were thoroughly cooked and broken into small pieces. Now, Mama stepped aside and Papa took over the position in front of the hot coal-burning stove.*

Yellow corn meal, not white, was the only kind permitted in the house. The left hand was used to sprinkle the corn meal gently over the surface of the simmering potato brew, while the right hand stirred with a wood stick about the thickness of a broom handle. To the eyes of a writer of recipes, the proportions were all guesswork, but not so with Papa! When the mixture began to be soupy, the left hand put down the corn meal. From here on the stirring was constant, but not arduous. Gradually the mixture became as thick as the batter for steamed pudding, but it was far from ready to eat! For at least 45 minutes the stirring must be continued. It was in this period of cooking that Papa's philosophy and humor entertained us all. He could not leave the pot, and we would not leave his stories.

During the last 15 minutes of cooking, the Polenta was digestible for his hungry children, but not perfection for a gourmet like Papa. Then it was that each of us would be given a big spoonful of hot Polenta. Into the center of our portion we would place a cube of aged, strong cheese, and roll the Polenta around it. These mounds were placed on one hot lid of the stove, which had been previously scrubbed by Mama and kept free for the very purpose of toasting these Cheese-Polenta prizes. When browned, the little balls were turned over and flattened to acquire a crisp, brown crust. We children loved these little taste-teasers almost as much as the treat to follow.

At the precise moment the Polenta was finished, Papa carried the kettle to the table and turned out the big golden ball onto a cloud-white tea towel, folded in four and laid on the bread board. Mama had timed her cooking so that all the food was on the table at one time: chicken cacciatore or veal or codfish prepared with a rich thin sauce seasoned with onions and garlic, "salada," Italian peas or green beans, a plate of cheese, and wine and milk. No one ever wanted dessert.

Papa served the Polenta. He used a clean string to cut the golden ball in two. Then with long sweeps of the string each half portion would be cut again. A knife was then used to cut the individual portions. Over this hot Polenta, each one ladled the day's special meat-and-sauce mixture. There was always more than we could eat, so the next day the leftover Polenta was sliced and fried just as Americans fry mush, but we think our Polenta is superior in flavor, due to the potatoes and the long cooking.

There was one more ceremony to the service of Polenta — licking the pot. We children peeled off strips of the thick, crisp crust on the bottom and sides of the pot. Mama always laughed and said it made dishwashing easier.

POLLO CON SALSA DE ALMENDRAS
Guatemalan Chicken with Almond Sauce
5 to 6 servings

1 5-pound hen	1 slice dry white bread
½ cup diced celery	1 No. 2 can tomatoes
1 onion, sliced thin	½ teaspoon cinnamon
1 teaspoon salt	6 whole cloves
1 cup blanched almonds	2 tablespoons vinegar
½ cup fat	¼ cup chopped stuffed olives
½ cup raisins	2 pimentos, chopped

Disjoint chicken; place in kettle and cover with water. Add diced celery, onion, and salt, and cook until tender. Remove meat from bones; cut meat into small pieces. Fry almonds in fat to light brown; remove and drain. In same fat, heat raisins until well puffed; remove from fat. Fry bread to light brown; remove and drain. Put each of these fried ingredients through the food chopper separately. Add to hot fat. Add tomatoes and spices. Pour in 2 cups of the strained chicken broth and add cut-up chicken meat. Simmer slowly 25 to 30 minutes, until sauce begins to thicken, and then add vinegar, olives, and pimentos. Let cook 5 to 10 minutes longer. Serve hot with toasted Tortillas (page 83).

SOUTHERN FRIED CHICKEN
4 servings

Select fryers of not over 2 pounds. Dress them carefully and cut into serving pieces. Chill thoroughly before frying. Add salt and pepper to flour and roll pieces in this. Then drop into deep hot fat (375°), fry until golden brown and chicken is done. Remove chicken and drain on absorbent paper. Serve hot with Chicken Gravy (page 131).

FRIED DUCKLING
4 to 5 servings

1 duckling, 3½ to 4 pounds	2 teaspoons paprika
1 cup flour	¼ cup butter
2 teaspoons salt	¼ cup fat
¼ teaspoon pepper	¼ cup water

Cut duckling into serving pieces, or, if quick-frozen, thaw according to directions on wrapper. Rinse in cold water, and drain. Mix flour, salt, pepper, and paprika in a paper sack. Shake 2 or 3 pieces of duckling at a time in sack in order to coat thoroughly with flour. Heat butter and enough of the fat in a heavy skillet to make a layer of fat ¼ inch deep. With kitchen tongs place duckling in hot fat, skin side down. Brown and turn. Add water and cover tightly. Reduce heat and cook slowly about 1½ hours, or until duckling is tender. To crisp the crust remove the cover during last 10 minutes.

ROAST DUCKLING

Long Island style and other specially raised ducklings are scientifically fed birds of fine flavor and tenderness. The skin is white and tender and the fat underneath is creamy white. Most ducklings on the market are 3½ to 4 pounds, ready-to-cook weight. Allowing about a pound per person, one is the buy for a small family, but two may be roasted and served side by side for a larger family.

Tart, well-seasoned stuffing combines well with rich duck meat. Some cooks fill the little bird with chopped onion and celery, or chopped onion and quartered apple. Some just put a whole, cored apple or a whole orange inside. Others prefer stuffing of rice and apricot or other dried fruit.

Roast a duck in an open pan, with no water, in an oven at 325° — moderately low heat. Because duck is fat, no basting is needed. Prick skin over back and around tail to let fat drain off in cooking. Pour off fat as it accumulates in the pan to keep drippings light-colored and delicately flavored. Allow at least 30 minutes per pound, then test for doneness. When well-done, the thick flesh on the drumstick feels soft when pressed, and leg joint moves easily.

GUINEA HEN DE LUXE

1 guinea hen, 2 pounds	1 tablespoon julienne green peppers
1 cup flour	8 ounces fresh mushrooms
Salt, as needed	1 tablespoon flour
¼ teaspoon paprika	1 cup bouillon
Butter for frying	2 tomatoes
1 tablespoon finely sliced green onion	6 cooked prunes
	1 egg yolk
1 tablespoon julienne red peppers	½ cup cream

Disjoint guinea. Coat with flour to which salt and paprika have been added. Fry very slowly in butter, in a skillet, until nicely browned and tender. Remove guinea and make sauce as follows: using same skillet, add onion, red and green peppers, and mushrooms. Cook until all are fairly well done, about 10 minutes. Add the tablespoon of flour and cook again for 2 minutes. Add bouillon, tomatoes, and prunes. Cook all together for 15 minutes or until of right consistency. Add egg yolk and cream. Serve browned guinea on French toast. Cover with sauce.

TURKEY SELECTION*

ALLOWANCE PER PERSON
Allow 1 pound of meat per person New York-dressed weight, which should give you enough turkey for two helpings apiece at the first meal and enough leftovers for a second meal.

STYLES OF TURKEY
New York or *Market Dressed*: Head and feet on; picked but not drawn.
Full Drawn: Ready to cook. It comes frozen or unfrozen; may or may not be individually packaged.

Buy a *hen* turkey if you want an 8- to 15-pound bird. Hen turkeys mature quickly and are usually better finished than toms of the same weight. Buy a *tom* if you want a 16- to 25-pound bird.

* From Poultry and Egg National Board

TURKEY STUFFING*

The turkey may be stuffed just before it goes into the oven or several hours in advance. When you stuff it ahead of time, cool hot dressing before putting it in the turkey; then wrap the stuffed bird loosely in waxed paper and refrigerate immediately.

Allow 1 cup of dressing per pound of bird *New York dressed,* or 1½ cups per pound *full-drawn weight,* to fill cavity and neck.

Don't pack dressing tightly. If you do, it will be soggy and bird may burst when dressing expands during cooking.

Turkeys may be roasted without dressing.

TIMETABLE FOR TURKEY ROASTING *

Oven Weight† (Pounds)	Oven Temperature	Cooking Time (Minutes per Pound)	Cooking Time (Hours per Bird)
8 to 10	325°	25 to 20	3 to 3½
10 to 14	325°	20 to 18	3½ to 4
14 to 18	300°	18 to 15	4 to 4½
18	300°	15 to 13	4½ to 5
20	300°	15 to 13	5 to 6

† The oven weight of a stuffed New York-dressed turkey approximates the purchase weight.

If you buy a drawn turkey, add 3 pounds to the purchase weight of an 8- to 14-pound turkey; add 4 pounds to the purchase weight of a 14- to 18-pound turkey to get the approximate oven weight of the stuffed bird.

TURKEY ROASTING*

For best results, follow these simple steps in roasting —
1. Rub cavity of bird with salt.
2. Put enough stuffing in neck to fill it out nicely and fasten neck skin to back with skewer.

* From Poultry and Egg National Board

3. Stuff cavity well, but do not pack tightly.
4. Truss bird and grease skin thoroughly with melted or softened cooking fat.
5. Place breast down on rack in shallow pan.
6. Cover top and sides of bird with fat-moistened cloth (preferably clean white cheesecloth).
7. Place in preheated oven set at proper temperature indicated on timetable for your size turkey.
8. Do not sear. Do not cover. Do not add water.
9. Moisten cloth with fat from bottom of pan if cloth dries slightly during cooking.
10. Turn bird breast up when about three-fourths done, so breast will brown nicely.

HOW TO TELL WHEN TURKEY IS DONE

To tell whether turkey is done, press the fleshy part of the drumstick with your fingers, protecting them with cloth or paper. If done, the meat feels soft. Or move the drumstick up and down. If the leg joint gives readily or breaks, the turkey is done.

If you use a meat thermometer, the turkey will be done when a thermometer placed in the center of the inside thigh muscle registers 190° or when one placed in the center of the dressing registers 180°.

SERVING

Take the turkey out of the oven 20 to 30 minutes before it is to be served, if possible. This gives the meat a chance to absorb the juices. Keep bird on warm platter until it is served.

TURKEY GRAVY
2 cups

3 tablespoons drippings	2 cups liquid
3 tablespoons flour	Salt and pepper

Pour drippings from roasting pan into a bowl. Skim off as much fat as possible and put 3 tablespoons into a saucepan. Measure 3 tablespoons of flour into the fat and blend thoroughly. Measure meat juice and add stock in which giblets were cooked, milk or water, to make up 2 cups. Cook fat and flour mixture over low heat, stirring constantly. Cook until frothy. Add cold liquid all at once, stirring constantly until thickened. Boil briskly about 5 minutes. Season to taste with salt and pepper. Serve hot.

Gravy may be cooked in the roasting pan, but this is not recommended, except for experienced cooks. If this is done, proceed as above, pouring out all the drippings, so you can measure accurately the quantity of fat and liquid needed.

TURKEY GIBLET GRAVY

Turkey giblets	1 small bay leaf
2 cups water	3 slices of onion
1 teaspoon salt	½ cup diced celery
3 peppercorns	½ cup diced carrot
3 cloves	

Cover gizzard and heart with water; add remaining ingredients and cook over low heat until tender, about 2 to 3 hours, or until heart can be pierced easily with a fork. Add liver 20 to 30 minutes before giblets are done, depending on size. Use broth in making turkey gravy. Chop giblets and add to gravy just before serving.

Stuffings for Poultry

APPLE STUFFING
About 6 cups

3 cups cubed bread	¼ cup chopped onion
½ cup turkey broth	¼ teaspoon sage
¾ cup melted butter	1 teaspoon salt
1 cup diced celery	Dash of pepper
2 cups pared chopped apples	

Moisten bread with broth and melted butter. Add other ingredients. Mix and stuff turkey or chicken.

CELERY AND CHESTNUT STUFFING
About 4 cups

1 pound chestnuts
4 tablespoons butter
1 cup diced celery
½ cup chopped onion
2½ cups diced dry bread

Boiling water
2 hard-cooked eggs, diced
Salt
1 tablespoon parsley
Paprika

Boil or roast chestnuts, shell and skin, then chop to make 1 cup. Melt butter in skillet and add diced celery and chopped onion. Cook slowly until lightly browned. Place diced bread in bowl and moisten with boiling water. Add browned onion and celery, eggs, chopped chestnuts, and seasonings. Mix all ingredients together and stuff chicken or turkey.

CORN BREAD STUFFING
About 6 cups

1 recipe corn bread (page 63), crumbled
1 cup cubed white bread
1 cup turkey or chicken broth
½ pound pork sausage meat

1 medium onion, finely chopped
3 hard-cooked eggs, diced
1½ teaspoons salt
½ teaspoon black pepper

Combine corn bread and diced white bread. Add broth and mix well. Cook sausage. Sauté onion in sausage fat until golden in color. Remove onion from fat. Add sausage, onion, hard-cooked eggs, and seasonings to corn bread mixture. Mix together lightly. Add more seasoning, if desired. Use as stuffing for chicken or turkey.

SAVORY STUFFING
About 4 cups

1 quart bread crumbs
1 teaspoon salt
Dash of pepper

2 teaspoons poultry seasoning
1 medium onion, finely chopped
1 cup butter

Mix bread crumbs, salt, pepper, and poultry seasoning. Chop onion and sauté in butter. Pour over bread crumbs. Mix thoroughly. Use to stuff chicken or turkey.

Fish and Shellfish

FISH

Baked Fish with Stuffing
Broiled Fish Steaks
Creole Halibut
Filipino Fried Fish in
    Vinegar Sauce
Fillet of Sole with Almonds
Fish Molee (India)
Fish Timbale with Mushrooms
Fried Fish

Fried Speckled Gulf Trout
Halibut Meunière
Halibut Mold with Cucumber
    Sauce
New England Codfish Balls
Planked Bass with Shrimp
    Sauce
Salmon Loaf
Salmon Soufflé

SHELLFISH

CLAMS
Clam Fritters

CRAB MEAT
Creamed Crab and
    Shrimp en Casserole
Creamed Crab in Avocado
Maryland Deviled Crab
Crab Meat Snug Harbor

LOBSTER
De luxe Lobster Casserole
Lobster Patties
Lobster Thermidor

SCALLOPS
Scallops Newburg

SHRIMP
Cooked Shrimp
Creole Shrimp in Rice Ring
Shrimp Curry
    Curry Accompaniments
French Fried Shrimp

STUFFINGS FOR FISH
Parsley and Egg
Plain
Vegetable

No LONGER do you have to live near the coasts to take advantage of the riches of the sea. Modern freezing and canning methods have made a wide variety of fish available even in remote inland towns.

It's wise to take stock of the kinds of fish at your market, then discover tasty ways to serve them. You'll find it will pay off, not only in wonderful eating, but also in plain dollars and cents. Many fish are budget-priced.

Fish

BAKED FISH WITH STUFFING
4 to 5 servings

Use pike, whitefish, or perch for baking. Plan ⅓ to ½ pound per person. Clean fish. Salt lightly inside and out.

Stuffing (for a 2-pound fish):

3 cups bread cubes
4 tablespoons chopped onions
⅓ cup chopped celery
1 teaspoon salt
½ teaspoon herb seasoning
⅛ teaspoon pepper
¼ cup, or more, melted fat
Mousseline Sauce (page 211)

To bread cubes add remaining ingredients and toss together lightly. Add more seasoning if necessary. Stuff fish, insert wooden picks, and lace with string. Wrap tail and fins in waxed paper. Brush with melted butter. Put into shallow baking pan and bake in moderate oven (350°) 40 to 45 minutes. Garnish with lemon wedges and parsley or water cress. Serve with Mousseline Sauce.

BROILED FISH STEAKS
8 servings

Purchase 6 slices of fish (halibut, salmon, cod, etc.) cut about ¾ inch thick. Skin and cook whole slices, or skin and bone to make two fillets from each slice. Dip the slices in cream and place on the bottom of a lightly greased broiling pan. Cover with a thin layer of fine soft bread crumbs and broil under moderate heat, without turning, for 15 minutes or until the fish is done. Dot over with bits of butter and continue broiling with more intense heat until the crumbs are a golden brown. Remove with spatula to a hot platter. Garnish with wedges of lemon and sprigs of parsley.

CREOLE HALIBUT
6 servings

6 slices halibut, ¾ inch thick
¼ cup butter
2 tablespoons oil or fat
1 cup chopped celery
1 small onion, chopped

1 green pepper, chopped fine
1 clove garlic, minced
Salt and pepper
1 No. 2 can tomatoes
Parsley

Sauté halibut in butter until nicely browned on both sides. Put oil or fat in another skillet and add celery, onion, green pepper, and garlic. Add salt and pepper to taste. Cook until onion is golden in color and green pepper is soft. Add tomatoes and cook until liquid has been reduced and thickened. Place halibut slices in shallow pan and pour the tomato mixture over them. Bake in moderate oven (350°) 15 to 20 minutes. Garnish with parsley.

FILIPINO FRIED FISH IN VINEGAR SAUCE
6 servings

6 fillets of sole
1 large green pepper
2 teaspoons chopped garlic
2 tablespoons fat
¾ cup finely chopped onion
1 cup water

1 teaspoon finely chopped ginger root
2 tablespoons vinegar
1 tablespoon brown sugar
Salt

Sauté fish until nicely browned on each side. Remove seeds and slice pepper in long slices ¼ inch wide. Mash garlic and brown in the fat. Remove garlic and fry pepper and onion until lightly browned. Add water, ginger, vinegar, sugar, and salt, and boil 10 minutes. Add the fried fish and simmer slowly 10 to 15 minutes. Serve hot.

This is a favorite method of preparing fish in the Philippines. The pungent sweet-sour sauce gives the fish a distinctive flavor.

FILLET OF SOLE WITH ALMONDS
4 servings

4 fillets of sole
Flour
Salt
Coarse black pepper
¼ cup butter
½ teaspoon finely chopped garlic
1 tablespoon finely chopped onion

½ cup butter
⅓ cup water
2 tablespoons lemon juice
Salt and pepper
½ cup blanched almonds, browned
    and chopped

Wipe fillets with damp cloth. Dry well. Dust very lightly with flour, salt, and coarse black pepper. Heat the ¼ cup of butter in heavy skillet. When foaming and just turning brown, put in the fillets. Cook to a golden brown on each side. Remove carefully from skillet and arrange on hot serving dish. Keep warm. Add garlic and onion to pan in which sole was cooked. Stir over low heat until golden brown. Add alternately the remaining ½ cup butter and the water and lemon juice, stirring frequently. Season to taste with salt and pepper. Add chopped browned almonds to sauce and heat sauce for about 2 minutes longer. Pour sauce over fish. Garnish platter with parsley or water cress and lemon wedges. Serve immediately.

Other fish fillets may be prepared in the same manner.

FISH MOLEE (INDIA)
4 servings

1 pound haddock fillet
½ cup flour
Dash of cayenne pepper
¼ teaspoon saffron

½ teaspoon salt
Dash of black pepper
¼ cup water

Blend flour and seasonings. Add water to make a thin batter. Dip fish fillets in batter and drain. Sauté in skillet in small amount of fat until nicely browned on both sides. Remove and set aside.

Molee:

4 thin slices onion
1 tablespoon fat
¾ teaspoon ground ginger
¼ teaspoon turmeric
3 cloves garlic, pounded

1 cup coconut milk
1 teaspoon salt
1 tablespoon lemon juice
1 medium onion, cut into eighths

Brown the slices of onion in hot fat with ginger, turmeric, and garlic. When golden brown, lower heat and add coconut milk that has been made by pouring 1 cup boiling water over ½ cup freshly grated coconut; then add salt, lemon juice, and onion. Simmer molee for 10 minutes. Place fish in sauce and simmer for 15 minutes over low heat. Serve hot.

FISH TIMBALE WITH MUSHROOMS
5 to 6 servings

1 cup cooked or canned fish	½ teaspoon salt
½ cup mushrooms	Dash of pepper
1 tablespoon butter	Dash of paprika
1 cup bread crumbs	Dash of nutmeg
2 cups cream	4 eggs, well beaten
½ cup butter	

Use any delicate fish, such as halibut or salmon. Remove the bones and skin and pound the meat very fine. Sauté mushrooms in butter and mix with the fish. Heat bread crumbs 10 minutes in cream, and add butter, salt, pepper, paprika, and nutmeg. When mixture is cold, add fish; beat whole mixture thoroughly. Add eggs; blend, and turn the mixture into buttered 1½-quart casserole. Place in a deep baking pan and pour hot water into the pan until it is within one inch of the top of the casserole. Bake uncovered in slow oven (325°) 45 to 60 minutes. Serve with Celery Sauce or Egg Sauce (page 215).

FRIED FISH
4 to 6 servings

1½ pounds fillet of haddock, cod or perch	1 cup corn meal
	2 eggs, beaten
Salt and pepper	Fat for deep fat frying

Sprinkle fish with salt and pepper; roll in corn meal, then in beaten egg, again in corn meal, and fry in deep hot fat (385°) 4 to 6 minutes. Serve with Drawn Butter (page 207), Tartare Sauce (page 214) or Chinese Meat Sauce (page 208).

FRIED SPECKLED GULF TROUT
4 servings

4 speckled gulf trout	1 cup corn meal
Salt and pepper	½ cup fat

Salt and pepper the trout and roll in corn meal. Melt fat in heavy skillet and fry trout in hot fat until nicely browned on both sides. Serve hot. Garnish with parsley and lemon wedges.

HALIBUT MEUNIERE
4 servings

4 slices halibut
Flour
½ cup butter
2 tablespoons finely chopped onion
1 teaspoon finely chopped garlic
⅓ cup tomato juice
1 teaspoon lemon juice

3 tablespoons finely chopped
  parsley
4 small peeled tomatoes
Salt and pepper
1 lemon, thinly sliced
Paprika

Roll halibut in flour. Heat ¼ cup of the butter in heavy skillet
and when foaming and just beginning to turn brown put the
halibut in skillet. Cook halibut until golden brown on each
side, then cover and cook over low heat for 3 or 4 minutes. Remove from skillet and arrange on hot serving platter. Add 2
more tablespoons of the butter to the skillet. Add onion and
garlic and sauté until golden in color. Add the tomato juice,
lemon juice, and parsley. Heat for several minutes and pour
over the halibut. Cut tomatoes in quarters and sauté in the remaining 2 tablespoons of butter; season with salt and pepper.
Garnish fish with the quartered tomatoes and thin slices of
lemon that have been dipped in paprika.

HALIBUT MOLD WITH CUCUMBER SAUCE
6 to 8 servings

2 pounds halibut
1 small onion, chopped fine
2 sprigs parsley
½ teaspoon peppercorns
1 bay leaf, broken into small pieces
4 egg whites, unbeaten

2½ cups heavy cream
½ teaspoon salt
Dash of pepper
Béchamel Sauce (page 204)
Cucumber Sauce (page 209)

Break halibut into pieces. Cover with cold water; add chopped
onion, parsley, peppercorns, and bay leaf. Simmer until fish is
tender, about 15 minutes. Remove fish (save fish stock for
Béchamel Sauce). Pound fish with wooden potato masher until
very fine; add egg whites one at a time and mix thoroughly. Add
cream, salt and pepper. Butter fish mold or ring mold. Pour
fish mixture into mold. Place in pan of hot water and bake in

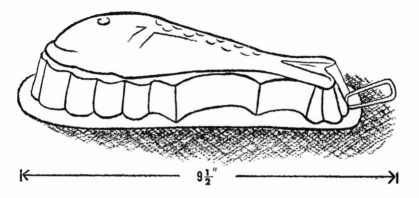

$9\frac{1}{2}''$

moderate oven (350°) 50 to 60 minutes or until done. Pour Béchamel Sauce over the halibut and put Cucumber Sauce in the center of the mold.

NEW ENGLAND CODFISH BALLS
1½ dozen

6 ounces dry salt codfish
2½ cups pared and diced potatoes
2 tablespoons butter

⅛ teaspoon pepper
1 egg, beaten

Soak codfish overnight in cold water. Next morning pour off water, place fish on cutting board and shred, using a fork. Cook potatoes until tender, drain thoroughly. Shake over heat until dry; mash, add butter and pepper, and beat with fork until very light. Add dry flaked codfish and egg and continue beating until mixture is light and fluffy. Add more salt if necessary. Dip with tablespoon and drop into deep hot fat (375°). Cook until light brown, about 1 minute. Cook a few at a time. Drain on absorbent paper. Serve with catsup or Tartare Sauce (page 214).

A hint from New Englanders: The codfish shreds more easily if it has been soaked at least 12 hours. Removal of as much water as possible from the potatoes and codfish is essential for a light and fluffy interior texture. For a touch of variety on your appetizer tray, form miniature codfish balls and fry in 1-inch deep fat — clever and delicious on the end of a toothpick.

These crisp golden brown balls have a melt-in-your-mouth quality.

PLANKED BASS WITH SHRIMP SAUCE
4 to 6 servings

3 pounds bass   2 tablespoons melted butter
Salt and pepper

Clean, split, and bone fish. Place skin-side down on heated, well-greased plank. Season with salt and pepper and brush over with melted butter. Broil under medium heat until lightly browned; move a little farther from the heat and broil 10 to 15 minutes longer. Serve Shrimp Sauce (page 213) with the fish.

As an accompaniment to the planked bass, serve Duchess Potatoes (page 185), broiled tomato wedges, and green beans. To prepare: Broil 3 small tomatoes cut in wedges. Cook 12-ounce package French-style green beans. Pipe a border of the Duchess Potatoes around fish and around edge of plank. Arrange broiled tomatoes and green beans between borders. Garnish with sprigs of parsley.

SALMON LOAF
6 to 8 servings

2 cups fresh or canned salmon   1 tablespoon melted butter
1 tablespoon lemon juice   ¾ cup soft bread crumbs
½ teaspoon salt   3 eggs, slightly beaten
⅛ teaspoon pepper   1 cup milk
½ teaspoon paprika   Parsley
1 tablespoon finely chopped onion   Lemon wedges

Flake the salmon; add lemon juice, salt, pepper, paprika, onion, and butter. Stir in bread crumbs, and then eggs and milk. Pack mixture into buttered loaf pan, 9½ x 5¼ x 2¾ inches, and bake in moderate oven (350°) 45 minutes. Turn out on oblong platter. Garnish with parsley and lemon wedges. Serve with Celery Sauce (page 215).

SALMON SOUFFLE
5 to 6 servings

3 tablespoons butter   1 cup canned salmon, flaked
3 tablespoons flour   1 tablespoon minced parsley
1 cup milk   1½ teaspoons grated onion
1 teaspoon salt   2 teaspoon lemon juice
½ teaspoon paprika   3 eggs, separated

Melt butter, add flour; blend well. Gradually add milk; continue to cook while stirring until thick and smooth. Add salt and paprika. Add flaked salmon, parsley, onion, and lemon juice. Remove from heat. Beat egg yolks; add to first mixture and set aside to cool. Beat egg whites until stiff but not dry; fold into salmon mixture. Pour into buttered 1½-quart casserole, place in pan of hot water and bake uncovered in slow oven (325°) about 50 to 60 minutes until well puffed and golden brown. Serve immediately.

Shellfish

CLAM FRITTERS
6 servings

1 cup fresh clams or 1 10½-ounce can clams, diced	1 teaspoon baking powder
½ teaspoon salt	1 egg, beaten
Dash of pepper	¼ cup milk
1 cup flour	¼ cup clam liquor

Drain clams. Add salt and pepper to clams. Sift flour and baking powder together. Combine the beaten egg, milk, and clam liquor. Add liquid to dry ingredients and mix just enough to dampen. Stir in the diced clams. Drop from tablespoon into deep hot fat (365°). Cook 2 to 3 minutes, or until nicely browned and cooked thoroughly. Serve hot.

CREAMED CRAB AND SHRIMP EN CASSEROLE
6 to 8 servings

2 6½-ounce cans crab meat	½ cup grated cheese
2 7-ounce cans shrimp	1 tablespoon grated onion
2½ cups well-seasoned Medium White Sauce (page 215)	½ teaspoon Worcestershire sauce
	½ cup buttered crumbs

Flake crab meat, remove black vein from shrimp. Add to white sauce grated cheese, onion, and Worcestershire sauce. Stir in lightly crab and shrimp. Place in baking shells or buttered 1½-quart casserole and top with buttered crumbs. Brown in very hot oven (450°) 5 to 6 minutes.

CREAMED CRAB IN AVOCADO
4 servings

1 6½-ounce can crab meat	Salt and pepper
1¼ cups milk	1 teaspoon lemon juice
3 tablespoons flour	2 large ripe avocados
3 tablespoons soft butter	3 tablespoons grated sharp cheese

Heat crab meat and milk in double boiler. Blend flour and butter until smooth, add to the hot milk and stir until smooth and thick. Add seasonings and lemon juice. Cut avocados in halves, peel, and place in shallow pan. Heap with the thick creamed crab meat and sprinkle with grated cheese. Pour hot water around avocados, enough to just cover the bottom of the pan; bake, uncovered, in moderate oven (375°) 15 minutes.

MARYLAND DEVILED CRAB
6 to 8 servings

1 pound cooked crab meat or 2 6½-ounce cans	Salt and pepper
¼ cup butter	1 tablespoon lemon juice
1 small onion, chopped	1½ cups Thick White Sauce (page 215)
2 tablespoons chopped green pepper	2 egg yolks
½ teaspoon Worcestershire sauce	⅓ cup mayonnaise
1 teaspoon chopped chives	1 teaspoon prepared mustard
Dash of cayenne pepper	½ cup buttered bread crumbs

Flake the crab meat. Melt butter in skillet. Add chopped onion and green pepper and cook until onion is golden in color. Add remainder of seasonings and white sauce. Add flaked crab meat. Beat egg yolks slightly and add to crab mixture. Fill crab shells or buttered 1½-quart casserole. Combine mayonnaise and prepared mustard. Spread this over crab mixture. Sprinkle with buttered bread crumbs and bake in hot oven (425°) 5 to 8 minutes or until crumbs are brown.

If you like crab meat, you'll like this Maryland deviled crab. Try it for your next party luncheon.

CRAB MEAT SNUG HARBOR
6 servings

½ cup hot Medium White Sauce
   (page 215)
3 teaspoons grated onion
1½ teaspoons Worcestershire sauce
½ cup cubed fresh bread
½ cup mayonnaise

2 teaspoons lemon juice
½ teaspoon salt
Dash of white pepper
2 tablespoons butter
1¼ pounds fresh lump crab meat
   or 3 6½-ounce cans

Blend together white sauce, onion, Worcestershire sauce, and bread cubes. Cool. Fold in mayonnaise, lemon juice, salt, and pepper. Put butter in saucepan and stir over low heat until browned. Add crab meat to browned butter and toss lightly together. Combine crab meat with sauce mixture. Turn into buttered 1½-quart casserole or into buttered shells. Brown in hot oven (450°) 10 to 15 minutes. Serve at once.

Crab meat Snug Harbor is a favorite luncheon dish with shoppers at Ayres Tea Room, in Indianapolis.

DE LUXE LOBSTER CASSEROLE
6 servings

½ cup hot Medium White Sauce
   (page 215)
2½ teaspoons onion juice
1 teaspoon Worcestershire sauce
½ cup cubed soft bread
½ cup mayonnaise

1 tablespoon lemon juice
¼ teaspoon salt
⅛ teaspoon pepper
2 tablespoons browned butter
3 6-ounce cans lobster

Blend white sauce, onion juice, Worcestershire sauce, and bread cubes. Cool. Fold in mayonnaise, lemon juice, salt and pepper. Put butter in skillet and brown. Gently toss lobster with browned butter. Add white sauce mixture and fold in lightly. Place in shells or buttered 1½-quart casserole and brown in very hot oven (450°) 15 minutes. Serve at once.

LOBSTER PATTIES
10 servings

Lobster Filling:

½ green pepper, chopped
2 shallots or 2 tablespoons chopped
   onion
4 tablespoons butter
3 6-ounce cans lobster
6 tablespoons flour

1½ cups Chicken Stock (page 45)
½ teaspoon paprika
¾ teaspoon salt
Dash of pepper
½ cup cream
2 egg yolks, well beaten

Cook pepper and shallots in butter until brown; add lobster
and cook 5 minutes. Add flour and blend. Add Chicken Stock
slowly, bring to boil and add seasonings. Before serving, add
cream and egg yolks. Reheat carefully in double boiler. Serve in
Patty Shells (page 427).

*Patricia Mooney of Minneapolis is responsible for the delectable
lobster filling recipe. When we serve tiny lobster patties at a tea,
they are one of the most popular savories.*

LOBSTER THERMIDOR
1 serving

1½ to 2-pound freshly cooked
   lobster, cold
3 tablespoons butter
1 tablespoon flour
½ teaspoon prepared mustard
¼ teaspoon salt
Dash of cayenne pepper

½ teaspoon paprika
1¼ cups cream
2 tablespoons lemon juice
½ pound fresh mushrooms
½ cup grated cheese
¼ cup cracker crumbs
1 tablespoon melted butter

Split lobster lengthwise. Remove meat and cut into ½-inch cubes.
Melt 1 tablespoon of the butter, add flour and seasonings. Blend
well; add cream and lemon juice, stirring constantly until sauce
has thickened. Clean and slice mushrooms, sauté in remaining 2
tablespoons butter. Add sautéed mushrooms and lobster to sauce
and mix well. Fill empty shell with mixture. Sprinkle with grated
cheese and buttered cracker crumbs. Place under broiler to
brown. Serve hot.

SCALLOPS NEWBURG
4 servings

1 pint scallops	¼ teaspoon salt
2 tablespoons butter	Dash of cayenne pepper
1 teaspoon lemon juice	½ cup plus 2 tablespoons cream
1 tablespoon butter	2 egg yolks, well beaten
2 teaspoons flour	½ cup buttered bread crumbs

Cook scallops in salted water 3 to 5 minutes. Drain and dry. Put the two tablespoons of butter in skillet and add scallops. Heat for three minutes and add lemon juice.

Make Cream Sauce as follows: Melt remaining tablespoon of butter. Add flour and stir until well blended. Add salt and cayenne pepper. Add the cream, stirring until mixture thickens. Remove from heat and add slowly to beaten egg yolks. Add scallops. Turn mixture into buttered 1½-quart casserole, sprinkle with buttered bread crumbs and brown in hot oven (425°) 10 minutes.

COOKED SHRIMP
3 servings

1 pound fresh shrimp	1 piece celery, sliced
2 sprigs parsley	1 small bay leaf
3 slices onion	4 peppercorns
1 carrot, sliced	1 tablespoon vinegar

Wash raw shrimp well in cold water. Drop into boiling salted water to cover, using 1 teaspoon salt to 1 quart water. Add vegetables, seasonings, and vinegar. Simmer, *tightly covered,* 5 minutes, or only until pink and tender. Drain, and rinse in cold water. Remove legs; peel shell from shrimp by breaking the under shell and opening from front to back. With sharp pointed knife remove black vein from center back of each shrimp.

CREOLE SHRIMP IN RICE RING
10 to 12 servings

2 cups rice
¼ cup butter
1 cup diced celery
1 onion, chopped
1 clove garlic, minced
2 tablespoons oil
1 No. 2½ can tomatoes
2 bay leaves

1 sprig thyme
Few drops of Tabasco sauce
1 teaspoon salt
½ teaspoon pepper
2 pounds Cooked Fresh Shrimp
 (page 155)
Parsley

Cook rice and add butter. Cook celery, onion, and garlic in oil. Add tomatoes and seasonings and cook 40 minutes. Remove bay leaves. Add shrimp, cook 10 minutes longer. Pack rice into well-greased ring mold and let stand 30 minutes. Unmold rice onto large round platter and pour shrimp mixture into center. Garnish with parsley.

If you do not have a ring mold, the rice may be put on the platter and the shrimp creole poured over it.

SHRIMP CURRY AND ACCOMPANIMENTS
4 to 5 servings

1½ pounds fresh shrimp
¼ cup butter
2 tablespoons finely chopped onion
2 teaspoons curry powder
¼ cup flour

2½ cups milk
1 teaspoon salt
2 tablespoons lemon juice
1 teaspoon finely chopped ginger
 root

Cook the shrimp (page 155). Melt butter; add onion and cook until golden brown in color. Stir in the curry powder and flour and blend until smooth. Add milk, stirring slowly until sauce thickens. Add salt, lemon juice, and ginger root. Add shrimp and let stand in sauce over low heat for about ½ hour before serving. Serve hot with rice and curry accompaniments.
NOTE: If desired, less curry powder may be used.

Curry Accompaniments

Chutney
Diced crisp bacon
Finely chopped hard-cooked egg whites
Finely chopped hard-cooked egg yolks
Finely chopped peanuts
Fried onion
Raisins
Ripe olives
Shredded coconut
Stuffed olives

Serve accompaniments in individual bowls with shrimp curry or Chicken Curry (page 126). Let each guest help himself.

To my way of thinking, the accompaniments make the curry.

FRENCH FRIED SHRIMP
4 to 5 servings

1 cup flour	1 egg, beaten
½ teaspoon sugar	1 cup water
½ teaspoon salt	1 pound Cooked Fresh Shrimp
Dash of black pepper	(page 155)

Combine all ingredients except shrimp; beat well to make smooth batter. Peel shell from shrimp, leaving last section and tail intact. Cut through back to divide in half, but do not sever; remove black vein. Dip shrimp in batter; fry in deep hot fat (375°) 2 to 3 minutes, until golden brown. Drain on absorbent paper. Serve with Tartare Sauce (page 214).

Shrimp are best if allowed to stand in batter for several hours.

Stuffings for Fish

PARSLEY AND EGG STUFFING

1 cup coarse dry bread crumbs
1 medium onion, chopped
2 tablespoons butter
1 cup chopped hard-cooked eggs

1 tablespoon minced parsley
¼ teaspoon minced thyme
½ bay leaf
Salt and pepper

Moisten crumbs. Fry onion slowly in the butter until golden in color. Add bread and hard-cooked eggs; continue to fry for a few minutes. Add herbs and seasonings; mix well and stuff fish.

PLAIN STUFFING

4 tablespoons butter, melted
3 tablespoons water
2½ cups soft bread crumbs
2 teaspoons grated onion

½ cup chopped celery
2 tablespoons lemon juice
½ teaspoon salt
½ teaspoon herb seasoning

Add melted butter and water to bread crumbs. Add all remaining ingredients and mix thoroughly. Stuff fish.

VEGETABLE STUFFING

½ cup fat
¾ cup ground carrots
¼ cup chopped onion
½ cup chopped celery
2 cups soft bread crumbs

1 teaspoon salt
⅛ teaspoon white pepper
2 tablespoons lemon juice
2 tablespoons chopped parsley

Put fat in skillet. Add carrots, onion, and celery. Sauté until onion is golden in color. Combine with remaining ingredients and mix well. Use to stuff fish, or stuffing may be put on fish steaks and baked.

Vegetables

ARTICHOKES
Artichoke Hearts with
  Hollandaise Sauce

ASPARAGUS
*Asparagus with Almond-
  Mushroom Sauce*
Asparagus à la Goldenrod

BEANS
Beans Fugarth (India)
Boston Baked Beans
French Green Beans
Frijoles Refritos
Green Beans with Mushrooms
Lyonnaise Green Beans
South American Lima Beans
Spanish Green Beans
Swedish Brown Beans
Sweet-and-Sour String Beans

BEETS
Baked Julienne Beets
Beets in Orange Sauce
Bieten Met Appelen

BROCCOLI
Broccoli à la Fiorentina
Broccoli Soufflé

BRUSSELS SPROUTS
*Brussels Sprouts with Chest-
  nuts*

CABBAGE
Cabbage with Capers
Coleslaw
Dutch Slaw
*Russian Stuffed Cabbage
  Leaves*
Savory Red Cabbage

CARROTS
Rantott Sargarepa
Sliced Carrots with Onion

CAULIFLOWER
*Baked Cauliflower with Cheese
  Sauce*
*Cauliflower with Mousseline
  Sauce*
French Fried Cauliflower
Fried Cauliflower (India)
Karfiol

CORN
Corn Custard Pudding
Mexican Corn Casserole
Mexican Corn Sauté

EGGPLANT
Spanish Eggplant

MUSHROOMS
How to Prepare
Deviled Mushrooms
Sautéed Mushroom Caps

ONIONS
*Baked Onions with Mustard
  Sauce*
Creole Onions
Pennsylvania Dutch Onion Pie
Planked Stuffed Onions

PEAS
Black-Eyed Peas
*Dhall Curry (India)
  Coconut Rice (India)*
Peas à la Française
Petits Pois à la Bourgeoise

PEPPERS
Chiles Rellenos

POORIS
Pooris (India)
Potatoes for Pooris

POTATOES
Boofers
Creamed Potatoes
Duchess Potatoes
Franconia Potatoes
Kartoffel Knödel
Mashed Potatoes
O'Brien Potatoes
Paprika Potatoes
Parsley Buttered Potatoes
Potato Cutlets (India)
Potato Puffs (India)
Pommes de Terre à la
    Hollandaise
Pommes de Terre à la
    Lyonnaise
Pommes de Terre Noisette
Pommes de Terre Variations
    Duxelle
    Julienne
    Lorette
    Maître d' Hôtel
    Parisienne
    Persillade

SWEET POTATOES
Candied Yams or Sweet
    Potatoes

French Fried Sweet-Potato
    Chips

Sweet Potatoes with Apples
Sweet Potatoes with Dates
Sweet Potato Soufflé

SPINACH
Gratin à la Maries
Mexican Baked Spinach
Spinach with Onion
Spinach Timbale on Tomato
    Slices

SQUASH
French Fried Zucchini
Zucchini Marinade

TOMATOES
Baked Tomatoes with Crab
    Meat Filling
Broiled Tomatoes
Fried Tomatoes in Cream
Southern Style Tomatoes
Stuffed Tomatoes

TURNIPS
Turnip Greens

VEGETABLE PLATTER

IT HAS BEEN said that folks eat "with an eye." That's just one reason why vegetables help to make a successful meal. Their bright colors add a cheery touch to the plate. Important, too, are their fresh flavors and bounty of health-giving vitamins and minerals.

Vegetables are delicious cooked quickly and seasoned generously with butter, salt, and pepper. But for the special occasion, they taste even better if you give them a new touch, a subtle seasoning, a gay garnish.

ARTICHOKE HEARTS WITH HOLLANDAISE SAUCE
4 to 5 servings

1 No. 2½ can artichoke hearts
1 cup bread crumbs
¼ cup melted butter

1 cup thick Hollandaise Sauce
  (page 209)
¼ cup grated sharp cheese
Paprika

Rinse artichoke hearts with cold water. Drain. Place standing up in a buttered 1½-quart casserole. Combine bread crumbs and melted butter. Sprinkle over artichoke hearts. Put in moderate oven (375°) about 15 minutes or until artichokes are heated through. Then cover with Hollandaise Sauce; sprinkle with cheese and a dash of paprika. Return to oven for 5 to 6 minutes to melt cheese and brown lightly. Serve at once.

ASPARAGUS WITH ALMOND MUSHROOM SAUCE
4 servings

1 pound fresh asparagus or 1
  12-ounce package frozen

Sauce:

2 tablespoons butter
¾ cup sliced mushrooms, fresh or
  canned
2 tablespoons flour
½ teaspoon salt

⅛ teaspoon pepper
1 cup rich milk
½ cup chopped toasted almonds
½ cup grated American cheese

Cook asparagus. Drain. To make sauce, melt butter, add mushrooms, and sauté; add flour and seasonings, and blend well. Add milk. Cook until thickened. Place asparagus in buttered 1½-quart casserole and pour sauce over asparagus. Sprinkle with toasted almonds and grated cheese. Put under broiler or in very hot oven (450°) 4 to 5 minutes until cheese melts. Serve at once.

ASPARAGUS À LA GOLDENROD
4 servings

2 tablespoons bacon drippings
2 tablespoons flour
½ teaspoon salt
Dash of pepper
1 cup liquid (asparagus water
    plus milk)

4 hard-cooked eggs
2 cups hot cooked fresh asparagus,
    cut in 1-inch lengths
4 slices crisp dry toast

Make a medium white sauce from bacon drippings, flour, salt, pepper, and liquid. Peel eggs and remove yolks from whites. Chop egg whites and add to white sauce. Arrange cooked asparagus on toast slices. Top with white sauce. Force egg yolks through a sieve and sprinkle over the white sauce. Sprinkle with a little paprika. Garnish plate with parsley. Serve hot.

BEANS FUGARTH (INDIA)
4 to 5 servings

1 pound fresh green beans
Boiling water
1½ teaspoons salt
1 green chilli pepper about 1½
    inches long

3 tablespoons butter
4 slices onion
½ cup grated fresh coconut

Clean and string the beans and cut them diagonally in pieces about ⅓ inch in width. Put beans in saucepan and add just enough boiling water to cover. Add salt and chilli pepper split lengthwise. Cook until just done but not soft. Drain beans. Heat butter in saucepan. Add onion and sauté until a golden brown in color. Add coconut and continue cooking for 2 minutes and then add beans. Stir quickly and cover pan for 2 minutes. Serve hot.

This combination of coconut and onions gives the beans an unusual flavor — a favorite flavor combination in India, where fresh coconuts are as common as potatoes. Okra, carrots, other varieties of beans, egg plant, potatoes, and green pumpkin are a few of the vegetables that can be prepared in this way, either singly or in combinations.

BOSTON BAKED BEANS
8 to 10 servings

1 pint pea beans
½ pound fat salt pork
1 teaspoon salt
2 tablespoons brown sugar

¾ cup molasses
2 tablespoons vinegar
1 teaspoon dry mustard
Boiling water

Wash and pick over beans. Soak overnight in cold water. In the morning, drain, cover with fresh water and simmer until skins begin to break; turn into bean pot. Cut pork into cubes and place on beans. Add salt, brown sugar, molasses, vinegar, and mustard. Add boiling water to just cover. Cover and bake in very slow oven (250°) for about 6 hours without stirring, adding water as necessary to keep beans covered. Uncover during last half hour to brown.

Can't you just smell the tantalizing aroma of these beans cooking? This is the way the New Englanders like them — molasses only, and no tomato sauce. For authentic Boston baked beans, they must be the small pea beans — no others will do. The baked beans and Boston brown bread are always served for Saturday night supper. If there are any beans left over, they are served for Sunday morning breakfast.

FRENCH GREEN BEANS
5 to 6 servings

2 tablespoons minced onion
3 tablespoons butter
2½ cups Frenched string beans, cooked
1 teaspoon salt

¼ teaspoon pepper
¼ teaspoon thyme, crushed
¼ cup Chicken Stock (page 45)
¼ cup cream
1 tablespoon flour

Fry onion in butter until golden in color. Add cooked string beans. Add salt, pepper, thyme, and the stock. Then add flour to cream and add to beans. Heat again until sauce is slightly thickened. Serve hot.

NOTE: To "French" beans, cut in two strips. Then cut each strip in two narrow strips.

FRIJOLES REFRITOS
Mexican Pork and Beans
4 to 6 servings

1 pound frijoles (pink or pinto beans)	1 clove garlic, mashed
Boiling water	1 teaspoon salt
½ pound diced salt pork	4 tablespoons fat
1 tablespoon chili powder	1 cup grated American cheese
	3 medium onions, sliced thin

Soak the frijoles in water overnight. Next day pour off the water; cover frijoles with boiling water and add diced salt pork. Cook slowly until tender, about 2 hours, adding more boiling water if needed. Add chili powder, mashed garlic, and salt. Put fat into large skillet; add frijoles a spoonful at a time, mashing thoroughly. Keep over a slow fire, stirring occasionally. If mixture becomes too dry, add some of liquid in which beans were cooked. Frijoles should become a dark rich brown in color. To serve, place frijoles in a large bowl. Cover with grated cheese and onion slices.

Once you try this Mexican version of pork and beans, you may completely forget the American style. The cheese is strictly an American variation but it adds flavor as well as color. Mexicans prefer to mash the beans before frying them.

GREEN BEANS WITH MUSHROOMS
6 to 8 servings

½ pound fresh mushrooms	1 pound small green string beans
1 tablespoon butter	Salt
½ cup cream	1 teaspoon sugar
Salt	1 tablespoon butter

Clean mushrooms and slice thin. Melt butter in a skillet and sauté mushrooms 4 to 5 minutes. Add the cream gradually, then cover and allow to simmer 10 minutes. Season with salt and, if desired, add a little pepper. Keep mushrooms hot. Wash and string the beans. Cut lengthwise, French style. Cook in slightly salted water for about 10 or 15 minutes, or until they are just tender. Drain. Sprinkle with salt and add sugar and butter. Combine with mushrooms and heat. Serve hot.

LYONNAISE GREEN BEANS
4 servings

1 10-ounce package frozen green beans or 1 pound fresh	2 tablespoons butter
1 small onion, sliced thin	½ teaspoon salt
	Dash of white pepper

Add just enough boiling water to cover the beans. Cook uncovered until beans are tender, 20 to 25 minutes. Drain. Sauté sliced onion in butter until golden in color. Add onion and butter to beans; add salt and pepper. Reheat and serve hot.

SOUTH AMERICAN LIMA BEANS
4 to 6 servings

1 cup dried lima beans	Dash of paprika
1 teaspoon salt	2 tablespoons oil
1 tablespoon minced onion	1 cup strained tomatoes
1 tablespoon minced parsley	½ teaspoon chili powder
2 tablespoons minced green pepper	Salt and pepper

Soak dried lima beans several hours, or overnight. Drain, cover with boiling water, and cook slowly until tender, adding salt when partly done. Cook onion, parsley, green pepper, and paprika in hot oil for 5 minutes. Add tomatoes, chili powder, and cooked limas. Season with salt and pepper. Pour into buttered 1½-quart casserole and bake in moderate oven (350°) 25 to 30 minutes.

SPANISH GREEN BEANS
5 to 6 servings

1 pound green beans	2 cups water
1 tablespoon butter	2 cups canned tomatoes
1 small onion, sliced thin	1 green pepper, chopped
1 clove garlic, crushed	1 teaspoon salt
1 tablespoon flour	¼ teaspoon pepper

Wash and dry green beans, string, and cut beans lengthwise, French style. Heat butter in skillet; add beans, sliced onion, and garlic. Cook 10 minutes, but do not let brown. Add flour, stirring well, and then water, tomato pulp, and chopped pepper; add salt and pepper and simmer until beans are tender. Cook until liquid has been reduced. Serve hot.

If you like green beans with a different flavor, try these Spanish green beans.

SWEDISH BROWN BEANS
6 to 8 servings

2 cups brown beans
2 quarts water
2 teaspoons salt

½ cup molasses
¼ cup white vinegar

Wash beans and allow to soak in 2 quarts of water for several hours. Cook slowly in the same water until beans are tender. The longer you soak the beans, the shorter the required cooking time. Season with salt, molasses, and vinegar.

Serve at the Smörgåsbord (page 460).

SWEET-AND-SOUR GREEN BEANS
5 to 6 servings

1 pound green beans
1 teaspoon salt
2 tablespoons fat
1 tablespoon flour

¼ teaspoon paprika
3 tablespoons lemon juice
1 tablespoon sugar

Clean, string, and cut beans into 2-inch pieces; just cover with boiling water and cook until tender. When nearly done, add salt. Melt fat, blend in flour, and brown slightly. Add paprika; then add lemon juice and sugar. Pour sauce over the beans. Cook together 5 minutes. Serve hot.

BAKED JULIENNE BEETS
4 to 6 servings

6 medium beets
½ cup boiling water
½ teaspoon salt

2 teaspoons lemon or lime juice
1 tablespoon butter
Dash of pepper

Scrub beets; peel and cut into julienne strips. Put in 1½-quart casserole. Add water and salt. Cook covered in moderate oven (350°) 30 to 45 minutes. Just before serving add lemon or lime juice, butter, and a dash of pepper.

dressed up with cauliflower . . .

Veal Steak Paprika, page 119.

a vegetable's favorite partner . . .

Baked Ham with Brown Sugar Glaze, page 112.

BEETS IN ORANGE SAUCE
4 servings

½ cup orange juice	1 tablespoon sugar
2 tablespoons lemon juice	1 tablespoon cornstarch
1 tablespoon vinegar	1 tablespoon cold water
½ teaspoon salt	1 No. 2 can small whole beets
Dash of pepper	2 tablespoons butter

Combine in double boiler orange juice, lemon juice, vinegar, salt, pepper, and sugar. Mix cornstarch and water to a smooth paste; add to juice. Cook until slightly thickened, stirring constantly. Add beets and heat thoroughly. Add butter and blend. Serve hot.

BIETEN MET APPELEN
Dutch Beets with Apples
4 to 6 servings

2 large cooked beets	4 sour apples
¼ cup butter	½ teaspoon salt
1 medium onion, sliced thin	¼ teaspoon nutmeg

Peel and slice beets. Melt butter in saucepan and add onions; sauté until lightly browned. Pare and chop apples. Combine with beets; add salt and nutmeg. Simmer until apples are done but not mushy.

BROCCOLI À LA FIORENTINA
Italian Broccoli
3 to 4 servings

1 pound fresh broccoli or 1 10-ounce package frozen	2 cloves garlic, finely chopped
¼ cup olive or salad oil	Salt and pepper

Cook broccoli in boiling salted water. When tender, remove and drain thoroughly. Chop coarsely. Put oil in a heavy skillet. When hot, add garlic; cook until golden in color. Add broccoli; season with salt and pepper. Cook for 15 to 20 minutes, stirring occassionally. If preferred, use less garlic.

BROCCOLI SOUFFLE
6 servings

1 pound fresh broccoli or 1 10-ounce package frozen	1 teaspoon salt
	Dash of nutmeg
3 tablespoons butter	Dash of white pepper
3 tablespoons flour	1 teaspoon lemon juice
1 cup milk	4 eggs, separated

Cook and chop broccoli. Melt butter in double boiler, add flour; blend well. Gradually add milk; continue to cook while stirring until thick and smooth; add salt, nutmeg, and pepper. Add broccoli and lemon juice. Remove from heat. Beat egg yolks; add to first mixture; set aside to cool. Beat egg whites until stiff but not dry; gradually fold egg whites into broccoli mixture. Turn into buttered 1½-quart casserole. Place casserole in a pan of hot water to depth of 1½ inches. Bake uncovered in slow oven (325°) 50 to 60 minutes or until done. Serve at once—a soufflé doesn't improve on standing.

Try this broccoli soufflé with baked or broiled ham.

BRUSSELS SPROUTS WITH CHESTNUTS
5 to 6 servings

1 quart Brussels sprouts	2 tablespoons flour
½ pound chestnuts	1 cup liquid
¼ cup butter	1 teaspoon salt
2 teaspoons sugar	Dash of white pepper

Cook sprouts and save liquid. Cover chestnuts with boiling water and boil about 20 minutes or until shell and skin can be easily removed. Cover blanched chestnuts with 1 cup boiling water to which ½ teaspoon salt has been added and cook until chestnuts are tender and water has evaporated. Brown the butter; add sugar and chestnuts. Cook until well browned, stirring constantly. Add flour to 1 cup of liquid in which sprouts have been cooked and add to chestnuts. Let sauce cook until thickened. Add sprouts and seasoning. Heat thoroughly and serve.

CABBAGE WITH CAPERS
6 servings

3 tablespoons fat	2 tablespoons capers
2 cloves garlic, chopped	1 tablespoon vinegar
¾ cup chopped onion	1 teaspoon salt
1 head cabbage (1½ pounds), shredded	½ teaspoon pepper
	2 large tomatoes
¼ cup chopped ham	½ cup buttered bread crumbs

Heat fat in skillet, add garlic and onion, cook until golden, 3 to 4 minutes. Add cabbage and sauté in covered pan. Add ham, capers, vinegar, salt, and pepper. While this is slowly simmering, broil tomatoes, remove skin, and chop very fine. Add to the cabbage. Put mixture into buttered 1½-quart casserole and sprinkle bread crumbs over the top. Bake in moderate oven (350°) about 20 minutes.

COLESLAW
6 to 8 servings

½ cup heavy cream	Dash of pepper
3 tablespoons vinegar	3 cups finely shredded cabbage
½ teaspoon salt	

Whip cream and add vinegar slowly, continuing to beat until stiff. Add salt and pepper. Pour over shredded cabbage. Toss together. Serve very cold.

DUTCH SLAW
6 servings

1 small head cabbage	½ teaspoon salt
1 teaspoon salt	Pepper
1 egg	¼ cup vinegar
1 tablespoon sugar	

Shred cabbage rather fine. Put in saucepan and sprinkle with salt. Cover pan and place over low heat; steam until tender. Beat egg, add sugar, salt, pepper, and vinegar, and pour over the steamed cabbage. Heat for 5 minutes. Serve at once.

RUSSIAN STUFFED CABBAGE LEAVES
6 to 8 servings

1 cup rice
2 cups chopped cooked meat
Salt and pepper
1 large head cabbage

¼ pound butter
4 cups tomato sauce or tomato
    soup

Cook rice and mix with meat. Add salt and pepper. Scald cabbage in boiling water, and separate leaves from each other. Trim down core on each leaf and fill leaf with 1 large tablespoon meat mixture; roll and tie with string. Brown rolls in butter. Place in buttered 1½-quart casserole. Cover with tomato sauce and bake in moderate oven (350°) 30 minutes.

SAVORY RED CABBAGE
6 servings

1 medium head red cabbage
3 medium cooking apples
3 tablespoons butter
½ cup diced onion
¼ cup cider vinegar

½ cup water
1 teaspoon salt
1 tablespoon sugar
Dash of pepper
Dash of nutmeg

Shred cabbage fine, removing core. Pare apples and chop. Melt butter in saucepan; add onion and cook 5 minutes. Add apples, vinegar, water, salt, sugar, pepper, and nutmeg. Toss in cabbage. Cover; cook slowly until cabbage is tender, about 15 to 20 minutes. Add a little more water if necessary during the cooking, so cabbage does not stick to bottom of pan. Serve at once. Good with pot roast of beef.

RANTOTT SARGAREPA
Hungarian Sweet-Sour Carrots
6 to 8 servings

2 bunches fresh carrots	½ cup vinegar
1 teaspoon salt	¾ cup sugar
Hot water	1 tablespoon chopped parsley
2 tablespoons butter	

Wash and scrape carrots. Cut into strips 3 by ½ inches. Place in saucepan, add salt and hot water to cover. Cook until tender; drain and add butter, vinegar, and sugar. Cook slowly until transparent. Serve hot. Garnish with chopped parsley.

Yes — something different! Carrots with a sweet-sour flavor. Try them with a veal or chicken dish.

SLICED CARROTS WITH ONION
6 servings

¼ cup butter	Dash of pepper
¼ cup chopped onion	½ teaspoon sugar
3 cups thinly sliced raw carrots	½ cup hot water
½ teaspoon salt	

Melt butter in saucepan; add onion. Cook 5 minutes. Add carrots, salt, pepper, sugar, and water; cover tightly. Simmer over very low heat 30 minutes, or until carrots are tender. Add more water if necessary during cooking.

BAKED CAULIFLOWER WITH CHEESE SAUCE

1 medium head cauliflower	1 recipe Cheese Sauce (page 215)
Buttered bread crumbs	

Remove outside leaves and cook head of cauliflower in boiling salted water until tender. Place whole cooked cauliflower in buttered 1½-quart casserole. Cover with buttered bread crumbs. Place in hot oven (400°) 8 to 10 minutes to brown. Remove from oven. Pour Cheese Sauce over cauliflower. Serve at once.

CAULIFLOWER WITH MOUSSELINE SAUCE
4 to 6 servings

1 medium head cauliflower
1½ cups Mousseline Sauce (page 211)

2 tablespoons finely minced parsley

Remove outside leaves and cook head of cauliflower in boiling salted water until tender. Place in serving dish. Pour Mousseline Sauce over cauliflower. Sprinkle minced parsley on top. Serve at once.

FRENCH FRIED CAULIFLOWER
4 to 5 servings

1 medium head cauliflower
1 cup fine bread crumbs

2 eggs, slightly beaten
¼ cup milk

Remove outside leaves of cauliflower. Separate cauliflower into flowerets. Cook in boiling salted water 10 minutes or until just tender. Drain and let cool. Roll each floweret in crumbs; then in beaten eggs to which milk has been added. Roll again in crumbs. Fry in deep hot fat (375°) to a delicate brown. Sprinkle lightly with salt. Drain on absorbent paper. Serve with well-seasoned Medium White Sauce (page 215), to which parsley has been added, or with Cheese Sauce (page 215).

FRIED CAULIFLOWER (INDIA)
6 to 8 servings

1 medium head cauliflower
1 cup flour
2 teaspoons salt

Dash of turmeric
Dash of cayenne
1 cup water

Wash cauliflower and break into flowerets. Sift together dry ingredients. Add water and mix to a smooth thin batter. Dip flowerets into batter; drain off excess batter. Drop into deep hot fat (375°) and fry to crisp golden brown.

KARFIOL
Hungarian Cauliflower with Cheese Sauce
5 to 6 servings

1 large head cauliflower	1 tablespoon lemon juice
1 quart water or more	½ teaspoon salt
1 teaspoon salt	Dash of pepper
3 tablespoons butter	2 egg yolks
3 tablespoons flour	½ cup toasted bread crumbs
1½ cups milk	½ cup grated American cheese
2 tablespoons grated Parmesan cheese	¼ cup melted butter

Boil cauliflower in enough salted water to cover it. Cook until tender, about 15 to 20 minutes. Drain. Prepare sauce while cauliflower is cooking. Melt butter and add flour. Add milk, cooking until smooth and thickened, stirring constantly. Add Parmesan cheese, lemon juice, salt and pepper, blending well together. Add several spoonfuls of sauce to beaten egg yolks, then combine with remaining sauce. Divide cauliflower into flowerets and place in buttered 1½-quart casserole. Cover with the sauce and sprinkle the toasted crumbs and grated American cheese over the top. Pour melted butter over all. Bake uncovered in moderate oven (350°) about 30 minutes or until crusty and golden brown.

CORN CUSTARD PUDDING
6 to 8 servings

3 eggs	2 tablespoons melted butter
1 No. 2 can whole kernel corn	1 tablespoon sugar
1 teaspoon salt	2 cups milk, scalded
⅛ teaspoon pepper	

Beat eggs slightly. Combine corn and liquid with other ingredients and add to eggs. Pour into buttered 1½-quart casserole. Set in pan of hot water. Bake in moderate oven (350°) 35 to 40 minutes or until firm. Serve this delicate corn custard in the casserole in which it was baked.

Corn custard is a favorite way of serving corn in the South.

MEXICAN CORN CASSEROLE
8 servings

2 tablespoons flour
1 teaspoon salt
½ teaspoon chili powder
⅛ teaspoon pepper
Dash of cayenne pepper
2 cups canned whole kernel corn
   or fresh corn

1 small onion, chopped fine
1 tablespoon fat
1 dozen ripe olives, chopped
1 cup hot Tomato Sauce (page 206)
1 cup grated cheese

Add flour and seasonings to corn. Brown onion in fat and add to corn. Add olives and thoroughly combine all ingredients. Turn mixture into buttered 1½-quart casserole. Pour the hot Tomato Sauce over mixture and sprinkle with cheese. Bake in moderate oven (350°) 10 to 15 minutes until cheese is melted.

MEXICAN CORN SAUTE
4 servings

1 No. 2 can whole kernel corn
3 tablespoons butter
1 tablespoon finely chopped green
   pepper

1 tablespoon chopped pimento
½ teaspoon salt
½ teaspoon chili powder

Drain corn and heat in butter. Add remaining ingredients. Simmer 10 to 15 minutes, stirring frequently. Serve hot.

A colorful corn dish, easily prepared. If desired, leave out chili powder.

SPANISH EGGPLANT
6 to 8 servings

1 large eggplant
4 slices bacon, diced
1 medium onion, finely chopped
1 green pepper, finely chopped
1 teaspoon salt

⅛ teaspoon pepper
1 6-ounce can tomato purée plus
   one can water
½ cup grated cheese
Buttered bread crumbs

Peel eggplant and cut into ½-inch cubes. Fry bacon until crisp and add onion and green pepper. Cook about 5 minutes; add eggplant, salt, pepper, tomato purée, and water. Cook until eggplant is tender. Turn mixture into buttered 1½-quart casserole. Sprinkle with grated cheese and top with buttered bread crumbs. Bake in moderate oven (350°) 35 to 45 minutes. Serve at once.

MUSHROOMS — HOW TO PREPARE

FRESH MUSHROOMS

Select firm, smooth, cream-colored mushrooms. Just before cooking wash mushrooms carefully in warm water to remove any soil. Place on paper towel to dry. It is not necessary to peel mushrooms unless skin of cap is tough and brown. The caps may be left whole or cut into lengthwise strips, depending on how they are to be used. The stems may be cut in pieces and should be cooked a little longer than the caps, as they are less tender.

CANNED MUSHROOMS

Drain mushrooms and sauté in butter before adding to sauce.

DEVILED MUSHROOMS

3 to 4 servings

1 pint fresh mushrooms	½ cup bread crumbs
Salt and pepper	1 tablespoon butter, softened
2 teaspoons lemon juice	Dash of Tabasco sauce
1 hard-cooked egg yolk	Parsley
1 raw egg yolk, beaten	

Wash and dry mushrooms carefully. Remove stems. Cut off tough ends. Place mushrooms caps and stems in buttered 1½-quart casserole. Season with salt, pepper, and lemon juice. Mash the hard-cooked egg yolk and add raw egg yolk. Combine with bread crumbs and softened butter. Add Tabasco sauce. Spread bread crumb mixture on top of mushrooms. Bake uncovered in moderate oven (350°) 15 to 20 minutes or until bread crumbs are brown. Garnish with parsley. Serve hot.

SAUTEED MUSHROOM CAPS

3 to 4 servings

1 pint fresh mushrooms	Dash of pepper
¼ cup butter	4 circles of toast
Salt	

Wash mushrooms carefully. Place on absorbent paper to dry. Remove stems. Melt butter in heavy skillet. Add mushroom caps. Sauté 10 minutes. Sprinkle with salt and pepper. Serve mushrooms on circles of crisp toast. Garnish with parsley. Serve hot.

BAKED ONIONS WITH MUSTARD SAUCE
4 servings

1 No. 2 can small white onions
¼ cup butter
3 teaspoons sugar
1 teaspoon dry mustard

Dash of cayenne pepper
½ teaspoon salt
2 tablespoons chopped parsley

Drain onions and place in buttered 1½-quart casserole. Combine the butter, sugar, mustard, pepper, and salt, and spread over onions. Bake in moderate oven (350°) about 25 minutes. Sprinkle with parsley. Serve at once.

This is an intriguing way to let an often-slighted vegetable come into its own. You'll soon give it a starring role in your menus, especially as a combination with pork. The long cooking with the rich tangy sauce mellows the onion flavor until it can be objectionable to no one. Be sure to choose the little white globe onions.

CREOLE ONIONS
8 servings

8 medium onions
1 slice bacon, diced
1 tablespoon finely chopped green
    pepper
Salt and pepper

½ cup chopped cooked ham
½ cup tomato purée
1 small clove garlic, minced
½ cup grated American cheese

Peel onions, cook in boiling salted water for 15 to 20 minutes or until tender. Drain. Place onions in buttered 1½-quart casserole. Sauté diced bacon until crisp and add green pepper; cook for 5 minutes. Sprinkle onions lightly with salt and pepper, add bacon, green pepper, ham, tomato purée, and garlic. Cover and bake in moderate oven (350°) 20 to 25 minutes. Remove the cover, sprinkle with cheese and return to oven to melt cheese. Serve at once.

PENNSYLVANIA DUTCH ONION PIE
6 to 8 servings

1½ pounds small white onions
3 slices bacon, diced
2 eggs, beaten
2 cups sour cream

¼ teaspoon salt
Dash of pepper
½ recipe Plain Pastry (page 433)
1 teaspoon caraway seeds

Cook onions in boiling salted water until tender. Fry diced bacon until crisp; drain. Combine beaten eggs, sour cream, salt, pepper, cooked onions, and bacon. Line a 9-inch pie pan with Plain Pastry. Pour onion mixture into pastry shell. Sprinkle caraway seeds over the top. Bake in hot oven (450°) 10 minutes. Reduce temperature to moderate (350°) and bake 30 to 35 minutes. Serve hot as a vegetable entree.

PLANKED STUFFED ONIONS
6 servings

6 large onions
3 tablespoons fat
1 pound can (2 cups) corned beef
    hash
Salt and pepper

Duchess Potatoes (page 185)
1 12-ounce package frozen peas,
    cooked
6 large mushroom caps

Peel and cook onions until almost tender in a large quantity of boiling water. Drain and let cool. Cut slice off top of each onion and lift out centers. Chop about ½ cup of the onion that has been removed and brown lightly in the fat. Add to hash and season to taste with salt and pepper. Stuff onions with this mixture and place in baking dish. Bake in hot oven (400°) about 20 minutes or until lightly browned.

Grease plank and heat it. Arrange stuffed onions in the center. Using a pastry bag, pipe a border of Duchess Potatoes around onions and around edge of plank. Brown in hot oven (400°) 15 to 20 minutes. Pile hot, buttered peas between potato borders; garnish tops of the onions with mushroom caps that have been sautéed lightly in butter. Serve at once.

BLACK-EYED PEAS
6 servings

1 pound dried black-eyed peas	4 cups boiling water
½ pound salt pork, cut into cubes	1 teaspoon salt

Cover peas with cold water and soak overnight. Drain peas; add salt pork, boiling water, and salt. Simmer for 2 hours, or until peas are done. Serve with some of the "pot likker" in which the peas were cooked.

It is a tradition in the South to serve black-eyed peas on New Year's Day for good luck.

DHALL CURRY (INDIA)
4 servings

1 cup split peas	1 green chilli pepper, cut in half
¼ medium onion, minced	1 teaspoon salt
⅛ teaspoon ginger	1 tablespoon butter
Dash of ground cloves	

Soak split peas overnight. Put soaked peas in a saucepan; add onion, seasonings, salt; cover with water 1½ inches above level of the peas. Cover the pan and cook over low heat until peas are soft and most of the water has evaporated. Mash peas and add butter and cook until thick but not dry. Serve with Coconut Rice.

This is one of the vegetarian curries of India and is interesting in texture and flavor. Gwendolyn Matthews, of Madras, says, "Indian food is as varied as the different sectional foods in the United States, but, in general, most of the food in India, when compared to that in America, has plenty of spices, seasonings, and hot green and red chillies. The staple article of diet in the South of India is rice while that of the North is wheat. South Indians eat rice in great quantities with curries and savoury vegetables and dried legume preparations. Non-vegetarians enjoy curry with their rice and this curry is usually made with either beef, mutton, chicken, or fish, and vegetables cooked in a hot spicy gravy. Non-vegetarians are comparatively few in India because the Hindus, who are a majority, are vegetarians. On the coasts fresh coconut is used in different vegetable and meat preparations and the juice of the fresh scraped coconut extracted with hot water is used in savoury and sweet dishes. Northerners eat pooris and chappatis — flat cakes made of wheat flour, without leavening — with meat and vegetable preparations. In general, salads as they are served in the States are not typical of Indian foods except for a few raw sliced vegetables like tomatoes and cucumbers. The nearest approach to salad is a preparation made with sour cream in which fresh sliced vegetables are marinated and served with the cream."

COCONUT RICE (INDIA) — 4 servings

1 medium coconut	Pinch of saffron (3 stamens)
2½ cups boiling water	1 teaspoon warm milk
½ teaspoon turmeric	1 teaspoon salt
1 bay leaf	1 cup rice
2 cloves	1 tablespoon butter

Split coconut in two. Remove shell and grate coconut meat. Pour the boiling water over freshly grated coconut, letting it stand for 10 minutes. Stir occasionally. The liquid should become milky white in color. Strain and discard grated coconut. Use the coconut milk to cook the rice in. Mix into it the turmeric, bay leaf broken into 2 pieces, cloves, the saffron dissolved in the warm milk, and the salt. Heat the milk; pour over the rice and add enough boiling water so that the liquid is about one inch above rice level. Cook rice until it is done and each grain is distinct. Melt butter and pour over rice. Serve hot with Dhall Curry.

PEAS À LA FRANÇAISE
6 to 8 servings

1 quart shelled green peas or 2 12-ounce packages frozen	2 tablespoons sugar
1 small head lettuce or outside leaves of 2 heads	¼ pound butter
½ cup small pickling onions	½ cup water
	Salt and pepper

Put peas in a heavy saucepan with close-fitting lid. Add the lettuce, onions, sugar, butter, and water. Season with salt and pepper to taste. Cook covered for about 15 minutes. Then remove lid and cook until liquid has just evaporated. Remove the lettuce. Serve peas in a hot dish and garnish with the onions.

Peas with a French flavor! Try them the next time you want something different for special guests.

PETITS POIS À LA BOURGEOISE
French Green Peas
4 servings

2 slices bacon
2 tablespoons flour
1½ cups Chicken Stock (page 45)
½ teaspoon salt
Dash of pepper

2 cups shelled green peas or 1
    12-ounce package frozen
4 sprigs parsley
2 small onions, sliced
½ pimento, cut into strips

Dice bacon, cook in skillet until crisp. Put 2 tablespoons of the bacon fat in saucepan; add 2 tablespoons flour and brown together. Add stock and seasoning and cook until smooth. Add the peas, parsley, and sliced onions. Cook until peas are tender, about 20 minutes. Add more seasoning, if necessary. Remove parsley before serving. Turn into serving bowl. Garnish with strips of pimento and crisp diced bacon.

CHILES RELLENOS
Guatemalan Stuffed Peppers
6 servings

6 large green peppers
¼ pound ground veal
¼ pound ground pork
½ cup raisins
1 tablespoon minced white onion
½ cup nuts, chopped fine

¼ cup minced green olives
2 tablespoons fat
½ cup fresh or canned tomatoes
3 eggs, separated
1 tablespoon flour
½ teaspoon salt

Heat green peppers over flame to blister. Wrap in towel. Let stand 15 minutes to loosen skin. Scrape off thin outside skin and remove all seeds and veins from peppers. Then place peppers in boiling salted water and cook for 5 minutes. To ground meat add raisins, onion, nuts, and olives. Fry this mixture in fat about 10 minutes. Add tomatoes and cook thoroughly. Stuff the peppers with meat mixture. Beat egg whites stiff. Beat the yolks; add flour and salt and fold into egg whites. Dip stuffed peppers in egg mixture and fry in deep hot fat (375°) until nicely browned. Drain on absorbent paper and serve hot.

POORIS (INDIA)
Puffed Bread Balls
About 2 dozen

2 cups flour
1½ teaspoons salt

2 teaspoons butter
Water

Sift flour and salt together. Add butter and mix into flour with a fork. Add about 4 tablespoons water and mix well. Dough should be the consistency of a rather stiff bread dough. Turn out on a board and knead well. Slap dough on board to develop gluten. Knead again. Let stand for ½ hour. Pinch off balls of dough about the size of marbles. Roll flat into rounds about ⅛ inch thick. Fry in deep hot fat (365°) until a delicate brown on each side.

The pooris will puff so that they look like a big puff ball. They should be taken right off the heat onto your plate and eaten with Potatoes for Pooris.

POTATOES FOR POORIS — 6 to 8 servings

4 large potatoes
1 cup frozen peas
2 medium onions
2 tablespoons fat
Dash of cayenne pepper
1 teaspoon mustard seed
½ teaspoon turmeric

2 cloves garlic, minced
⅛ teaspoon ginger
6 tablespoons water
2 teaspoons salt
1 green chilli pepper, diced
1 teaspoon lemon juice

Cook potatoes and peas separately. Dice potatoes. Cut ½ of an onion into thin slices for browning. Cut the remainder of the onions into larger pieces. Heat the fat; add onion slices, cayenne pepper, and mustard seed. Cover the pan for a few minutes until seeds pop. Add turmeric, minced garlic, ginger and larger pieces of onion; cook until onions are golden. Add water, cook for about 3 minutes longer. Add salt, diced chilli pepper, and potatoes. Stir until potatoes are done but not too soft. Potatoes should retain their shape. Add more fat if potatoes seem dry. Add lemon juice and more seasoning, if necessary. Add peas last. Serve hot with Pooris.

BOOFERS
Pennsylvania Dutch Potato Fritters
4 to 6 servings

2 cups grated raw potatoes	Dash of pepper
1 small onion, grated	1 tablespoon chopped parsley
1 egg, beaten	½ teaspoon baking powder
¼ teaspoon salt	4 tablespoons flour

Place potatoes in a strainer to drain off all liquid. Add grated onion, egg, salt, pepper, parsley, baking powder, and flour. Mix well. Drop by spoonfuls into deep hot fat (375°) and fry 5 to 6 minutes or until brown. Drain the fritters on absorbent paper.

NOTE: If the fritter batter should separate when dropped into the fat, add just enough flour to bind.

These are little oyster-sized golden brown balls of French fries with just enough onion to be interesting and just enough parsley to be colorful. Serve with Sauerbraten (page 98) for a meal with a real Pennsylvania Dutch flavor. They're equally good with pot roast or Swiss steak.

CREAMED POTATOES
4 to 6 servings

4 medium potatoes, pared and cooked	Paprika
1½ cups Medium White Sauce (page 215)	1 tablespoon chopped parsley

Cut the potatoes in ¾-inch cubes and add to the well-seasoned Medium White Sauce. Heat in double boiler until potatoes are warmed through, stirring as little as possible to prevent mushing. Turn into serving bowl. Sprinkle with paprika and garnish with parsley.

When new potatoes are in season, cook 1 pound with skins on. Peel and add to white sauce.

dolled up by Duchess potatoes . . .

Planked Broiled Lamb Chops, page 101.

always as good as it looks . . .

Planked Steak with Duchess Potatoes, page 96.

DUCHESS POTATOES
5 to 6 servings

5 or 6 medium potatoes
¼ cup melted butter
½ teaspoon salt
Dash of pepper
2 egg yolks, slightly beaten

⅓ cup cream
1 egg, beaten
2 teaspoons water
2 tablespoons melted butter

Pare potatoes. Cook in boiling salted water until done. Drain. Put through ricer to be sure there are no lumps. Add butter, salt, pepper, egg yolks, and cream to riced potatoes. Beat until light and fluffy. Use rose tube in canvas pastry bag and fill bag ¾ full of potato mixture. Force potato mixture onto greased baking sheet into rosette forms. Brush with beaten egg to which water has been added. Put in hot oven (425°) to brown. Brush with melted butter after removing from oven. Serve with broiled lamb chops, roast lamb, or pork.

Duchess potatoes may be formed into cone shape and browned in the oven or used as a potato border on a plank.

FRANCONIA POTATOES
8 servings

8 medium potatoes

Pare potatoes and parboil 10 minutes; drain and place in pan with Rolled Rib Roast of Beef (page 96). Bake until done and nicely browned, about 45 minutes. Turn potatoes several times during baking period and baste with fat in pan.

KARTOFFEL KNODEL
German Potato Balls
6 to 8 servings

4 medium potatoes	Dash of pepper
¼ cup milk	Flour
2 tablespoons butter	1 egg yolk, slightly beaten
2 egg yolks, slightly beaten	½ cup milk
½ teaspoon salt	2 cups fine bread crumbs

Cook the potatoes. Put through ricer. Add milk, butter, and egg yolks, and mix lightly. Season with salt and pepper. Shape into small balls about 1 inch in diameter. Roll in flour, then dip in egg yolk to which milk has been added. Drain. Put bread crumbs in shallow pan. Drop potato balls into bread crumbs and coat lightly with crumbs. Fry in deep hot fat (375°) until golden brown. Drain on absorbent paper. Serve hot.

MASHED POTATOES
6 to 8 servings

6 medium potatoes	Dash of white pepper
2 tablespoons butter	½ cup hot cream
½ teaspoon salt	

Pare potatoes and just cover with water; cook until done. Drain off water; let potatoes stand in a warm place uncovered, for a few minutes, to dry out thoroughly. Mash the potatoes or put them through a ricer. Add butter, salt and pepper to taste. Pour in the hot cream a little at a time, whipping it in until all has been used and potatoes are light and fluffy. Add more hot cream if potatoes are not moist enough. Serve hot.

O'BRIEN POTATOES
5 to 6 servings

1 quart raw potato balls	3 pimentos
Salt	½ cup diced green pepper
2 slices onion	1 tablespoon chopped parsley
2 tablespoons butter	

Pare potatoes and shape with French vegetable cutter into balls ½ inch in diameter. Soak in cold water and drain well. Fry in deep hot fat (375°) until brown and tender. Drain and sprinkle with salt. Fry onion in butter until golden brown. Remove onion, add pimentos and green pepper; cook 3 to 4 minutes, then add the potatoes. Serve hot with finely chopped parsley over all.
NOTE: By removing the onion, you have the flavor but not the discolored onion which develops when left in.

PAPRIKA POTATOES
6 to 8 servings

6 to 8 potatoes	Salt
2 tablespoons butter	¾ cup sour cream
2 small onions, finely chopped	1 tablespoon chopped parsley
½ teaspoon paprika	

Pare potatoes and cut into small cubes. Put butter in skillet and add onions; cook until onions are yellow; then add paprika, potatoes, and salt. Cover and cook until potatoes are tender. Add a little water to keep potatoes from sticking. Add cream. Do not stir, but shake the saucepan to prevent potatoes from sticking to pan. Simmer until done. Serve hot, garnished with parsley.

PARSLEY BUTTERED POTATOES

Allow one medium potato or 3 or 4 small new potatoes for each person. Pare potatoes and cook until just tender. Place in serving bowl, pour melted butter over potatoes and then sprinkle with finely minced parsley. Serve at once.

POTATO CUTLETS (INDIA)
About 12

6 large potatoes
1 tablespoon butter
1 tablespoon milk
1 pound lean beef
1 large onion
2 bunches green onions
2 tablespoons fat
½ teaspoon turmeric
½ teaspoon ginger
½ teaspoon chopped mint

½ green chilli pepper, diced
2 teaspoons salt
½ cup tomato purée
1 teaspoon flour
2 tablespoons lemon juice
2 eggs, beaten (for dipping)
1 cup bread crumbs
1 12-ounce package Brussels sprouts, cooked
3 tomatoes, sliced in ¼-inch slices

Cook potatoes and mash. Add butter and milk. Grind beef through fine knife of the meat grinder so that it is finely minced. Cut ½ of the onion into thin slices for frying; mince remainder of the onion. Cut green onions and tops into thin slices. Heat fat in a saucepan; when hot, drop in the onion slices, turmeric, ginger, mint, and chilli, and cook until onions are golden in color. Add beef. Brown for 5 minutes; then add the remainder of onion, green onions, salt, and tomato purée. Pour in sufficient water to barely cover meat mixture. Cover and cook until meat is tender and water evaporated. Add the flour to thicken mixture a bit. When meat mixture is almost dry, add lemon juice, and salt to taste. Remove from heat and cool. Drain thoroughly to remove any excess liquid.

For each potato cutlet use about ½ cup of the mashed potatoes. Flatten slightly. Put 1 tablespoon meat mixture into center of mashed potatoes and enclose meat. Shape potato and meat mixture into cutlet shape. Roll in beaten egg and then in bread crumbs. Fry in fat in hot skillet until brown on one side. Turn and brown the other side. Arrange on large platter with cooked Brussels sprouts in the center of the dish and sliced tomatoes around the edge. Serve hot with tomato catsup.

This is an Anglo-Indian dish which may be prepared with a mixed vegetable, shrimp, or fish filling instead of meat. Sometimes the filling is used to stuff hollowed fresh tomatoes, green peppers, or egg plants cut in half lengthwise, cooked, and scooped out to form a shell.

POTATO PUFFS (INDIA)
8 to 10 puffs

¼ cup cashew nuts
4 tablespoons fat
Dash of cayenne pepper
Dash of ground ginger
2 medium potatoes, cooked and
    diced

1 cup cooked beets
1 cup diced cooked carrots
1 teaspoon salt
2 tablespoons lemon juice
1 recipe Plain Pastry (page 433)

Cut cashew nuts into large pieces and sauté in 2 tablespoons of the fat until golden brown. Heat remaining 2 tablespoons fat and add cayenne pepper and ginger; add potatoes, beets, and carrots, and cook until seasoned. Add salt, lemon juice, and cashew nuts. Remove from fire; use as filling for potato puffs.

Roll pastry ⅛ inch thick. Cut into circles 4 inches in diameter. Place a generous tablespoon of the vegetable mixture on half of the pastry round. Fold other half over and press edges together with a hollow key to make design around edge. (Fork tines may be used if key is not available.) Prick top of pastry with fork. Bake in hot oven (400°) 12 to 15 minutes or until nicely browned.

POMMES DE TERRE À LA HOLLANDAISE
6 to 8 servings

6 medium potatoes
½ cup melted butter
1 tablespoon lemon juice
1 teaspoon salt

Dash of white pepper
Dash of nutmeg
2 tablespoons minced parsley

Pare potatoes. Cut into 1-inch cubes. Cook potatoes until tender. Drain well. Melt butter, add lemon juice, and pour over potatoes. Sprinkle salt, pepper, and nutmeg on potatoes. Toss potatoes lightly and turn into serving dish. Sprinkle with parsley and serve at once.

Potatoes with a slightly different flavor!

POMMES DE TERRE À LA LYONNAISE
6 to 8 servings

1 tablespoon butter
1 tablespoon oil
2 ounces salt pork, finely diced
2 small onions, sliced thin

3 cups cooked potatoes, sliced thin
Salt and pepper
¼ cup cream
1 tablespoon minced parsley

Heat butter and oil in skillet. Add salt pork and cook until slightly browned. Add onions and cook slowly until tender and golden brown. Add potatoes, salt and pepper. Let brown a little, then turn. Repeat until potatoes are nicely browned. Drain off any extra fat. Add cream. Cook 2 to 3 minutes longer. Turn into serving dish. Sprinkle with finely chopped parsley. Serve at once. Nice with roast beef.

Men like these lyonnaise potatoes — golden brown with a robust onion flavor.

POMMES DE TERRE NOISETTE
5 to 6 servings

6 large potatoes
½ cup butter

Salt
Paprika

Cut the potatoes with a round ball cutter into balls the size of a hazelnut. Cook them in butter until golden brown and until potatoes are cooked through. Sprinkle lightly with salt and paprika. Serve with roast meat.

POMMES DE TERRE VARIATIONS

Duxelle — Cook and mash potatoes. Add cream, salt, pepper, and onion, and form into cone shape. Roll in eggs and crumbs and fry in deep fat.

Julienne — Cut potatoes in matchlike strips and fry in deep fat.

Lorette — Cook and mash potatoes; mix with egg. Form into cigar shape. Roll in egg and crumbs; fry in deep fat.

Maître d'Hôtel — Slice potatoes. Cook in butter and milk, and season with fine herbs.

Parisienne — Cut potatoes in small round balls with ball cutter, and fry in deep fat.

Persillade — Cut potatoes with ball cutter; steam. Serve with drawn butter and parsley.

CANDIED YAMS OR SWEET POTATOES
6 servings

6 medium yams or sweet potatoes
⅓ cup butter
½ cup brown sugar

½ cup pineapple or other
    fruit juice
2 tablespoons butter

Cook yams or sweet potatoes in jackets until done but not soft. Peel and cut in half lengthwise. Put into buttered 2-quart casserole. Melt butter; add sugar and pineapple juice. Pour over potatoes. Dot with the 2 tablespoons butter. Bake in moderate oven (350°) 25 to 30 minutes. Baste with syrup several times during cooking so potatoes will be nicely glazed.

FRENCH FRIED SWEET-POTATO CHIPS

1 pound sweet potatoes
1 pint oil or fat for frying

1 tablespoon confectioners' sugar

Pare the potatoes and slice crosswise into very thin slices. Soak in cold water for 15 minutes and drain thoroughly; dry. Fry in deep hot fat (375°) until the chips are a delicate brown. Drain on absorbent paper; sprinkle with confectioners' sugar.

These delicately brown, crisp sweet-potato chips can be very successfully used as a cocktail accompaniment.

SWEET POTATOES WITH APPLES
6 to 8 servings

6 sweet potatoes
6 apples
½ cup maple syrup

¼ cup water
2 tablespoons butter

Wash sweet potatoes. Cook in boiling water until tender; drain and peel potatoes. Cut slices crosswise, 1 inch thick. Core, pare, and cut apples into ½-inch rounds. Place the potatoes in buttered 2-quart casserole and place a slice of apple on top of each. Pour over potatoes the maple syrup and water, and dot with butter. Bake in moderate oven (350°) 35 to 45 minutes or until apples are tender. Serve as a luncheon dish with pork sausage or ham loaf.

SWEET POTATOES WITH DATES
6 to 8 servings

3 pounds sweet potatoes
¼ cup cream
¼ teaspoon cinnamon

¾ teaspoon salt
¾ cup chopped pitted dates
¼ cup butter, melted

Cook sweet potatoes until tender. Peel and mash while hot. There should be no lumps. Add cream, cinnamon, salt, dates, and butter. Mix well and turn into buttered 1½-quart casserole and bake in moderate oven (350°) 20 to 25 minutes or until light brown. Serve with roast chicken or turkey.

The light touch of cinnamon and the dates give this sweet-potato dish a distinct flavor all its own.

SWEET POTATO SOUFFLE
6 to 8 servings

2 cups boiled, mashed sweet
    potatoes
¾ teaspoon salt
1 cup rich milk

½ cup honey
2 tablespoons cornstarch
3 eggs, beaten
¾ cup pecans, coarsely chopped

Blend all ingredients in order given. Place in buttered 1½-quart casserole. Bake in slow oven (300°) 30 to 40 minutes until set. *NOTE*: If the sweet potatoes have a tough grain, it is better to sieve them after cooking.

Try this delicate sweet potato soufflé as an added attraction with Baked Ham (page 112) for your next dinner party. Such a combination will give an authentic touch of the "Deep South." Betty Johnson, a graduate student from Ruston, Louisiana, added this to our repertory of recipes. It has been adopted by us Yankees with much enthusiasm.

GRATIN À LA MARIES
Spinach with Mushrooms and Cheese
6 to 8 servings

2 pounds fresh spinach or 2
   12-ounce packages frozen
½ pound fresh mushrooms,
   cleaned and sliced
2 tablespoons butter
1 teaspoon lemon juice
1 cup chopped cooked ham

1 cup Medium White Sauce (page
   215)
2 egg yolks, beaten
¾ cup grated Swiss or American
   cheese
½ cup buttered bread crumbs

Remove tough stems from fresh spinach. Cook spinach in a very little salted water for 5 minutes. Drain. Cook mushrooms in butter and lemon juice; add to spinach. Chop ham and mix with spinach and mushrooms. Put into buttered 1½-quart casserole. Make 1 cup well-seasoned Medium White Sauce. Add beaten egg yolks to white sauce. Pour over the spinach mixture. Sprinkle with grated cheeese and buttered bread crumbs. Bake in moderate oven (350°) about 20 minutes. Serve at once.

MEXICAN BAKED SPINACH
4 to 6 servings

1 pound spinach
2 green peppers, chopped
2 cups chopped cooked celery
¼ cup tomato juice
2 tablespoons raisins, chopped
1 teaspoon salt
1 teaspoon sugar

1 teaspoon chili powder
⅛ teaspoon cinnamon
Dash of cayenne pepper
¼ cup grated cheese
4 tablespoons buttered bread
   crumbs

Wash spinach thoroughly and remove any tough stems. Cook slowly with peppers in covered saucepan, using no other water than that which clings to leaves. Drain and chop fine. Mix with celery, tomato juice, raisins, and seasonings. Put in buttered 1½-quart casserole, sprinkle with grated cheese and buttered crumbs. Bake in moderate oven (350°) 20 to 25 minutes.

Spinach with the Mexican touch!

SPINACH WITH ONION
6 to 8 servings

2 pounds spinach
2 tablespoons salad oil
1 clove garlic, crushed
2 tablespoons chopped onion

1 teaspoon salt
½ cup water
2 hard-cooked eggs

Remove tough stems of spinach and wash thoroughly. Heat oil in saucepan, fry garlic and onions slightly. Add spinach and cook for a few minutes, stirring constantly; add salt and water, and cook 8 to 10 minutes. Turn into serving dish and garnish with sliced hard-cooked eggs. Serve lemon wedges with spinach.

SPINACH TIMBALE ON TOMATO SLICES
8 servings

2 cups cooked spinach, chopped
    fine
2 tablespoons butter
3 eggs, slightly beaten
1 cup milk
⅔ teaspoon salt
⅛ teaspoon pepper

Few drops onion juice
2 teaspoons vinegar
8 slices tomatoes, 2½ inches in
    diameter
8 bread rounds, 2½ inches in
    diameter, sautéed in butter
Hollandaise Sauce (page 209)

Put spinach in bowl and add butter, eggs, milk, salt, pepper, onion juice, and vinegar. Mix lightly. Fill buttered 6-ounce custard cups ¾ full of the spinach mixture. Place cups in pan of hot water to depth of about 1½ inches. Bake in slow oven (300°) 25 to 30 minutes or until firm to the touch. Let stand 5 minutes before removing from cup. Place slice of tomato on sautéed round of bread. Turn spinach mold out on tomato slice. Top with 1 teaspoon Hollandaise Sauce and sprinkle with paprika.

For your next buffet supper try these colorful spinach timbales. They taste as good as they look.

FRENCH FRIED ZUCCHINI

Slice zucchini squash into thin strips, soak in salt water ½ hour. Drain, drop (2 to 3 in a cluster) into a fritter batter made by combining 1 cup flour, 1 cup milk, and 1 well-beaten egg. Fry until golden brown in deep fat (365°). Drain, serve hot.

ZUCCHINI MARINADE
Fried Italian Squash
4 servings

1 medium zucchini squash	2 tablespoons vinegar
3 tablespoons butter	

Cut young zucchini squash in ¼-inch slices. Sauté in butter and pour vinegar over them. Serve hot, garnished with a few sprigs of mint.

BAKED TOMATOES WITH CRAB MEAT FILLING
6 servings

6 medium tomatoes	½ cup cream
1 tablespoon butter	1 cup flaked crab meat
1 tablespoon flour	1 tablespoon finely chopped green
½ teaspoon salt	pepper
Dash of pepper	1 tablespoon diced pimento
¼ teaspoon paprika	¼ cup toasted chopped almonds
½ teaspoon onion juice	1 cup buttered bread crumbs

Remove a slice from the top of each tomato; scoop out some of the pulp. Sprinkle inside of tomato with salt. Invert and let stand ½ hour. Melt butter; add flour, salt, pepper, paprika, and onion juice; blend and add cream. Cook until sauce has thickened and add crab meat, green pepper, pimento, and almonds. Fill tomatoes with mixture and sprinkle with buttered bread crumbs. Bake in moderate oven (375°) 10 to 15 minutes or until done. Serve at once. Garnish with parsley.

Serve as a luncheon entree and your guests will be delighted with the crab meat and baked tomato combination.

BROILED TOMATOES
6 servings

6 tomatoes
Salt and pepper

1½ cups fine bread crumbs
2 eggs, beaten

Cut thin slice from each end of tomato. Cut each tomato into 4 thick slices. Sprinkle with salt and pepper, dip in crumbs, egg, and crumbs again. Broil 6 to 8 minutes, or bake in hot oven (425°) 10 minutes.

FRIED TOMATOES IN CREAM
6 servings

3 large tomatoes
Flour
¼ cup butter

Salt and pepper
½ cup cream
6 rounds of toast

Cut tomatoes in thick slices and dip in flour. Melt butter in skillet. Sauté tomato slices in butter. Sprinkle with salt and pepper. Pour in cream. Bring to boiling point; simmer for 5 minutes and serve at once on toast rounds.

SOUTHERN STYLE TOMATOES
6 servings

6 ripe medium tomatoes
2 tablespoons butter
3 tablespoons flour
½ teaspoon salt

⅛ teaspoon pepper
1 cup cream
1 teaspoon lemon juice
1 tablespoon chopped parsley

Prick each tomato several times. Put in baking dish and bake in moderate oven (350°) 15 to 20 minutes or until soft. Make cream sauce of butter, flour, salt, pepper, and cream. Cook until thickened. Add lemon juice. When tomatoes are done, remove skins, arrange on serving dish and pour cream sauce over them. Sprinkle with chopped parsley. Serve hot.

STUFFED TOMATOES
6 servings

6 tomatoes	½ cup tomato pulp
6 tablespoons chopped green pepper	¼ teaspoon salt
	⅛ teaspoon pepper
3 tablespoons butter	Few drops onion juice
¾ cup soft bread crumbs	Buttered bread crumbs

Remove stem end from each tomato. Take out seeds and most of the pulp; sprinkle inside of tomatoes with salt; invert and let stand 20 minutes. Cook green pepper for 5 minutes in butter. Add bread crumbs, tomato pulp, salt, pepper, and onion juice. Fill tomatoes with this mixture and cover with buttered bread crumbs. Place in buttered 1½-quart casserole and bake in very hot oven (450°) 15 minutes.

TURNIP GREENS
6 servings

2 pounds turnip greens	1-inch cube salt pork

Plunge greens into boiling salted water to cover. Slice cube of salt pork several times almost through and add to vegetable while cooking. Cook until tender, 15 to 20 minutes after water returns to a boil. Serve with vinegar.

In southern homes there is always a bottle of pepper sauce on the table to use on turnip greens, mustard greens, or collards which are so popular in that part of the country. The pepper sauce is made by pouring vinegar over hot red peppers and allowing it to stand until it acquires some of the hotness from the peppers. A dash of this pepper sauce is added to the greens to suit the taste of each member of the family.

A favorite saying in the South is that the greens aren't good unless they "take" the seasoning that is added to them. Some greens do and some don't!

VEGETABLE PLATTER
6 to 8 servings

1 medium head cauliflower	6 tablespoons melted butter
2 bunches carrots	Salt and pepper
2 12-ounce packages frozen peas	Chopped parsley

Remove outside leaves of cauliflower. Cook cauliflower whole, drain, and place in center of round platter. Cut carrots in strips 3 to 4 inches long. Cook until done. Cook peas. Add melted butter to each vegetable. Sprinkle lightly with salt and pepper. When arranging carrots and peas around cauliflower, divide into thirds. Let carrots extend lengthwise from head of cauliflower and place peas between carrot strips to give interesting effect. Sprinkle cauliflower with chopped parsley. Serve with Hollandaise Sauce (page 209) for added flavor and color.

When preparing this vegetable platter, time the cooking of the vegetables carefully so each one will be done at just the right time.

Your most discriminating guests should be pleased when this colorful vegetable platter makes its appearance at the dinner table.

Sauces and Relishes

SAUCES

Allemande
Almond Mushroom
Amandine
Barbecue
Béarnaise
Béchamel
  Yellow Béchamel
Bread

BROWN OR ESPAGNOLE

Brown, with Mushrooms
Creole
Périgueux
Tomato
Brown Roux for 1 Pint

BUTTER

Anchovy
Beurre Noir
Beurre Noisette
Drawn Butter
Lemon Butter
Maître d'Hôtel
  Caper
Paprika
Shrimp or Lobster

Caper Cream
Chinese Meat
Currant Jelly
Fresh Cucumber
Hollandaise
Horse-Radish

Hot Tartare
Lög (onion)
Meunière
Mint
Mock Hollandaise
Mornay
Mousseline
Mustard
Orange
Raisin
Russian
Sea Food Cocktail
Shrimp
Soubise
Sweet-Sour
Tartare
Velouté

WHITE

Thin
Medium
Thick
Celery
Cheese
Egg
Mushroom

SUGGESTIONS FOR SAUCES

Beef
Fish
Poultry
Sweetbreads
Vegetables

RELISHES

Pickled beets
Spiced beets
Cranberry Jelly
Cranberry Sauce

Green Tomato Pickles
Pineapple Chutney
Spiced Prunes

SAUCES have been called The Sonnet of the Table. The simplest dish can be enhanced and made more palatable by the accompaniment of a smooth, creamy, well-blended sauce that lifts it out of the ordinary. Sauces are the test of the culinary art of the cook. It takes patience to make a good sauce, for the cooking cannot be hurried.

Sauces

SAUCE-MAKING

There are several types of sauces, each with its own variations. Foundation or medium white sauce is made from milk thickened with a *roux* (equal parts of fat and flour). Cream sauce substitutes cream for milk in the same recipe. Brown sauce has browned flour in place of white flour.

The smooth consistency of a sauce starts with the proper blending of the fat, flour, and seasonings, and then the blending with the liquid to make a smooth sauce. The hot or cold liquid is added slowly to the roux and cooked with constant stirring until the sauce is smooth and thickened.

COOKING PLAIN SAUCES

Allow the sauce to cook at least ten minutes from the time the liquid is added. When a sauce is cooked less than that time, the flour will not have had time to cook completely. The butter then separates, which gives an oily appearance to the sauce.

Sauces that have a high proportion of butter and eggs, as Hollandaise and Mousseline sauce, require careful technique in making so that they do not separate. Follow the directions for the sauce carefully. Cook this type of sauce in a double boiler and over low heat. Sauces of the Hollandaise type do not keep well on standing and should be served at once.

SEASONING

A plain sauce may be spoiled by overseasoning or by too spicy a seasoning. The sauce should be seasoned just enough to bring out the natural flavor.

CHARACTER OF THE SAUCE

No matter what the flavoring, whether the sauce is plain or rich, the rule for seasoning and flavoring should be the same; the ingredients used for this purpose should be so proportioned that no one flavor predominates over the other.

AMOUNT TO SERVE

Only a small amount of sauce is needed with most foods; it is the accompaniment to the food, not the food itself. The right sauce complements the food and becomes an integral part of the dish.

ALLEMANDE SAUCE
About 1½ cups

2 tablespoons butter
3 tablespoons flour
1 cup Veal Stock (page 46) or
   Chicken Stock (page 45)
¼ teaspoon salt

Dash of white pepper
⅓ cup cream
1 egg yolk, beaten
1 tablespoon lemon juice
Dash of nutmeg

Melt butter in double boiler; add flour and blend thoroughly. Add stock and season with salt and pepper. Cook until thick. Add cream. Pour some of the sauce over beaten egg yolk. Combine with remainder of sauce and return to double boiler to thicken. Remove from heat. Add lemon juice and nutmeg. Serve hot over cooked fish, salmon loaf, or asparagus.

ALMOND MUSHROOM SAUCE
3 cups

4 tablespoons butter
1 tablespoon chopped onion
1 cup chopped fresh mushrooms
4 tablespoons flour
½ teaspoon salt

Dash of pepper
2 cups Chicken Stock (page 45)
2 teaspoons lemon juice
½ cup chopped toasted almonds

Melt butter; add onion and mushrooms. Sauté, then add flour and blend well. Add salt, pepper, and Chicken Stock. Cook until thick and smooth. Add lemon juice and almonds. Serve over Chicken Loaf (page 127).

AMANDINE SAUCE
About ½ cup

6 tablespoons butter
⅓ cup slivered blanched almonds

1 teaspoon lemon juice

Melt butter in a small skillet. Add almonds and sauté until delicately browned. Add lemon juice. Serve with fish or sweetbreads. The sauce may also be served with broccoli, green beans, or cauliflower.

BARBECUE SAUCE
About 1½ quarts

½ cup diced green pepper
2 medium onions, minced
2 cloves garlic, crushed
¼ cup oil
2 cups tomato catsup
1 cup chili sauce
½ cup water
½ cup beefsteak sauce
2 teaspoons prepared mustard

1 teaspoon grated horse-radish
½ cup lemon juice
¼ cup vinegar
½ cup sugar
½ teaspoon paprika
1 teaspoon salt
½ teaspoon black pepper
⅛ teaspoon cayenne pepper

Sauté green pepper, onion, and garlic in oil. Add remaining ingredients. Simmer over low heat for 1 hour or more. Stir occasionally while cooking.

This is a good spicy sauce to use when you barbecue ribs or chicken.

BEARNAISE SAUCE
1 cup

3 tablespoons water
3 tablespoons tarragon vinegar
½ medium onion, chopped
4 slightly beaten egg yolks

½ teaspoon salt
⅛ teaspoon paprika
4 tablespoons butter

Put water, vinegar, and onion in a small saucepan. Heat to boiling point. Remove onion and pour liquid gradually on egg yolks. Add seasonings. Cook in double boiler, stirring constantly, until mixture begins to thicken. Add butter, 1 tablespoon at a time, stirring constantly. This sauce has a piquant flavor and is nice to serve with fish.

Béarnaise sauce was named for Béarn, the town in the Pyrenees where Henri IV was born. It was introduced in 1835 by the chef of the Pavilion of Henri IV.

BECHAMEL SAUCE
2½ cups

3 tablespoons butter
4 tablespoons flour
½ to 1 teaspoon salt
¼ teaspoon paprika
1¼ cups Chicken Stock (page 45)

¾ cup cream or cream and
    mushroom liquid
½ cup mushrooms, chopped,
    canned or fresh

Make as a white sauce, adding cream slowly after mixture has thickened. Sauté mushrooms and add. Serve over Cheese Timbales (page 260), or Chicken Croquettes (page 126).

YELLOW BECHAMEL SAUCE — About 3 cups

1 recipe Béchamel Sauce   2 egg yolks, slightly beaten

Add a small amount of the hot Béchamel Sauce to the egg yolks, stirring well. Combine with remaining sauce in double boiler; cook for a few minutes, stirring constantly. The sauce must be served immediately so that it does not separate or curdle. Serve with fish.

Béchamel sauce was named after Louis de Béchamel, Lord Steward of the Household at the Court of Louis XIV.

BREAD SAUCE
About 2 cups

1½ cups milk
1 small onion
4 cloves
⅓ cup fresh bread crumbs
1 teaspoon salt

⅛ teaspoon pepper
Dash of cayenne pepper
2 tablespoons butter
½ cup dry bread crumbs

Scald milk in double boiler. Add onion stuck with cloves. Add fresh bread crumbs and cook over low heat for 20 minutes. Remove onion. Add salt, pepper, and cayenne pepper. Heat butter, add dry bread crumbs, and stir until well browned. Stir into milk mixture. Serve with roast chicken.

BROWN OR ESPAGNOLE SAUCE
About 3 cups

2 tablespoons butter
2 tablespoons finely chopped carrot
2 tablespoons finely chopped onion
2 tablespoons finely chopped celery
2 tablespoons finely chopped
    parsley
2 tablespoons flour

Small piece bay leaf
1 clove
½ teaspoon peppercorns
2½ cups Beef Stock (page 45)
4 tablespoons Brown Roux
    (page 206)

Cook in the butter the carrot, onion, celery, and parsley. After mixture is lightly browned, thicken with flour. Add bay leaf, clove, and peppercorns, and continue browning. Heat Beef Stock and add above mixture to it. Simmer together 10 or 15 minutes. Strain through fine sieve and add to Brown Roux. Cook until thickened.

BROWN SAUCE WITH MUSHROOMS

To Brown Sauce (page 205) add ¾ cup fresh or canned mushrooms sautéed in 1 tablespoon butter.

CREOLE SAUCE

To Brown Sauce (page 205) add 2 tablespoons chopped red peppers and 2 tablespoons chopped green peppers, sautéed in butter.

PERIGUEUX SAUCE

To Brown Sauce (page 205) add ¼ cup chopped truffles.

TOMATO SAUCE

In Brown Sauce recipe (page 205) reduce Beef Stock to 1¼ cups and add 1¼ cups tomatoes.

BROWN ROUX FOR 1 PINT SAUCE

¼ cup butter	5 tablespoons flour

Melt butter, add flour, and let cook over a low heat, stirring often, until the mixture attains a rich but light mahogany color. It is important that the cooking be done slowly, and the stirring be repeated at very short intervals. If the mixture becomes the least bit burned it cannot be used.

ANCHOVY BUTTER

¼ cup butter	1 teaspoon anchovy paste
½ teaspoon onion juice	1 teaspoon lemon juice

Cream butter and blend in other ingredients. Spread on fish or steak just before serving.

BEURRE NOIR
Black Butter

Heat ¼ cup butter in a small pan until dark brown (almost black). Add 1 teaspoon lemon juice or wine vinegar. Use on fish or vegetables.

BEURRE NOISETTE
Nut-Brown Butter

Heat ¼ cup butter in a small pan until it is a delicate brown. Use on fish or vegetables.

DRAWN BUTTER

Drawn butter is melted butter. Put ¼ cup of butter in a small pan; set in a warm place where it will melt gradually, and will not brown. Pour over fish or vegetables.

LEMON BUTTER

½ cup butter
2 tablespoons lemon juice

1 tablespoon chopped parsley
Paprika

Melt butter and add lemon juice, parsley, and paprika. Serve with baked or broiled fish.

MAITRE D'HOTEL BUTTER

¼ cup butter
½ teaspoon salt
Dash of pepper

1 tablespoon finely chopped
parsley
1 teaspoon lemon juice or tarragon
vinegar

Cream butter; add salt, pepper, and parsley, and blend well. Add lemon juice slowly. Spread on fish or steak just before serving.

CAPER BUTTER

In Maître d'Hôtel Butter recipe substitute capers for parsley.

PAPRIKA BUTTER

¼ cup butter
½ teaspoon paprika

½ teaspoon lemon juice
½ teaspoon wine vinegar

Cream butter and blend in paprika. Gradually add lemon juice and wine vinegar. Spread on fish before serving.

SHRIMP OR LOBSTER BUTTER

¼ cup butter
1 tablespoon finely chopped shrimp
or lobster

1 teaspoon lemon juice
Dash of salt
Dash of pepper

Blend ingredients. Spread on fish just before serving.

CAPER CREAM SAUCE
2½ cups

¼ cup butter
¼ cup flour
1½ cups milk
1 teaspoon salt

1 tablespoon lemon juice
3 tablespoons capers
½ cup cream
2 eggs, slightly beaten

Melt butter in double boiler, add flour and blend thoroughly. Add milk and cook, stirring constantly, until mixture thickens. Add salt, lemon juice, and capers. Then add cream mixed with slightly beaten eggs. Continue cooking over low heat 2 minutes longer. Serve hot with Broiled Fish Steaks (page 144).

CHINESE MEAT SAUCE FOR FRIED FISH
6 servings

½ pound ground beef
¼ pound ground ham
1 tablespoon fat
2 tablespoons flour

1 piece fresh ginger cut into long
    thin slices
⅓ cup bamboo shoots
1½ cups hot water

Add ground beef and ham to fat in skillet; sauté until beef is cooked. Add flour and stir until blended with meat. Add ginger, bamboo shoots, and water. Cook for 15 minutes or until sauce has thickened slightly and is well blended. Serve over Fried Fish (page 147) for Chinese Filipino Dinner (page 454).

CURRANT JELLY SAUCE
About 3 cups

¼ cup butter
1 bay leaf
1 sprig parsley
¼ cup diced celery
½ cup flour

2 cups cold Veal Stock (page 46)
1 teaspoon salt
Dash of pepper
1 cup currant jelly
2 teaspoons lemon juice

Heat butter in skillet until light brown; add bay leaf, parsley, and celery. Add flour and brown to a golden color. Add the stock and cook until slightly thickened. Strain sauce and add seasoning. Add currant jelly to the brown sauce, stirring until dissolved. Stir in lemon juice. Serve with roast lamb.

FRESH CUCUMBER SAUCE
1½ cups

½ cup heavy cream
Salt and pepper

1 teaspoon vinegar
1 peeled cucumber, finely chopped

Whip cream; add other ingredients.

HOLLANDAISE SAUCE
About 1¼ cups

½ cup butter
3 egg yolks
1 tablespoon lemon juice

⅓ cup boiling water
¼ teaspoon salt
Dash of cayenne pepper

Divide butter into 3 pieces. Put one piece in double boiler with egg yolks and lemon juice. Cook over hot water on low heat, stirring constantly until butter is melted. Add a second piece of butter, and as the mixture thickens, a third piece. Add boiling water slowly. Cook 1 minute. Remove from heat and season. Serve with broccoli or asparagus.

HORSE-RADISH SAUCE
About 1 cup

¼ cup grated horse-radish
1 tablespoon lemon juice
1 teaspoon vinegar

¼ teaspoon salt
Dash of cayenne pepper
½ cup heavy cream

Drain horse-radish to remove any excess liquid. Combine horse-radish, lemon juice, vinegar, salt, and cayenne pepper. Chill. Just before serving, whip cream and fold in horse-radish mixture. Serve with Baked Ham (page 112) or cold meats.

HOT TARTARE SAUCE
About 1½ cups

½ cup Medium White Sauce (page 215)
½ cup mayonnaise
1 tablespoon tarragon vinegar
1 teaspoon finely chopped onion

1 tablespoon finely chopped pickles
1 tablespoon finely chopped olives
1 tablespoon finely chopped parsley
1 tablespoon finely chopped capers

Add all ingredients to white sauce. Stir constantly over hot water until thoroughly heated, but do not boil. Serve with baked fish or Broiled Fish Steaks (page 144).

LOG SAUCE
Onion Sauce
5 to 6 servings

1 cup Medium White Sauce (page 215)
4 small onions, peeled and sliced
3 sprigs parsley
½ teaspoon salt

⅛ teaspoon thyme
Dash of nutmeg
Dash of white pepper
Dash of paprika

Add just enough boiling water to cover onions; add remainder of seasonings and cook until onions are soft. Drain and rub through a wire sieve. Add the onion purée to the white sauce. Heat in double boiler and stir until well blended. Serve with Frikadeller (page 93).

MEUNIERE SAUCE (FOR FISH)

Melt 3 tablespoons butter and cook slowly until brown. When the fish is cooked, sprinkle a few drops of fresh lemon juice on it, also some finely minced parsley, and then pour the melted brown butter over it.

MINT SAUCE
½ cup

¼ cup water
2 tablespoons confectioners' sugar

⅓ cup finely chopped mint leaves
¼ cup white vinegar

Heat water and sugar. Pour over mint leaves. Add vinegar and let stand 30 minutes to infuse. Serve with roast lamb.

MOCK HOLLANDAISE SAUCE
About 2 cups

1 cup Medium White Sauce (page 215)
2 egg yolks, beaten slightly

4 tablespoons butter
1 tablespoon lemon juice

Stir the hot white sauce into the egg yolks; add butter, a tablespoon at a time. Add lemon juice and blend. Serve immediately.

MORNAY SAUCE
About 3 cups

2½ cups hot Béchamel Sauce
   (page 204), made with Fish
   Stock (page 46)

2 ounces Gruyère cheese
2 ounces Parmesan cheese
½ cup butter

Beat cheese into hot Béchamel Sauce. Let sauce remain over heat until cheese is melted; then remove and gradually beat in the butter. Serve with fish.

MOUSSELINE SAUCE
About 1½ cups

¼ cup butter
4 egg yolks
¼ cup cream
¼ teaspoon salt

Dash of cayenne pepper
2 tablespoons lemon juice
¼ cup butter

Cream the ¼ cup of butter; add egg yolks one at a time, beating into butter thoroughly. Add cream, salt, and cayenne pepper. Cook in a double boiler over low heat, stirring constantly until the sauce thickens. Remove from heat and add lemon juice slowly. Add remaining ¼ cup butter and blend into sauce. Keep warm, but do not heat again. Serve with baked or broiled fish. This sauce is equally good with vegetables such as asparagus or broccoli, or with Spinach Timbales (page 194).

MUSTARD SAUCE
About 2 cups

3 egg yolks
2 tablespoons sugar
2 tablespoons water
¼ cup vinegar
1 teaspoon salt

1 tablespoon dry mustard
2 tablespoons butter
2 tablespoons grated horse-radish
1 cup heavy cream, whipped

Beat egg yolks. Add sugar, water, vinegar, salt, and mustard. Cook in double boiler until thick. Add butter and horse-radish; stir until well blended. Cool. Fold into whipped cream. Serve with Baked Ham (page 112) or Glazed Ham Loaves (page 113).

ORANGE SAUCE
2½ cups

½ cup fat (use at least part of fat
from baking ham)
¼ cup flour
¾ cup water

1¾ cups orange juice
½ cup brown sugar
2 tablespoons grated orange peel
1 tablespoon grated lemon peel

Melt fat in double boiler, add flour and blend. Add water, orange juice and brown sugar slowly, stirring well until mixture thickens slightly. Cook 15 to 20 minutes, stirring occasionally. Remove from heat and add grated orange and lemon peel. If fat has a tendency to separate, stir in a little warm water until the mixture is again smooth. Serve with Baked Ham (page 112). Garnish each serving with slice of orange.

Leftover sauce may be kept in refrigerator and reheated in double boiler.

This orange sauce recipe, a favorite with the students, was contributed by Pearl Jackson Aldrich of Michigan State College.

RAISIN SAUCE
About 2 cups

½ cup sugar
¼ cup water
½ cup raisins
1 tablespoon butter
2 tablespoons vinegar

½ teaspoon Worchestershire sauce
½ teaspoon salt
Dash of pepper
1 cup currant jelly
Red food coloring

Combine sugar and water and bring to boil in saucepan. Add remaining ingredients and simmer gently for about 5 minutes or until jelly is melted. Stir in a small amount of red food coloring to give a pretty red color. Serve warm with Baked Ham (page 112).

RUSSIAN SAUCE
About 2½ cups

1 cup Velouté Sauce (page 214)
1 teaspoon chives or 1 teaspoon
finely chopped onion
1 teaspon prepared mustard
1 teaspoon grated horse-radish

¼ teaspoon salt
Dash of white pepper
¼ cup cream
1 teaspoon lemon juice

Add chives or onions, mustard, horse-radish, salt, and pepper to the Velouté Sauce. Cook 2 minutes; strain. Add cream, then lemon juice. Reheat before serving. Serve with baked fish or Broiled Fish Steaks (page 144).

SEA FOOD COCKTAIL SAUCE
8 to 10 servings

1 cup chili sauce	Dash of Tabasco sauce
1 teaspoon Worcestershire sauce	⅛ teaspoon white pepper
1 teaspoon grated horse-radish	2 tablespoons lemon juice

Mix ingredients and chill thoroughly. Serve over sea food cocktail, or use as a dip for shrimp.

SHRIMP SAUCE
About 2½ cups

2 tablespoons butter	½ cup cream
3 tablespoons flour	½ teaspoon Worchestershire
½ teaspoon paprika	sauce
½ teaspoon salt	1 cup diced Cooked Shrimp (page
⅛ teaspoon pepper	155)
Dash of cayenne pepper	1 teaspoon lemon juice
1 cup milk	1 tablespoon minced parsley

Melt butter in double boiler; add flour, paprika, and seasonings, and blend well. Add milk and cream. Stir until well blended and smooth. Cook 10 to 12 minutes. Add Worcestershire sauce and diced shrimp. Add lemon juice. Pour sauce over baked fish; sprinkle with minced parsley.

SOUBISE SAUCE
About 2 cups

1 cup sliced onions	½ cup cream
1 cup Velouté Sauce (page 214)	Salt and pepper

Cover onions with boiling water and cook until soft. Drain and rub through a sieve. Add to the Velouté Sauce, then add cream. Season.

This is an especially good sauce with fish, if you like an onion flavor.

SWEET-SOUR SAUCE
About 1½ cups

¾ cup water
2 tablespoons vinegar
1 tablespoon soy sauce
¼ cup sugar

¼ teaspoon salt
1 tablespoon cornstarch
2 tablespoons water

Combine water, vinegar, soy sauce, sugar, and salt. Heat to boiling. Add cornstarch to water to make paste. Stir slowly into boiling mixture. Cook over low heat 2 to 3 minutes, until sauce is clear and thickened. If sauce of darker color is desired, replace 1 tablespoon water with 1 tablespoon soy sauce. The sauce may be served with Egg Roll (Page 105).

TARTARE SAUCE
1 cup

1 cup Mayonnaise (page 251)
½ teaspoon prepared mustard
1 teaspoon grated onion
2 tablespoons chopped parsley

2 tablespoons finely chopped dill
    pickle
½ clove garlic, finely minced

Combine Mayonnaise and mustard, and add other ingredients. Place in refrigerator to chill. Serve with fish.

VELOUTE SAUCE
1 cup

2 tablespoons butter
2 tablespoons flour
1 cup Chicken Stock (page 45)
    or Veal Stock (page 46)

¼ teaspoon salt
Dash of white pepper
5 mushroom caps

Melt butter, add flour and blend. Add stock and seasonings. Cook until thick. Add mushroom caps, sliced and cooked. Serve over Egg Timbales (page 260) or Chicken Loaf (page 127).

A delicious Velouté sauce may be made by adding ⅛ cup cream just before serving.

WHITE SAUCE
About 1 cup

Thin:

1 tablespoon butter	⅛ teaspoon pepper
1 tablespoon flour	1 cup milk
½ teaspoon salt	

Medium:

2 tablespoons butter	⅛ teaspoon pepper
2 tablespoons flour	1 cup milk
½ teaspoon salt	

Thick:

4 tablespoons butter	⅛ teaspoon pepper
4 tablespoons flour	1 cup milk
½ teaspoon salt	

Melt butter in double boiler and blend in flour, salt, and pepper. Add milk gradually, stirring constantly until mixture thickens and there is no starch flavor. Cover and let remain over low heat until ready to serve.

CELERY SAUCE

Add to Medium White Sauce 1 cup diced cooked celery and 1 tablespoon minced parsley.

CHEESE SAUCE

To 1 cup hot Medium White Sauce add 1 cup grated American cheese. Stir until melted.

EGG SAUCE

Add to Medium White Sauce 2 diced hard-cooked eggs, 1 tablespoon minced parsley, and dash of cayenne pepper.

MUSHROOM SAUCE

Sauté ½ pound sliced fresh mushrooms, or ¾ cup canned mushrooms, and 1 teaspoon finely chopped onion for 5 minutes in the butter to be used in making Medium White Sauce. Then blend in flour and seasonings; proceed as for Medium White Sauce.

SUGGESTIONS FOR SAUCES
To Serve with Meat, Fish, Poultry, and Vegetables

Beef:

"Boiled beef" with Horse-radish

Broiled beef with:
Béarnaise, Brown Mushroom, Brown Tomato, Horse-radish, Maître d'Hôtel Butter

Croquettes with:
Soubise, Tomato

Leftover meat with Périgueux

Fish:

Baked fish with:
Béchamel, Cheese, Hollandaise, Shrimp

Broiled fish with:
Cucumber, Hollandaise, Lobster Butter, Maître d'Hôtel, Paprika Butter, Tartare

Creamed fish with Mornay

Croquettes with Tartare

Fried fish with:
Béarnaise, Cucumber, Tartare

Salmon, baked, with:
Anchovy Butter, Caper Butter, Drawn Butter, Hollandaise

Salmon loaf with:
Hollandaise, Tomato, Drawn Butter and slices of hard-cooked egg or chopped pickles and capers

Scalloped fish with Béchamel

Steamed fish with:
Caper, Cheese, Hollandaise, Velouté

Timbales with Hollandaise

Poultry:
   Broiled chicken with Perigueux
   Planked chicken with:
      Cream, Hollandaise
   Roast chicken with Bread
   Chicken soufflé with:
      Béchamel, Mushroom

Sweetbreads:
   Broiled sweetbreads with Velouté
   Cutlets with:
      Tomato, Velouté
   Grilled sweetbreads with:
      Maître d'Hôtel, Mushroom, Tomato

Vegetables:
   Broccoli with Mousseline
   Brussels sprouts with:
      Cream, Hollandaise, Mousseline
   Cauliflower with:
      Cheese, Cream, Drawn Butter, Hollandaise, Mousseline
   Green Beans with Amandine

Relishes

PICKLED BEETS
2 pints

4 cups sliced cold cooked beets
2 cups vinegar
⅓ cup sugar
½ teaspoon salt
3 sticks whole cinnamon

½ teaspoon allspice
1 teaspoon whole cloves
2 teaspoons white mustard seed
1 teaspoon celery seed

Combine vinegar, sugar, and salt. Tie spices loosely in a cheese-cloth bag; add to vinegar. Add mustard seed and celery seed. Heat to boiling. Remove cheesecloth bag. Fill clean, hot pint jars with beets and pour over hot spiced vinegar. Seal jars and let stand for 36 hours before using.

SPICED BEETS
4 to 6 servings

1 pound fresh beets
½ cup vinegar
½ cup water
½ cup sugar

1 teaspoon salt
1 stick cinnamon
⅓ teaspoon whole allspice
3 whole cloves

Wash beets. Cut off top leaves. Cook beets in boiling water until tender. Remove skins, roots, and tops. Slice beets, or if the beets are small they may be left whole. Tie the spices loosely in a cheesecloth bag. Heat vinegar, water, sugar, salt, and spices to boiling. Add beets and boil 5 minutes. Let stand 30 minutes. Beets may be served hot or cold, or sealed in a jar while hot.

CRANBERRY JELLY
8 to 10 servings

1 quart cranberries
2 cups water

2 cups sugar

Pick over and wash cranberries. Add water. Cook until berries burst. Press pulp through a coarse sieve. Add sugar and stir until dissolved. Let cook 3 to 5 minutes longer. Pour into small molds or ring mold. Chill and serve with roast turkey.

CRANBERRY SAUCE
10 to 12 servings

2 cups sugar   4 cups cranberries
2 cups water

Boil sugar and water together for 5 minutes. Add washed cranberries and boil without stirring until skins pop open, 10 to 15 minutes. Continue to cook 5 minutes longer. Pour into bowl to chill.

GREEN TOMATO PICKLES
About 3 pints

4 pounds green tomatoes, sliced   1 teaspoon dry mustard
4 medium onions, sliced   1 teaspoon whole allspice
4 tablespoons salt   ¼ teaspoon black pepper
1 teaspoon whole cloves   2 cups vinegar
1 teaspoon mustard seed   1 cup sugar

Add 2 tablespoons of the salt to the tomatoes and remaining 2 tablespoons salt to the onions. Let stand overnight; drain well. Tie spices loosely in a cheesecloth bag and put in kettle with vinegar and sugar. Heat to boiling point; add tomatoes and onions and let simmer slowly 20 minutes. Pack into clean hot jars and seal immediately.

PINEAPPLE CHUTNEY
About 2 pints

1 No. 2½ can sliced pineapple   ¾ cup slivered blanched almonds
1 cup vinegar   ½ cup seedless raisins
1 cup brown sugar   ½ green pepper, chopped fine
½ teaspoon salt   2 tablespoons finely chopped
1 small clove garlic, chopped fine   crystallized ginger

Cut sliced pineapple in ¾-inch pieces. Add vinegar, brown sugar, and salt, and cook slowly for 20 to 30 minutes. Stir in remaining ingredients and continue cooking over low heat until thickened. Stir occasionally, to prevent scorching. Serve with Baked Ham (page 112), Shrimp Curry (page 156), or Chicken Curry (page 126).

SPICED PRUNES
4 cups

1 pound prunes	1 teaspoon whole allspice
4 cups water	2 peppercorns
2 lemons	1½ cups sugar
4 blades mace	½ cup vinegar
2 teaspoons whole cloves	

Wash prunes thoroughly and soak in water 3 hours or until plump; do not drain. Extract juice of lemons and chop peel. Tie spices in cloth bag and add with lemon peel to prunes. Simmer for 1 hour. Remove spice bag and add lemon juice, sugar, and vinegar. Boil 5 minutes. Serve with roast pork or other roast meat. May be sealed in sterilized jars and used later.

Salads and
Salad Dressings

SALADS

Apple
Avocado and Grapefruit
Cabbage
Cantaloupe Ring with Melon
    Balls
Chicken
Chinese
Cranberry-Orange
Ensalada Estilo Sombrero
Filipino Stuffed Tomato
Frozen Fruit
Fruit Salad
Grapefruit Jellied
Guacamole
Hot Potato
Italian
Julienne Vegetable and
    Cheese Salad Bowl
Lakewood
Lime Gelatin
Lime Ring Mold
Mexican Cabbage
Mexican Tomato and Onion
Mexican Vegetable
Molded Grapefruit-Almond
Nut (India)
Pannonia Salata
Potato
Red Plum
Russian Coleslaw

Shrimp
Spanish Chicken
Spring
Summer
Supper
Swedish Herring
Tomato Aspic with Avocado
    and Celery
Tomato, Cucumber, and Egg
    on Curly Endive
Tomato, Onion, and
    Cucumber (India)
Tomatoes Stuffed with
    Potato Salad
Tossed Green

SUGGESTIONS FOR FRUIT SALAD PLATES

Banana
Melon Ball
Melon Ring
Winter

SUGGESTIONS FOR SALAD COMBINATIONS

Chicken
Fish
Fruit
Frozen Fruit
Jellied Fruit
Molded Vegetable
Vegetable

SALAD DRESSINGS

Chiffonade
Cooked
Currant Jelly
Egg and Green Pepper

FRENCH
French Variations
Cottage Cheese
Garlic
Lemon
Piquant

Fruit
Green Goddess
Honey

Italian
Lime-Honey

MAYONNAISE
Piquant
Variations
Pennsylvania Dutch Hot Bacon
Poppy-Seed
Roquefort
Russian
Russian Sour Cream
Thousand Island
Thousand Island French

Aᴍᴇᴀʟ needs a salad. It needs the crisp, cool texture of chilled salad greens, the bright color of fresh fruits and vegetables, the piquant flavor of a well-seasoned dressing.

Salad can be simple — as easy-to-make as a tray of crunchy relishes or mixed greens tossed with oil and vinegar. Or it can be a real showpiece such as a fancy fruit plate.

The dressing for your salad must be just right. Its job is to point up the flavor of the fruits or vegetables, to enhance them, not to overpower them. Be a miser with it. Nothing can ruin a salad more quickly than too much dressing. For a tossed salad use just enough to coat each leaf and leave it sparkling and shiny, and with no excess dressing left in the bowl.

Salads

APPLE SALAD
6 servings

4 red tart apples, not pared
¼ cup lemon juice
¼ cup mayonnaise
¼ cup Fruit Salad Dressing
  (page 250)

2 cups chopped celery
½ cup chopped pecans
6 marshmallows, cubed

Cube apples, cover with lemon juice to prevent turning dark. Mix mayonnaise and Fruit Salad Dressing together. Drain apples; combine ingredients with dressing. Serve on lettuce leaf.

AVOCADO AND GRAPEFRUIT SALAD
6 servings

2 large grapefruit
2 ripe avocados
1 pomegranate

1 head lettuce
French Dressing (page 249)

Peel and section grapefruit. Drain and chill thoroughly. Peel avocados and cut into 12 slices each. Peel pomegranate and remove seeds. Arrange 4 sections of grapefruit and 3 or 4 slices of avocado in overlapping sections on bed of shredded lettuce in lettuce cup. Garnish with pomegranate seeds. Serve French Dressing made with lemon juice with this salad.

This makes an attractive Christmas salad with its contrast of green avocado and shiny red pomegranate seeds.

CABBAGE SALAD
6 to 8 servings

1 small head cabbage, cut fine
1 pimento, chopped
1 green pepper, chopped

½ teaspoon salt
Dash of pepper
Cooked Salad Dressing (page 248)

Combine ingredients, chill thoroughly. Moisten with dressing. Serve on lettuce leaf.

CANTALOUPE RING WITH MELON BALLS
8 to 10 servings

3 large cantaloupe
½ honeydew melon
¼ watermelon
1 tablespoon sugar
½ cup lemon juice

½ cup pineapple juice
¾ pound bing cherries
Lettuce
Sprigs of mint
Lemon French Dressing (page 250)

With a French ball cutter, make balls from one cantaloupe, the honeydew, and watermelon. Add sugar to lemon juice and pineapple juice and pour over melon balls. Chill thoroughly. Drain before serving. Cut two of the cantaloupe into ½-inch slices. Peel and chill. When arranging salad, place lettuce on plate, put melon slice on lettuce; cut in two and spread apart slightly. Fill center with melon balls; garnish plate with a few bing cherries with stems left on, and a sprig of mint. Serve Lemon French Dressing with this salad.

CHICKEN SALAD
6 servings

2 cups diced cooked chicken
½ cup diced celery
½ cup chopped toasted almonds
½ cup mayonnaise

2 tablespoons cream
½ teaspoon salt
Dash of pepper
1 tablespoon lemon juice

Combine ingredients. Let stand an hour or two before serving. Serve on crisp lettuce leaf garnished with mayonnaise and a few chopped almonds.

This chicken salad may be used for the center of the Lime Ring Mold (page 232).

CHINESE SALAD
4 to 6 servings

2 cups cooked rice
1½ tablespoons minced onion
1 cup French Dressing (page 249)
1 3¾-ounce can sardines, drained
¼ cup vinegar
1 head lettuce

2 hard-cooked eggs
3 gherkins, chopped
2 tablespoons chili sauce
1 tablespoon capers
1 teaspoon minced parsley

Combine rice, onion, and ½ cup of the French Dressing; chill. Marinate sardines in vinegar 10 minutes. Put 3 to 4 tablespoons rice in mound on each lettuce leaf, arrange sardines alternately over salad; dice egg yolks and whites separately and sprinkle over salad. Garnish with gherkins and serve with dressing made by combining remaining French Dressing with chili sauce, capers, and parsley.

CRANBERRY-ORANGE SALAD
10 to 12 servings

1 package cherry-flavored gelatin	1 orange, ground fine
1 cup hot water	1 cup drained crushed pineapple
¾ cup sugar	1 cup chopped celery
1 tablespoon lemon juice	½ cup chopped pecans
1 cup pineapple juice	Lettuce
1 cup ground raw cranberries	½ cup mayonnaise

Dissolve gelatin in hot water; add sugar, lemon juice, and pineapple juice. Stir to dissolve. Chill until partially set, add remaining ingredients. Pour into individual molds. Unmold on lettuce leaf. Garnish with mayonnaise.

ENSALADA ESTILO SOMBRERO
Mexican Sombrero Salad
6 servings

2½ cups cottage cheese	6 slices pineapple, well drained
1 teaspoon salt	Green pepper and pimento strips
½ teaspoon chili powder	Mayonnaise
½ cup pineapple juice	Lettuce

Season cottage cheese with salt, chili powder, and enough pineapple juice to moisten. Mold into cones about 2 inches in diameter; place cone on each slice of pineapple; put dent in cone to look like hat. At base arrange strips of green pepper for hat band and pimento for the bow. Serve on crisp lettuce leaf with mayonnaise to which whipped cream has been added.

FILIPINO STUFFED TOMATO SALAD
6 servings

6 medium tomatoes
½ teaspoon salt
1 cup crushed pineapple
⅓ cup chopped peanuts

⅓ cup finely diced celery
2 tablespoons French dressing
6 lettuce leaves

Scald tomatoes and peel. Cut slice from top and remove some of pulp. Sprinkle the tomato with salt, drain, and chill thoroughly. Combine pineapple, peanuts, diced tomato pulp, celery, and French dressing; place in cavity of the tomatoes. Arrange on lettuce leaves and serve cold.

FROZEN FRUIT SALAD
10 to 12 servings

1 cup diced pineapple
½ cup diced peaches
½ cup white cherries, cut in halves
¼ cup maraschino cherries, cut in quarters
½ cup diced pears
½ cup pecans, coarsely chopped
1 teaspoon chopped crystallized ginger (if desired)
12 marshmallows, cut in fourths

¼ cup orange juice
1 tablespoon lemon juice
½ cup mayonnaise
½ cup Fruit Salad Dressing (page 250)
¼ cup confectioners' sugar
¼ teaspoon grated lemon peel
1 cup heavy cream
Lettuce

Have fruit well drained. Combine fruit, nuts, ginger, and marshmallows. Combine juices, mayonnaise, salad dressing, sugar, and lemon peel. Whip cream until stiff. Fold into salad dressing and then fold this into fruit mixture. Put in molds or paper cartons and freeze. Unmold, cut into slices, and serve on lettuce leaf. Garnish with Fruit Salad Dressing to which some whipped cream has been added (about a teaspoonful on each salad). Top with mint leaf and half a maraschino cherry for color.

FRUIT SALAD
6 servings

4 red apples, diced
¼ cup lemon juice
½ pound white grapes, seeded and cut in half, or 4 slices pineapple, diced

4 bananas, sliced
6 tablespoons Fruit Salad Dressing (page 250)
½ cup heavy cream
⅓ cup pecans

Add lemon juice to apples and let stand while preparing other fruit. Drain apples; combine with grapes and bananas. Whip cream; fold in Fruit Salad Dressing. Serve on crisp lettuce leaf and sprinkle a few pecans on each salad.

NOTE: This fruit salad should not be prepared too far in advance because both apples and bananas are apt to discolor.

GRAPEFRUIT JELLIED SALAD
6 to 8 servings

1 tablespoon (1 envelope)
   unflavored gelatin
½ cup cold water
1 cup boiling water
6 tablespoons sugar
½ teaspoon salt

1½ cups grapefruit juice
2 tablespoons lemon juice
2 pimentos
1 cup grapefruit sections
Lettuce
Mayonnaise

Soften gelatin in cold water a few minutes. Add boiling water, stir until dissolved. Add sugar and salt and stir well. Add grapefruit juice and lemon juice. Cut pimento into thin strips and arrange alternately with sections of grapefruit in bottom of mold. Pour in enough of the gelatin mixture to cover. Chill quickly. Add another layer of fruit and pimento and remainder of gelatin. Chill; when set, turn out on lettuce leaf. Garnish with mayonnaise and pimento strip.

GUACAMOLE
Peppery Avocado Spread
About 1 cup

1 ripe avocado, well mashed
1 green Mexican pepper or
   1 pimento, chopped
1 tablespoon finely chopped onion

1 clove garlic, mashed
1 large peeled tomato, chopped fine
Salt and pepper
¼ cup mayonnaise

Combine ingredients. Mix well. Serve on lettuce leaf. This is a highly flavored salad.

For a party spread, use this unusual paste on thin crackers or potato chips.

HOT POTATO SALAD
6 to 8 servings

6 medium potatoes
¼ cup finely minced onion
2 tablespoons finely chopped green
    pepper
3 hard-cooked eggs, chopped

4 slices bacon, diced
¼ cup vinegar
1 teaspoon salt
⅛ teaspoon white pepper

Cook potatoes with skins on; drain and peel. Break apart carefully with fork; add onion, green pepper, and diced eggs. Fry bacon until crisp but not too brown. Add vinegar and seasonings to hot bacon fat; heat thoroughly and pour over potatoes. Serve hot garnished with paprika.

ITALIAN SALAD
4 servings

1 head lettuce
4 tablespoons salad oil
2 tablespoons red wine vinegar

1 teaspoon prepared mustard
3 anchovy fillets, mashed

Lettuce should be very crisp. Break into chunks; place in salad bowl. Mix remaining ingredients for dressing. Just before serving, dress lettuce with this anchovy salad dressing. Do not have excess dressing in bowl.

This salad is an excellent companion to Italian Spaghetti (page 94).

JULIENNE VEGETABLE AND CHEESE SALAD BOWL
8 to 10 servings

2 heads crisp lettuce
1 cup fresh spinach
1 raw carrot, cut in julienne strips
1 piece celery, cut in julienne strips
½ cup thinly sliced red radishes
¼ cup thinly sliced green onions

4 ounces sharp Cheddar cheese, cut
    in julienne strips
Salt
Coarse black pepper
Garlic French Dressing (page 249)

Remove outside leaves of lettuce and line salad bowl. Break remainder of lettuce into pieces the size of a walnut. Place in bowl. Tear spinach apart, removing stem. Put spinach in bowl and add remainder of vegetables and, lastly, the cheese. Sprinkle lightly with salt and a very little coarse black pepper. At serving time toss lightly with just enough Garlic French

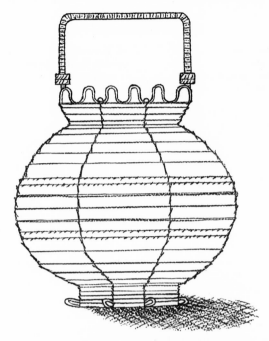

This artistic type of wire basket is used in France and neighboring countries for rinsing and particularly for drying or removing excess water from lettuce, endive, and other salad materials. After washing, the leaves are put into the basket, rinsed in cold water, and the whole is whirled to remove extra water. The maid usually steps into the courtyard to do this. Afterwards the basket may be hung up until the salad greens are needed.

Dressing to coat vegetables. There should be no excess dressing in bowl.

Sliced breast of chicken, turkey, or veal, cut in julienne strips, may be used instead of the cheese.

LAKEWOOD SALAD
6 to 8 servings

4 large grapefruit
1 head lettuce
2 cups white grapes, seeded
½ cup pecans

½ pimento, cut in thin strips
½ cup Roquefort Salad Dressing
(page 253)

Peel grapefruit, and section. Arrange 4 or 5 overlapping sections in cup of lettuce. Garnish with grapes, pecans, and a strip of pimento. Chill thoroughly and serve with Roquefort Salad Dressing.

LIME GELATIN SALAD
8 to 10 servings

1 package lime-flavored gelatin
1¾ cups boiling water or pineapple
juice
3 tablespoons lemon juice
½ cup heavy cream
½ cup cottage cheese

2 tablespoons mayonnaise
½ cup well-drained crushed
pineapple
½ cup slivered blanched almonds
½ teaspoon salt

Dissolve flavored gelatin in boiling water or fruit juice. Add lemon juice. Whip cream. When the gelatin is nearly set, whip until light; then fold in the whipped cream and the remaining ingredients. Pour into individual molds and let stand until set.

LIME RING MOLD SALAD
6 servings

1 package lime-flavored gelatin
1 cup hot water
1 cup fruit juice

1 3-ounce package cream cheese
1 8-ounce can spiced white grapes
½ cup pecans

Add hot water to lime gelatin and stir until dissolved; add fruit juice. Let stand until partially set and pour into individual ring molds. Cut cream cheese into small cubes. Drain white grapes. Just before gelatin sets, place a few grapes, cubes of cream cheese, and pecans in each ring mold. The consistency of the gelatin should be stiff enough to hold the fruit, cheese, and pecans in place. Let stand until set. When ready to serve, turn out on crisp lettuce leaf or curly endive and fill center with Chicken Salad (page 226).

This colorful ring mold topped with chicken salad was the suggestion of Evelyn Irving, graduate student in Education, for our May Day Tea.

from the fruits in season . . .

Melon Ring Salad, page 241.

on a sultry day . . .

Banana Salad, page 241.

MEXICAN CABBAGE SALAD
6 servings

2 cups cabbage, shredded fine	1 medium onion, finely diced
¼ cup diced green pepper	¼ cup mayonnaise
¼ cup diced pimento	¼ cup chili sauce
½ cup stuffed olives, chopped	Lettuce

Combine cabbage, pepper, pimento, olives, and onion. Chill. Mix together mayonnaise and chili sauce. Add to other ingredients. Mix lightly. Serve in lettuce cups; garnish with a strip of pimento.

MEXICAN TOMATO AND ONION SALAD
6 servings

1 head lettuce	3 tablespoons oil
1 pound ripe tomatoes, peeled and sliced	1 tablespoon vinegar
3 small onions, sliced thin	Salt and pepper

Arrange on lettuce leaves in bowl a slice of tomato, then a thin slice of onion, until bowl is filled. Mix oil, vinegar, salt and pepper to taste, and pour over salad. Place in refrigerator until ready to serve.

MEXICAN VEGETABLE SALAD
6 to 8 servings

¼ cup salad or olive oil	2 tablespoons minced green pepper
1 clove garlic, crushed	1 teaspoon salt
1 cup soft bread cubes	1 teaspoon chili powder
2 tablespoons vinegar	1 head lettuce
½ cup diced celery	Garnish with:
1 pimento, cut in strips	Paprika
1 cup diced cooked potatoes	Pimento strips
½ cup diced onion	Sliced stuffed olives
½ cup grated carrot	

Heat 1 tablespoon of the oil in skillet; sauté garlic and bread cubes until bread is golden in color. Remove garlic. Add remainder of salad oil to vinegar. Combine other ingredients and add toasted bread cubes, oil and vinegar. Toss lightly together. For salad bowl, line bowl with lettuce leaves and heap salad in bowl. Garnish with paprika, strips of pimento, and sliced stuffed olives. May be served on individual salad plates and garnished in same manner.

MOLDED GRAPEFRUIT-ALMOND SALAD
6 servings

1 package lemon-flavored gelatin
1 cup hot water
1 cup fruit juice
2 medium grapefruit

⅓ cup whole blanched almonds
¼ cup sliced stuffed olives
Mayonnaise

Add hot water to gelatin; stir until dissolved and add fruit juice. Section grapefruit and drain. When gelatin is just beginning to set add grapefruit, almonds, and olives. Pour into individual salad molds. Let stand in refrigerator until set. Unmold onto crisp lettuce leaf. Garnish with mayonnaise to which cream has been added.

NUT SALAD (INDIA)
6 servings

4 large red apples
½ cup lemon juice
½ cup chopped nuts
½ cup chopped dates
½ cup shredded coconut

½ cup raisins
¼ cup melted butter
1 head curly endive
½ cup mayonnaise

Quarter 2 of the apples and remove core. Dice apples into ½-inch cubes. Pour ½ of the lemon juice over diced apples. Cut three ½-inch slices from each of the remaining apples. Cover with rest of lemon juice. Combine nuts, dates, coconut, raisins, and melted butter. Arrange endive on salad plate. Put slice of apple on each plate. Put mound of mixed fruit on apple slice. Garnish with mayonnaise and a sprinkle of paprika.

PANNONIA SALATA
Hungarian Fruit Salad
6 servings

3 bananas
1 cup diced fresh or canned pineapple
3 oranges, sectioned
1 apple, diced

½ cup French Dressing (page 249)
6 red maraschino cherries, cut in quarters
6 green minted maraschino cherries, cut in quarters

Cut bananas in two lengthwise. Save banana skins to serve salad in. Dice bananas into ½-inch cubes. Toss diced bananas, diced pineapple, orange sections, and diced apple together lightly. Add French dressing and let stand 15 to 20 minutes. Drain fruit. Heap fruit in banana skins. Arrange salad on crisp lettuce leaf or curly endive. Garnish each salad with a few sections of red and green cherries.

This fruit salad is used in our Hungarian Dinner (page 456). The colorful fruit in its banana skin boat is an effective way of serving the salad.

POTATO SALAD
6 servings

4 medium potatoes, cooked in jackets	¼ cup chopped onion
½ cup French dressing	3 hard-cooked eggs, diced
1 teaspoon salt	1 tablespoon chopped parsley
Dash of white pepper	½ cup mayonnaise
¾ cup chopped celery	1 teaspoon prepared mustard

Peel cooked potatoes and, while still warm, break apart carefully with fork. Pour French dressing over potatoes; add salt and pepper and let stand for several hours. Combine with other ingredients. Add more salt and pepper, if necessary. Add mayonnaise and mustard and blend ingredients. Serve on crisp lettuce leaf. Garnish with parsley and sprinkle with paprika.

RED PLUM SALAD
4 servings

1 No. 2½ can red plums	Orange juice
1 3-ounce package cream cheese	2 oranges, sectioned
¼ cup chopped pecans	6 lettuce cups
1 teaspoon chopped candied ginger	Mayonnaise

Drain plums; remove pits. Mix cream cheese, chopped pecans, chopped ginger, and enough orange juice to moisten; fill the plums. Arrange three stuffed plums in each lettuce cup with sections of orange. Garnish with mayonnaise to which whipped cream has been added.

RUSSIAN COLESLAW
6 servings

2½ cups finely shredded cabbage
1 teaspoon salt
1 medium apple
1 small carrot
1 teaspoon minced onion

1 teaspoon parsley
2 tablespoons mayonnaise
1 teaspoon sugar
½ cup sour cream

Sprinkle shredded cabbage lightly with salt and let stand 15 minutes. Chop unpared apple. Grate the carrot. Mix all ingredients together; let stand 30 minutes to chill before serving.

SHRIMP SALAD
4 servings

4 lettuce cups
8 thin slices cucumber, not pared
16 small or 8 large cooked shrimp
 (½ 7-ounce can)

8 slices (2 whole) tomato
2 slices American cheese
French dressing

Arrange lettuce cups on chilled salad plates. Alternate cucumber slice, shrimp, and tomato slice until there are two of each on each plate. Slice cheese in julienne strips. Arrange 5 or 6 strips beside each salad. Serve 1 teaspoon French dressing on each salad.

SPANISH CHICKEN SALAD
4 servings

4 lettuce cups
1 cup (8-ounce can) chicken
1 cup chopped celery
½ cup (2 medium) grated carrots
12 stuffed olives, sliced
¼ cup blanched, toasted, chopped
 almonds

1 tablespoon finely grated onion
2 slices diced pineapple
2 chopped hard-cooked eggs
Dash of salt
2 tablespoons French dressing
2 tablespoons mayonnaise

Dice chicken; combine with remaining ingredients. Refrigerate for 1 hour. Serve in lettuce cups.

SPRING SALAD
6 to 8 servings

1 package lemon-flavored gelatin	4 slices pineapple
1½ cups boiling water or pineapple juice	¼ cup lemon juice
	½ cup blanched almonds
1 small cucumber	Lettuce
3 pieces celery	Mayonnaise

Dissolve lemon gelatin in boiling water or pineapple juice. Cool. Dice cucumber, celery, and pineapple in ⅓-inch cubes. Marinate with the lemon juice. Blanch and chop almonds coarsely. When gelatin has partially set, add fruit, vegetables, and almonds. Pour into individual molds to chill. To unmold dip entire mold quickly into very hot water. Serve on crisp lettuce leaf. Garnish with mayonnaise.

Cucumbers, green peppers, celery, and carrots, or any desired combination, may be used.

SUMMER SALAD
Cucumber Sherbet in Tomato Cups
6 servings

6 medium tomatoes	Onion juice
½ teaspoon salt	Salt
2 large cucumbers	Dash of white pepper
4 tablespoons vinegar	

Cut slice from top of tomato and scoop out inside. Drain well. Salt inside of tomato lightly. Chill thoroughly. Pare cucumbers, cut lengthwise, and scrape out the seeds. Grate the cucumbers (should have about 2 cups of the grated pulp and juice), add vinegar, a dash of onion juice, salt and pepper to taste. Freeze to a mush in a refrigerator tray. Don't let sherbet get too hard or it will be icy. When ready to serve, fill the tomatoes with the cucumber sherbet. Serve on a lettuce leaf.

Refreshing on a hot day!

SUPPER SALAD
4 servings

1 cup chopped corned beef
1 cup grated carrots
1 cup finely shredded cabbage
¼ cup chopped sweet pickle
¼ cup chopped cucumber

2 tablespoons Garlic French
    Dressing (page 249)
3 tablespoons mayonnaise
Paprika
Parsley

Mix corned beef, carrots, cabbage, pickle, and cucumber. Marinate in Garlic French Dressing. Add mayonnaise and heap salad in lettuce cups. Sprinkle with paprika and garnish with parsley.

Other chopped cooked meat may be used instead of the corned beef, if desired.

SWEDISH HERRING SALAD
6 to 8 servings

1 cup diced cooked herring
1 cup diced cold boiled potatoes
½ cup diced cooked beets
½ cup diced apples, not pared
½ cup diced sweet pickles

⅓ cup vinegar
¼ teaspoon salt
Dash of white pepper
1 teaspoon sugar
1 teaspoon prepared mustard

Mix herring, potatoes, beets, apples, and sweet pickles together lightly. Combine vinegar, salt, white pepper, sugar, and prepared mustard, and pour over salad.

Salad Garnish:

½ cup finely chopped cooked beets
3 hard-cooked eggs, yolks and
    whites chopped separately

¼ cup capers
¼ cup chopped parsley

Place salad pyramid-shape on platter and garnish with chopped beets, yolks and whites of eggs, capers, and parsley. Serve salad with a bowl of Mayonnaise (page 251), if desired.

This is the type of herring salad to serve at the Smörgåsbord (page 460).

TOMATO ASPIC SALAD WITH AVOCADO AND CELERY
6 to 8 servings

2 tablespoons (2 envelopes) unflavored gelatin	1 tablespoon lemon juice
½ cup cold water	4 whole cloves
2 cups tomato juice	2 teaspoons sugar
1 medium onion, sliced	½ teaspoon salt
3 sprigs parsley	½ cup diced ripe avocado
2 tablespoons cider vinegar	½ cup diced celery
	Mayonnaise

Soften gelatin in cold water. Combine remaining ingredients except avocado and diced celery. Simmer slowly for about 15 minutes and then strain. Add gelatin to hot juice and stir. Let chill until partially set and add avocado and celery. Pour into individual molds or one large ring mold and chill until firm. Use curly endive or lettuce cup on salad plate. Unmold salad. Serve with mayonnaise.

Crab meat or shrimp may be used instead of the avocado.

TOMATO, CUCUMBER, AND EGG SALAD
ON CURLY ENDIVE
6 servings

1 head curly endive	3 hard-cooked eggs
3 medium tomatoes	French Dressing (page 249)
1 cucumber	

Wash curly endive and pull apart. Wrap in damp cloth; put in refrigerator and let remain until crisp. Peel tomatoes and cut into ¼-inch slices. Pare cucumber and cut into thin slices. Peel hard-cooked eggs and slice. For individual servings, place 2 or 3 pieces of curly endive on plate; arrange 2 slices of tomato and 2 thin slices of cucumber on endive. Garnish with 2 or 3 slices of hard-cooked egg. Just before serving, put a teaspoon of French dressing over salad.

For the English High Tea (page 455), add a piece of Pork Pie (page 106) and a Sausage Roll (page 112) to each plate. Garnish plate with parsley.

TOMATO, ONION, AND CUCUMBER SALAD (INDIA)
6 to 8 servings

1 medium onion
2 medium tomatoes
1 small cucumber
1 cup sour cream

2 teaspoons vinegar
2 teaspoons salt
1 teaspoon sugar

Slice onion into fine thin slices; soak in water for 10 minutes and drain well. Dice tomatoes. Pare cucumber, cut thin slices, then cut each slice in half. To sour cream add vinegar, salt, and sugar. Mix in the vegetables and set aside for 1 hour. Serve a small amount in sauce dishes as salad.

TOMATOES STUFFED WITH POTATO SALAD
4 servings

2 medium potatoes
½ cup chopped celery
¼ cup finely chopped parsley
¼ cup French dressing
2 chopped hard-cooked eggs
1 teaspoon salt

2 tablespoons mayonnaise
2 tablespoons deviled ham
1 anchovy fillet
4 tomatoes
4 lettuce cups

Cook potatoes in jackets until easily pierced with a fork. Drain, peel, and cut in cubes while hot. Add celery, parsley, and French dressing. Toss lightly and let stand 10 minutes to marinate. Add eggs and salt. Combine mayonnaise, deviled ham, and anchovy fillet. Mix with other ingredients just enough to blend in mayonnaise. Chill for at least one hour. To serve, cut the tops from the tomatoes about ¼ inch down, scoop out tomatoes and invert for about 5 minutes. Fill each tomato with potato salad and serve immediately on lettuce leaf.

TOSSED GREEN SALAD
6 servings

1 head crisp lettuce
1 head curly endive
1 cup fresh spinach
1 cucumber, sliced thin

2 green onions, chopped
Dash of salt
French Dressing (page 249)

Remove six leaves of lettuce for garnishing plates. Break remainder of lettuce into chunks. Pull apart curly endive. Remove stems from spinach leaves and tear into pieces. Toss lettuce, endive, spinach, cucumber, and chopped onions together. Sprinkle with salt. Add just enough French dressing to moisten.

SUGGESTIONS FOR FRUIT SALAD PLATES

Banana Salad
Arrange lettuce leaf on luncheon plate. Peel and split banana lengthwise. Garnish with strawberry halves. Add a mound of cottage cheese, fresh pineapple wedges, and orange slices sprinkled with coconut. Place ripe olives in center. Serve with Fruit Salad Dressing (p. 250).

Melon Ball Salad
Arrange two lettuce cups on luncheon plate. Place a mound of cottage cheese in one; surround with orange slices and orange sections. Place melon balls in the other lettuce cup and a sprig of water cress. Put two finger sandwiches on either side of melon balls. Garnish plate with balls of cream cheese pressed between walnut halves. Serve with Lemon French Dressing (page 250).

Melon Ring Salad
Arrange lettuce on luncheon plate. Cut 1-inch-thick ring of chilled cantaloupe and place on plate. Fill center with strawberries or fruit in season. Arrange slices of orange around melon ring. Serve chilled with a sweet French dressing, made by combining ¼ cup each of salad oil, lemon juice, and honey or red jelly, with salt to taste.

Winter Salad
Place a crisp lettuce cup at back of salad plate. Fill this with a banana, cut diagonally into sixths or eighths. On one side of plate, arrange a row of slices of unpared, red-skinned apple. Top with 3 dates, 2 rows of orange slices in center of plate and 3 walnut halves to complete the salad. To prevent discoloration, dip banana and apple in the juice saved in slicing oranges. Serve with Lemon French Dressing (page 250).

SUGGESTIONS FOR SALAD COMBINATIONS

Chicken Salads

Chicken with:
  Browned pecans, pimento, celery
  Celery
  Celery, Brazil nuts
  Celery, ham
  Cucumber, artichoke hearts, truffles
  Peas, celery
  Pimento, celery
  Veal, celery
  Veal, radishes, olives, hard-cooked eggs

Fish Salads

Crab meat with:
  Celery
  Celery, tomatoes
  Cucumber
  Grapefruit
  Olives, celery
  Orange, grapefruit
  Shrimp, celery

Lobster with:
  Celery
  Celery, capers
  Olives, celery
  Shrimp, hard-cooked eggs
Salmon, hard-cooked eggs, parsley, olives
Sardines, potatoes, hard-cooked eggs, garlic
Shrimp, celery, tomato
Tuna with:
  Celery
  Celery, green peppers

Fruit Salads

Apple with:
Banana, pineapple
Celery, Brazil nuts
Celery, nuts
Celery, pimento
Celery, pineapple, white grapes
Cheese, pimento
Pear, peaches, maraschino cherries
Pineapple, cucumber, mayonnaise
Pineapple, pistachio nuts, cream dressing
Red grapes, bananas, pineapple
Apricot, pineapple, pear
Bananas, fresh mint leaves, cheese, French dressing
Cherries with:
Half peach, maraschino cherries
Half pear, mayonnaise
Pecan, cream cheese
Pineapple
Dates stuffed with cream cheese
Figs (canned) stuffed with cream cheese mixed with pecans
Grapefruit with:
Apricot, French dressing
Artichoke hearts, French dressing
French dressing
Green pepper, celery, walnuts
Oranges, white grapes, pecan meats, Blue cheese, French
dressing
Tomato, French dressing
Orange with:
Grapefruit sections, French dressing
Pineapple
Pear with:
Cheese, mayonnaise
Cream cheese, nuts
Dates and pecans
White grapes, maraschino cherries

Pineapple with:
  Celery, orange, nuts
  Cream cheese, currant jelly
  Grapefruit, celery, walnuts
  Neufchâtel cheese, maraschino cherries
Prunes stuffed with:
  Pecans, sprinkled with lemon juice
  Cheese, nuts

Frozen Fruit Salads

Cream cheese, lemon juice, walnuts, pimento, green pepper,
  celery, whipped cream
Oranges, peaches, cherries, mayonnaise, whipped cream
Peaches, bananas, maraschino cherries, whipped cream
Pineapple, apricots, bananas, maraschino cherries, mayonnaise,
  whipped cream

Jellied Fruit Salads

Apple, pineapple, celery, chopped olives
Cranberry jelly, celery, nuts
Diced pineapple, diced cucumber
Pear, lemon juice, candied ginger, ginger ale
Pineapple, grapefruit, almonds, ginger

Molded Vegetable Salads

Cabbage, green peppers, pimento, mayonnaise
Cucumbers, cooked carrots, potatoes, mayonnaise
Cucumbers, tomatoes, onion juice, truffles
Tomato aspic, mayonnaise

Vegetable Salads

Artichoke hearts, tomatoes, French beans, French dressing
Asparagus with:
  A band of finely chopped hard-cooked egg, olives, green
    pepper, pimento
  Pimento and French dressing
Avocado, grapefruit, French dressing
Beets, string beans, onions, French dressing

Cabbage with:
    Celery, pimento, green peppers
    Celery, pimento, onion in tomato jelly
    Cheese, cucumber, pickles, pimento, French dressing
Carrots (raw) with:
    Green peas, string beans, French dressing
    Raisins, French dressing
Cauliflower with:
    Carrots, French beans, truffles
    Carrots, peas, celery, tomato, French dressing
    Chiffonade dressing
Celery with:
    Cabbage, green peppers
    Hard-cooked eggs, pimento or green peppers
    Peas, beets, mayonnaise
    Peas, nuts

Cucumber with:
  Apple, pineapple
  Grapefruit, French dressing
  Pineapple
  Sweetbreads, French dressing
  Tartare sauce
  Tomato
  Water cress, French dressing
Potatoes with:
  Celery, green peppers, pimento
  Celery, ham, mushrooms, fine herbs
  Celery, hard-cooked eggs, red peppers, pickles
  French beans, tomatoes, capers, olives
  Hard-cooked egg, pickle, celery, parsley, chives
  Hard-cooked egg, red peppers, chives
  Pickled red cabbage, celery, mayonnaise
Tomato with:
  Artichoke hearts, asparagus tips
  Blue cheese, French dressing
  Cucumber, green peppers
  Grapefruit, French dressing
  Grapefruit, green peppers, romaine
  Green peppers, onion, French dressing
Tomatoes stuffed with:
  Asparagus, tomato, green pepper, red pepper
  Chicken, celery, stuffed olives
  Crab meat, celery
  Cream cheese, olives, pimentos
  Diced cucumbers, green peppers
  Diced pineapple, celery
  Peas, celery, chicken
  Pineapple, apple, celery
  Shrimp, celery

Salad Dressings

CHIFFONADE DRESSING
About 1½ cups

1 cup French Dressing (page 249)
2 teaspoons finely chopped parsley
2 teaspoons finely chopped pimento
1 teaspoon chopped capers

2 hard-cooked eggs, yolks and whites chopped separately
¼ teaspoon salt
Dash of cayenne pepper

Just before serving, combine French Dressing with parsley, pimento, capers, and finely chopped hard-cooked egg yolks and whites. Shake well before using.

COOKED SALAD DRESSING
About 2 cups

½ cup flour
3 tablespoons sugar
2 teaspoons dry mustard
¾ teaspoon salt
⅛ teaspoon paprika

1⅓ cups water
2 eggs or 4 egg yolks
½ cup vinegar
2 tablespoons butter

Add seasonings to flour; mix well. Add water to the dry ingredients gradually to prevent lumping. Mix until smooth. Cook in double boiler until thick and there is no starchy taste, about 30 minutes. Beat eggs or egg yolks. Add part of the cooked mixture to beaten eggs; combine both mixtures and cook 3 minutes longer. Remove from heat and add vinegar and butter. Stir into salad dressing and beat until smooth. This is a thick salad dressing and may be combined with mayonnaise, whipped cream, or sour cream.

CURRANT JELLY SALAD DRESSING
About 1½ cups

¼ cup currant jelly
1 cup French Dressing (below)

¼ cup heavy cream
½ teaspoon grated lemon peel

Beat jelly with fork until smooth before adding the other ingredients. Mix, chill, and shake thoroughly. Serve on fruit salad.

EGG AND GREEN PEPPER SALAD DRESSING
About 1½ cups

1 cup Mayonnaise (page 251)
2 hard-cooked eggs, finely chopped
1 teaspoon onion juice

1 tablespoon finely chopped
green pepper

Combine and serve on hearts of lettuce.

FRENCH DRESSING
1½ cups

1 cup olive oil or salad oil	Dash of pepper
½ cup lemon juice or vinegar	Dash of cayenne pepper
½ teaspoon salt	1 teaspoon paprika

Combine and beat or shake thoroughly before using. Add 1 teaspoon sugar if desired. Serve with hearts of lettuce or tossed salad.

FRENCH DRESSING VARIATIONS

French Dressing combined with:

> Chili sauce
> Horse-radish
> Roquefort or Blue cheese
> Worcestershire sauce
> Finely chopped hard-cooked eggs, olives, parsley, pimento, onion
> Finely chopped red and green peppers, onion juice

COTTAGE CHEESE FRENCH DRESSING
About 3 cups

1¼ cups creamed cottage cheese	⅓ cup mild vinegar
¼ cup sugar	1 tablespoon water
1 teaspoon salt	2 teaspoons Worcestershire sauce
2 teaspoons dry mustard	1 teaspoon grated onion
1 teaspoon paprika	1 clove garlic, mashed
¾ cup salad oil	Dash of Tabasco sauce
¼ cup catsup	

Put cottage cheese in mixing bowl and beat until creamy. Blend dry ingredients into cottage cheese. Add other ingredients and mix until well blended. Serve on hearts of lettuce or on any tossed green salad.

This recipe came from Helen Penner, a former member of our staff, who first introduced it at our staff Christmas party. We have unanimously adopted it.

GARLIC FRENCH DRESSING

Use recipe for French Dressing (above). Warm oil slightly. Mash 1 clove of garlic with the salt and add to warm oil. Let stand several hours. Add remaining ingredients. Shake well. Strain before using.

LEMON FRENCH DRESSING
About 1 cup

½ cup lemon juice
½ cup salad oil
½ teaspoon salt

1 teaspoon paprika
2 tablespoons honey

Combine ingredients and shake well. Use as dressing for fruit salad.

PIQUANT FRENCH DRESSING
About 2 cups

1½ cups French Dressing
    (page 249)
2 tablespoons finely chopped green
    pepper

2 teaspoons capers
2 tablespoons finely chopped
    pickled beets
2 teaspoons finely chopped parsley

Mix and chill. Shake thoroughly before using.

FRUIT SALAD DRESSING
About 2½ cups

⅓ cup orange juice
⅓ cup pineapple juice
2 tablespoons lemon juice
2 eggs, slightly beaten

½ cup sugar
¼ teaspoon salt
1 cup heavy cream, whipped

Mix fruit juices; add to beaten eggs and add sugar and salt. Cook in double boiler for 3 to 5 minutes or until thickened. Cool, fold in whipped cream. Serve on Fruit Salad (page 228).

GREEN GODDESS SALAD DRESSING
1½ cups

3 anchovy fillets
1 tablespoon chopped capers
1 small clove garlic, finely minced
1 tablespoon chopped chives
¼ cup finely chopped parsley

1 tablespoon finely chopped onion
1 tablespoon tarragon vinegar
1 tablespoon lemon juice
1 cup stiff Mayonnaise (page 251)

Mash anchovy fillets. Combine mashed anchovy, capers, garlic, chives, parsley, and onion. Blend vinegar and lemon juice into Mayonnaise. Add other ingredients. Serve on hearts of lettuce or a tossed green salad.

HONEY DRESSING FOR FRUIT SALAD
About 2 cups

2 eggs
½ cup strained honey
2 tablespoons lemon juice

⅛ teaspoon salt
⅛ teaspoon paprika
½ cup heavy cream, whipped

Beat whites and yolks separately. Whip honey, lemon juice, salt, and paprika with yolks. Put in double boiler and stir until the mixture thickens. Chill. Fold in beaten egg white and the whipped cream. Serve on fruit salad.

ITALIAN SALAD DRESSING
About 2½ cups

1½ cups olive oil
¾ cup wine vinegar

1 tablespoon prepared mustard
4 anchovy fillets, mashed

Combine and shake well before using. Serve on green salad.

LIME-HONEY FRUIT SALAD DRESSING
1⅔ cups

⅓ cup lime juice
⅓ cup strained honey
1 cup salad oil
½ teaspoon paprika

½ teaspoon prepared mustard
½ teaspoon salt
Grated peel of 1 lime

Combine all ingredients in a bowl. Beat with rotary beater. Keep in fruit jar. Chill before serving. Serve on fruit salad.

MAYONNAISE
About 2 cups

1 teaspoon salt
¼ teaspoon paprika
Dash of cayenne pepper
1 teaspoon prepared mustard

2 egg yolks
2 tablespoons vinegar
2 cups salad oil
2 tablespoons lemon juice

Mix the dry ingredients and prepared mustard; add the egg yolks and beat well. Beat vinegar into egg yolk mixture. Add oil, very slowly at first, beating with a rotary beater, until ½ cup has been added. Add 1 tablespoon of the lemon juice and beat well. Continue to add remaining oil and lemon juice until all has been used.

MAYONNAISE PIQUANT
About 1½ cups

1 cup Mayonnaise (page 251)
2 tablespoons finely chopped green olives

2 tablespoons chopped sweet pickles
2 tablespoons chopped pimento

Combine ingredients. Serve on lettuce salad.

MAYONNAISE VARIATIONS

Mayonnaise combined with:
Capers, shallot, parsley, water cress
Chili sauce, pimento, green peppers
Chutney
Olives, pickles
Onion, chili sauce, tarragon vinegar
Pimentos, chives, chili sauce, tarragon vinegar
Roquefort or Blue cheese, Worcestershire sauce
Tomato catsup and green peppers
Whipped cream

PENNSYLVANIA DUTCH HOT BACON DRESSING
About 1 cup

6 slices bacon
¼ cup minced onion
¾ cup vinegar
¼ teaspoon salt, or to taste

Dash of pepper
½ teaspoon sugar
½ teaspoon prepared mustard
2 hard-cooked eggs, diced

Cut bacon into small pieces with scissors. Put into skillet. Cook slowly until crisp. Strain to remove bacon; add onion to bacon fat and sauté until golden in color. Add vinegar, seasonings, and prepared mustard, and bring to a boil. Cool slightly and pour over the salad. Sprinkle crisp bacon on top and diced eggs over all. Serve with lettuce or any green salad.

For added zest at any meal, serve this peppy, tart bacon dressing on your potato salad. It's especially delightful to the salad-minded family in the wintertime. The dressing is also complementary to dandelion greens, chicory, or romaine.

POPPY-SEED DRESSING
About 2 cups

½ cup sugar
1 teaspoon dry mustard
1 teaspoon salt
⅓ cup vinegar

1½ tablespoons onion juice
1 cup oil
1½ tablespoons poppy seed

Mix sugar, mustard, salt, and vinegar together. Add onion juice and mix well. Gradually add oil, beating constantly. Add poppy seed last.

ROQUEFORT SALAD DRESSING
About 2 cups

1 cup salad oil
½ cup lemon juice
1 teaspoon onion juice
1 tablespoon vinegar
¼ teaspoon dry mustard

½ teaspoon salt
2 teaspoons paprika
Dash of pepper
¼ pound Roquefort or Blue cheese

Beat all ingredients except cheese with egg beater until well blended. Crumble cheese into dressing. Store in refrigerator in covered jar until ready to use. Shake well before serving. Use on green salad or on grapefruit sections.

RUSSIAN DRESSING
About 1½ cups

1 cup Mayonnaise (page 251)
1 tablespoon lemon juice
4 tablespoons chili sauce
1 teaspoon Worcestershire sauce

½ teaspoon onion juice
¼ teaspoon salt
Dash of cayenne pepper

Fold remaining ingredients into Mayonnaise. Serve on hearts of lettuce.

RUSSIAN SOUR CREAM SALAD DRESSING
About ¾ cup

½ cup sour cream
3 tablespoons vinegar
½ teaspoon paprika

Dash of salt
1 teaspoon finely minced chives

Beat sour cream, vinegar, paprika, and salt together until thick and smooth. Add minced chives. May be served with cucumber or cabbage salad.

THOUSAND ISLAND DRESSING
About 1½ cups

1 cup Mayonnaise (page 251)
¼ cup chili sauce
2 hard-cooked eggs, chopped
2 tablespoons chopped pimento

1 teaspoon grated onion
¼ teaspoon Worcestershire sauce
1 tablespoon chopped stuffed olives

Combine ingredients. Serve on head lettuce or tomato salad.

THOUSAND ISLAND FRENCH DRESSING
About 1 cup

½ cup salad oil
3 tablespoons lemon juice
½ teaspoon salt
¼ teaspoon paprika
¼ teaspoon prepared mustard
1 teaspoon onion juice
½ teaspoon Worcestershire sauce

1 tablespoon finely chopped parsley
¼ cup finely chopped stuffed
   olives
2 tablespoons finely chopped
   pimento
1 tablespoon finely chopped green
   pepper

Mix ingredients, chill, shake thoroughly before using.

Casseroles
and Supper Dishes

CASSEROLES

CHEESE CASSEROLES

Cheese Custard
Cheese Omelet
Cheese Soufflé

EGG CASSEROLES

Curried Eggs
Eggs Mornay
Egg Timbales
Mexican Stuffed Eggs

MEAT CASSEROLES

Beef Ball
Broccoli-Beef Surprise
Broccoli-Ham
Hot Chicken Salad
Meat Casserole à la Carol
Quick Corned Beef Hash

Savory Sausage
Surprise

RICE CASSEROLES

Chicken-Vegetable
Dixie
Jambalayah
Mexican Rice
Rice Pilaf

SEA FOOD CASSEROLES

Clam Soufflé
Crab Meat
Nippy Salmon
Salmon
Shrimp Delight
Tuna Corn Bread
    Upside-Down

SUPPER DISHES

Arroz y Frijoles Colorados
Beef Pancakes au Gratin
Canadian Meat Pie
Corn Fritters
Eggs Benedict
Enchiladas — American Style
Enchiladas — Mexican Style

Guatemalan Rice
Italian Spaghetti
Jean's Hearty Noodles
Noodles Romanoff
Snappy Frankfurters
Spanish Rice
Tasty Beef Hash

L ET's face it. Everyone is busy these days. You want to entertain and yet you can't find the time. Informal entertaining is the solution to your problem. Extend hospitality to your friends with a simple luncheon or an informal after-the-game party.

For a mixed group you'll want a main dish that's hearty and filling and will satisfy the inner man. Plan plenty, so when your guests ask for more you won't be embarrassed. Top off the party with one of your favorite desserts. When your guests depart happy and satisfied you'll know your hostessing rates a blue ribbon.

Casseroles

CHEESE CUSTARD
6 servings

2 cups milk, scalded
1 cup grated American process
   cheese

4 eggs, separated
½ teaspoon salt

To scalded milk add grated cheese, stirring carefully until cheese melts. Cool. Beat egg yolks until light and add milk and cheese mixture. Add salt. Beat egg whites until stiff but not dry and fold into cheese mixture. Pour into buttered 1½-quart casserole. Set in a pan of hot water and bake uncovered in moderate oven (350°) 40 to 60 minutes or until firm to the touch. Serve immediately.

CHEESE OMELET
6 servings

4 slices bread
2 tablespoons butter
1 cup milk
½ teaspoon salt

Dash of pepper
1 cup grated American cheese
4 egg yolks
4 stiffly beaten egg whites

Butter the bread, cut into 1-inch cubes, put into buttered 1½-quart casserole, and add milk. If dry bread is used, more milk may be required. Sprinkle with salt, pepper, and grated cheese. Beat egg yolks until light and stir into bread mixture. Fold in beaten whites. Bake uncovered in slow oven (325°) 30 to 35 minutes.

This is an easy-to-make cheese dish — nourishing, too.

CHEESE SOUFFLE
4 to 5 servings

3 tablespoons fat
3 tablespoons flour
½ teaspoon salt
Dash of cayenne pepper
1 cup rich milk

1 cup grated American cheese
½ teaspoon prepared mustard
3 egg yolks, well beaten
3 egg whites, beaten until stiff, but
   not dry

Melt fat in double boiler, stir in flour, salt, and cayenne. Blend well. Add milk gradually, stirring constantly. Cook over hot water for 5 minutes. Remove from heat. Add cheese;

stir until melted. Add the prepared mustard. When mixture is almost cool, stir in the well-beaten egg yolks. Fold in the stiffly beaten egg whites — carefully, until the whites just disappear. Pour into well-greased 1½-quart casserole. Set casserole in a pan of hot water to depth of about 1 inch. Bake uncovered in slow oven (325°) 50 to 60 minutes until firm to the touch.

NOTE: The soufflé loses some of its volume on standing, so serve at once.

This light, fluffy cheese soufflé, with its delicate brown crust, is a perfect luncheon dish. Just add a buttered green vegetable, a crisp tossed salad, a fruit dessert, and you'll have a meal to please an epicure.

CURRIED EGGS
4 servings

2 tablespoons butter	½ cup chopped onion
¼ teaspoon curry	¼ cup chopped green pepper
1½ teaspoons salt	1 clove garlic, finely minced
½ teaspoon sugar	2 cups (1 No. 2 can) tomatoes
½ teaspoon prepared mustard	½ cup water
Dash of cayenne pepper	4 hard-cooked eggs

Melt butter in saucepan and add to it the dry ingredients; blend well. Add onion, green pepper, and garlic, and cook about 5 minutes or until onion and green pepper are soft. Pour in tomatoes and water, and cook until sauce has thickened, about 15 minutes. Cut hard-cooked eggs in quarters; place in buttered 1½-quart casserole. Pour tomato sauce over eggs and heat in moderate oven (350°) 10 minutes. Serve as a luncheon or supper dish.

EGGS MORNAY
4 servings

8 eggs	½ cup grated Parmesan cheese
½ cup Mornay Sauce (page 211)	

Poach eggs, allowing 2 per person. Place poached eggs in a buttered 1½-quart casserole. Cover the eggs with Mornay Sauce; sprinkle generously with grated Parmesan cheese. Put under broiler for a few minutes to brown. Serve at once. Garnish with parsley.

EGG TIMBALES
6 servings

4 eggs	1 teaspoon salt
1 cup rich milk	Dash of pepper
1 teaspoon onion juice	

Beat eggs slightly. Add remaining ingredients and blend. Butter individual 6-ounce custard cups. Fill ¾ full. Set the cups in pan of hot water; bake in slow oven (325°) 20 to 25 minutes or until firm. Serve with Cheese Sauce (page 215), Mushroom Sauce (page 215), or Velouté Sauce (page 214).

CHEESE TIMBALES

Add ½ cup grated American cheese to Egg Timbale mixture before adding seasonings.

CHICKEN OR HAM TIMBALES

Chicken or ham timbales may be made by adding ½ cup of either to Egg Timbale mixture.

SPANISH OR CREOLE TIMBALES

Line buttered mold with whole canned pimentos. Fill with Egg Timbale mixture and bake same as Egg Timbales. Remove timbales from the water and let stand 5 minutes before unmolding.

MEXICAN STUFFED EGGS
4 servings

4 hard-cooked eggs	2 teaspoons lemon juice
1 tablespoon finely chopped onion	2 tablespoons mayonnaise
2 tablespoons finely chopped green pepper	Dash of Tabasco sauce
1 teaspoon minced parsley	4 stuffed olives
¼ teaspoon salt	½ cup tomato sauce or tomato soup
Dash of pepper	

Cut the hard-cooked eggs in half lengthwise. Remove yolks and put through sieve. Combine with remaining ingredients, except stuffed olives and tomato sauce, and mix well. Add more seasoning if desired. Refill the whites with the yolk mixture and top with half a stuffed olive. Place the stuffed eggs in buttered 1½-quart casserole and pour around them the tomato sauce or tomato soup. Bake uncovered in slow oven (325°) 10 to 15 minutes or until eggs are heated through. Serve at once.

BEEF BALL CASSEROLE
8 servings (3 meat balls per serving)

2 pounds ground beef
1 teaspoon salt
½ teaspoon pepper
1 cup chopped onion
2 eggs, beaten
24 stuffed olives
¼ cup fat
¼ cup flour

½ cup warm water
2 cups sour cream
1 teaspoon lemon juice
½ teaspoon Worcestershire sauce
1 teaspoon chopped parsley
¼ teaspoon paprika
¼ teaspoon salt

Combine ground beef, salt, pepper, chopped onion, and beaten eggs, and mix well. Form mixture into 1½-inch balls with an olive in the center of each. Brown meat balls in fat. When nicely browned remove from skillet; place in 1½-quart casserole. Pour off fat in skillet, reserving 3 tablespoons. Add flour and blend with fat. Add water, sour cream, and the remaining seasonings, and cook until thickened, stirring constantly. Pour sauce over meat; heat in moderate oven (350°) 10 minutes.

BROCCOLI-BEEF SURPRISE
4 to 6 servings

1 pound fresh broccoli or
    10-ounce package frozen
2 tablespoons butter
3 tablespoons flour
2 cups milk
1 cup (2½-ounce glass) dried beef

¾ teaspoon Worcestershire sauce
¼ teaspoon pepper
2 cups cooked (1½ cups uncooked)
    noodles
2 tablespoons butter
½ cup bread crumbs

Cook broccoli. Combine butter, flour, and milk to make a white sauce. Add dried beef, Worcestershire sauce, and pepper; cook one minute, stirring constantly. Remove from range. Cut the cooked broccoli in 1-inch pieces and add to white sauce. Put drained, cooked noodles in buttered 1½-quart casserole. Pour broccoli and beef sauce over noodles and top with buttered bread crumbs. Bake in moderate oven (350°) 20 minutes.

BROCCOLI-HAM CASSEROLE
5 to 6 servings

1 pound fresh broccoli or 10-ounce
    package frozen
3 tablespoons butter
3 tablespoons flour
½ teaspoon salt
1½ cups milk
1 cup chopped cooked ham
1 tablespoon chopped parsley

2 tablespoons chopped green pepper
2 hard-cooked eggs, chopped
¼ cup grated American cheese
1 teaspoon finely chopped onion
4 teaspoons lemon juice
2 tablespoons melted butter
½ cup bread crumbs

Cook broccoli. Make a white sauce by melting butter, adding flour and salt, and cooking one minute. Add milk, stirring constantly, and cook until the consistency of medium white sauce. Cut the cooked broccoli in one-inch pieces and place in buttered 1½-quart casserole. Combine ham, parsley, green pepper, chopped eggs, cheese, onion, and lemon juice. Cover broccoli with ham mixture. Pour white sauce on top. Combine melted butter with bread crumbs and sprinkle over sauce. Bake in moderate oven (350°) 20 minutes. Green beans or asparagus may be substituted for broccoli.

HOT CHICKEN SALAD EN CASSEROLE
6 to 8 servings

2 cups chopped cooked chicken
2 cups chopped celery
½ cup blanched, chopped, salted
    almonds
⅓ cup chopped green pepper
2 tablespoons chopped pimento

2 tablespoons minced onion
½ teaspoon salt
2 tablespoons lemon juice
½ cup mayonnaise
2 cups crushed potato chips
⅓ cup grated Swiss cheese

Blend chicken, celery, almonds, green pepper, pimento, onion, salt, lemon juice, and mayonnaise. Put alternate layers of chicken mixture and crushed potato chips into buttered 1½-quart casserole. Top with layer of crushed potato chips and grated cheese. Bake in moderate oven (350°) 20 to 25 minutes, or until cheese is melted.

MEAT CASSEROLE A LA CAROL
6 to 8 servings

¼ cup chopped onion	1½ teaspoons Worcestershire sauce
1 clove garlic, finely minced	4 tablespoons crumbled Blue
1 pound pork sausage meat	cheese
1 pound ground beef	1 cup canned mushrooms
1 teaspoon basil	2 cups cooked spaghetti
2 cups tomato purée	1 cup corn flakes
2 tablespoons sugar	½ cup chopped, blanched almonds

Sauté onion, garlic, sausage, and ground beef in skillet until brown. Drain off excess fat. Add basil, tomato purée, sugar, and Worcestershire sauce. Simmer for five minutes over low heat. Remove from heat and mix in cheese and mushrooms. Turn cooked spaghetti into buttered 1½-quart casserole. Pour hot meat mixture over spaghetti. Top with cornflakes. Bake in moderate oven (350°) 20 minutes. Remove from oven. Sprinkle with almonds and return to oven for 5 minutes. Serve immediately.

Meat casserole à la Carol was worked out by Carol Peterson, of Ellsworth, Iowa, Institution Management major. Carol and Jean Bartrug of Iowa Falls worked diligently to create distinctive casserole dishes.

QUICK CORNED BEEF HASH
4 servings

1-pound can corned beef hash	¼ teaspoon celery seed
¼ cup finely chopped parsley	Dash of sage
¼ cup (2 whole) chopped pimentos	¼ teaspoon Worcestershire sauce
1 small clove garlic	Dash of Tabasco sauce
1 tablespoon lemon juice	¼ teaspoon salt
½ cup cream	½ cup crushed potato chips

Combine corned beef hash, parsley, pimento, garlic, and lemon juice. Turn into buttered 1½-quart casserole. Mix cream with celery seed, sage, Worcestershire sauce, Tabasco sauce, and salt. Pour over hash mixture. Top with crushed potato chips. Bake in moderate oven (350°) 20 minutes.

SAVORY SAUSAGE CASSEROLE
5 to 6 servings

1½ pounds pork sausage meat	1 bay leaf
⅔ cup chopped onion	¼ teaspoon dry mustard
2 tablespoons flour	Dash of nutmeg
1 cup milk	½ teaspoon salt
1 cup water	⅛ teaspoon pepper
2 tablespoons lemon juice	¼ cup canned mushrooms

Shape sausage into 1½-inch balls and brown in skillet. When brown remove balls and pour off fat, reserving about ¼ cup. Place sausage balls in 1½-quart casserole. Sauté the onions in the ¼ cup of sausage fat until golden in color. Stir flour into fat and cook one minute. Add milk, water, lemon juice, and seasonings, and cook until slighly thickened, stirring constantly. Add mushrooms. Pour sauce over sausage balls and heat in moderate oven (350°) 10 minutes. Serve with rice, if desired.

SURPRISE CASSEROLE
4 to 6 servings

1 cup chopped pork sausage links	1 cup peas
2 tablespoons flour	1 tablespoon chopped onion
¾ teaspoon salt	1 tablespoon chopped parsley
¼ teaspoon pepper	¾ cup grated American cheese
1 cup sour milk	2 tablespoons chopped pimento
1 cup water	2 tablespoons melted butter
2 cups noodles	½ cup bread crumbs

Cut sausages in small pieces and sauté. Mix flour, salt, and pepper. Add sour milk and water, cook over medium heat, stirring constantly until of medium white sauce consistency. Cook noodles and drain. Spread a layer of cooked noodles in buttered 1½-quart casserole. Add peas, sausage, onion, parsley, grated cheese, and chopped pimento. Put remaining noodles on top. Pour sauce over noodles. Combine melted butter with bread crumbs and sprinkle on top. Bake in moderate oven (350°) 20 minutes.

CHICKEN-VEGETABLE CASSEROLE
5 to 6 servings

1 cup diced cooked chicken	2 tablespoons fat
1 cup chopped stuffed olives	2 tablespoons flour
1 cup cooked peas	2 cups milk
½ cup diced cooked celery	1½ cups cooked rice
1½ teaspoons salt	2 tablespoons melted butter
¼ teaspoon pepper	½ cup bread crumbs
1 tablespoon lemon juice	

Combine chicken, olives, peas, celery, salt, pepper, and lemon juice. Melt fat and add flour; add milk, stirring constantly to avoid lumping. Cook until consistency of thin white sauce. Add chicken mixture to white sauce. Put cooked rice in buttered 1½-quart casserole. Pour white sauce mixture over rice. Combine melted butter and bread crumbs; sprinkle over sauce. Bake in moderate oven (350°) 25 minutes.

DIXIE CASSEROLE
4 to 6 servings

⅔ cup (4-ounce can) chopped ripe olives	1 teaspoon salt
½ cup grated American cheese	Dash of pepper
½ cup cubed cooked ham	1½ cups milk
2 tablespoons pimento	2 cups cooked rice
2 tablespoons fat	2 tablespoons melted butter
2 tablespoons flour	½ cup bread crumbs

Combine olives, cheese, ham, and pimento. Melt fat and add flour, salt, and pepper. Add milk, stirring constantly to avoid lumping; cook until thickened. Put rice in buttered 1½-quart casserole. Add olive mixture to white sauce and pour over rice. Combine butter with bread crumbs; sprinkle over top of casserole. Bake in moderate oven (350°) 25 minutes or until crumbs are nicely browned.

JAMBALAYAH
6 to 8 servings

1½ cups diced cooked chicken,
    ham, or veal
1 cup cooked rice
1½ cups canned tomatoes
1 large onion

½ green pepper
2 pieces celery
4 tablespoons butter
Salt and pepper
½ cup buttered bread crumbs

Mix together the chicken, rice, and tomatoes, and allow them
to cook for 10 minutes. Then chop the onion, green pepper,
and celery, and sauté in butter for a few minutes. Add these
to the chicken and rice mixture, then add salt and pepper to
taste. Turn the mixture into buttered 1½-quart casserole and
cover with buttered bread crumbs. Bake uncovered in moderate oven (350°) about 1 hour. Serve hot.

*Jambalayah has many variations, and in most Creole kitchens it is
made according to whatever the cook has on hand, the one necessary
ingredient being rice. The word itself comes from "jambon," French
for the bit of ham that usually goes into it for flavor. This is an excellent way of utilizing leftover chicken, turkey, pork, shrimp, or crab.*

MEXICAN RICE (using leftover rice)
6 to 8 servings

3 cups cooked rice
4 tablespoons fat
1 teaspoon salt

1 teaspoon chili powder
1 cup chili sauce
½ cup grated American cheese

Brown cooked rice in hot fat; season with salt and chili
powder. Add chili sauce to rice. Sprinkle with grated cheese.
Mix carefully. Turn into buttered 1½-quart casserole. Bake
uncovered in hot oven (400°) 15 to 20 minutes. Serve hot.

RICE PILAF
5 to 6 servings

2 thick slices salt pork, finely diced
1 cup rice
2 medium onions, cut fine
3 cups hot water

2 cups canned tomatoes
4 tablespoons minced parsley
Salt, pepper, and paprika

Fry salt pork until it is lightly browned. Wash and drain rice, add to pork, and stir until rice is a golden brown; add onion and continue cooking. Add hot water gradually, cover, and cook until rice is done. Add the remaining ingredients. Place mixture in buttered 1½-quart casserole and bake uncovered in moderate oven (350°) 30 minutes.

Here is the distinctive flavor achieved only with browned rice. We might call it a version of Spanish rice, but no matter what it's called, it is excellent for a luncheon main dish.

CLAM SOUFFLE
4 to 6 servings

¾ cup (10½-ounce can) minced
    clams
2 tablespoons butter
2 tablespoons flour
½ teaspoon salt
Dash of pepper
2 teaspoons grated onion

1 tablespoon lemon juice
½ cup milk
½ cup bread crumbs
3 eggs, separated
Medium White Sauce (page 215)
Parsley

Drain clams, reserving ½ cup of the liquid. Melt butter; add flour, salt and pepper, and cook 1 minute. Add grated onion and lemon juice; blend well. Gradually add the ½ cup of clam liquid and the milk. Cook until thickened, stirring constantly. Remove from range; cool slightly and stir in the minced clams and bread crumbs. Beat egg yolks until light; blend into sauce mixture. Beat egg whites to soft peak stage and fold in. Turn mixture into buttered 1½-quart casserole. Place in pan of hot water; bake in slow oven (325°) 40 to 45 minutes.

Serve with well-seasoned Medium White Sauce to which finely chopped parsley has been added.

This is a favorite recipe of Mrs. Grace Shugart of Manhattan, Kansas, former Institution Management staff member at Iowa State College. This light, delicately flavored clam soufflé is a welcome change for a Friday luncheon dish.

CRAB MEAT CASSEROLE
4 to 6 servings

1 cup (6½-ounce can) crab meat, flaked
1½ cups (3 to 4) chopped hard-cooked eggs
½ cup (4-ounce can) mushrooms
2 tablespoons chopped onions
3 tablespoons melted butter
2 teaspoons lemon juice
Dash of curry powder
¼ pound American cheese, grated
1 cup cooked peas
½ teaspoon salt
2 cups Thin White Sauce (page 215)
½ cup bread crumbs

Combine flaked crab meat, chopped eggs, and mushrooms. Sauté onion in 1 tablespoon of the melted butter until golden brown; add to crab meat mixture. Mix in lightly the lemon juice, curry powder, grated cheese, peas, and salt. Turn the mixture into buttered 1½-quart casserole. Pour White Sauce over the top. Combine remaining 2 tablespoons of butter with bread crumbs. Sprinkle buttered crumbs over top and bake in moderate oven (350°) 25 minutes.

NIPPY SALMON CASSEROLE
4 to 6 servings

1 cup cooked (¾ cup uncooked) noodles
2 tablespoons chopped onion
¼ cup melted butter
3 tablespoons flour
1½ teaspoons salt
¼ teaspoon pepper
2 cups milk
2 tablespoons horse-radish
¼ teaspoon Worcestershire sauce
1 cup (8-ounce can) salmon, flaked
½ cup (4-ounce can) mushrooms
2 tablespoons (2 whole) pimentos
1 cup cooked peas
½ cup bread crumbs

Sauté onion in 2 tablespoons of the butter until golden brown. Stir in flour, salt, and pepper. Gradually add the milk, stirring constantly to avoid lumping; cook until thickened. Remove from heat and add horse-radish and Worcestershire sauce. Toss together salmon, mushrooms, pimentos, peas, and noodles with white sauce and pour into buttered 1½-quart casserole. Combine remaining 2 tablespoons of butter with bread crumbs. Sprinkle on top of casserole. Bake in moderate oven (350°) 20 minutes.

SALMON CASSEROLE
6 servings

2 cups (16-ounce can) pink
    salmon
½ cup chopped green pepper
½ cup minced onion
½ teaspoon salt
⅛ teaspoon pepper
Dash of chili powder
1 egg, beaten

1 cup tomato purée
½ cup bread crumbs
1 cup mushroom soup
2 tablespoons chopped parsley
2 tablespoons lemon juice
2 tablespoons melted butter
½ cup bread crumbs

Combine in a skillet the salmon, green pepper, onion, salt, pepper, chili powder, beaten egg, tomato purée, and ½ cup of bread crumbs. Simmer for five minutes. Add the mushroom soup, parsley, and lemon juice, and simmer five minutes longer. Pour into buttered 2-quart casserole. Combine melted butter and remaining ½ cup bread crumbs; sprinkle on top of casserole. Bake in moderate oven (350°) 20 minutes.

SHRIMP DELIGHT
4 to 6 servings

⅓ cup (3¼-ounce can) mush-
    rooms
¼ cup melted butter
1 cup (7-ounce can) shrimp,
    flaked
1½ cups grated American cheese
3 tablespoons chili sauce
½ teaspoon Worcestershire sauce

½ teaspoon salt
Dash of pepper
2 tablespoons (2 whole) diced
    pimentos
½ cup cream
1½ cups cooked rice
½ cup bread crumbs

Cook mushrooms in 2 tablespoons of the butter for 2 minutes. Add shrimp, cheese, chili sauce, Worcestershire sauce, salt, pepper, and pimentos, and stir together carefully. Pour in cream and cook 1 minute longer. Put cooked rice into buttered 1½-quart casserole. Pour shrimp mixture over the rice. Combine remaining 2 tablespoons of melted butter with bread crumbs and sprinkle on top of casserole. Bake in moderate oven (350°) 25 minutes.

TUNA CORN BREAD UPSIDE-DOWN
4 to 6 servings

1 cup (7-ounce can) tuna, flaked
⅓ cup (3¼-ounce can) mushrooms
2 cups cooked mixed vegetables
2 cups Medium White Sauce
   (page 215)
¼ cup flour

¾ cup yellow corn meal
1 teaspoon baking powder
1 tablespoon sugar
½ teaspoon salt
¼ teaspoon soda
¾ cup sour milk
1½ tablespoons melted shortening

Combine tuna, mushrooms, and mixed vegetables. Season well.
Put into buttered 1½-quart casserole and pour White Sauce
over vegetables. Mix flour, corn meal, baking powder, sugar,
salt, and soda. Add sour milk to dry ingredients; stir in shortening and mix until smooth. Spread lightly over top of casserole.
Bake in moderate oven (350°) 25 minutes or until corn bread
is done. Remove from oven and invert on a hot serving plate.
Serve as main dish for luncheon or supper.

Supper Dishes

ARROZ Y FRIJOLES COLORADOS
Rice and Red Beans
6 servings

1 cup red beans	1 teaspoon chili powder
¼ pound salt pork, diced	1 teaspoon salt
1 quart boiling water	1½ cups cooked rice
1 medium onion, chopped fine	

Cook beans with salt pork in boiling water until tender; add onion, chili powder, and salt to taste. Simmer until beans are done. Add rice and serve.

This is a favorite dish in the Southwest.

BEEF PANCAKES AU GRATIN
10 servings

½ pound ground beef	1 cup sifted flour
4 tablespoons minced onion	1 teaspoon baking powder
2 tablespoons fat	1 egg, well beaten
1½ teaspoons salt	1½ cups milk
Dash of garlic salt	½ cup (4 ounces) grated American
1 teaspoon lemon juice	cheese
½ teaspoon Worcestershire sauce	

Sauté ground beef and onion in hot fat until brown. Add salt, garlic salt, lemon juice, and Worcestershire sauce; simmer until beef is cooked, about 10 minutes. Cool to lukewarm. Sift flour and baking powder together twice. Combine well-beaten egg and milk and blend gradually into dry ingredients, mixing until free of lumps. The batter will be very thin. Drain fat from cooked meat. Combine meat mixture with batter. Use ⅓ cup batter for each pancake and bake in a skillet or on a hot griddle, lightly greased. Brown well on both sides. Each pancake requires 5 to 7 minutes to bake. Remove from griddle and spread with butter and finely chopped parsley. Roll up jelly-roll fashion. Place rolled pancakes in a pan. Sprinkle with grated American cheese. Put under broiler until cheese melts. Serve hot, with a mushroom sauce if desired.

CANADIAN MEAT PIE

1 pound pork (¾ lean, ¼ fat)	½ teaspoon pepper
3 cups cold water	¼ teaspoon celery salt
½ cup sliced onion	Dash of powdered sage
1 teaspoon salt	Dash of nutmeg
½ cup dry bread crumbs	1½ teaspoons lemon juice
1½ cups stock	

Cut pork in 1-inch cubes. Cook until tender in water to which onion and salt have been added. Reserve 1½ cups stock from cooked pork. Grind pork and onion through fine knife of meat grinder. Combine with bread crumbs, stock, pepper, celery salt, sage, nutmeg, and lemon juice. Simmer slowly 10 minutes.

Pastry:

2 cups sifted flour	½ cup fat
1 teaspoon salt	½ cup cold water
1 teaspoon baking powder	

Sift flour, salt, and baking powder. Cut in fat until mixture is in pea-size pieces. Make a well in the center and add water all at once. Stir with circular motion with a fork until blended. Remove dough to a lightly floured board. Knead 10 times. Divide into 2 equal parts and roll to fit a 9-inch pie pan. Both crusts will be thicker than ordinary pie crusts. Line pie pan with bottom crust. Fill with meat mixture. Top with perforated crust. Bake in moderate oven (375°) 35 minutes. Cut in pie-shape wedges and serve hot or cold for luncheon or supper.

I was introduced to Canadian meat pie in the home of a San Diego friend after Christmas Eve service. Hot, flaky wedges of the meat pie were served with Ambrosia, following the family tradition of the hostess, Kathleen Binet Fitzpatrick. With all the excitement of the Christmas festivities, I failed to request the recipe.

On returning to Iowa State College, I appealed to one of our Canadian graduate students, Nellie Patson of Saskatoon, Saskatchewan, to see if she could locate such a recipe for me. Nellie immediately wrote to one of her French Canadian friends, Mrs. W. Toupin of Storthoaks, Saskatchewan, who obligingly sent this recipe. At the top of the page she wrote "Canadian Meat Pie — Good Luck U.S.A."

Mrs. Toupin added, "Some people add cooked potatoes instead of bread, and spice it to taste with sage, nutmeg, and cloves. Those recipes were given from mother to daughter for generations."

CORN FRITTERS
Makes 18 to 20

1¼ cups flour	2 eggs, separated
2 teaspoons baking powder	⅓ cup milk
1 teaspoon salt	1 cup drained whole kernel corn
1 teaspoon paprika	

Sift flour, baking powder, salt, and paprika together. Beat egg yolks and add milk and corn. Stir into dry ingredients just enough to dampen. Beat egg whites until stiff but not dry and fold into batter. Drop from tablespoon into deep hot fat (375°). Fry to a golden brown 5 to 6 minutes or until done in the center. Drain on absorbent paper. Serve with crisp bacon.

EGGS BENEDICT
4 servings

4 eggs	2 tablespoons butter
4 thin slices boiled ham	½ cup Hollandaise Sauce
2 English muffins	(page 209)

Poach the eggs. Cut ham into rounds and sauté in butter. Split the muffins with a fork and toast the cut side. Butter muffins and put round slice of ham on hot muffin. Top the ham with the poached egg and put a tablespoon of Hollandaise Sauce on each. Sprinkle with chopped parsley and serve at once.

ENCHILADAS—AMERICAN STYLE
12 servings

Tortilla Filling:

½ pound American cheese   ½ teaspoon salt
2 medium white onions, minced

Grate cheese and chop onions. Mix cheese, onions, and salt.

Sauce for Tortillas:

2 tablespoons fat   1 No. 2 can tomatoes
1 small onion, chopped fine   ½ teaspoon salt
1 tablespoon flour   Dash of Tabasco sauce
3 cloves garlic, mashed   ½ cup fat
3 tablespoons chili powder   12 Tortillas (page 83)

Melt the 2 tablespoons fat in skillet, add chopped onion. Fry
until golden in color. Add flour, garlic, chili powder, tomatoes,
salt, and Tabasco sauce. Let simmer until thick. Add more
seasoning, if necessary. Heat the ½ cup fat in small saucepan
and have fat and sauce in adjoining pans on range. Dip Tortillas into hot fat for a few seconds, using spatula to remove.
Then put tortillas into sauce; when thoroughly soaked, remove
to heated pan. Put about 2 tablespoons of the cheese and onion
mixture on each tortilla. Roll and place on serving platter
and cover with remaining sauce. Sprinkle more cheese and
onion mixture over them. Serve at once.

ENCHILADAS—MEXICAN STYLE
4 servings

Sauce for Tortillas:

¼ cup fat   3 cups water
¼ cup flour   1 pound fat
½ teaspoon salt   1½ pounds grated American cheese
Dash of Tabasco sauce   2 cups finely chopped onions
1 10-ounce bottle chili sauce   12 Tortillas (page 83)

Heat the ¼ cup of fat in saucepan; add flour, salt, and Tabasco
sauce, and blend. Add chili sauce and water and cook 5 to 10

minutes or until sauce is well blended. Heat the pound of fat in shallow saucepan slightly larger than Tortillas (about 6 inches in diameter). Place pan with sauce at right of pan of hot fat on range. Have a pancake turner for each. Dip the tortillas, one at a time, in and out of the hot fat; then into the chili sauce, and remove to hot plate. Sprinkle each tortilla with cheese and finely chopped onion. Arrange in stacks of three, topped with a fried egg and several tablespoons of the chili sauce. Serve with a lettuce and tomato salad.

NOTE: Drop eggs into deep fat and flip grease over them so yolk is completely covered with white.

This is the authentic Mexican version of the enchilada which Laurene Bealer of New Mexico made for us in Catering Class. It was an entirely new dish to most of the girls from the Middle West. Laurene was perfectly at home flipping the tortillas in and out of the fat and sauce and it was easy to see that she knew the Mexican cuisine. It was fun to watch her make up the stacks of tortillas into enchiladas.

GUATEMALAN RICE
6 servings

1 cup rice	2 cups peeled fresh tomatoes or
4 tablespoons fat	canned tomatoes
1 small onion, chopped fine	2 cups hot water
1 clove garlic, minced	1 teaspoon salt
	1 small green pepper, chopped fine

Wash rice thoroughly. Fry in hot fat until light brown, stirring constantly so each grain will cook separately. Add onion and garlic and fry until golden in color. Then cut tomatoes into cubes and add with the hot water, salt, and green pepper. Add more hot water in small quantities as necessary until rice is cooked, shaking but not stirring — it breaks grains to stir when moist. Simmer slowly until rice is thoroughly cooked.

ITALIAN SPAGHETTI
4 to 6 servings

½ cup chopped onions
1 pound ground beef
1 tablespoon fat
¾ cup chopped celery
1 clove garlic, finely minced
1 tablespoon chili powder
1 bay leaf
3 teaspoons salt
¼ teaspoon pepper

1 cup tomato sauce
½ cup (7-ounce can) tomato paste
1 cup canned tomatoes
2 cups cold water
1 pound long spaghetti
2 quarts boiling water
2 teaspoons salt
Parmesan cheese

Sauté onions and ground beef in fat until brown. Add celery, garlic, chili powder, bay leaf, salt, and pepper. Mix well and add tomato sauce, tomato paste, tomatoes, and water. Simmer for 2 hours, adding more water if necessary. Cook spaghetti in the boiling, salted water until tender. Drain and rinse with hot water. Arrange on a hot platter or on individual plates. Pour sauce over spaghetti. Sprinkle generously with grated Parmesan cheese.

JEAN'S HEARTY NOODLES
6 to 8 servings

2 cups noodles
4 slices bacon, chopped
3 hard-cooked eggs
2½ tablespoons butter
2½ tablespoons flour
¼ teaspoon salt
¼ teaspoon paprika

1 cup milk
½ teaspoon Worcestershire sauce
1 cup grated American cheese
2 tablespoons pimento
2 tablespoons finely chopped parsley

Cook noodles in salted water; drain. Sauté bacon until crisp and remove from skillet. Sauté noodles in bacon grease until lightly browned. Separate whites and yolks of hard-cooked eggs. Chop whites and force yolks through wire sieve. To make sauce: Melt butter, add flour, salt, and paprika; cool 1 minute. Add milk and cook over low heat, stirring constantly until thickened. Remove from range; cool. Add Worcestershire sauce, cheese, pimento, and chopped egg white; blend and reheat for 1 minute. Pile noodles on platter and pour sauce over noodles. Garnish with parsley, riced egg yolks, and bacon strips.

NOODLES ROMANOFF
6 servings

6 ounces broad noodles	½ teaspoon salt
1 cup sour cream	Dash of pepper
1 cup cottage cheese	1 cup sour cream
1 clove garlic, chopped fine	⅓ cup chopped chives
1 medium onion, chopped fine	Parmesan cheese
1 teaspoon Worcestershire sauce	

Cook noodles until tender; drain. Add sour cream, cottage cheese, garlic, onion, and seasonings. Mix carefully and turn into buttered 1½-quart casserole. Sprinkle generously with paprika. Bake in moderate oven (350°) 45 minutes. Caution: Do not overcook! Combine sour cream with chopped chives and put a tablespoon on each serving of noodles. Sprinkle generously with Parmesan cheese.

This recipe for noodles Romanoff comes from Marion Roy Acklin of Lancaster, Pennsylvania, an Institution Management graduate of Iowa State College, who is famous for her excellent food.

SNAPPY FRANKFURTERS
4 servings

4 frankfurters	1 slice American process cheese
2 teaspoons prepared mustard	4 slices bacon

Place frankfurters in boiling water; cover. Remove from heat; let stand 8 to 10 minutes. Drain and split lengthwise. Spread lightly with mustard. Put ¼ slice of cheese in each. Close frankfurter and wrap a strip of bacon around each, securing each end with a wooden pick. Put under broiler for 5 minutes or until bacon is cooked and crisp. Serve in buns.

SPANISH RICE
6 servings

¼ cup olive oil or salad oil
¼ cup minced onion
1 clove garlic, mashed
1 cup rice, washed and drained
3 cups tomato juice
1 6-ounce can tomato paste
2 pimentos, chopped

¼ cup chopped green pepper
1 teaspoon salt
3 teaspoons paprika
Dash of cayenne pepper
¼ teaspoon Worcestershire sauce
½ cup diced cooked bacon

Heat oil in heavy skillet. Add onion and garlic and cook until golden in color. Add raw rice, stirring frequently, and cook to a light brown. Add remaining ingredients except bacon. Cover skillet and cook until rice is tender. Stir occasionally. Add diced bacon just before rice is served.

This method of cooking rice gives a flavor that is different than when rice is cooked in either water or milk. Watch closely and stir often to prevent the rice from becoming too brown.

TASTY BEEF HASH
4 to 5 servings

5 tablespoons fat
2 tablespoons finely chopped onion
2 cloves garlic, finely minced
2 tablespoons chopped green pepper

⅓ cup grated raw carrots
2 cups cubed cooked potatoes
2 cups chopped cooked beef
½ teaspoon salt
⅛ teaspoon pepper
½ cup cream

Melt fat in skillet. Add onion and garlic and sauté until golden in color. Add green pepper and carrots and cook 2 minutes longer. Add cubed potatoes, chopped beef, salt, and pepper, and cook over slow fire about 5 minutes, stirring occasionally. Pour cream over mixture and cook until mixture is dry and slight crust is formed on bottom.

Sandwiches

TEA SANDWICHES

Nut Sticks
Ribbon Sandwiches
   Filling Combinations
Rolled Sandwiches

SAVORY SPREADS

Anchovy Butter
Blue Cheese
Chicken Pecan
Crab, Shrimp, or Lobster
Cream Cheese
Creole Butter
Cucumber Butter
Ham and Tartare Sauce
Liver Paste
Mushroom Butter
Mushroom and Deviled Ham
Parsley Butter
Pimento Cheese
Piquant Cheese
Ripe Olive and Nut
Sardine Butter
Savory Butter
Savory Cream Cheese
Tongue

SUGGESTIONS FOR SAVORY SPREADS

SWEET SPREADS

Cranberry
Cream Cheese
   Apricot
   Date
   Ginger, Nut
   Maraschino Cherry
   Marmalade
   Pineapple
   Raspberry Jam
Lemon Curd

HEARTY SANDWICHES

Barbecued Crab Meat
Barbecued Tuna on Buns
Broiled Hamburger-Cheese Buns
Cheese-Bacon Special
Cheese and Ham Rolls
Chicken-Cheese-Tomato-Bacon
Crab Meat Salad
Denver Special
French Fried Tuna Salad
Meat Salad in Buns
Zesty Ham

NOTHING else is quite so versatile as a sandwich. It can make a meal or late evening snack. Or a tray of festive sandwiches can be the highlight of an afternoon tea.

You'll want to serve sandwiches that fit the occasion. One that's a supper in itself should be the hearty, stick-to-the-ribs kind — plenty of meat, cheese, or whatever fixings you choose on plump buns or generous slices of bread.

But sandwiches that go to a tea party must be dainty, and just as pretty to look at as they are delicious. Contrast adds interest, so plan to vary the fillings, shapes, and garnishes. Display them attractively on trays or platters. Then your guests will toss bouquets your way.

SANDWICH PREPARATION FOR A TEA OR PARTY

The bread for sandwiches should be preferably one day old, as it will cut more easily than fresh bread. Sandwich loaves cut to the best advantage and may be used for open or closed sandwiches. Boston brown bread, date, nut or prune bread, cut thin and spread with softened butter or cream cheese, are a welcome addition to a tea tray of sandwiches.

If you cannot purchase the sandwich bread sliced to the desired thickness, then a sharp knife and a good cutting board will be necessary. When making sandwiches for a party, you will save time by having all of the bread sliced before any of the actual sandwich making is done. Cut the bread lengthwise of the loaf, since it is easier to spread a few long pieces of bread than so many smaller ones, as must be done if the bread is cut crosswise. Remove all but the bottom crust before slicing. The bread will be easier to slice with the bottom crust left on. To prevent the bread from drying out, keep the slices stacked and store them in pans that have been lined with a damp cloth and covered with a layer of waxed paper. Put another layer of waxed paper over the bread and cover with a damp cloth. Keep in the refrigerator until ready to use. If fancy sandwiches are to be made, they may be cut ahead of time and stored in the same manner.

Prepare the fillings ahead of time and store in small covered bowls or jars in the refrigerator. If butter is to be used on the sandwiches, it should be creamed until of the proper consistency to spread and kept at room temperature. The butter should never be melted as it soaks into the bread. Garnishes should be prepared ahead of time, also. With careful planning and organization of the materials needed the actual job of making the sandwiches will be comparatively simple.

MAKING THE SANDWICHES

Arrange slices of bread or bread cutouts on a bread board. Spread with softened butter and then spread generously with the filling, bringing it to the edge of the bread. The filling should be of good spreading consistency. Use a thin flexible spatula to spread filling on bread. For *open sandwiches*, bring the filling neatly down to the edge. Decorate as desired. *Ribbon sandwiches* can be made up in alternate slices, two whole-wheat and two white, using contrasting filling. Press each stack firmly together. For *rolled sandwiches,* spread each lengthwise slice of bread with softened butter and then one of the spreads. Roll up, beginning with short end of bread, as for a jelly roll. Wrap the uncut rolls in waxed paper. Chill in refrigerator until ready to serve.

QUANTITY GUIDE — BREAD*

1¼ pound loaf white bread cuts 19 (⅝″) slices, without end crust.

1½ pound loaf white bread cuts 24 (⅝″) slices, without end crust.

2 pound sandwich loaf white bread cuts 28 (½″) slices, or 36 (⅜″) slices, without end crust.

3 pound sandwich loaf white bread cuts 44 (½″) slices, or 56 (⅜″) slices, without end crust.

1 pound loaf whole wheat bread cuts 16 (⅝″) slices, without end crust.

2 pound loaf whole wheat bread cuts 28 (½″) slices, without end crust.

3 pound loaf whole wheat bread cuts 44 (½″) slices, or 56 (⅜″) slices, without end crust.

1 pound loaf rye bread cuts 23 (¾″) slices, without end crust.

2 pound loaf rye bread cuts 33 (¾″) slices, without end crust.

NOTE: The thickness and number of slices will vary in different localities.

---

* From American Institute of Baking

Tea Sandwiches

NUT STICKS

Cut slices of white bread ½ inch thick and cut in strips 2 to 3 inches in length. Spread rather thickly on four sides and ends with creamed butter or cream cheese, then roll in chopped nuts. Blanched and browned almonds are delicious. Pecans may be used. Add a little salt to nuts to improve flavor.

These nut sticks are a great favorite for afternoon tea and are especially good with Reception Chocolate (page 299).

RIBBON SANDWICHES

Remove crusts from a loaf of graham bread and a loaf of white bread. Cut slices lengthwise, about ⅜ inch thick. Spread slice of graham bread with cheese spread, lay on it a slice of buttered white bread and spread with deviled ham. Continue in alternate layers until four are used. Press firmly together, cover with a damp cloth and leave in cold place. When ready to serve, cut slices about ¼ inch thick. These slices may be cut in two again. Fillings in contrasting color and texture should be used. Fillings should be of a consistency to spread easily and should be spread thickly, so slices will stick together and not fall apart when cut.

FILLING COMBINATIONS

Pimento Cheese Spread on graham bread — Ripe Olive and Nut Spread on white bread (page 287)

Parsley Butter on whole-wheat bread — Sardine Butter on white bread (page 287)

Cranberry Spread on white bread — Cream Cheese and Pineapple Spread on graham bread (page 289)

ROLLED SANDWICHES

Remove all but the bottom crust from bread. It will slice easier with bottom crust on. Cut bread lengthwise of loaf in ¼-inch slices. Remove remaining crust after bread has been sliced. Put a damp cloth and waxed paper on a tray and place sliced bread on this. Cover with waxed paper and another damp cloth so bread will not dry out and will roll easily.

When ready to make sandwiches, spread each slice with Savory Butter (page 287) or any other soft spread: Anchovy Butter (page 286), Cream Cheese and Maraschino Cherry Spread (page 289), Shrimp Butter (page 286), or deviled ham. Filling should be of a consistency that will spread easily. Spread filling to edges of bread, roll up crosswise of slice, being careful not to break bread. When sandwich is rolled, lay between damp cloths, edge down so it will stay rolled. Put in cold place until ready to serve. Cut into ⅓-inch slices. Put tiny sprig of parsley in center, if desired. Serve as tea sandwiches or as salad accompaniment.

For nice variety on your sandwich tray, place several sprigs of water cress across one end of slice of buttered bread. Let water cress extend beyond edge. Roll up and place between damp towels until time to serve.

SAVORY SPREADS

Anchovy Butter. Blend together ¼ cup softened butter, 2 teaspoons anchovy paste, and 1 teaspoon lemon juice.

Blue Cheese. Combine ¼ pound Blue cheese, two 3-ounce packages cream cheese, 2 tablespoons mayonnaise, and 2 tablespoons crisp diced bacon.

Chicken Pecan. Combine 1 cup finely minced chicken, ¼ cup coarsely chopped pecans, ¼ cup chopped celery, ¼ cup finely chopped stuffed olives, ½ cup mayonnaise, and ½ teaspoon salt. Minced turkey may be used instead of chicken.

Crab, Shrimp, or Lobster. Combine 1 cup finely shredded crab meat, shrimp or lobster with 1 cup finely cut celery, ¼ cup chopped green pepper, ½ cup Savory Butter (page 287), ½ cup mayonnaise, and lemon juice to taste.

Cream Cheese, Green Pepper, and Pimento. Combine two 3-ounce packages cream cheese, 1 tablespoon finely chopped green pepper, 1 tablespoon finely chopped pimento, and 1 tablespoon mayonnaise.

Creole Butter. Combine 2 tablespoons finely chopped green olives, 2 tablespoons finely chopped pickles, and 2 tablespoons chopped pimentos. Stir in 2 teaspoons lemon juice, 1 teaspoon French mustard, and 1 teaspoon paprika. Add this to 1 cup creamed butter.

Cucumber Butter. Pare cucumber and dice finely. Combine with ½ cup softened butter, 1 teaspoon lemon juice, and ¼ teaspoon salt.

Ham and Tartare Sauce. Combine 1 cup finely minced ham with ⅓ cup Tartare Sauce (page 214).

Liver Paste. Mash ¼ pound liver sausage; add 2 tablespoons mayonnaise and ¼ teaspoon salt.

Mushroom Butter. Combine ½ cup softened butter with 2 tablespoons finely chopped sautéed mushrooms and 2 teaspoons lemon juice.

Mushroom and Deviled Ham. Combine two 3-ounce cans deviled ham with ¼ cup chopped fresh mushrooms that have been sautéed in butter; stir in 2 tablespoons mayonnaise and ¼ teaspoon salt.

Parsley Butter. Combine ½ cup softened butter with 1 tablespoon lemon juice, ¼ cup very finely chopped parsley, and ¼ teaspoon salt. Chopped water cress, chives, or olives may be used in the same way.

Pimento Cheese. Combine 1 cup grated American cheese with ¼ cup finely chopped pimento, 1 tablespoon French dressing, ¼ teaspoon onion juice, and ⅛ teaspoon salt.

Piquant Cheese. Combine ½ pound grated cheese with 1 hard-cooked egg and 1 tablespoon grated onion. Add ¼ cup mayonnaise, ¼ cup chili sauce, and Worcestershire sauce or other seasonings.

Ripe Olive and Nut. Combine 1 cup chopped ripe olives with ½ cup chopped nuts and ¼ cup mayonnaise.

Sardine Butter. Mash one 3¾-ounce can of sardines to a smooth paste; blend with ¼ cup softened butter and 1 teaspoon lemon juice.

Savory Butter. Cream 1 pound butter, add 3 tablespoons boiling water a few drops at a time and continue beating. Stir in 3 tablespoons lemon juice, add 1 tablespoon prepared mustard, dash of cayenne, and ¼ teaspoon Worcestershire sauce. Beat until light and fluffy. This may be used as a spread for fish and meat sandwiches or for finger sandwiches. *Other savory butters* may be made using these flavorings alone or in combinations: Prepared mustard, paprika, celery salt, onion juice, Worcestershire sauce, catsup, curry paste or powder, chopped parsley, chives, grated horse-radish, pimento.

Savory Cream Cheese. Combine two 3-ounce packages cream cheese with ¼ cup chopped salted almonds, 1 tablespoon finely chopped sweet pickle, and 1 tablespoon chutney.

Tongue. Combine 1 cup finely minced cooked tongue, ⅓ cup mayonnaise, ¼ teaspoon Worcestershire sauce, ¼ teaspoon onion juice.

SUGGESTIONS FOR SAVORY SPREADS

Celery, toasted almonds, mayonnaise
Cheese, finely chopped ripe olives, green pepper
Cheese, Worcestershire sauce, onion juice, lemon juice
Chicken Salad (page 226)
Chopped stuffed olives, chopped celery, mayonnaise
Cottage cheese, Worcestershire sauce, chili sauce, minced green
    olives
Egg, celery, green pepper, pimento, mayonnaise
Flaked tuna fish and Tartare Sauce (page 214)
Sardine paste, lemon juice, Tabasco sauce

SWEET SPREADS

Cranberry. Put 1 cup cranberries through fine knife of food chopper; add 1 teaspoon grated orange peel and ¼ cup sugar. Set aside for 2 hours; drain well before spreading mixture on buttered bread.

Cream Cheese and Apricot. Blend one 3-ounce package cream cheese with 3 tablespoons apricot pulp, 1 teaspoon lemon juice, ½ teaspoon sugar, and ⅛ teaspoon salt.

Cream Cheese and Date. Blend two 3-ounce packages cream cheese with ⅓ cup cream. Add ½ cup chopped dates and ½ cup chopped nuts.

Cream Cheese, Ginger, and Nut. Blend one 3-ounce pack-cream cheese with 1 tablespoon finely chopped crystallized ginger, 2 tablespoons chopped walnuts, and ⅛ teaspoon salt.

Cream Cheese and Maraschino Cherry. Blend one 3-ounce package cream cheese with ½ cup chopped well-drained maraschino cherries, ¼ cup finely chopped blanched almonds, and ⅛ teaspoon salt.

Cream Cheese and Marmalade. Blend one 3-ounce package cream cheese with 1 tablespoon marmalade, 1 tablespoon chopped pecans, and ¼ teaspoon salt.

Cream Cheese and Pineapple. Blend one 3-ounce package cream cheese with well-drained grated pineapple, maraschino cherries, and ginger.

Cream Cheese and Raspberry Jam. Blend one 3-ounce package cream cheese with 2 tablespoons raspberry jam and ⅛ teaspoon salt.

Lemon Curd (English). Grate peel of two lemons and extract juice. Melt 2 tablespoons butter in double boiler and add 4 beaten egg yolks, ¾ cup sugar, the grated peel, and lemon juice. Cook until thick.

Hearty Sandwiches

BARBECUED CRAB MEAT SANDWICHES
8 servings

½ cup chili sauce
1 3-ounce package cream cheese
1 cup crab meat (fresh or canned)
½ teaspoon horse-radish
½ teaspoon Worcestershire sauce

1 teaspoon finely chopped onion
2 teaspoons lemon juice
4 round buns
½ cup grated American cheese

Mix chili sauce with cream cheese. Add crab meat and other ingredients, except cheese. Add more seasonings, if desired. Cut buns in two. Butter cut surface. Heap crab-meat mixture on buns. Sprinkle a teaspoon of grated cheese on each one. Put under broiler or in hot oven (425°) to melt cheese.

Tuna fish may be substituted for crab meat.

BARBECUED TUNA ON BUNS
6 servings

½ cup tomato purée
½ cup wine vinegar
2 tablespoons soy sauce
¼ cup melted butter
1 clove garlic, finely chopped

½ teaspoon marjoram
2 7-ounce cans (2 cups) flaked
   tuna
6 hamburger buns

Combine tomato purée, vinegar, soy sauce, butter, garlic, and marjoram. Simmer over low heat for 15 minutes. Add tuna. Let mixture stand 15 minutes to blend flavor. Split buns in half. Butter lightly and place buttered side down in hot skillet until brown. Remove to hot serving platter, placing browned side up. Spread with barbecued tuna. Serve immediately.

This sauce may be used with salmon, pork, or chicken and served in the same manner.

BROILED HAMBURGER-CHEESE BUNS
8 servings

1 pound ground beef
2 small cloves garlic, finely minced
1 teaspoon salt
¼ teaspoon pepper

1 cup milk
8 hamburger buns
4 teaspoons prepared mustard
8 slices process American cheese

Combine beef, garlic, salt and pepper, and mix well. Add as

much of the milk as is needed to give a mixture of good spreading consistency. Split buns and place under broiler until lightly browned. Spread 2½ tablespoons of meat mixture on the buns. Place on baking sheet, put under broiler, and let remain until meat mixture is cooked through. Remove from broiler; spread ½ teaspoon mustard on meat and place a slice of cheese on top. Put under broiler again and allow to remain until cheese has melted. Serve immediately.

Mrs. Jane Stebbins is responsible for this recipe, which is a favorite with her two sons, Bob and Bruce.

CHEESE-BACON SPECIAL
6 servings

2 eggs, well beaten	1 teaspoon lemon juice
2 cups (1 pound) grated American cheese	Dash of garlic salt
½ teaspoon salt	Dash of celery salt
⅛ teaspoon pepper	6 strips bacon
½ teaspoon paprika	6 hamburger buns
½ teaspoon Worcestershire sauce	3 tablespoons mayonnaise

Combine eggs, cheese, salt, pepper, paprika, Worcestershire sauce, lemon juice, garlic salt, and celery salt. Cut bacon strips in half and cook slowly until lightly browned. Split buns in half. Butter and place buttered side down in a hot skillet until brown. Turn browned side up. Spread egg and cheese mixture on one half of each bun. Spread the other half with mayonnaise and top with 2 bacon strips. Place under broiler until cheese is melted and bacon is crisp. Remove to hot serving platter and serve immediately.

CHEESE AND HAM ROLLS
8 servings

8 hard French rolls	1 large onion, chopped
1 pound sharp Cheddar cheese	4 teaspoons chopped green pepper
1 cup ground cooked ham	8 stuffed olives, chopped
½ cup tomato sauce	½ cup salad oil

Cut top lengthwise from French rolls and hollow out centers. Mix all ingredients together and fill rolls with mixture. Heat in moderate oven (350°) 10 to 15 minutes. These rolls are good to serve at an informal buffet meal. They are practically a whole meal in themselves.

CHICKEN-CHEESE-TOMATO-BACON SANDWICHES
4 servings

1 cup (½ pound) grated American cheese
½ teaspoon salt
¼ teaspoon pepper
½ teaspoon paprika
½ teaspoon Worcestershire sauce
1 teaspoon lemon juice
Dash of garlic salt
Dash of celery salt
4 slices bacon
4 hamburger buns
1 cup (4-ounce can) sliced boned chicken
2 tablespoons mayonnaise
2 tomatoes, sliced

Combine cheese, salt, pepper, paprika, Worcestershire sauce, lemon juice, garlic salt, and celery salt. Cut bacon strips in half; sauté until lightly browned. Split buns in half. Butter each half lightly and place buttered side down in hot skillet until brown. Turn browned side up. Cover one half of each bun with chicken and top with cheese mixture. Spread the other half with mayonnaise and top with tomatoes and bacon strips. Place under broiler until cheese melts. Remove to hot serving platter and serve immediately with potato chips and celery hearts.

Sliced turkey, ham, or luncheon meat may be substituted for the chicken.

CRAB MEAT SALAD SANDWICHES
6 servings

1 cup (6-ounce can) flaked crab meat
1 cup (½ pound) grated process cheese
1 cup finely chopped celery
2 tablespoons mayonnaise
2 teaspoons lemon juice
Dash of garlic salt
12 stuffed olives, chopped
1 teaspoon horse-radish
6 hamburger buns

Combine crab meat and remaining ingredients; mix well. Split buns in half. Butter lightly and place buttered side down in a hot skillet until brown. Turn browned side up and spread with crab-meat salad mixture. Place under broiler and broil until the cheese melts. Remove to hot serving platter and serve immediately.

DENVER SPECIAL SANDWICHES
6 servings

1 3¼-ounce can deviled ham
2 tablespoons chopped green
  pepper
2 tablespoons (1 whole) pimento
½ tablespoon finely chopped onion
¼ teaspoon salt

Dash of pepper
3 eggs, slightly beaten
3 hamburger buns
3 tablespoons butter
Dash of curry powder

Combine deviled ham, green pepper, pimento, onion, salt, and pepper. Stir beaten eggs into deviled ham mixture. For each sandwich pour ¼ cup of mixture into greased skillet and cook as you would pancakes. Brown well on both sides. Split hamburger buns in half. Spread with butter seasoned with curry powder. Grill buttered side down in a hot skillet. Remove to a hot serving platter. Place one pancake on each half bun; serve immediately.

FRENCH FRIED TUNA SALAD SANDWICHES
5 to 6 double sandwiches

1 8-ounce can tuna
2 hard-cooked eggs, chopped
1 sweet pickle, chopped
¼ cup finely chopped celery
½ teaspoon onion juice

Mayonnaise
10 to 12 slices bread
2 eggs
2 tablespoons cream
4 tablespoons fat

For sandwich filling, combine tuna, chopped eggs, pickle, celery, and onion juice. Moisten with mayonnaise. Spread on bread to make sandwiches. Beat eggs until light and add cream. Melt fat in heavy skillet. Lower one side of the sandwich into the egg mixture, turn it over and dip in the other side. Place in hot fat and fry until light brown.

Try this crisp French fried tuna salad sandwich as a change from grilled sandwiches. Your family is sure to like it.

MEAT SALAD IN BUNS
6 servings

¾ cup chopped luncheon meat
1 cup (2 whole) chopped hard-cooked eggs
1 cup chopped celery
¼ cup chopped sweet pickle
¼ cup chopped dill pickle
⅓ cup mayonnaise
½ teaspoon horse-radish

½ teaspoon prepared mustard
Dash of garlic salt
1 teaspoon lemon juice
¼ teaspoon Worcestershire sauce
6 wiener buns
1 tablespoon butter
¼ cup grated American cheese

Combine meat, eggs, celery, sweet and dill pickles. Mix mayonnaise with horse-radish, mustard, garlic salt, lemon juice, and Worcestershire sauce. Combine mayonnaise and meat mixtures. Cut the tops off buns. Scoop out the soft part, leaving only a shell. Fill each bun with sandwich filling. Brush the edge of each bun with butter. Top with grated cheese and put under broiler until cheese has melted. Remove to a hot serving platter and serve immediately.

ZESTY HAM SANDWICHES
4 servings

½ cup (4) chopped sweet pickles
½ cup (3) chopped dill pickles
3 tablespoons (2 large) pimentos
1 cup (½ pound) grated American cheese

⅓ cup mayonnaise
4 slices bread
4 thin slices cooked ham

Combine sweet and dill pickles, pimentos, cheese, and mayonnaise. Butter bread lightly and place buttered side down in hot skillet until lightly browned. Turn browned side up. Place 1 slice of ham on each slice of bread and top with pickle-cheese mixture. Place under broiler until cheese melts. Remove to hot serving platter and serve immediately.

Dried beef, chicken, or salami may be used instead of ham.

Beverages

Bohemian Tea
Cocoa
Coffee
Grenadine Punch
Lemonade

Mexican Chocolate
Pineapple Punch
Reception Chocolate
Spiced Cider
Tea

N<small>O MATTER</small> what kind of party you give, from the most formal reception to a spontaneous gathering, you'll want to pass something to drink.

Let the thermometer dictate your choice. A long, cool drink and the tinkle of ice in glasses will help your summer guests forget the heat. On a frigid winter day, a steaming beverage is as inviting and heart-warming as a blazing fire on the hearth.

It's as easy to prepare fruit drinks, coffee, tea, or chocolate for a crowd as for your family. The secret is to know the right proportion of ingredients. You'll find a guide to pleasant refreshment in this chapter.

The following recipes are for quantity serving, because of many requests for beverage recipes to serve large groups.

BOHEMIAN TEA
18 to 20 servings

1½ teaspoons ground cinnamon
1½ teaspoons ground cloves
1 cup sugar
2 quarts boiling water

2 tablespoons orange pekoe tea
1½ cups orange juice
½ cup lemon juice

Tie ground cinnamon and cloves loosely in a muslin bag. Add spice bag and sugar to boiling water; boil together 5 minutes. Remove from heat. Tie tea in a muslin bag. Add to syrup. Cover and let stand 5 minutes. Remove spices and tea bag. Add juice of oranges and lemons. Serve hot.

COCOA
25 servings

1 cup cocoa
½ teaspoon salt
1¼ cups sugar
2 cups boiling water

1¼ gallons milk
1 teaspoon vanilla
Dash of cinnamon

Mix cocoa, salt, and sugar together. Add the water and mix until smooth. Cook together for about 5 minutes. Scald the milk in a double boiler; add cocoa mixture to scalded milk and stir until well blended. Cook 15 minutes. Just before serving add vanilla and cinnamon. Whip to a froth and serve hot.

A marshmallow may be added to each cup, if desired.

COFFEE
25 servings

¾ pound regular grind coffee
½ cup cold water
1 egg, slightly beaten

1½ gallons cold, freshly-drawn
   water
½ cup cold water

Mix coffee with cold water and egg. Tie loosely in a large cloth sugar sack. As soon as water comes to full, rolling boil, remove pot from direct heat and immediately drop coffee sack into water. Push sack up and down to force water through ground coffee.

Cover kettle and allow coffee to brew for 12 to 15 minutes, moving sack up and down frequently during brewing. At end of brewing time, lift sack out of kettle, permitting it to drain thoroughly. Add ½ cup cold water to settle grounds.

If it is necessary to postpone the serving, maintain a uniform temperature in the kettle somewhat below boiling point. Do not allow the brew to boil—this destroys the flavor of the coffee.

GRENADINE PUNCH
About 20 to 24 servings

2 cups orange juice
1 cup lemon juice
1 cup grenadine

1½ quarts chilled pale dry ginger ale

Mix fruit juices and grenadine and pour over block of ice to chill. Just before serving add ginger ale. Use bing cherries and slices of oranges and limes to garnish punch bowl.

The deep red of the grenadine gives this punch a holiday color.

LEMONADE
20 to 25 servings

4 cups sugar
2 cups boiling water

2 cups lemon juice
1 gallon ice water

Cook the sugar and the boiling water together to a thin syrup, about 5 minutes. Chill. Strain the lemon juice, add the chilled syrup and the ice water.

MEXICAN CHOCOLATE
6 servings

2 ounces (2 squares) unsweetened chocolate
2 tablespoons hot water
⅔ cup sugar
1 teaspoon cornstarch

½ teaspoon salt
2 teaspoons cinnamon
2 cups strong coffee
3 cups hot milk
1 teaspoon vanilla

Place chocolate and hot water in top of double boiler. Heat until chocolate is melted. Combine sugar, cornstarch, salt, and cinnamon. Add to chocolate. Add coffee and stir until smooth. Cook 5 minutes longer. Combine with hot milk to which vanilla has been added. Cook in double boiler over low heat about 30 minutes to blend. Whip to a froth and serve hot.

PINEAPPLE PUNCH
About 25 servings

3 tablespoons green tea
2 cups orange juice
3 cups lemon juice
1 quart pineapple juice

4 cups sugar
3 cups water
1 quart pale dry ginger ale
1 quart lime ice

Pour 3 cups of freshly boiled water over the tea. Brew for about 3 minutes. Strain and cool. Extract juice from oranges and lemons. Add the pineapple juice and tea infusion. Boil sugar and water for 10 minutes to make a thin syrup. Chill and add to the fruit juice. Add ice and water to make 2 gallons. Add ginger ale just before serving.

A tablespoon of lime or orange ice may be added to each serving to give color and flavor.

RECEPTION CHOCOLATE
8 to 10 servings

1 cup sugar
1 cup cocoa
1 cup boiling water
1 quart heavy cream

2 quarts milk
1 teaspoon vanilla
¼ teaspoon salt

Mix sugar and cocoa, stir to a smooth paste with the boiling water. Heat over the direct flame and then cook in a double boiler for about 30 minutes or until a thick paste is formed. Chill. Whip cream. Fold in cocoa paste. Scald milk in double boiler, add vanilla and salt. When serving chocolate, put chocolate mixture in bowl and hot milk in pitcher. Put a large spoonful of chocolate mixture in cup; add hot milk. (Be sure milk is scalding hot, otherwise beverage will be lukewarm because of cold paste that is added.)

For your next reception or tea try reception chocolate. It's a glorified way of serving this favorite beverage.

SPICED CIDER
About 25 servings

8 2-inch pieces cinnamon bark
1 tablespoon cloves
1 tablespoon allspice
½ teaspoon mace

½ teaspoon salt
Dash of cayenne pepper
1 cup brown sugar
1 gallon cider

Tie spices loosely in a cheesecloth bag. Add spices and brown sugar to cider. Bring slowly to boiling point. Simmer 15 minutes. Remove spice bag. Serve hot.

TEA
20 to 25 servings

2½ tablespoons tea   3 cups boiling water

Pour boiling water over tea; steep for 10 minutes to make strong tea essence. Strain to remove tea leaves. Keep tea essence hot. Use 1 cup of tea essence to 1½ quarts of boiling water, which should give tea of proper strength. If too strong add a little boiling water.

This should be sufficient tea essence to make 1½ gallons of hot tea.

Desserts

FOREIGN AND SECTIONAL DESSERTS

Angel *Pie*
Baba au Rhum
Coconut Pancakes *(India)*
Cream Puffs
    Chocolate Glaze
Crème Brûlée

Crêpes Suzette
Date Torte
English Trifle
Hungarian Nut Torte
New England Maple Fritters
Polachinkas

FROZEN DESSERTS

Avocado Melon Mold
Avocado Orange Sherbet
Biscuit Tortoni
Cranberry Sherbet
    Cranberry and Apple
    Sherbet
French Vanilla Ice Cream
    Coconut Ice Cream
Fresh Strawberry Ice
   Strawberry Ice *(Using*
    Frozen Berries)
Ginger Lemon Sherbet

Loganberry Sherbet
Manhattan Ice Cream
Marron Bombe
Orange Almond Mousse
Pistachio Bombe
Rhubarb Banana Ice Cream
Spumoni
Strawberry Melba
Strawberry Mousse
Strawberry Parfait Amour
    Strawberry Parfait

FRUIT DESSERTS

Ambrosia
Apple Dumplings
Apple Fritters
Apple Pan Dowdy
Apple Strudel
Dutch Tart
Fresh Peach Cobbler
Fried Green Bananas

Fried Peaches
Hawaiian Glacé Bananas
Meringue Pears or Peaches
Pesche Ripiene
Pizza Figliati
Plantain Fritters *(India)*
Rhubarb Scallop with
    Meringue

PUDDINGS

Almendrada
Almond and Pineapple
Baked Indian
Blueberry Slump
Brood Met Appelen
Burnt Almond Sponge
Cherry Crème
    Macaroon Crème
Chocolate Fudge
Cranberry Crisp
    Apple Crisp
Frozen Lemon

Fruited Syllabub
Goureff Kacha
Grape Sponge
Lemon Chiffon
Lemon Crackle
Ostkaka
Pineapple Fluff
Plum
Pudin de Laranjas
Shrikand (India)
Soft Custard
    Snow Custard

SOUFFLES

Chocolate
Coconut

Orange
Pecan

DESSERT SAUCES

Foamy
Hard
Hot Fudge
Lemon

Mocha
Oriental
Sabayon
Vanilla

DESSERT IS the happy ending to a meal. It will keep your guests talking about your wonderful dinner as they leave the table. That's why you should choose a dessert to fit your meal.

After a luncheon or light dinner, or at a dessert party, you'll make a hit with a rich, glamorous treat. But a light, simple dessert is the natural follow-up to an elaborate dinner. Your guests will eat it with pleasure and not out of a sense of duty.

You may want to plan a dessert you can make in advance, such as a smooth frozen mousse, a refreshing ambrosia, or a velvety pudding. That leaves you with less detail to fuss over when your guests arrive. But once in a while you'll find producing a dramatic dessert — Crêpes Suzette or Baba au Rhum — well worth the last-minute effort.

Foreign and Sectional Desserts

ANGEL PIE
12 to 14 servings

6 egg whites (¾ cup)	1 tablespoon vinegar
¼ teaspoon salt	1 teaspoon vanilla
2 cups sugar	

Beat egg whites until foamy. Add salt. Add 1 cup of the sugar slowly while beating constantly. Then beat in remaining cup of sugar alternately with vinegar and vanilla. Beat until stiff. Pour into 2 buttered 9-inch pie pans and shape like a pie crust. Bake in very slow oven (275°) 1 hour. Top with fresh berries or a favorite tangy dessert sauce and a spoonful of whipped cream.

On cooling the angel pie, the shell will crack. The outside is crusty but not tough; the inside is moist, soft, and spongy.

BABA AU RHUM
8 to 10 servings

½ cake compressed yeast
½ cup warm milk
½ cup sifted flour
½ cup shortening
3 tablespoons sugar

1 teaspoon grated lemon peel
¼ teaspoon salt
3 eggs
1½ cups sifted flour

Soften yeast in warm milk. Beat in the ½ cup of flour; cover and let sponge rise until light. Cream together shortening, sugar, lemon peel, and salt. Add eggs, one at a time; beat well after each addition. Add the remaining 1½ cups of flour slowly; add sponge and mix well. Pour into greased ring mold and let stand until triple in bulk. Bake in moderate oven (350°) 25 minutes. When baked, prick baba with a fork, pour sauce over it, and let stand until sauce is absorbed. Pour apricot glaze over baba just before serving. Decorate with glacé fruit.

Sauce for Baba:

2 cups sugar
4 cups water
4 teaspoons rum flavoring

1 teaspoon lemon juice
¼ teaspoon almond extract

Boil sugar and water for 8 to 10 minutes. Remove from heat and add flavorings. Pour sauce over baba at intervals and let stand until all of sauce is absorbed.

Apricot Glaze:

1½ cups dried apricots
2 cups water
¼ cup sugar

2 tablespoons light corn syrup
⅛ teaspoon salt

Cook apricots in water until soft. Put through strainer to make apricot purée. Add sugar, corn syrup, and salt. Cook for 5 minutes. Cool.

COCONUT PANCAKES (INDIA)
About 3 dozen

Batter:

4 eggs
1 teaspoon salt
1½ cups milk

1 cup flour
3 tablespoons melted butter

Beat eggs until light. Add salt, milk, and flour, and beat until smooth. This is a very thin batter. Heat iron skillet and brush lightly with oil. Pour about 2 tablespoons batter into skillet for each pancake. They should be about 3 to 4 inches in diameter. Brown lightly on one side only. Spread unbrowned side with melted butter. Put 1 tablespoon coconut mixture on each pancake and roll up. Serve warm as dessert.

Coconut Filling:

1 cup grated fresh coconut
2 tablespoons sugar
2 cardamom seeds, pounded

½ cup raisins
½ cup chopped nuts

According to Gwendolyn Matthews, of Madras, Indian women love to cook delicacies, in particular, but many educated women do not do so because of abundant native help. Indian women, however, believe that one of the most important factors of good cookery is the particular "touch" of a good cook who can turn edible foods into superb dishes!

CREAM PUFFS
About 1 dozen, large

½ cup butter
1 cup boiling water
1 cup sifted flour

¼ teaspoon salt
4 eggs, unbeaten

Combine butter and water in saucepan and bring to boil. Add flour and salt and stir constantly until mixture leaves sides of pan in smooth compact mass. Remove from heat and cool slightly. Add eggs, one at a time, beating thoroughly after each addition. Beat steadily until mixture is smooth and satiny. Shape with a pastry bag or drop from tablespoon 2 inches apart on ungreased cooky sheet, 15½ x 12 inches. Bake in hot oven (450°) 10 to 15 minutes, then reduce heat to moderate (350°) and bake about 25 minutes longer. When cool, cut slit in side of each puff and fill with whipped cream or Cream Pie Filling (page 424). Top with Chocolate Glaze.

Chocolate Glaze:

2 tablespoons butter
2 squares unsweetened chocolate
3 tablespoons hot milk

1 cup confectioners' sugar
Dash of salt

Heat butter and chocolate in double boiler until melted. Combine milk, confectioners' sugar, and salt. Add to chocolate mixture gradually, stirring until smooth.

For *tiny cream puffs* to serve at teas, use about ½ teaspoon batter for each puff and bake in the same manner, only for a shorter time. Bake in hot oven (450°) 6 to 8 minutes, then in moderate oven (350°) about 15 to 20 minutes. These miniature puffs may be filled with tuna fish salad or Chicken Salad (page 226) and used on an assorted sandwich tray. If you would like to use them with cookies and cakes, fill with a dab of cream filling and top with a bit of colored frosting.

These tiny cream puffs give a professional touch to your party cakes.

CREME BRULEE
4 to 6 servings

2 cups cream
4 egg yolks
2½ tablespoons sugar

1 teaspoon vanilla
¼ cup light brown sugar

Heat cream in double boiler. Beat egg yolks, adding sugar gradually. Remove cream from heat and pour very slowly into egg yolk mixture, stirring constantly. Add vanilla. Pour into 1½-quart casserole. Place in pan of hot water and bake uncovered in slow oven (325°) about 45 to 50 minutes or until done. When custard is set, sprinkle with brown sugar. Place under broiler for a minute or so until sugar melts. Chill. Serve plain or with fruit.

This is a rich smooth custard and should be served very cold.

CREPES SUZETTE
8 to 10 servings

2 eggs
1½ cups milk
½ cup butter, melted

1 tablespoon oil
1 cup sifted flour

Beat eggs until light and add milk. Add butter and oil. Stir in flour and beat until batter is smooth. Heat skillet and grease lightly. Pour batter into greased skillet to make thin pancakes about 4 inches in diameter. When brown on one side, turn over and brown lightly on other side. Keep warm until served.

Filling:

½ cup butter
½ cup sugar
¼ cup orange juice

1 tablespoon lemon juice
2 teaspoons grated orange peel
1 teaspoon grated lemon peel

Cream butter and sugar and add orange and lemon juice and grated peels. Spread each crêpe or pancake with this filling. Roll up and sprinkle with confectioners' sugar. If preferred, spread with currant jelly or raspberry jam. Serve 3 crêpes per person.

This is an easy-to-make American version of the famous French Crêpes Suzette.

DATE TORTE
6 to 8 servings

3 egg yolks
¼ teaspoon salt
1¾ cups confectioners' sugar
1 teaspoon baking powder
¼ cup bread crumbs

½ cup coarsely chopped nuts
½ pound pitted dates, chopped
½ teaspoon vanilla
3 egg whites
1 cup heavy cream, whipped

Beat egg yolks until light. Add salt and confectioners' sugar and blend. Add baking powder, bread crumbs, nuts, dates, and vanilla, and mix well. Beat egg whites to soft peak stage and fold into mixture. Pour into buttered 9-inch square pan. Bake in slow oven (325°) 20 to 25 minutes. Cool. Break torte into pieces the size of a walnut and fold into whipped cream. Serve in sherbet dishes.

ENGLISH TRIFLE
12 to 14 servings

1 recipe Sponge Cake (page 409)
1½ cups raspberry jam
2½ cups pineapple juice
1 tablespoon lemon juice
½ teaspoon almond extract
1 cup slivered blanched almonds

1 recipe Soft Custard (page 339), chilled
1 cup heavy cream
2 tablespoons confectioners' sugar
½ teaspoon vanilla
½ cup glacé cherries

Bake Sponge Cake in oblong pan, 13 x 9½ x 2 inches. Cut cake into slices about ⅓ inch thick and spread slices generously with raspberry jam. Place one slice on top of another, sandwich fashion. Cut into 2-inch pieces. Place pieces in sherbet dish. Combine pineapple juice, lemon juice, and almond extract. Pour two tablespoons pineapple juice over cake in each cup (more if necessary, to moisten cake). Sprinkle with a few slivered almonds. Add enough Soft Custard to cover cake; chill. Whip cream and fold in confectioners' sugar and vanilla. Garnish with whipped cream and ½ of a glacé cherry. Sprinkle a few almonds on top.

HUNGARIAN NUT TORTE
6 to 8 servings

Torte:

¼ cup butter
¾ cup sugar
2 teaspoons vanilla
1½ ounces (6 tablespoons) grated unsweetened chocolate

¼ cup bread crumbs
¼ cup flour
¾ cup ground nuts
8 egg whites

Cream butter and sugar together until light and fluffy. Stir into creamed mixture the vanilla, grated chocolate, bread crumbs, flour, and nuts. Mix well. This will be a crumbly mixture. Beat egg whites to soft peak stage. Fold carefully into bread crumb mixture. Turn into 2 greased 8-inch round cake pans. Bake in slow oven (325°) 30 to 35 minutes. Let stand 10 minutes. Remove from pan and cool.

Filling:

¼ cup butter, softened
1 cup confectioners' sugar
2 tablespoons warm cream
1 tablespoon cocoa

¼ teaspoon salt
½ teaspoon vanilla
½ cup finely chopped nuts

Cream butter, add confectioners' sugar, cream, cocoa, salt, and vanilla. Mix until smooth and add chopped nuts. Spread filling between layers of torte. Frost top and sides with Mocha Frosting (page 415). Sprinkle with grated chocolate, if desired.

NEW ENGLAND MAPLE FRITTERS
About 16 fritters

2 cups sifted flour
2 teaspoons baking powder
½ teaspoon salt

1 cup milk
1 egg, well beaten
Confectioners' sugar

Sift dry ingredients together. Add milk to beaten egg and pour into flour mixture. Stir just enough to blend ingredients. Drop from tablespoon into deep hot fat (365° to 375°) 5 to 6 minutes or until well puffed and golden brown. Drain on absorbent paper. Sprinkle with confectioners' sugar. Serve warm with hot maple syrup.

NOTE: For best results, fry only a few fritters at a time. Too many lower the temperature of the fat and increase the cooking time, causing the fritters to become grease soaked. Drain excess grease from the fritters by placing them on a paper towel as they come out of the fat. Deep fat frying calls for constant attention, for the tender, golden brown crust and even shape result from turning fritters often in fat and removing at just the right stage.

Although you may never have considered the lowly fritter as a dessert, you'll count this among your favorites once you try it. Maple syrup is the perfect complement for the light, puffy golden brown balls.

POLACHINKAS
Yugoslavian Crêpes Suzette
6 servings; 3 per serving

2 eggs	1 cup raspberry jam
½ teaspoon salt	½ cup sugar
¾ cup milk	½ teaspoon cinnamon
½ cup sifted flour	¾ cup sour cream
4 tablespoons melted butter	

Beat eggs until light. Add salt, milk, flour, and butter, and beat until smooth. This is a very thin batter. Heat skillet and brush lightly with oil. Pour about 2 tablespoons of batter into skillet for each pancake, which should be about 3 to 4 inches in diameter. When light brown on one side, turn and brown the other side. Spread each pancake generously with jam. Roll and stack in a 1½-quart casserole. Mix sugar and cinnamon and sprinkle over pancakes; pour on sour cream. Bake uncovered in moderate oven (350°) 35 minutes or until most of cream has been absorbed. Serve hot.

Polachinkas are the Yugoslavian version of the Crêpes Suzette. This recipe came from Mildred Rasul, a student, whose grandmother brought the recipe from Yugoslavia.

Frozen Desserts

MELON MOLDS

Melon Molds are so called because of the shape. They are also called Bombes.

TO LINE OR FILL A MOLD

Chill the melon mold. Line the mold with ice cream, using a spoon dipped in hot water. Spread evenly on bottom and sides of mold ¾ to 1 inch thick. Put second mixture in center and fill mold. Cover with waxed paper. Put lid on mold.

TO FREEZE BOMBE OR MOLD

Place in freezing-compartment for 24 hours.

TO UNMOLD BOMBE OR MOLD

Dip entire mold quickly in and out of very hot water. Wipe off; remove cover and waxed paper. Run knife around edge to loosen.

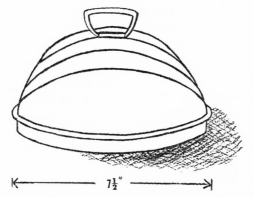

7½"

Invert mold onto pan that has been covered with waxed paper; set in freezing-compartment again to harden, as ice cream becomes slightly runny when mold is dipped into hot water.

TO SERVE BOMBE OR MOLD

Slip mold onto glass plate that has been chilled. Decorate base of mold with fresh fruit or flowers and serve immediately.

AVOCADO MELON MOLD
10 to 12 servings

1½ cups mashed avocado pulp (2 large ripe avocados)	½ cup sugar
	½ teaspoon salt
3 tablespoons lemon juice	1½ cups cream
1 teaspoon grated lemon peel	¼ teaspoon green food coloring
1 tablespoon orange juice	2 egg whites

Combine mashed avocado pulp, lemon juice, lemon peel, orange juice, sugar, salt, and cream. Add coloring. Put into container of ice cream freezer. Pack with ice and salt. Freeze. When partially frozen, add egg whites that have been beaten to frothy stage. Continue freezing until firm. Use this avocado ice cream to line a quart melon mold. Fill the center with Loganberry Sherbet (page 316). Cover mold with waxed paper before putting on lid. Place in freezing-compartment for 24 hours. Unmold onto chilled glass plate. If desired, decorate the base of the mold with small flowers such as daisies.

Here's one way to have "watermelon" out-of-season. The deep loganberry sherbet center is a pleasing color contrast to the olive green avocado-flecked outer ring, and a more pleasing flavor contrast couldn't be imagined. These fancy melon molds make an ideal dessert to serve at a buffet party.

AVOCADO ORANGE SHERBET
8 to 10 servings

1½ cups mashed avocado pulp
½ cup pineapple juice
¾ cup orange juice
½ cup lemon juice
2 teaspoons grated lemon peel

1¼ cups sugar
1 cup milk
¼ teaspoon salt
Few drops of almond extract
Green food coloring

Add fruit juices and lemon peel to mashed avocado; then add sugar, milk, salt, and almond extract. Add green coloring to tint delicate green. Freeze.

Crisp almond cookies make a perfect accompaniment to this tangy sherbet.

BISCUIT TORTONI
8 to 10 servings

¾ cup sugar
½ cup water
3 egg whites
6 egg yolks
2 teaspoons unflavored gelatin
¼ cup cold water
1½ cups heavy cream
½ teaspoon vanilla

½ teaspoon lemon extract
½ teaspoon almond extract
½ teaspoon salt
¾ cup cake crumbs or vanilla
    wafer crumbs
½ cup chopped blanched almonds
½ cup toasted coconut

Boil sugar and water to first thread stage (234°). Beat egg whites to soft peak stage and pour ½ of syrup over the whites and beat until fluffy. Beat egg yolks until light and add other half of syrup slowly, beating constantly. Add to yolk mixture the gelatin which has been softened in cold water and melted over hot water. Fold into egg whites; whip cream and fold in. Add vanilla, lemon and almond extract, salt, cake crumbs, almonds, and coconut. Fill fluted paper cups ¾ full of mixture and put into freezing-compartment to harden.

A very rich dessert!

CRANBERRY SHERBET
8 to 10 servings

1 pound (4 cups) cranberries
2½ cups water
2¼ cups sugar
½ cup cold water

1 tablespoon (1 envelope)
    unflavored gelatin
⅓ cup lemon juice

Cook cranberries and water until skins pop. Rub through sieve, add sugar and heat to boiling. Soften gelatin in cold water, add to hot cranberry mixture and stir until dissolved. Cool and add lemon juice. Freeze.

CRANBERRY AND APPLE SHERBET

Use 2 cups diced apples and 2 cups cranberries instead of 4 cups cranberries and proceed as for Cranberry Sherbet.

FRENCH VANILLA ICE CREAM
6 to 8 servings

½ cup sugar	2 cups milk, scalded
⅛ teaspoon salt	1 cup cream
4 egg yolks, slightly beaten	1 tablespoon vanilla

Mix together sugar, salt, and slightly beaten egg yolks. Stir scalded milk slowly into egg yolks. Cook in double boiler until mixture coats a spoon, about 3 minutes. Cool and strain. Add cream and vanilla. Freeze.

COCONUT ICE CREAM

Add ¾ cup grated fresh coconut or ¾ cup toasted shredded coconut to French Vanilla Ice Cream about 5 minutes before it is frozen.

The French version of ice cream is as fluffy and airy as foam itself, with an unsurpassed, rich custard flavor.

FRESH STRAWBERRY ICE
4 to 6 servings

1 cup sugar	1 tablespoon lemon juice
1 cup water	¼ teaspoon salt
1 pint fresh strawberries, mashed	

Boil sugar and water together for 5 minutes. Cool. Add strawberries, lemon juice, and salt. Freeze. Use 8 parts ice, 1 part salt.

Fresh strawberry ice may be used for parfaits, with French Vanilla Ice Cream (above).

STRAWBERRY ICE (USING FROZEN BERRIES)

2 12-ounce boxes frozen strawberries	1 cup water
	1 tablespoon lemon juice

Put frozen strawberries through a wire sieve. Add water and lemon juice. Proceed as for Fresh Strawberry Ice.

GINGER LEMON SHERBET
4 to 6 servings

3 cups milk
¾ cup sugar
3 tablespoons finely chopped
    candied ginger

¼ cup lemon juice
1 tablespoon grated lemon peel
3 tablespoons lime juice

Combine milk and sugar. Add ginger, lemon juice, lemon peel, and lime juice. The mixture may have a curdled appearance, but this will not affect the texture. Freeze. Serve in crystal sherbet glasses and garnish with a mint leaf.

LOGANBERRY SHERBET
4 servings

1 No. 2 can loganberries
2 teaspoons lemon juice

¼ cup water

Press loganberries through a wire sieve to remove seeds and pulp. Add lemon juice and water. Freeze. If frozen berries are used, two 12-ounce packages and ½ cup water will be needed.

This loganberry sherbet is used as a center for Avocado Melon Mold (page 313).

MANHATTAN ICE CREAM
6 servings

2 cups sliced fresh peaches
½ cup confectioners' sugar

3 tablespoons rum flavoring
1 quart vanilla ice cream

Add to peaches the confectioners' sugar and rum flavoring. Chill. Let stand 2 or 3 hours. Put half of ice cream into refrigerator tray; cover with the fruit and remaining ice cream. Let stand 3 or 4 hours in refrigerator. When serving, garnish with sliced fresh peaches.

MARRON BOMBE
10 to 12 servings

2 teaspoons unflavored gelatin
½ cup water
½ cup sugar
¼ teaspoon salt
2 egg whites
1 cup marrons, cut into small
    pieces*

1½ cups heavy cream
1 teaspoon vanilla
¼ teaspoon almond extract
1 tablespoon lemon juice
Green food coloring
1½ quarts vanilla ice cream

Soak gelatin in ¼ cup of the water. Cook sugar, salt, and the remaining ¼ cup water together for 3 minutes. Cover saucepan for a minute or two to dissolve sugar crystals on sides of pan. Beat egg whites to soft peak stage; gradually add hot syrup, beating constantly. Dissolve soaked gelatin over hot water and beat into egg white mixture until of the consistency of boiled frosting. Let stand until it begins to set. Stir occasionally. Add marrons. Whip cream; add vanilla, almond extract, and lemon juice. Fold egg white mixture carefully into whipped cream. Add a small amount of green food coloring. Line 1-quart melon mold with the vanilla ice cream. Fill center with marron mixture. Cover with waxed paper and place in freezing-compartment for 24 hours. Unmold onto a crystal plate and decorate as desired. Cut into 1-inch slices to serve.

On the outside, smooth vanilla ice cream — inside, a refreshing mint-green mixture with pebbles of chestnuts. Slices of this bombe make such a pretty dessert plate. Like all frozen desserts, half its beauty to the busy hostess is in the fact that it can be prepared well in advance of the party. If you don't have chestnuts, substitute pecans or almonds.

* Marrons are chestnuts that have been preserved in a syrup. They should be drained before using.

ORANGE ALMOND MOUSSE
10 to 12 servings

1 cup sugar	1 cup orange juice
2 tablespoons grated orange peel	¼ cup lemon juice
⅓ cup boiling water	½ cup glacé cherries
1 tablespoon unflavored gelatin	2 cups heavy cream
¼ cup cold water	1 cup chopped blanched almonds

Put sugar, grated orange peel, and boiling water into saucepan. Stir and boil 1 minute. Soak gelatin in the cold water for a few minutes. Dissolve soaked gelatin in hot syrup. Add orange and lemon juice. Let stand until jelly-like in consistency. Cut cherries into quarters. Whip cream. Fold whipped cream, cherries, and nuts into the thickened gelatin mixture. Place in refrigerator and let stand several hours or overnight. If frozen mousse is preferred, put mixture into freezing-compartment. Serve in sherbet glasses.

The recipe for this creamy, luscious orange almond mousse was brought from Avon, New York, by one of my first students at Iowa State College, Harriet Anderson.

PISTACHIO BOMBE
8 to 10 servings

2 cups milk
3 egg yolks
1 cup sugar
¼ teaspoon salt
1⅓ cups heavy cream

2 teaspoons vanilla
½ teaspoon almond extract
½ cup chopped pistachio nuts*
Green food coloring
Strawberry Mousse (page 320)

Scald milk in double boiler. Beat egg yolks and add sugar and salt. Add scalded milk slowly to egg yolks. Return to double boiler and cook until mixture thickens, about 3 minutes longer. Cool. Add the cream, vanilla, almond extract, and nuts. Add enough green coloring to tint mixture a delicate green. Freeze. Use mixture to line 1-quart melon mold. Fill the center with Strawberry Mousse. Cover mold with waxed paper. Put lid on

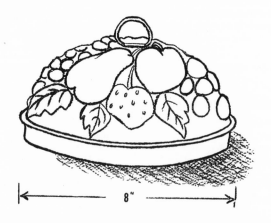

8″

mold and place in freezing-compartment. Let stand until set. Unmold and decorate with whole fresh strawberries.

Tint the mixture only the coolest green and choose any pretty, fancy mold.

This dessert is most delectable when fresh strawberries can be used in the mousse but frozen berries are also good. An inspiring specialty for a dessert party.

* Use blanched almonds if pistachio nuts are not available.

RHUBARB BANANA ICE CREAM
8 to 10 servings

1½ cups Rhubarb Sauce*
Red food coloring
1 cup cream

1 egg, beaten
1 banana, sliced
2 tablespoons lemon juice

Add a small amount of red coloring to Rhubard Sauce to give a delicate pink color. Combine with the cream and beaten egg; add sliced banana and lemon juice. Freeze.

*Rhubarb Sauce:

1 pound rhubarb, cut in 1-inch
   pieces

¾ cup sugar
½ cup hot water

Combine rhubarb, sugar, and water in saucepan. Cover and cook slowly until tender, 20 to 25 minutes. If frozen rhubarb is used, it will take two 12-ounce packages plus 2 tablespoons sugar.

Here's an unusual partner for your fresh spring rhubarb. The bland banana balances nicely with the tangy rhubarb for a different flavor treat. It's such a pretty, fluffy-looking ice cream, too.

SPUMONI
Italian Ice Cream
10 to 12 servings

Cream Filling:

1½ cups heavy cream, whipped
½ cup sugar
½ cup maraschino cherries,
   drained and cut into quarters

3 tablespoons candied orange peel,
   cut into thin strips
1 teaspoon lemon juice

Fold sugar, maraschino cherries, orange peel, and lemon juice into whipped cream. Put in refrigerator tray to harden.

Lining for Mold:

1½ quarts vanilla ice cream
½ cup chopped blanched almonds

¼ teaspoon almond extract

Add chopped nuts to ice cream, then flavor with almond extract. If ice cream becomes soft, put in freezer to harden.

To Pack Spumoni:

First chill 1-quart melon mold, then line with ice cream to depth of 1 inch. Bring ice cream well up on sides of mold and leave hollow in center. Fill mold with whipped cream mixture. Cover with waxed paper, fit lid on tightly and put in freezing-compartment for 24 hours. Unmold onto chilled plate and garnish as desired. Cut into 1-inch slices for serving.

STRAWBERRY MELBA
6 servings

1 pint fresh strawberries
¼ cup sugar

1 cup heavy cream, whipped
1 quart vanilla ice cream

Wash and hull strawberries. Mash and add sugar. Fold strawberries into whipped cream. Serve ice cream on chilled plate. Top with a heaping tablespoon of strawberry-cream mixture, and pour over this the Strawberry Melba Sauce.

Strawberry Melba Sauce:

2 teaspoons cornstarch
2 tablespoons sugar
¼ cup light corn syrup

1 cup fresh or frozen raspberries
1 pint fresh strawberries, crushed
1 tablespoon lemon juice

Mix cornstarch, sugar, and corn syrup together. Add raspberries and cook until clear and somewhat thickened. Cool. Strain to remove raspberry seeds; mix with strawberries and lemon juice.

Good, but oh so-o rich!

STRAWBERRY MOUSSE
10 to 12 servings

2 cups fresh strawberries or 12-ounce package frozen
¾ cup sugar
1 teaspoon lemon juice

¼ teaspoon salt
2 egg whites, beaten
1½ cups heavy cream

Wash and hull fresh strawberries. Cook berries with the sugar and force through a strainer. If frozen berries are used, defrost overnight in refrigerator and put through strainer. Do not add any sugar to frozen berries. Add lemon juice and salt to strawberry purée. Beat egg whites to soft peak stage and fold into strawberry purée. Whip cream and fold into mixture. Pour into refrigerator trays. Let stand until frozen. Use for center of Pistachio Bombe (page 318).

STRAWBERRY PARFAIT AMOUR
10 to 12 servings

3 cups heavy cream
¾ cup confectioners' sugar
2 teaspoons vanilla

1 cup peanut brittle broken into small pieces
½ teaspoon salt

Whip cream. Fold in confectioners' sugar, vanilla, peanut brittle, and salt. Pour into a 1-quart ring mold; cover with waxed paper.

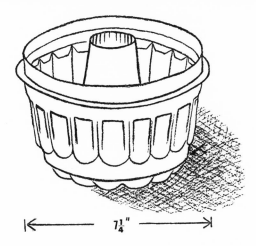

Put cover on mold and place in freezing-compartment for 24 hours. Unmold, pile Strawberry Parfait in center and garnish with fresh strawberries.

STRAWBERRY PARFAIT — 10 to 12 servings

1 quart fresh strawberries or 2 cups frozen	2 egg whites
2 cups sugar	½ teaspoon salt
½ cup water	1 teaspoon lemon juice
	2 cups heavy cream

Clean and mash fresh strawberries, sprinkle with 1 cup of the sugar. Cover and let stand 30 minutes to 1 hour; then force through a fine sieve. If frozen berries are used, let stand overnight in refrigerator to defrost, then put through a sieve, but do not add any extra sugar. Pour strawberry purée into refrigerator tray and freeze to a mush. Boil ½ cup water and the remaining 1 cup of sugar to soft ball stage (238°) or until syrup threads from spoon. Beat egg whites to soft peak stage and add syrup gradually, beating constantly. Add salt and lemon juice. Fold into frozen strawberry purée. Whip cream until stiff and fold into strawberry mixture. Pour into refrigerator trays and freeze. Stir several times during freezing period. Use as center for Strawberry Parfait Amour.

Everyone loves this rich, crunchy, nut ice-cream ring heaped high with frothy pink strawberry parfait. Cooling and refreshing on a summer day — but don't count either calories or pennies with this dessert.

Fruit Desserts

AMBROSIA
6 to 8 servings

6 seedless oranges	⅓ cup sugar
1½ cups shredded fresh coconut	

Peel oranges. Slice crosswise in ¼-inch slices. Place orange slices and coconut alternately in crystal sherbet glasses. Sprinkle with sugar. Chill thoroughly. Serve very cold. If desired, ambrosia may be put into a crystal bowl and served at the table.

In the South, ambrosia is a favorite dessert at Christmastime. Thin slices of rich, dark fruit cake are served with it.

APPLE DUMPLINGS
9 servings

Syrup:

1 cup granulated sugar	4 tablespoons butter
1 cup brown sugar	2 cups boiling water

Combine granulated sugar, brown sugar, butter, and water. Bring to boil and cook 5 minutes.

Dumplings:

2 cups sifted flour	⅔ cup milk
3 teaspoons baking powder	2 tablespoons butter
½ teaspoon salt	6 to 8 apples, pared and chopped
2 tablespoons sugar	¾ cup sugar
4 tablespoons shortening	1 teaspoon cinnamon

Sift flour, baking powder, salt, and sugar together. Cut in shortening and add milk to make a soft dough. Turn out on floured board and knead gently, about 25 to 30 times. Roll into rectangle ¼ inch thick. Cut into 5-inch squares; brush each square with butter. Mix sugar and cinnamon together. Place about ¼ cup chopped apples in center of each square and sprinkle 1 teaspoon sugar and cinnamon mixture over the apples. Enclose apples with dough, sealing tightly. Pour syrup into baking pan, 13 x 9½ x 2 inches. Drop dumplings 1 inch apart, sealed side down, into the syrup and bake in hot oven (400°) 20 to 25 minutes. The top will rise out of the syrup and will brown. Serve with whipped cream, ice cream, or cream to which vanilla, sugar, and nutmeg have been added.

These golden brown dumplings of flaky pastry and spicy apples in their well-flavored sauce were introduced to us by Mrs. Ruth Gaertner, graduate student from Charleston, Illinois. Mrs. Gaertner has charge of the cafeteria at Eastern Illinois College. She says they can hardly keep the counter supplied with these mouth-watering morsels when they are on the menu, they are such a great favorite with the students.

APPLE FRITTERS
About 3 dozen

5 to 6 medium apples   **Juice of 1 lemon**
¼ cup sugar

Core and pare apples and slice into thin circles. Place in bowl and sprinkle with sugar. Add lemon juice and let stand until ready for use.

Fritter Batter:

½ cup milk   **2 tablespoons melted butter**
2 egg yolks, well beaten   **1½ tablespoons lemon juice**
⅞ cup sifted flour   **1 teaspoon vanilla**
1 teaspoon salt   **2 egg whites, stiffly beaten**
¼ teaspoon nutmeg   **Confectioners' sugar**

Pour milk into beaten egg yolks. Sift together flour, salt, and nutmeg, and add to milk mixture; add melted butter, lemon juice, and vanilla. Stir until well blended. Fold in egg whites. Drain apple slices on absorbent paper, dip each circle into batter separately, and drop into deep hot fat (375°) 4 to 5 minutes or until golden. Sprinkle with confectioners' sugar and serve hot.

These crisp, crunchy fritters make an ideal accompaniment to Baked Ham (page 112) or pork chops. They may also be served with a lemon sauce as a dessert. The delicate fritters are at their best while still crisp, so be sure to serve them as soon as possible after they have been fried.

APPLE PAN DOWDY
8 to 10 servings

Pastry:

2 cups sifted flour
1 teaspoon salt

⅔ cup shortening
5 to 6 tablespoons cold water

Filling:

1 quart pared, sliced apples
¼ cup sugar
¼ teaspoon cinnamon
¼ teaspoon nutmeg

¼ teaspoon salt
¼ cup dark molasses
½ cup water
2 tablespoons butter

Sift flour and salt together and cut in shortening. Add water one tablespoon at a time, blending with a fork until mixture holds together. Chill. Use ⅔ of pastry dough, rolled ⅛ inch thick, to line a 1½-quart casserole. Mix sugar, spices, and salt. Fill casserole with alternate layers of apples and spice mixture. Mix molasses and water and pour over apples. Dot with butter. Cover apples with other ⅓ of pie crust rolled ⅛ inch thick; trim and flute edges, and press to rim of casserole. Bake in hot oven (425°) 20 minutes.

Remove from oven and chop mixture with a knife, being sure the pie crust is thoroughly mixed with the apples. Add ½ cup water, return to oven, and bake 20 to 30 minutes in slow oven (325°) or until apples are tender. Serve with cream to which a little nutmeg has been added.

APPLE STRUDEL
10 to 12 servings

2 cups sifted flour
3 teaspoons baking powder
½ teaspoon salt
2 tablespoons sugar
4 tablespoons shortening

⅔ cup milk
2 tablespoons melted butter
3 cups pared, chopped apples
⅔ cup sugar
1 teaspoon cinnamon

Frosting:

2 cups confectioners' sugar
1 teaspoon cinnamon
1 tablespoon butter, softened

3 tablespoons cream
¼ cup chopped nuts

Sift together the flour, baking powder, salt, and the 2 tablespoons of sugar. Cut in shortening and add milk to make a soft dough.

Turn out on floured board and knead 25 to 30 times. Roll dough ¼ inch thick. Brush with melted butter; cover with chopped apples. Mix the ⅔ cup of sugar with the cinnamon and sprinkle over the apples. Roll up like a jelly roll and form into a semicircle on a greased cooky sheet. Bake in hot oven (425°) 25 to 35 minutes. While warm spread with frosting made of the confectioners' sugar, cinnamon, butter, and cream. Sprinkle chopped nuts over the frosting. Cut roll into 1-inch slices and serve warm or cold.

This is our American version of apple strudel.

DUTCH TART
12 to 14 servings

Filling:

6 tart apples	1 teaspoon grated orange peel
2 oranges	1 teaspoon grated lemon peel
1 cup sugar	Juice of 2 lemons
½ cup shredded pineapple	

Pare and slice apples. Cook in small amount of water until done. Force through strainer. Peel oranges, section and add to apple pulp. Add sugar, shredded pineapple, orange and lemon peel and lemon juice. Cook again for a few minutes.

Pastry:

1 pound butter	5 cups sifted flour
2 cups sugar	2 teaspoons lemon extract
6 eggs	1 teaspoon grated lemon peel

Cream butter, add sugar gradually, and mix until light and fluffy. Beat eggs until light. Add flour to creamed butter and sugar mixture alternately with beaten eggs and continue until all have been added. Add lemon extract and grated lemon peel. Mix until smooth. Pour batter into 2 buttered 9-inch square cake pans in alternate layers with the fruit filling. Bake in moderate oven (350°) 35 to 40 minutes or until done. Cut in squares and serve with whipped cream.

This is a rich, rather heavy dessert.

FRESH PEACH COBBLER
6 to 8 servings

2 cups sifted flour	2 tablespoons sugar
3 teaspoons baking powder	4 tablespoons shortening
½ teaspoon salt	⅔ cup milk

Sift together the flour, baking powder, salt, and sugar. Cut in shortening and add milk to make a soft dough. Turn out on floured board and knead 25 to 30 times.

Filling:

3 pounds (about 5 cups) fresh peaches, peeled and sliced	½ teaspoon salt
1 cup sugar	¼ cup corn syrup
1 tablespoon cornstarch	¼ teaspoon almond extract

Mix together sugar, cornstarch, and salt, and sprinkle over sliced peaches. Mix corn syrup and almond extract. Add to peaches.

Roll ⅔ of dough ¼ inch thick to fit a 9-inch square baking pan. Put dough into pan and trim to fit. Add peach filling. Dot with butter. Roll remainder of dough ¼ inch thick. Cut into strips ½ inch wide and about 9 inches long. Moisten ends of strips. Place strips on top lattice-fashion and press into pastry. Bake in hot oven (400°) 25 to 30 minutes or until peaches are tender. Serve cobbler hot or cold with heavy cream or ice cream.

FRIED GREEN BANANAS
4 servings

4 green bananas

Peel bananas. Slice about ⅛ inch thick. Fry in deep hot fat (375°) until browned.

FRIED PEACHES
6 servings

6 fresh peaches	¼ cup brown sugar
2 tablespoons butter	

Peel and split the peaches. Remove pit. Melt the butter in a skillet and put peach halves in skillet. Fill the hollow halves with the brown sugar and let simmer until done, but not too soft.

So versatile and so good. Add whipped cream or ice cream and you have a colorful and luscious dessert; serve with meat and you have the perfect accompaniment. And, best of all, you can use either fresh or canned peaches, so they're always in season. You may like to try flavored syrup with the peaches for variety.

HAWAIIAN GLACE BANANAS
6 servings

4 tablespoons butter
6 bananas, peeled and left whole
4 tablespoons guava jelly

1 tablespoon lemon juice
½ cup pineapple juice

Put butter in skillet to melt, add bananas and sauté until light golden brown. Add guava jelly, and when it has melted add lemon and pineapple juice. Baste bananas with the sauce and leave in pan until well glazed, but not too soft. Serve with Shrimp Curry (page 156) or Baked Ham (page 112).

MERINGUE PEARS OR PEACHES
6 servings

12 halves of pears or peaches,
    canned or fresh
¼ cup sugar
1½ teaspoons grated lemon peel

¼ cup orange juice
1 tablespoon chopped candied
    ginger

Drain the fruit and place in a 9-inch square pan. Combine sugar, grated peel, juice, and ginger. Fill cavities of pears with the mixture.

Meringue:

3 egg whites

6 tablespoons sugar

Make a meringue of the egg whites and sugar. Pile meringue on the pears and bake in slow oven (325°) 12 to 15 minutes or until a delicate brown. Serve hot or cold as a fruit dessert. Garnish with currant jelly.

PESCHE RIPIENE
Italian Stuffed Peaches
8 servings

4 lady fingers or 4 strips (1" x 2")
    stale sponge cake
¾ cup chopped blanched almonds
¼ cup finely chopped fruit peel

½ teaspoon lemon extract
¼ teaspoon almond extract
8 fresh peaches
½ cup sugar

Break lady fingers or sponge cake into small bits. Combine with almonds and fruit peel. Add extracts and mix. Fill peach halves with this mixture. Put halves together, hold with wooden picks. Sprinkle with sugar. Bake in hot oven (400°) 10 minutes. Serve with whipped cream or ice cream.

PIZZA FIGLIATA
Italian Fruit-Nut Roll
6 to 8 slices

1 recipe Plain Pastry (page 433)
½ cup honey
¾ cup chopped nuts
1 cup mixed candied fruit peel
2 tablespoons sugar
½ teaspoon cinnamon
Confectioners' sugar

Roll pastry into rectangle ¼ inch thick. Spread with honey; sprinkle with chopped nuts and candied fruit peel. Combine sugar and cinnamon and sprinkle over peel. Roll up length-wise, jelly-roll fashion; twist roll in a spiral. Place on lightly greased cooky sheet, 15½ x 12 inches. Bake in moderate oven (350°) 30 to 35 minutes or until done. Dust with confectioners' sugar. Cut roll into 1-inch slices and serve for dessert.

PLANTAIN FRITTERS (INDIA)
About 3 dozen

3 ripe plantain or bananas
½ cup cake flour
2 tablespoons sugar
2 teaspoons baking powder
¼ teaspoon salt
2 eggs, beaten
¼ cup sweetened condensed milk
1 teaspoon vanilla
¼ cup coarsely chopped salted nuts
½ cup raisins

Mash bananas with a fork, leaving fairly small pieces. Sift dry ingredients together. Combine beaten eggs, milk, and vanilla; add to flour mixture and stir just enough to blend. Fold in banana pulp, nuts, and raisins. This batter should be the con-sistency of drop cookies. Add a little more flour, if necessary, to make of proper consistency. Drop into deep hot fat (365°) and fry for 2 to 3 minutes or until golden brown in color and cooked through. Serve as dessert.

RHUBARB SCALLOP WITH MERINGUE
8 servings

1 pound rhubarb
1 cup sugar
1 tablespoon grated orange peel
2 tablespoons confectioners' sugar
¼ teaspoon salt
1 small sponge cake
2 egg whites
¼ cup sugar

Cut rhubarb in 1-inch pieces and cook with ½ cup water for about 5 to 10 minutes. Add the 1 cup of sugar, grated orange peel, confectioners' sugar, and salt, and cook 3 to 4 minutes longer. Cut the sponge cake in thin slices. Line bottom of buttered 1½-quart casserole with sliced sponge cake. Cover with alternate layers of rhubarb mixture and cake slices. Bake uncovered in moderate oven (350°) 25 to 30 minutes. Make meringue of egg whites and the remaining ¼ cup of sugar. Pile meringue on baked pudding and put in hot oven (425°) 8 to 10 minutes to brown meringue. Serve warm or cold.

Puddings

ALMENDRADA
Mexican Molded Fruit Gelatin
6 to 8 servings

1 tablespoon (1 envelope) unflavored gelatin	2 tablespoons **chopped maraschino cherries**
½ cup pineapple juice	¼ cup shredded pineapple
4 egg whites	⅓ cup chopped blanched **almonds**
¼ teaspoon salt	½ teaspoon vanilla
¾ cup sugar	¼ teaspoon almond extract

Soften gelatin in cold pineapple juice. Dissolve over hot water. Beat egg whites until foamy; add salt and sugar gradually and continue beating until soft peak stage is reached. Add the dissolved gelatin to egg whites and beat until thick and of a marshmallow consistency. Add vanilla and almond extract. Divide into 3 parts. Color one part pink and add the maraschino cherries; color one part green and add pineapple, and add chopped almonds to the remainder. Mold in oblong loaf pan, 9½ x 5¼ x 2¾ inches, putting white layer on bottom, then green, then pink, to represent Mexican flag colors. Let stand until set. Cut in slices and garnish with whipped cream, or serve with a custard sauce.

The delicate pink, green, and white colors in this light, fluffy dessert represent those of the Mexican flag; but the colors may be changed to those you wish to use to carry out the theme for any party.

ALMOND AND PINEAPPLE PUDDING
6 to 8 servings

3 cups milk
1 cup chopped blanched almonds
½ cup sugar
1 piece whole cinnamon
15 graham crackers

2 egg yolks
½ cup diced pineapple
2 teaspoons lemon juice
¼ teaspoon salt

Heat milk in double boiler. Add chopped almonds, sugar, and cinnamon. Heat about 15 minutes. Remove cinnamon. Roll graham crackers to make crumbs. Beat the egg yolks until light; add some of the scalded milk mixture, then combine with remainder of the milk and cook in double boiler until slightly thickened and custard-like in consistency. Add graham cracker crumbs, pineapple, lemon juice, and salt. Cook 5 minutes longer. Cool. Garnish with whipped cream and half of a maraschino cherry.

BAKED INDIAN PUDDING
6 to 8 servings

1 quart milk
½ cup yellow corn meal
1 teaspoon salt
¼ cup molasses

½ cup sugar
¼ teaspoon cinnamon
2 tablespoons butter

Scald 3 cups of the milk; pour over corn meal to which salt has been added. Add molasses, sugar, cinnamon, and butter. Mix thoroughly. Turn into buttered 1½-quart casserole. After pudding has been in oven 20 minutes, pour in the remaining cup of cold milk and stir carefully. Bake in very slow oven (250°) 5 to 6 hours. Serve warm with whipped cream or ice cream.

NOTE: To insure proper consistency, stir carefully four or five times during first 1½ hours of baking. The pudding is very thin when put in the oven, but don't be alarmed — it will thicken and caramelize as it bakes.

The long slow baking is the secret of success with this old-fashioned New England pudding. It brings out the smooth caramel flavor and a texture like velvet. Hurried cooking at high temperature fails to develop the delicate flavor and the product will be syrupy and tasteless.

BLUEBERRY SLUMP
6 to 8 servings

1 No. 2 can (2½ cups) blueberries
  or 2½ cups fresh blueberries
1 cup sugar
¼ cup flour

⅛ teaspoon salt
1 tablespoon lemon juice
1 tablespoon butter
½ recipe Plain Pastry (page 433)

Combine blueberries, sugar, flour, salt, and lemon juice. Pour into 8-inch square pan. Dot with butter. Roll pastry ¼ inch thick. Cut to fit top of pan. Cut 2 slits in pastry. Cover berries with pastry. Bake in hot oven (450°) 10 to 12 minutes or until crust is nicely browned. Serve warm with thick cream or ice cream.

Betty James, a graduate student from Connecticut, introduced us to this blueberry slump. "More blueberries and less crust," says Betty, "and serve with plenty of good thick cream or ice cream." This is a dessert especially well liked where blueberries grow in great profusion, as they do in Massachusetts and Connecticut.

BROOD MET APPELEN
Pennsylvania Dutch Bread Pudding with Apples
8 to 10 servings

8 slices bread
1½ cups hot milk
¼ cup butter
5 eggs
¼ teaspoon salt
¾ cup granulated sugar

½ teaspoon cinnamon
½ teaspoon nutmeg
1 cup seedless raisins
1 cup pared, diced apples
½ cup brown sugar

Toast bread and cut into ½-inch cubes. Turn into buttered 1½-quart casserole. Add hot milk and butter, and let stand 30 minutes. Beat eggs until light. Add salt, sugar, cinnamon, nutmeg, raisins, and apples; pour over the bread mixture and stir in. Sprinkle brown sugar over top of pudding and bake uncovered in slow oven (300°) 45 minutes. Serve with Lemon Sauce (page 343) or cream.

You won't even recognize bread pudding when it's all spruced up with apples and raisins and a crusty brown sugar top. Here's an appealing way to use up dried bread. It's good by itself but even better with cream. Occasionally use whipped cream or ice cream with it for a special occasion.

BURNT ALMOND SPONGE
6 to 8 servings

¾ cup sugar
1 tablespoon (1 envelope)
    unflavored gelatin
½ cup cold water
¾ cup scalded milk
¼ cup sugar

½ teaspoon salt
1 teaspoon vanilla
2 cups heavy cream
1 cup blanched and browned
    almonds, coarsely chopped

Put the ¾ cup of sugar in heavy skillet. Heat and stir until sugar becomes dark brown and caramelized. Soften gelatin in the cold water. Add caramelized sugar slowly to scalded milk; then add gelatin and stir until dissolved. If mixture becomes curdled, strain. Add remaining ¼ cup sugar, the salt, and vanilla to gelatin mixture and chill until mixture is jelly-like in consistency. Whip until frothy. Whip cream and fold carefully into gelatin mixture. Add ½ cup of the almonds. Chill until set. To serve, garnish with whipped cream and the remaining ½ cup browned almonds.

CHERRY CREME
10 to 12 servings

1 tablespoon (1 envelope)
    unflavored gelatin
¼ cup cold water
½ cup boiling water
1 cup sugar
½ teaspoon grated lemon peel

⅓ cup lemon juice
½ cup glacé cherries
2 cups heavy cream
12 marshmallows, cut into quarters
1 cup chopped blanched almonds

Soften gelatin in cold water for 5 minutes. Dissolve in boiling water. Add sugar, lemon peel, lemon juice, and cherries which have been cut in small pieces. Let gelatin mixture chill until thick and jelly-like in consistency. Whip cream; fold in marshmallows and almonds and then carefully fold in gelatin mixture. Pour into buttered 1-quart mold or individual molds. Chill.

MACAROON CREME

Omit lemon peel, lemon juice, and chopped nuts. Add 6 almond macaroons, rolled fine, or ½ cup cake crumbs, 1 teaspoon vanilla, ¼ teaspoon almond extract, and 2 teaspoons rum flavoring.

CHOCOLATE FUDGE PUDDING
8 to 10 servings

¼ cup butter
1 cup sugar
1 teaspoon vanilla
1 ounce (1 square) unsweetened
   chocolate, melted

1½ cups sifted flour
½ teaspoon salt
3 teaspoons baking powder
¾ cup milk
½ cup chopped nuts

Cream butter and sugar. Add vanilla and melted chocolate and mix until well blended. Sift flour, salt, and baking powder together. Add all of flour, then all of milk to the chocolate mixture. Add chopped nuts and mix well. Pour batter into greased 9-inch square pan.

Topping Mixture:

1 cup granulated sugar
1 cup brown sugar
¼ cup cocoa

½ teaspoon salt
2 cups boiling water

Mix together the granulated sugar, brown sugar, cocoa, and salt. Sprinkle over cake batter. Pour the boiling water over the batter. Do not stir. Bake in moderate oven (350°) 40 to 45 minutes. This will separate into two layers, crust on top and chocolate fudge on the bottom. Serve crust-side down with the chocolate sauce on top. Garnish with whipped cream.

CRANBERRY CRISP
9 servings

1 cup uncooked rolled oats
½ cup sifted flour
¼ teaspoon salt
1 cup light brown sugar
1 teaspoon grated orange peel

⅓ cup butter
Pound can (1⅔ cups) cranberry
   sauce
1 pint vanilla ice cream

Mix together rolled oats, flour, salt, brown sugar, and orange peel. Add butter and mix until crumbly. Place half of mixture in greased 8-inch square pan. Cover with cranberry sauce. Sprinkle with remaining crumb mixture. Bake in moderate oven (350°) 40 to 45 minutes. Cut in squares and serve warm with vanilla ice cream.

APPLE CRISP

Use 1½ cups of thick applesauce instead of the cranberry sauce.

FROZEN LEMON PUDDING
6 to 8 servings

¾ cup (about 12) crushed vanilla
wafers
3 egg yolks
½ cup sugar
4 tablespoons lemon juice

2 teaspoons grated lemon peel
3 egg whites
2 tablespoons sugar
1 cup heavy cream

Butter refrigerator tray and sprinkle with crushed wafers. Beat egg yolks, gradually adding ½ cup sugar, and beat until light. Heat in double boiler and stir until thick. Remove from heat. Cool. Add lemon juice gradually and grated lemon peel. The mixture becomes thin. Beat egg whites and add the 2 tablespoons sugar gradually, beating until soft peak stage is reached. Whip cream until thick. Fold egg whites into whipped cream and fold in lemon custard slowly. Pour lemon mixture over crushed wafers. Freeze in refrigerator tray. To serve, cut into rectangular pieces, garnish with whipped cream if desired. A few red raspberries sprinkled over the whipped cream make an attractive garnish.

FRUITED SYLLABUB
10 to 12 servings

2 cups heavy cream
4 egg whites
½ cup confectioners' sugar
¼ teaspoon salt
½ cup chopped blanched almonds

½ cup glacé cherries, chopped fine
½ cup orange juice
1 teaspoon lemon juice
¼ teaspoon almond extract

Whip cream. Beat egg whites to soft peak stage. Combine with the whipped cream. Fold in sugar and salt. Add the almonds and cherries. Combine juices and almond extract and fold into mixture. Chill until very cold. Serve in parfait or sherbet glasses.

GOUREFF KACHA
Russian Farina Fruit Pudding
10 servings

3 cups milk
1 cup cream
¾ cup farina
½ teaspoon salt
½ cup sugar
½ cup seedless raisins, chopped

1 cup crushed pineapple, well
drained
1½ cups chopped pecans
⅓ teaspoon almond extract
¾ cup heavy cream, whipped

Scald milk and cream in double boiler. Add farina. Cook until mixture thickens and is smooth, about 15 minutes. Add salt, sugar, fruit, nuts, and flavoring. Pour mixture into buttered 6-ounce custard cups. Place in hot water and bake in moderate oven (350°) 15 minutes. Chill. To serve, unmold and garnish with whipped cream.

This is a favorite pudding in Russia and was served at our Russian Dinner (page 459). We had to vary the original recipe a little and adapt it to our own method of serving.

GRAPE SPONGE
9 to 10 servings

1½ tablespoons unflavored gelatin
⅓ cup cold water
½ cup boiling water
¾ cup sugar
⅛ teaspoon salt

1½ cups grape juice
4 tablespoons lemon juice
3 egg whites
1 cup heavy cream

Soften gelatin in cold water and dissolve in boiling water. Add sugar and salt. Cool slightly. Add grape juice and lemon juice. Chill until jelly-like in consistency. Beat egg whites to soft peak stage. Whip cream until thick. Whip grape juice mixture until frothy and smooth and fold in whipped cream. Fold mixture slowly into egg whites. Pour into 1-quart mold or into individual molds and let stand until set.

LEMON CHIFFON PUDDING
6 servings

2 tablespoons flour
¾ cup sugar
¼ teaspoon salt
1 tablespoon grated lemon peel
1 tablespoon softened butter

2 egg yolks
¼ cup lemon juice
1 cup milk
2 egg whites

Mix flour, sugar, salt, lemon peel, and softened butter together. Beat egg yolks until light and lemon colored and add to first mixture. Add lemon juice and milk. Mixture may have a curdled appearance, but this will not affect texture. Beat egg whites until stiff but not dry and fold into lemon mixture. Pour into buttered 1½-quart casserole. Place in pan of hot water. Bake uncovered in slow oven (325°) 40 to 45 minutes or until set. Chill and serve plain or with whipped cream, if desired.

This pudding will have a fluffy cake topping and a custard layer on the bottom. It has a pleasing lemon flavor and is a real taste treat.

LEMON CRACKLE
9 servings

Filling:

½ teaspoon salt	2 eggs, beaten
2 tablespoons cornstarch	¼ cup butter
1 cup sugar	½ teaspoon vanilla
1 cup cold water	½ cup lemon juice (2)

Combine salt, cornstarch, sugar, and cold water. Cook over moderate heat until thick. Put in double boiler and cook 10 to 12 minutes, stirring occasionally. Add slowly to beaten eggs, return to double boiler. Cook 4 to 5 minutes longer. Remove from heat. Add butter, vanilla, and lemon juice. Cool.

Cake:

¾ cup soda cracker crumbs (10 crackers)	1 cup sifted flour
1 cup brown sugar	½ teaspoon soda
½ cup melted butter	1 cup shredded coconut

Mix cracker crumbs and brown sugar, and add melted butter. Mix flour, soda, and coconut together, add to cracker crumb mixture. Put ¾ of this mixture into a buttered 9-inch square cake pan. Pour lemon filling over this. Sprinkle the remaining mixture on top. Bake in moderate oven (350°) 15 to 20 minutes or until lightly browned. Chill. Cut in squares.

The recipe for this attractive party dessert came from Seattle with Edna Crothers when she came to Iowa State College to do graduate work. It is one of her favorite company desserts. If you like desserts with a lemon flavor you'll like this tangy, crunchy lemon crackle.

OSTKAKA
Swedish Pudding
8 to 10 servings

1½ rennet tablets	1 cup sugar
½ cup sifted flour	1 teaspoon vanilla or almond extract
6 quarts milk	½ teaspoon salt
4 eggs	
1 pint cream	

Dissolve rennet tablets in 2 tablespoons cold water. Mix flour and 1 cup milk into a paste. Heat the rest of the milk to lukewarm, add flour and milk paste and rennet solution. Stir until flour and rennet are mixed with milk; let stand in warm place until whey separates. Drain curd thoroughly. Beat eggs slightly, add cream, sugar, extract, and salt, then curd of milk. Pour mixture into buttered 1½-quart casserole. Set in pan of hot water and bake in slow oven (325°) 55 to 60 minutes.

PINEAPPLE FLUFF
10 to 12 servings

5½ cups milk	1 tablespoon vanilla
½ cup flour	4 egg whites
½ cup sugar	½ cup sugar
¼ teaspoon salt	⅔ cup drained crushed pineapple
4 egg yolks	(No. 1 can)

Scald milk in double boiler. Mix flour, ½ cup of sugar, and the salt. Stir into hot milk. Cook until thick, 20 to 25 minutes. Beat egg yolks. Add some of hot mixture to yolks and then combine both mixtures. Cook in double boiler 3 to 5 minutes longer. Cool. Add vanilla. Beat egg whites to frothy stage; add remaining ½ cup sugar gradually and beat until stiff. When cooked mixture is cold, fold in beaten egg whites and add pineapple. This mixture is a pretty yellow color. Divide into thirds. Color ⅓ a delicate green, and another ⅓ a delicate pink. Fill tall parfait glasses alternately green, yellow, pink. Garnish top with ½ of a maraschino cherry and 2 mint leaves. Or, if desired, decorate with whipped cream rosettes put through pastry tube.

This airy, delicately colored pineapple fluff is a recipe from Pearl Jackson Aldrich, graduate student from East Lansing, Michigan. She made the pineapple fluff for a catering dinner and it has been a favorite dessert ever since.

PLUM PUDDING
12 to 14 servings

1½ cups milk
3 egg yolks
1¼ cups sugar
2 cups bread crumbs
½ cup shortening, melted
1 teaspoon salt
½ teaspoon soda
1 teaspoon cloves
1½ teaspoons cinnamon

½ cup sifted flour
1 cup chopped nuts
1 cup currants
1 cup raisins
1 cup chopped pitted dates
½ cup candied fruit peel
2 teaspoons grated lemon peel
¼ cup lemon juice
3 egg whites

Heat milk. Beat egg yolks until light. Add sugar while beating. Add hot milk to egg mixture. Mix with the bread crumbs and add melted shortening. Combine salt, soda, spices, flour, nuts, currants, raisins, dates, fruit peel, lemon peel, and lemon juice. Add to bread crumb mixture and mix well. Beat egg whites to soft peak stage and fold into mixture. Pack well-greased brown bread cans ¾ full. Steam 3 hours. Slice and serve hot with Foamy Sauce or Hard Sauce (page 342).

Plum pudding has had a rather interesting career. In early days it was merely a soft, squashy mash extracted from fresh plums and mixed with butter, rice, and barley. The whole grains were included to inspire a good harvest for the coming year.

The next step produced a pudding made from meat broth, spices, and dried raisins. By the early 19th century there were plum puddings similar to the ones made today; however, they were boiled in a cloth instead of being steamed. Even today, some families like their plum pudding boiled.

PUDIN DE LARANJAS
Pan-American Orange Pudding
8 to 10 servings

1 tablespoon grated orange peel
1 teaspoon grated lemon peel
1½ cups orange juice
5 eggs
1 cup sugar

4 oranges, sectioned
6 red maraschino cherries, cut into quarters
6 green minted maraschino cherries, cut into quarters

Combine orange peel, lemon peel, and orange juice. Cover and allow to stand 15 to 20 minutes. Strain. Beat eggs and add sugar gradually; continue beating until all of sugar has been added. Add orange juice slowly, beat while adding. Pour into buttered 1½-quart casserole. Set in pan of hot water. Bake in slow oven (325°) 35 to 45 minutes or until custard is set. Chill. To serve, garnish with orange sections and a few red and green cherries.

This is a colorful dessert for a Pan-American party and is on the menu of the Pan-American Buffet Supper (page 459).

SHRIKAND (INDIA)
Creamy Dessert
4 to 5 servings

1 pint sour cream
¼ teaspoon pounded cardamom seeds

1 cup sugar
1 cup whole salted nuts

Put sour cream into cheesecloth bag and let drain overnight. The curd should be quite dry before it is mixed with the other ingredients. Add cardamom and sugar to the curd and blend. Place in a mound on a glass plate and cover with the nuts. Serve as a dessert.

This is a creamy, rich dessert — a small amount will suffice. At our Buffet Featuring Foods of India (page 454), we served the shrikand in small paper soufflé cups with a few of the nuts on top.

SOFT CUSTARD
6 servings

2 eggs
¼ cup sugar
⅛ teaspoon salt

2 cups milk, scalded
½ teaspoon vanilla
Nutmeg

Beat eggs slightly, add sugar and salt. Stir hot milk slowly into egg mixture. Cook in double boiler on low heat, stirring constantly until mixture is thick enough to coat spoon. Remove from heat. Add vanilla. Turn at once into a cold bowl and chill. Serve in sherbet glasses. Sprinkle a little nutmeg over the top. This custard may be used as a sauce, if desired.

NOTE: If cooked too long, the custard may curdle. If this should happen, beat with a rotary egg beater to a smooth consistency.

SNOW CUSTARD

Omit vanilla. Heat 1 stick cinnamon in milk and add ½ teaspoon shredded orange peel. After custard has cooked, remove from heat, strain into cold bowl. Before serving, whip two egg whites to soft peak stage and fold into custard.

Souffles

Who doesn't marvel at the beauty of a puffy, top-hatted, golden brown soufflé? Whether a fruit soufflé, a vegetable soufflé, or a dessert soufflé, there are certain rules which make the product a breath-taking success or a flat, soggy failure.

First of all, beat the egg yolks until they are thick and lemon-colored like creamy mayonnaise. The egg whites should be beaten until the peaks are slightly rounded. A deft, quick hand in the mixing is necessary so that little air is lost before it reaches the oven. A spatula with a flexible blade is a help here. Butter the bottom but not the sides of a straight-sided casserole for a large volume. For a soufflé with a top hat, cut a circle around the top of the mixture about two or three inches from the edge just before baking.

CHOCOLATE SOUFFLE
6 servings

¼ cup butter
2 ounces (2 squares) unsweetened
   chocolate
¼ cup flour
¼ teaspoon salt
1 cup milk

3 egg yolks
½ cup sugar
¼ teaspoon mace
1 teaspoon vanilla
3 egg whites

Melt butter and chocolate in double boiler; add flour and salt and blend thoroughly. Add milk slowly, stirring constantly. Cook until thick. This will be a very stiff white sauce. Beat egg yolks; add sugar gradually and beat until light. Add mace and vanilla. Add the white sauce to the egg yolk mixture and stir until well blended. Beat egg whites to soft peak stage and fold carefully into sauce mixture. Pour into buttered 1½-quart casserole. Place casserole in pan of hot water to depth of 1 inch. Bake in slow oven (325°) 50 minutes to 1 hour. Serve at once with Mocha Sauce (page 343).

Like chocolate cake, chocolate soufflé is a winner every time with its rich flavor and delicate texture.

COCONUT SOUFFLE
6 servings

¼ cup butter
5 tablespoons flour
¼ teaspoon salt
1 cup milk
3 egg yolks

⅓ cup sugar
1 teaspoon vanilla
1 cup shredded coconut
3 egg whites

Melt butter in double boiler; add flour and salt and blend together. Add milk slowly, stirring constantly. Cook until thick. This will be a stiff white sauce. Beat egg yolks; add sugar gradually and beat until light. Add vanilla. Fold white sauce into egg yolk mixture and stir until well blended. Stir in shredded coconut. Beat egg whites to soft peak stage and fold carefully into sauce mixture. Pour into buttered 1½-quart casserole. Place casserole in pan of hot water. Bake in slow oven (325°) 50 minutes to 1 hour. Serve with Foamy Sauce (page 342).

Soufflés should be served as soon as possible after they are removed from the oven, while still light and puffy.

ORANGE SOUFFLE
6 servings

¼ cup butter
6 tablespoons flour
¼ teaspoon salt
1 cup milk
3 egg yolks

½ cup sugar
3 tablespoons orange juice
1 tablespoon lemon juice
1 tablespoon grated orange peel
3 egg whites

Melt butter in double boiler; add flour and salt and blend thoroughly. Add milk slowly, stirring constantly. Cook until thick. This will be a very thick white sauce. Beat egg yolks; add sugar gradually and beat until light. Add orange and lemon juice and orange peel. Add egg yolk mixture to white sauce and stir until well blended. Cool. Beat egg whites to soft peak stage and fold carefully into sauce mixture. Pour into buttered 1½-quart casserole. Place casserole in pan of hot water. Bake in slow oven (325°) 1 hour. Serve at once with Sabayon Sauce (page 344).

For the final touch to the menu — a soufflé with a delicate fruit flavor.

PECAN SOUFFLE
6 to 8 servings

4 tablespoons butter
4 tablespoons flour
½ teaspoon salt
1 cup milk
3 egg yolks

½ cup sugar
1 cup coarsely chopped pecans
1 teaspoon vanilla
3 egg whites

Melt butter in double boiler. Add flour and salt. Add the milk gradually, stirring constantly. Cook until thick. Beat egg yolks until light; add sugar, pecans, and vanilla. Add egg yolk mixture to the white sauce and stir until well blended. Beat egg whites until stiff, but not dry. Fold the egg whites carefully into sauce mixture. Turn into buttered 1½-quart casserole. Place casserole in pan of hot water and bake in slow oven (325°) 50 minutes to 1 hour. Serve with Mocha Sauce (page 343).

Dessert Sauces

FOAMY SAUCE
About 1½ cups

½ cup butter
1 cup confectioners' sugar
⅛ teaspoon salt

1 egg, well beaten
1 teaspoon vanilla

Cream butter; add sugar gradually and mix until light and fluffy. Add salt and egg to creamed mixture and blend well. Heat in double boiler and beat with rotary egg beater until sauce is light and foamy. When sauce is foamy, remove from heat. Add vanilla. Serve with Coconut Soufflé (page 341).

HARD SAUCE
About 2 cups

½ cup butter
2 cups sifted confectioners' sugar

1½ teaspoons vanilla

Cream butter until very light; add sifted confectioners' sugar gradually and cream until light and fluffy. Add vanilla. Mix well. Put in refrigerator and serve very cold on steamed puddings or baked apples.

HOT FUDGE SAUCE
About 3 cups

1½ cups evaporated milk
2 cups sugar
4 ounces (4 squares) unsweetened chocolate

¼ cup butter
1 teaspoon vanilla
½ teaspoon salt

Heat milk and sugar to a rolling boil and boil 1 minute. Add chocolate. When melted, beat with an egg beater until smooth. The sauce may have a slightly curdled appearance until you begin to beat — beat *hard* and you will have a creamy smooth sauce. Remove from heat and add butter, vanilla, and salt. Cool. Use hot on ice cream or desserts.

The sauce may be stored in a jar in the refrigerator and heated in a double boiler before serving.

This easy-to-make fudge sauce is the answer for a good, rich fluffy sauce that will delight your family, especially the teen agers.

LEMON SAUCE
About 2½ cups

1 cup sugar
2 tablespoons cornstarch
¼ teaspoon salt
2 cups boiling water

2 tablespoons butter
2 tablespoons lemon juice
2 teaspoons grated lemon peel

Mix sugar, cornstarch, and salt. Gradually add water, and cook over low heat until thick and clear. Remove from heat. Add butter, lemon juice, and grated peel; blend thoroughly. Serve with steamed puddings.

MOCHA SAUCE
About 1 cup

¼ cup butter
1 cup confectioners' sugar
2 teaspoons cocoa

⅛ teaspoon salt
2 tablespoons strong coffee
1 teaspoon vanilla

Cream butter until light. Combine confectioners' sugar, cocoa, and salt. Add to creamed butter and blend until smooth and creamy. Add strong coffee and vanilla; mix well. Serve with Chocolate Soufflé (page 340).

ORIENTAL SAUCE
About 1 quart

4 cups sugar
2 cups water
1 orange (juice and grated peel)
1 lemon (juice and grated peel)

½ cup candied ginger (cut in small pieces)
1 cup slivered blanched almonds

Make a syrup of the sugar, water, fruit juices, and grated peel. Add ginger and cook until medium thick in consistency. Add the almonds last.

If you're looking for something different in the way of an ice cream sauce, try this oriental sauce with its intriguing flavor.

SABAYON SAUCE
About 1 cup

2 tablespoons lemon juice
½ cup orange juice
1 teaspoon grated lemon peel
2 egg yolks

⅓ cup sugar
2 egg whites
⅛ teaspoon salt

Mix fruit juices and grated peel. Beat egg yolks; add sugar gradually, beating until light and lemon colored. Add fruit juices and lemon peel. Cook in double boiler until thick, stirring frequently. Add salt to egg whites and beat to soft peak stage. Fold cooked mixture into egg whites. Serve with Orange Soufflé (page 341).

VANILLA SAUCE
About 2½ cups

1 cup sugar
2 tablespoons cornstarch
¼ teaspoon salt

2 cups boiling water
2 tablespoons butter
1 teaspoon vanilla

Mix sugar, cornstarch, and salt; gradually add water, and cook over low heat until thick and clear. Remove from heat. Add butter and vanilla; blend thoroughly. Serve warm with steamed puddings.

Cookies
and Small Cakes

Acorn Nut Meringues
Almond Cinnamon Squares
Almond Fingers
Almond Macaroons
Almond Twists
Ann's Meringues
   Chocolate Chip
   Coconut
   Holiday
   Meringue Shell Cookies
   Lime Meringue Pie
Applesauce Spice Cup Cakes

Banbury Tarts
Berlinerkransar
Butter Pecan Cookies
Butterkuchen
   Almond Paste Filling
Butterscotch Pecan Squares

Carrot Drop Cookies
Cherry Cake Tarts
Cherry Pecan Balls
Chilean Molasses Cookies
Chinese Almond Cookies
Chocolate Macaroons
Chocolate Mint Wafers
   Mint Filling
Cinnamon Crisps
Cocoa Brownies
Coconut Bars
Coconut Circles
Cream Horns
Creole Kisses

Date Pecan Cup Cakes
Date Swirls

Eccles Cakes
English Rolled Wafers

Fattigmand
Filled Cookies
   Apricot-Orange Filling
   Cinnamon-Prune Filling
   Date-Cherry-Orange Filling

   Raisin Filling
   Walnut-Fig Filling
Firelighters
Frosted Coffee Bars
Fruit Drops
   Peanut Fruit Drops
Ginger Cup Cakes
Hungarian Filled Crescents
Jeelobis
Josephines and Napoleons
   Vanilla Cream Filling
Klejner
Krumkage
Kulkuls
Lebkuchen
Lemon-Caraway Cookies
Marmalade Drop Cookies
Mocha Fingers
Oreilles de Cochon
Pecan Bars
Pecan Fudge Squares
Pepparkakor
Petits Fours
Quick Tea Dainties
Richmond Maids of Honor
Rolled Wafers
Rolled Pecan Nut Wafers
Rosettes
Rye Drop Cakes
Sand Bakkels
Sand Bars
Scotch Shortbread
Spritz
Sugar Cookies
   Christmas Cookies
Swedish Cream Lilies
Swedish Nut Cookies
Tea Cakes
   Butterfly Tea Cakes
Walnut Slices
   Orange Frosting

COOKIES are popular with everyone — from your junior cooky-jar raiders to your bridge or church group members. And what easier and friendlier hospitality could you offer when friends drop in than a plate of freshly-baked cookies with fragrant coffee or tea or chilled milk?

So take down the flour and sugar canisters, get out the spices and nuts, and bake a batch of cookies. Be certain that the family is around to kibitz and sample when you pull the cooky sheet out of the oven. You may want to bake an old favorite or try something new. The field is wide — crisp rolled cookies, rich little bars, handy refrigerator goodies, delicious tea cakes.

Every country has its distinctive cookies. America has adopted the favorite recipes of many lands, carried long ago in sailing ships and covered wagons to cozy pioneer kitchens. To these old-fashioned treasures, our cooks have added their delicacies, stamped with a New World flavor.

The combination or double-acting type of baking powder has been used in these recipes. About one-third of the leavening gas is released in the mixing, the remainder when heated. To adjust the baking powder to another type, follow the manufacturer's directions.

ACORN NUT MERINGUES
About 3½ dozen

3 egg whites
1 tablespoon vinegar
½ teaspoon salt

1 cup sugar
4 ounces semi-sweet chocolate
1 cup finely chopped almonds

Combine egg whites, vinegar, and salt. Beat to soft peak stage and add sugar gradually, beating until stiff. Shave or grate chocolate on coarse grater. Fold chocolate and nuts into meringue mixture. Drop from teaspoon onto lightly greased baking sheet, 15½ x 12 inches. Shape into oblong shape so they will look like acorns. Bake in slow oven (275°) 15 to 20 minutes or until meringues are done. Remove from baking sheet to cooling rack.

For Decorating Meringues:

6 ounces semi-sweet chocolate,
   melted

½ cup finely chopped almonds
¼ cup green decorating sugar

When meringues are thoroughly cooled, spoon some of melted chocolate over one end, so it covers about ¼ of the meringue. Sprinkle chocolate with chopped nuts and a little of the green sugar.

This recipe for acorn nut meringues is a favorite of my sister-in-law, Mrs. Dennis J. Sullivan. She often serves them for afternoon tea when she entertains the navy wives.

ALMOND CINNAMON SQUARES
About 2½ dozen

1½ cups sifted flour
½ teaspoon salt
¼ teaspoon cinnamon
½ cup shortening
¾ cup sugar
2 egg yolks, beaten
2 tablespoons milk

½ teaspoon lemon extract
½ teaspoon grated lemon peel
2 egg whites, slightly beaten
¼ cup confectioners' sugar
¼ teaspoon cinnamon
⅓ cup chopped blanched almonds

Sift together dry ingredients. Cream shortening; add sugar gradually and continue creaming until light. Combine egg yolks, milk, lemon extract and peel. Add liquid to dry ingredients and blend thoroughly. Turn into 2 greased 8-inch square pans. Add confectioners' sugar and cinnamon to egg whites. Spread over surface of dough. Sprinkle nuts on top. Bake in moderate oven (350°) 25 to 30 minutes. Cut into squares while still warm.

ALMOND FINGERS
3½ dozen

½ cup butter
¼ cup sugar
1 egg, separated
1 tablespoon warm water
1½ cups sifted flour
1 teaspoon cream of tartar

½ teaspoon soda
⅛ teaspoon salt
¼ teaspoon vanilla
¾ cup sifted confectioners' sugar
½ cup finely chopped blanched almonds

Cream butter and sugar until light; add beaten egg yolk, which has been combined with 1 tablespoon warm water, and mix well. Sift flour, cream of tartar, soda, and salt together. Add to the creamed mixture and blend thoroughly. Chill dough in refrigerator about 30 minutes. Roll ⅛ inch thick. Beat egg white to soft peak stage and fold in confectioners' sugar and vanilla to make a thin frosting. Spread frosting over dough and sprinkle surface with almonds. Cut into strips 1 inch wide and 3 inches long. Lay strips carefully on ungreased cooky sheet, 15½ x 12 inches, and bake in moderate oven (325°) 10 to 12 minutes or until a very light brown.

ALMOND MACAROONS
About 1½ dozen

8 ounces almond paste
3 egg whites, unbeaten
½ cup granulated sugar

¾ cup confectioners' sugar
2 tablespoons cornstarch

Combine almond paste and 1 egg white and beat until smooth. Stir in ¼ cup of granulated sugar and another egg white and mix well. Add remaining ¼ cup granulated sugar, confectioners' sugar, and cornstarch. Stir in remaining egg white and mix until smooth. Add another tablespoon cornstarch if mixture is runny. Cover cooky sheet, 15½ x 12 inches, with waxed paper. Drop macaroon mixture from teaspoon onto waxed paper 1 inch apart. The macaroons should be about 1 inch in diameter. Bake in slow oven (300°) 20 to 25 minutes until light brown and firm to the touch. Let stand about 5 minutes before removing from waxed paper.

ALMOND TWISTS
About 3 dozen

2 cups ground blanched almonds
3 tablespoons sugar

3 tablespoons grated lemon peel
3 egg whites

Mix together ground almonds, sugar, and lemon peel. Beat egg whites to soft peak stage. Fold in almond mixture. Put in pastry bag and force out in little twists on lightly greased cooky sheet, 15½ x 12 inches. Bake in moderate oven (350°) 12 to 15 minutes.

ANN'S MERINGUES
10 to 12 individual meringues

6 egg whites
¼ teaspoon salt

Pinch of cream of tartar
1½ cups granulated sugar

Place egg whites in mixer bowl. Turn on second speed of the electric mixer and beat until a froth has begun to form. Second speed makes a finer texture. Add salt and cream of tartar. Continue beating for 5 minutes or until soft peak stage. Add one-half of the sugar gradually, shaking gently out of a cup or pie pan. Continue to beat 5 minutes after one-half of sugar is in. Add other half of sugar as above. Continue beating for a total of 35 to 38 minutes, counting from the time of starting. The meringue should be beaten until the sugar has completely dissolved. Remove whip and remove all meringue from it. Shape meringues with a pastry tube or a spoon, as desired. Bake on brown paper on cooky sheet in very slow oven (250°) 1 hour or more, depending on size of meringue. When done, the meringue should lift off the paper easily.

Store in airtight tin so meringues will not absorb moisture and become soft. They should be crisp and dry and have a very fine texture. Fill individual meringues with ice cream and top with fresh berries.

I call this recipe Ann's Meringues because Ann Baker, graduate student in Institution Management, worked so painstakingly to produce a crisp, delicate meringue that came up to her idea of what a meringue should be. She found that the long, slow beating gave the texture she wanted and the low temperature, that is really just a drying-out process, gave a nice white meringue without a tinge of brown.

CHOCOLATE CHIP MERINGUES

Add 1 cup chocolate chips to ½ recipe Ann's Meringues (page 350). Drop from teaspoon onto cooky sheet, 15½ x 12 inches, that has been covered with heavy paper. Bake as directed for meringues.

COCONUT MERINGUES

Add 1 cup shredded coconut to ½ recipe Ann's Meringues (page 350).

HOLIDAY MERINGUES

Force Ann's Meringues (page 350) through pastry tube to make rosettes, or drop from teaspoon. Sprinkle with red or green sugar. Bake as directed for meringues.

These bright, airy meringues give a nice holiday air to a tray of assorted Christmas cookies.

MERINGUE SHELL COOKIES

1 recipe Ann's Meringues	½ recipe Butter Frosting
(page 350)	(page 412)

Use rosette tube in pastry bag and fill bag with meringue. Shape meringue into small rosettes. Bake as directed for Ann's Meringues. Tint Butter Frosting delicate pink, green, or yellow. Spread flat end of meringue shell with frosting and put shells together in this manner.

These meringue shells are quite decorative on a tea tray.

LIME MERINGUE PIE WITH FRESH COCONUT

Marjory Arkwright, who has had charge of the food service at Punahou School in Honolulu, uses the recipe for Ann's Meringues (page 350) and bakes them in pie pans. She fills the meringue with a tart lime or lemon filling and tops the pie with whipped cream and fresh coconut. On the mainland, we don't always have fresh coconut, but the shredded coconut can be used instead.

APPLESAUCE SPICE CUP CAKES
4 dozen

½ cup butter	¼ teaspoon salt
1 cup sugar	½ teaspoon cloves
1 egg, beaten	1 teaspoon cinnamon
¾ cup thick applesauce	¾ cup raisins, chopped
1¾ cups sifted cake flour	½ cup chopped walnuts
1½ teaspoons baking powder	8 to 10 glacé cherries
½ teaspoon soda	

Cream butter and add sugar; beat until light and fluffy. Stir in egg and ¼ cup of the applesauce and beat well. Sift flour, baking powder, soda, salt, and spices together. Add alternately with remaining applesauce and mix until smooth. Fold in raisins and nuts. Fill 2-inch greased muffin pans ⅔ full. Bake in moderate oven (350°) 20 minutes. Frost with thin Confectioners' Frosting (page 413) flavored with lemon. Decorate with bits of glacé cherry.

BANBURY TARTS
About 3 dozen

Cut circles of dough as for Eccles Cakes (page 363); place teaspoon of filling in center; fold dough over on each side to cover filling. Fold ends to make points. Turn over and prick pastry. Bake as for Eccles Cakes. This is the typical Banbury tart shape.

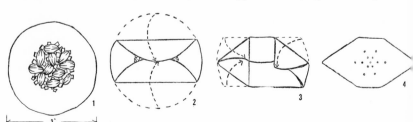

BERLINERKRANSAR
Norewegian Cookies
About 4 dozen

1 cup butter
½ cup sugar
2 hard-cooked egg yolks
2 raw egg yolks

2½ cups sifted flour
1 egg white, slightly beaten
6 cubes sugar, crushed

Cream butter; add sugar and continue creaming until light and fluffy. Force hard-cooked yolks through a wire sieve. Add sieved egg yolks and raw egg yolks to creamed butter and sugar mixture. Mix thoroughly. Add flour and mix until smooth. Chill dough for several hours. Pinch off small balls of dough about the size of a marble. Roll into strips 4 to 5 inches long and about the thickness of a lead pencil. Tie each strip into a knot and brush with egg white. Place on lightly greased cooky sheet, 15½ x 12 inches. Sprinkle with crushed sugar. Bake in moderate oven (350°) 8 to 10 minutes or until light brown in color. Remove carefully from baking sheet with spatula because the berlinerkransar are fragile and break easily.

BUTTER PECAN COOKIES
4 dozen

1 cup butter
½ cup brown sugar
½ teaspoon salt
1 egg yolk, beaten
2½ cups sifted flour

½ teaspoon vanilla
1 egg, beaten
2 tablespoons milk
½ cup pecan halves

Combine butter, sugar, and salt, and mix until light and fluffy. Add egg yolk. Stir in flour and blend well. Add vanilla. Roll dough into balls ¾ inch in diameter. Place 2 inches apart on greased cooky sheet, 15½ x 12 inches. Add milk to beaten egg and dip fork into this mixture. Press fork down on each cooky until ¼ inch thick. Place pecan in center. Bake in moderate oven (350°) 10 to 12 minutes or until cookies are golden brown in color.

BUTTERKUCHEN
Flaky Butter Tarts
About 3½ dozen

1 cup butter
2 cups sifted flour

1 egg, beaten
2 tablespoons water

Crumble butter into flour and blend until the mixture is about the size of peas. Combine egg and cold water. Add to butter and flour mixture and stir with fork until just blended. Knead lightly. Roll into rectangle, 12 x 15 inches, and fold into thirds. Roll out again. Repeat three times. Roll ¼ inch thick and cut into circles 2½ inches in diameter. Fit pastry rounds into 2-inch muffin pans. Fill ⅔ full of Almond Paste Filling. Bake in hot oven (425°) 5 minutes, then in moderate oven (350°) 8 to 10 minutes.

Almond Paste Filling:

8 ounces almond paste
1¾ cups confectioners' sugar
1 egg white

½ teaspoon rose water
2 tablespoons water

Mix almond paste and sugar together in bowl until consistency of corn meal. Beat egg white until foamy and add rose water and water; beat to soft peak stage. Combine with almond paste mixture.

This recipe for butterkuchen is one of many fine old German family recipes possessed by Helen Penner of Beatrice, Nebraska. Miss Penner, a graduate of Kansas State College, was a member of our Institution Management Staff and also director of the Ames High School Cafeteria.

BUTTERSCOTCH PECAN SQUARES
About 1½ dozen

1 cup brown sugar
1 cup butter

1 egg, well beaten
2 cups sifted flour

Cream together the brown sugar and butter until light. Add the egg and mix well. Add flour gradually, mixing well after each addition. Spread mixture in greased cake pan, 13 x 9½ x 2 inches.

Topping:

1 egg, well beaten
½ cup brown sugar

1 cup coarsely chopped pecans
½ cup brown sugar

Brush over the top the well-beaten egg, then sprinkle with ½ cup of the brown sugar and the coarsely chopped pecans; cover with remaining ½ cup brown sugar. Bake in moderate oven (350°) 20 to 25 minutes. Cut into 1½-inch squares.

CARROT DROP COOKIES
4 dozen

1 cup shortening
¾ cup sugar
1 egg, beaten
1 cup cooked, mashed carrots
½ teaspoon lemon extract

1 teaspoon vanilla
2 cups sifted flour
½ teaspoon salt
2 teaspoons baking powder

Cream shortening and sugar; add beaten egg, mashed cooked carrots, lemon extract, and vanilla. Mix well. Add dry ingredients which have been sifted together. Drop from teaspoon 1 inch apart onto greased cooky sheet, 15½ x 12 inches. Bake in moderate oven (350°) 12 to 15 minutes. While warm, frost with Confectioners' Frosting (page 413) tinted orange.

These carrot drop cookies make an ideal cooky for a Halloween party for the lollipop crowd. They have a bright orange color and are effective frosted and topped with a pumpkin face made with melted chocolate. Sina Faye Fowler from Kansas contributed this colorful recipe.

CHERRY CAKE TARTS
2½ dozen

½ recipe Plain Pastry (page 433)
1 cup cherry jam

½ recipe Butter Cake batter (page 394)

Roll pastry about ⅛ inch thick. Cut into rounds 3 inches in diameter. Fit pastry rounds into 2-inch muffin pans. Put scant teaspoon jam in each tart and cover with about ½ teaspoon of cake batter. Bake in hot oven (450°) 10 minutes or until cake is delicate brown and pastry is baked. Remove tarts from muffin pans. Frost with Lemon Confectioners' Frosting (page 415).

This recipe is one of the many versions of English pastries that Mrs. Walter Barlow served to Iowa State College students at church teas.

CHERRY PECAN BALLS
4 dozen

½ cup shortening
½ cup butter
½ cup sugar
2 egg yolks, beaten
2 tablespoons grated orange peel
2 teaspoons grated lemon peel

2 teaspoons lemon juice
2½ cups sifted cake flour
½ teaspoon salt
2 egg whites, slightly beaten
1½ cups finely chopped pecans
½ pound glacé cherries

Cream shortening, butter, and sugar. Add egg yolks, orange and lemon peel, and lemon juice; blend well. Stir in sifted flour and salt. Chill dough about 30 minutes. Form into balls ¾ inch in diameter; dip in egg whites and roll in chopped nuts. Place on greased cooky sheet, 15½ x 12 inches. Make an impression for cherry in the center of each. Cut cherries in half and press into cookies. Bake in slow oven (325°) 15 to 20 minutes.

CHILEAN MOLASSES COOKIES
3 dozen

¾ cup sugar
½ cup shortening
2 eggs, well beaten
½ cup molasses
2½ cups sifted flour

½ teaspoon soda
½ teaspoon salt
1 teaspoon ground ginger
½ cup boiling water

Cream sugar and shortening until light and fluffy. Add eggs and molasses and beat well. Sift dry ingredients together and add gradually to molasses mixture. Stir in boiling water and mix well. Drop from teaspoon 2 inches apart onto greased cooky sheet, 15½ x 12 inches. Bake in hot oven (425°) 12 to 15 minutes.

CHINESE ALMOND COOKIES
About 5 dozen

4 cups sifted flour
2 cups sugar
1 teaspoon baking powder
1 teaspoon salt
1½ cups shortening

1 egg, well beaten
2 tablespoons water
½ teaspoon almond extract
¾ cup blanched whole almonds

Sift dry ingredients together twice. Cut in shortening as for pie dough. Combine beaten egg with water and add to dry ingredients; add almond extract. Mix well. If dough is too crumbly, add a little more water. Divide into small balls about the size of a walnut. Flatten each ball ¼ inch thick and about 2 inches in diameter. Press whole blanched almond into center of each cooky. Place on ungreased cooky sheet, 15½ x 12 inches. Bake in moderate oven (350°) 15 to 20 minutes. This is a rich cooky dough; watch carefully so that they do not brown, as they should be cream colored to be authentic Chinese almond cookies.

This is the type of almond cooky that you buy at Chinese stores.

CHOCOLATE MACAROONS
5 to 6 dozen

½ cup salad oil
4 1-ounce squares unsweetened
    chocolate, melted
2 cups sugar
½ teaspoon salt

4 eggs
2 teaspoons vanilla
2 cups sifted flour
2 teaspoons baking powder
1 cup confectioners' sugar

Combine salad oil, chocolate, sugar, and salt. Beat in eggs one at a time and add vanilla; mix well. Add sifted flour and baking powder. Chill. Drop a teaspoon of mixture into a cup of confectioners' sugar; roll in cup to shape round. Place two inches apart on greased cooky sheet, 15½ x 12 inches. Bake in moderate oven (375°) 12 to 15 minutes. The macaroons will flatten out when baked.

CHOCOLATE MINT WAFERS
4 dozen

⅔ cup shortening
1 cup sugar
1 egg, beaten
2 cups sifted flour
1 teaspoon baking powder

½ teaspoon soda
½ teaspoon salt
¾ cup cocoa
¼ cup milk

Cream shortening and sugar until light and fluffy. Add egg and mix. Add sifted dry ingredients and milk alternately; blend thoroughly. Shape into rolls 1 inch in diameter. Wrap the rolls in waxed paper and chill for several hours or overnight. Cut in ⅛-inch slices. Place on ungreased cooky sheet, 15½ x 12 inches. Bake in slow oven (325°) 10 to 12 minutes. Remove from cooky sheet while still warm. When cool, put the cookies together in pairs with mint filling.

Mint Filling:

2 cups confectioners' sugar
⅛ teaspoon salt
¼ cup cream

¼ teaspoon peppermint extract
Green food coloring

Combine confectioners' sugar and salt. Add cream and stir until well blended. Add flavoring and just enough coloring to make a light green.

CINNAMON CRISPS
6 dozen

1 cup shortening
1 cup confectioners' sugar
1 egg, beaten
4 cups sifted flour

½ teaspoon salt
2 teaspoons cinnamon
1 cup coarsely chopped blanched almonds

Cream shortening and sugar until light and fluffy. Add egg and mix well. Sift dry ingredients together and add. Stir in chopped almonds. Mix well. Form into rolls 1½ inches in diameter. Wrap in waxed paper and place in refrigerator overnight. Slice ⅛ inch thick. Place on greased cooky sheets, 15½ x 12 inches. Bake in moderate oven (350°) 10 to 15 minutes.

COCOA BROWNIES
1½ dozen

1 cup shortening	¾ teaspoon baking powder
1¼ cups sugar	1 teaspoon salt
2 eggs, beaten	3 tablespoons corn syrup
1 cup sifted flour	1 teaspoon vanilla
½ cup cocoa	1 cup coarsely chopped nuts

Melt shortening; add sugar and mix thoroughly. Stir in beaten eggs. Sift flour, cocoa, baking powder, and salt together. Add to sugar mixture and mix well. Add corn syrup, vanilla, and nuts, and stir into chocolate mixture. Turn into greased 9-inch square pan. Bake in slow oven (325°) 30 to 35 minutes. Half of the nuts may be added to the batter and the other half sprinkled on top, if desired. Cut into 1½-inch squares while still warm.

For those who like less sweet and less chocolate, this brownie will be preferable to those made with chocolate. The cocoa gives a much milder flavor and a lighter color. The texture is more like that of cake. Don't omit the nuts because they are needed for extra flavor and texture.

COCONUT BARS
About 3 dozen

Pastry:

¾ cup butter	1½ cups sifted flour
¾ cup brown sugar	

Mix butter, brown sugar, and flour together, and blend. Divide into 2 equal parts and spread about ¼ inch thick in bottoms of two ungreased 8-inch square pans. Bake in slow oven (325°) 10 minutes or until lightly browned.

Cooky Filling:

3 eggs	¾ teaspoon baking powder
1½ cups brown sugar	½ teaspoon salt
1½ teaspoons vanilla	2¼ cups coconut
3 tablespoons flour	1 cup chopped nuts

Beat eggs; add brown sugar and vanilla; beat until light and fluffy. Sift together dry ingredients. Add to coconut and nuts. Stir into egg and sugar mixture and mix thoroughly. Pour half of mixture over baked pastry in each pan. Spread evenly. Bake in moderate oven (350°) about 15 minutes or until filling is firm. Cool. Cut into bars about 1 inch wide and 3 inches long.

COCONUT CIRCLES
About 2 dozen

½ cup butter
½ cup sugar
2 eggs, beaten
2 cups sifted flour
½ teaspoon salt
¼ teaspoon baking powder
½ cup ground blanched almonds

½ teaspoon vanilla
¼ teaspoon almond extract
½ recipe Butter Frosting
(page 412)
2 cups browned* or colored†
coconut

Cream butter; add sugar and continue creaming until light and fluffy. Add eggs and blend into creamed mixture. Sift flour, salt, and baking powder together, and stir into creamed mixture. Add almonds, vanilla, and almond extract, and mix well. Roll cooky dough ¼ inch thick. It may be a little sticky, so use enough flour on board to handle cookies easily. Cut with a 1½-inch cutter. Place on greased cooky sheet, 15½ x 12 inches. Bake in moderate oven (350°) 10 to 12 minutes. Place on cooling rack. When cold spread with Butter Frosting and place two circles together, sandwich-fashion. Spread the sides and top rather generously with the butter frosting and toss into either browned or colored coconut, so that top and sides of cooky are coated with coconut. Let stand an hour or so before serving so frosting will dry and cookies can be more easily handled.

This is a way to dress up any wafer cooky — sandwich-style with frosting. Colored coconut adds a festive touch, and chopped almonds give a different flavor. You may want to vary the shape, according to the occasion and the season.

---

* To *brown* coconut, spread coconut thinly on the bottom of a shallow pan; place in hot oven (400°) for a few minutes. Watch closely as coconut burns easily. Stir coconut so it will brown evenly.

† To *color* coconut, put a few drops of food coloring in a pie pan; add about 2 teaspoons water; toss ½ cup coconut into pan and stir quickly. Try not to get coconut too wet. Remove from pan onto absorbent paper until thoroughly dry.

patience produced perfection . . .

Ann's Meringues, page 350.

mouthfuls of goodness . . .

Josephines and Napoleons, page 371.

CREAM HORNS
About 1½ dozen

½ recipe Quick Puff Pastry
(page 434)
½ cup heavy cream, whipped

1 tablespoon confectioners' sugar
½ teaspoon vanilla

Roll pastry into 8-inch square, ¼ inch thick. Cut into ¾-inch strips; brush one edge with water and wind around cream horn tins. If you do not have tins, cut 5-inch squares of heavy paper and cut in two, diagonally, to obtain triangle. Roll into cone shape, folding over points, so paper will not unroll. Wind pastry strips around paper cones. Place pastry horns on ungreased cooky sheet, 15½ x 12 inches. Bake in moderate oven (375°) 12 to 15 minutes until a delicate brown. Let stand about 5 minutes after taking out of oven. Remove pastry from horns and allow to cool. Before serving, fill with whipped cream to which confectioners' sugar and vanilla have been added.

Cream horns, Eccles Cakes (page 363), and Banbury Tarts (page 352) make an attractive assortment to serve with afternoon tea. All are types of English tea cakes.

CREOLE KISSES
About 5 dozen

¾ cup light brown sugar, firmly
packed
½ cup granulated sugar
3 egg whites

1 teaspoon vanilla
1 teaspoon vinegar
½ cup finely chopped nuts

Sift brown sugar before measuring so it is free from lumps. Combine brown sugar and granulated sugar. Beat egg whites until frothy; add sugar gradually and continue beating to soft peak stage. Beat in vanilla and vinegar. Fold nuts into meringue. Cover cooky sheet, 15½ x 12 inches, with unglazed paper. Drop meringue from teaspoon onto paper about 1 inch apart. Bake in very slow oven (250°) 25 to 30 minutes. Allow to remain on pan about 5 minutes after removing from oven so that they will dry. Remove carefully from paper. Store kisses in tightly covered container.

These puffy bits which resemble miniature macaroons should have an even, faintly tanned surface and a dry, tender interior structure. They are made slightly crunchy by bits of finely chopped nuts but they still dissolve like cotton candy in your mouth. Both guests and family will enjoy their delicately caramelized, toasted flavor.

DATE PECAN CUP CAKES
5 dozen

¼ cup butter
1 cup sugar
1 teaspoon vanilla
4 eggs, separated
1 tablespoon milk
1 cup sifted flour

2 teaspoons baking powder
¼ teaspoon salt
1 pound pitted dates, chopped
1 pound pecans, chopped
Butter Frosting (page 412)

Cream butter and sugar until light and fluffy. Blend in vanilla. Add beaten egg yolks and milk, and mix thoroughly. Add sifted dry ingredients and mix to a smooth batter. Fold in chopped dates and pecans. Beat egg whites to soft peak stage and fold into batter. Fill 2-inch greased muffin pans ⅔ full of batter. Bake in moderate oven (350°) 25 to 30 minutes. Spread with Butter Frosting and serve as afternoon tea cakes.

NOTE: The batter may be baked in a 9-inch square pan, cut into squares, and served as a dessert. Top with whipped cream.

This is an old southern recipe and, as you can see, is just chuck-full of pecans and dates. Mary Leidigh, of Stillwater, Oklahoma, contributed the recipe.

DATE SWIRLS
About 3 dozen

½ cup butter
½ cup brown sugar
½ cup white sugar
1 egg, beaten

2 cups sifted flour
½ teaspoon soda
½ teaspoon salt
½ teaspoon lemon extract

Cream butter; add brown and white sugar, and mix until light and fluffy. Stir in egg and blend well. Add sifted dry ingredients; mix until smooth. Blend in lemon extract. Roll dough into rectangle, 12 x 18 inches, and ¼ inch thick. Spread with date filling and roll up like jelly roll. Chill for one hour. Cut into ¼-inch slices. Place on greased cooky sheet, 15½ x 12 inches. Bake in moderate oven (350°) 12 to 15 minutes.

Filling:

8 ounces pitted dates	½ cup sugar
½ cup water	1 tablespoon lemon juice

Mix ingredients together. Cook for about 5 minutes. Cool.

ECCLES CAKES
3 dozen

1 recipe Quick Puff Pastry
   (page 434)

Roll ⅛ inch thick. Cut in circles 3 inches in diameter.

Filling:

1 cup granulated sugar	¼ teaspoon nutmeg
½ cup butter, melted	¼ teaspoon cinnamon
1 cup finely chopped candied peel	1 egg, beaten
2 cups currants	2 tablespoons milk

Mix all ingredients but egg and milk, and place a scant teaspoon of filling in center of circle. Pinch edges of dough together, turn over, flatten lightly, and prick top with fork. Place on greased cooky sheet. Brush with egg and milk mixture. Bake in moderate oven (350°) 15 to 20 minutes.

Eccles cakes are similar to filled cookies. They are good served with afternoon tea.

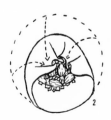

ENGLISH ROLLED WAFERS
4 dozen

1 cup sifted flour	½ cup light molasses
⅔ cup sugar	½ cup butter
½ teaspoon ginger	¾ cup finely chopped nuts

Sift together flour, sugar, and ginger. Heat molasses to boiling point, and immediately add butter. Slowly add flour mixture to molasses, stirring constantly. The mixture will resemble caramel icing in consistency and texture. Stir in nuts. Turn a baking pan, 13 x 9½ inches, upside down, and grease the bottom of it. Drop mixture from teaspoon onto the greased surface. Bake only three cookies at a time, as they are somewhat difficult to handle. Bake in slow oven (300°) 10 minutes. The wafers will have spread out and formed a thin lacy pattern. They should be only very lightly browned. Remove from oven and allow to cool slightly. Test with spatula for exact time at which wafer is cool enough to be removed from pan, and yet warm enough to be pliable.

Wrap wafer loosely around handle of a large wooden spoon so that top of wafer will be on outside of roll. Remove from handle of spoon and place rolled wafers on absorbent paper to cool. The finished wafers will be thin and brittle. The only difficult part of this recipe is in finding just the right moment at which the wafers can most successfully be rolled.

NOTE: Lightly grease the baking pan and don't place the cookies too near the edge because they both spread and slide on the slippery surface. Allow the cookies to set by cooling partially for a minute or two but roll them while they are slightly warm.

Be prepared to experiment a little because success doesn't come easily with these crisp lacy-looking cookies. You'll be pleased with the variety that they add to your tea table.

FATTIGMAND
Scandinavian Fried Cookies
About 2½ dozen

6 egg yolks	1 teaspoon vanilla
2 tablespoons sugar	½ teaspoon ground cardamom
2 tablespoons cream	¾ to 1 cup sifted flour
¼ teaspoon salt	

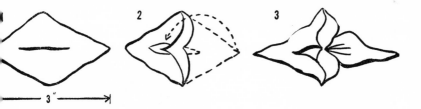

Beat egg yolks until light and lemon colored. Add sugar, cream, salt, vanilla, and cardamom. Add ¾ cup flour and mix to make a stiff dough. Add remaining ¼ cup flour if dough is sticky. Turn dough out on lightly floured board and roll ⅛ inch thick. Cut in diamond shape about 4 inches long. Make a slit about 1½ inches long in the center of the diamond and pull one corner through. Fry in deep hot fat (360°) 3 to 4 minutes or until lightly browned. Sprinkle with powdered sugar before serving.

This is a Scandinavian version of the doughnut but it's in a fancier shape. Since the dough is rolled out thin, it has a crisp texture all the way through and should be a golden brown.

FILLED COOKIES
2½ dozen

Foundation Sugar Cookies:

6 tablespoons butter	2¼ cups sifted flour
½ cup sugar	3 teaspoons baking powder
1 egg, well beaten	¼ teaspoon salt
1 teaspoon lemon extract	¼ cup milk
Grated peel of 1 lemon	

Cream butter and sugar until light and fluffy. Add well-beaten egg, lemon extract, and grated peel. Then add sifted dry ingredients alternately with milk. Beat after each addition until smooth. Chill for 1 hour. Roll ⅛ inch thick. Cut with 2½-inch cooky cutter. Place one teaspoon of filling on the circle, and place another circle on top, pressing edges together. Prick center of cooky with a fork or make a slit in top. Place on greased cooky sheet. Bake in hot oven (400°) 8 to 10 minutes.

FILLINGS FOR COOKIES

Apricot-Orange Filling:

¾ cup water
1½ cups sugar
3 tablespoons flour
1½ teaspoons grated orange peel

¼ teaspoon salt
4½ cups chopped dried apricots
¾ cup orange juice

Mix together and cook until thick. Cool.

Cinnamon-Prune Filling:

1 medium orange, peeled and diced
½ cup prune juice
½ cup sugar
1½ teaspoons cinnamon

¼ teaspoon salt
2 tablespoons melted butter
¾ cup chopped walnuts
2 cups chopped prunes

Mix together and cook until thick. Cool.

Date-Cherry-Orange Filling:

1 tablespoon flour
1 cup sugar
1 cup water

1 cup chopped raisins
1 cup chopped pitted dates
15 chopped glacé cherries

Mix together and cook until thick. Cool.

Raisin Filling:

2 cups chopped seedless raisins
⅔ cup sugar
1 tablespoon butter
1 tablespoon flour

⅔ cup boiling water
1 tablespoon lemon juice
¼ teaspoon salt
Grated peel of 1 lemon

Mix together and cook until thick. Cool.

Walnut-Fig Filling:

1¼ cups water
1 cup light corn syrup
½ cup sugar
4 tablespoons flour
¼ teaspoon salt

¾ cup chopped walnuts
2 cups chopped figs
2 tablespoons lemon juice
2 teaspoons grated lemon peel

Mix together and cook until thick. Cool.

FIRELIGHTERS
1½ dozen

1¾ cups rolled oats
¼ teaspoon baking powder
¼ teaspoon salt
⅓ cup coconut

½ cup butter, melted
1 tablespoon light corn syrup
½ cup brown sugar
1 teaspoon vanilla

Mix together rolled oats, baking powder, salt, and coconut. Combine butter, syrup, sugar, and vanilla. Pour into rolled-oat mixture and mix together. Press into greased, 9-inch square pan. The mixture should be about ½ inch thick. Bake in slow oven (325°) 25 to 30 minutes. Allow to cool slightly; mark into bars 1½ x 4 inches.

NOTE: Watch closely — these burn quickly. They should be a delicate golden brown color.

A great favorite in England, these are a specialty of Miss Joan Smith of the School of Domestic Economy, at Manchester, England. Their interesting name stems from the fact that they look like chips of wood with which to light fires. But the resemblance ends there, for they have a delicious crunchy texture and are tasty as only oatmeal cookies can be. Children are especially delighted by both the shape and flavor.

FROSTED COFFEE BARS
2½ dozen

4 tablespoons shortening
1 cup brown sugar
1 egg, beaten
½ cup warm coffee
1½ cups sifted cake flour
½ teaspoon baking powder

½ teaspoon soda
½ teaspoon cinnamon
¼ teaspoon salt
½ cup seedless raisins
¼ cup chopped nuts

Cream shortening and sugar until light and fluffy. Add beaten egg and mix well. Add warm coffee. Sift dry ingredients together and add to the creamed mixture. Mix thoroughly. Stir in chopped raisins and nuts. Pour into greased 9-inch square pan. Bake in moderate oven (350°) 20 to 25 minutes. Frost while warm with Lemon Confectioners' Frosting (page 415) and when cool cut in bars 2½ inches by 1 inch.

FRUIT DROPS
About 2 dozen

1 cup sweetened condensed milk	1 teaspoon vanilla
2 cups shredded coconut	¼ teaspoon salt
1 cup chopped dates	

Combine ingredients and mix well. Drop from teaspoon one inch apart on well-greased cooky sheet, 15½ x 12 inches. Bake in moderate oven (350°) 10 to 12 minutes or until nicely browned. Remove carefully from pan because they are apt to stick. The fruit drops are a macaroon-like cooky.

One cup of chopped prunes or apricots may be used instead of the dates.

PEANUT FRUIT DROPS — About 3 dozen

2½ cups salted peanuts	1⅓ cups sweetened condensed milk
1 cup dried apricots	2 tablespoons lemon juice

Grind peanuts and apricots; add condensed milk and lemon juice. Mix well. Drop from teaspoon onto greased cooky sheet, 15½ x 12 inches. Bake in moderate oven (350°) 15 to 20 minutes.

GINGER CUP CAKES
About 3 dozen

1 cup butter
¾ cup sugar
2¼ cups sifted cake flour
2 teaspoons baking powder

½ teaspoon salt
¾ cup preserved ginger
4 eggs, well beaten
1 teaspoon vanilla

Cream butter; add sugar gradually and continue creaming until light and fluffy. Sift flour, baking powder, and salt together. Cut ginger into small pieces and add to the flour mixture. Add dry ingredients to creamed mixture and mix well. Add beaten eggs and vanilla and blend into cake batter. Fill well-greased 2-inch muffin pans about ½ full of batter. Bake in slow oven (325°) 15 to 20 minutes. Remove from pans and cool on wire rack. Frost with Fluffy White Frosting (page 414).

If you like a real ginger flavor, experiment with increasing the amount of ginger. They're good without frosting, too. The little cakes will have a fine texture if you handle the dough carefully and work rapidly.

HUNGARIAN FILLED CRESCENTS
About 4 dozen

½ cup butter
1 tablespoon shortening
2 cups sifted flour
¼ teaspoon salt
2 egg yolks

½ cup sour cream
½ cup currant jelly
1 egg, beaten
3 tablespoons milk
Confectioners' sugar

Add butter and shortening to flour and salt. Mix together with fork or pastry blender until consistency of coarse corn meal. Beat egg yolks slightly; add sour cream. Pour into flour and fat mixture and mix thoroughly. Wrap in waxed paper. Chill for several hours or overnight. Roll ⅛ inch thick on lightly floured board. Cut into rounds 3 inches in diameter. Place about ½ teaspoon jelly near edge of each round. Fold other edge over to completely cover jelly. Press down to seal; roll up jelly-roll fashion. Shape into crescents. Place on lightly greased cooky sheet, 15½ x 12 inches. Brush with egg and milk mixture. Bake in moderate oven (375°) 12 to 15 minutes. Remove from pan while warm; sprinkle with confectioners' sugar.

Be a miser with the jelly because it runs out of the crescents if more than ½ teaspoon is used.

JEELOBIS (INDIA)
Deep-fat Fried Sweet
About 2 dozen

½ cup sour cream
2 cups flour
¼ pound Rolong (farina)
1 cup water

½ teaspoon saffron
2 tablespoons hot milk
Few drops yellow food coloring
Fat for deep fat frying

Syrup:

3 cups sugar   1 cup water

Mix sour cream, wheat flour, and farina with the water. Cover and set in a warm place overnight. The next day make the syrup by cooking the sugar and water together to a heavy syrup (about the consistency of corn syrup). Mix the saffron with the hot milk until it dissolves. Add saffron and yellow coloring to sour cream and flour mixture. If the mixture is too thick for squeezing through a pastry bag, add a little more water. The mixture should be a little thinner than a muffin batter. Heat the fat. Put mixture in pastry bag fitted with a tube that has a round hole in the end. Squeeze mixture from pastry bag into deep hot fat (375°) with a continuous flow to form a coil with the batter about 2 to 2½ inches in diameter. Fry until golden brown in color. Remove and drop immediately into the warm syrup. Cook in syrup 1 to 2 minutes. Remove at once to wire cooling rack to drain.

NOTE: If the syrup is too thin, the jeelobi will become soggy. The jeelobi should be crisp with the sugar syrup soaked into the tunnels. Serve cold as a sweet for the Buffet Featuring Foods of India (page 454).

Jeelobis are a popular sweet in India. Indian women often use a coconut shell with a hole made in it to pour the batter into the hot fat. The basis for a host of Indian tea-time savories and sweets is flour of wheat or rice, or any of the different cereals and pulses found in India. Indian sweets are numerous in variety and several require much skill and technique in making, with a good many hours spent in preparation. Baking is not a very popular method of cooking due to no facilities for good baking; consequently, deep fat frying and steaming are the typical methods of Indian cookery.

JOSEPHINES AND NAPOLEONS
1 dozen of each

½ recipe Quick Puff Pastry
(page 434)

Roll pastry ⅛ inch thick.

To Make 1 Dozen Napoleons:

Cut 24 oblongs, 2 x 3 inches, from the pastry. (Use remainder of pastry for Josephines.) Prick with fork. Place on ungreased cooky sheet, 15½ x 12 inches. Bake in very hot oven (475°) 8 to 10 minutes or until delicately browned.

Vanilla Cream Filling:

½ cup sugar	2¼ cups milk
2 tablespoons cornstarch	2 egg yolks, slightly beaten
2 teaspoons flour	1 tablespoon butter
½ teaspoon salt	1 teaspoon vanilla

Combine in double boiler sugar, cornstarch, flour, and salt; stir milk in gradually. Cook until thick, stirring constantly. Stir part of the mixture into the egg yolks; combine both mixtures and cook 2 to 3 minutes longer. Remove from heat. Blend in butter and vanilla. Cool.

Spread all of oblongs with Vanilla Cream Filling. Sprinkle half of oblongs with chopped nuts. Put together in pairs, using nut-covered oblongs for the tops.

To Make 1 Dozen Josephines:

Cut remaining pastry into strips, 1 x 4 inches. Wrap each strip around a glacé cherry. Place on ungreased cooky sheet, 15½ x 12 inches. Bake in very hot oven (475°) 5 to 6 minutes or until delicately browned.

KLEJNER
Danish Cookies
About 6 dozen

½ cup butter	2½ cups sifted flour
½ cup sugar	¼ teaspoon salt
1 tablespoon cream	1 teaspoon grated nutmeg
2 eggs, slightly beaten	1 tablespoon grated lemon peel

Cream butter; add sugar and cream and mix together until light and fluffy. Add eggs and blend into mixture. Sift flour, salt, and nutmeg together. Add to creamed mixture and mix thoroughly. Stir in grated lemon peel. Divide dough in half and turn out onto lightly floured board. Roll each half of

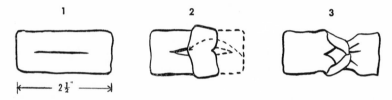

dough into rectangular shape ⅛ inch thick. Cut into strips 2½ inches long and 1 inch wide. Make a slit about 1½ inches long down the center and pull one end through the slit. Handle carefully. Fry in deep hot fat (360°) until light brown. Sprinkle with confectioners' sugar.

Here are cookies with a doughnut flavor but with a crustier brown layer. Be sure to keep the fat temperature low so that a golden crust is formed without burning or darkening the outside. They are excellent either plain or dipped in powdered sugar, and they're just as good for dunking as regular doughnuts.

KRUMKAGE
Norwegian Ice Cream Cones
6 dozen

5 eggs	1 cup heavy cream
1 cup sugar	2 cups flour
1 cup melted butter	

Beat eggs until light; add sugar gradually, beating constantly. Pour in melted butter and cream. Blend well. Add flour and beat until batter is smooth. Heat krumkaga iron. Pour batter on iron until it reaches the edges. Bake 1 minute on each side. When nicely browned, remove krumkaga from iron. Roll into cone shape. Just before serving, put a heaping tablespoon of whipped cream into each krumkaga.

NOTE: A krumkaga iron resembles a waffle grid except that it is thinner and has a finely traced design on both sides.

KULKULS
Christmas Sweet of India
About 4 dozen

3 cups flour	½ cup milk
1½ teaspoons baking powder	Water (about ¼ cup)
½ teaspoon salt	1 tablespoon melted butter
2 eggs, beaten	¾ teaspoon vanilla

Sift flour, baking powder, and salt together. Combine eggs, milk, and water; stir into flour mixture with just enough strokes to blend. Add melted butter and vanilla and blend into batter. This batter will be about the consistency of bread dough. Let stand for ½ hour. Pinch off pieces of dough about the size of a marble. Flatten on the back of a fork so that dough extends over entire length of fork tines. Start rolling dough at end near handle of fork and roll kulkul off back of fork into a curl. Drop into deep hot fat (365°) and fry about 2 minutes or until golden brown in color. Cool kulkuls and when cold drop into a heavy sugar syrup and stir until entirely coated with the syrup. Remove at once and spread on a wire rack to dry.

Syrup:

2 cups sugar	½ cup water

Cook sugar and water together to hard-crack stage (305°). This will be a thick sugar syrup. Drop the kulkuls into this syrup.

Kulkuls are connected very specially with Christmas. Families start making a good supply of these cookies a few weeks before Christmas and serve them to friends who drop in for a visit during the holidays.

LEBKUCHEN
German Christmas Cookies
5 dozen

3½ cups brown sugar
2 eggs, beaten
½ cup dark molasses
1 cup cold water
7 cups sifted flour
1 tablespoon soda
2 teaspoons salt

1 tablespoon cinnamon
1 tablespoon nutmeg
1 tablespoon cloves
1 cup chopped citron and candied
    peel
2 cups chopped nuts

Add sugar gradually to eggs. Then add molasses and water. Stir sifted dry ingredients into egg mixture. Blend well. Stir in the candied fruit and nuts. Place in refrigerator overnight. Roll ¼ inch thick on floured board; cut into 2-inch circles. Place on greased cooky sheet. Bake in slow oven (250°) 30 to 35 minutes. Sprinkle with confectioners' sugar or frost with Confectioners' Frosting (page 413).

NOTE: These cookies may be stored for a long time. They become very hard, but may be softened by placing in a jar with half an apple.

LEMON-CARAWAY COOKIES
5 dozen

½ cup shortening, softened
1 cup sugar
1 egg, beaten
2 tablespoons lemon juice

3 teaspoons caraway seeds
3 cups sifted cake flour
½ teaspoon soda
½ teaspoon salt

Cream shortening; add sugar and continue creaming until light and fluffy. Add egg and mix well. Add lemon juice and caraway seeds. Sift the dry ingredients together and add to creamed egg and sugar mixture. Form into a roll 1½ inches in diameter and wrap in waxed paper. Chill 30 minutes to 1 hour. Cut into ¼-inch slices. Place on greased cooky sheet. Bake in moderate oven (375°) 10 minutes.

MARMALADE DROP COOKIES
About 4 dozen

½ cup shortening
1 cup sugar
2 eggs, well beaten
3 cups sifted flour
½ teaspoon soda

½ teaspoon salt
1 cup thick orange marmalade
⅓ recipe Orange Confectioners'
    Frosting (page 416)

Cream shortening; add sugar and continue creaming until light. Add eggs and mix well. Sift flour, soda, and salt together. Stir into creamed mixture. Add marmalade and blend thoroughly. Drop from teaspoon 1 inch apart onto greased cooky sheet. Bake in moderate oven (350°) 12 to 15 minutes. Remove to cooling rack. When cold frost with Orange Confectioners' Frosting.

MOCHA FINGERS
About 4 dozen

1 recipe Coconut Circles (page 360)
½ cup raspberry jam
½ cup finely chopped almonds

⅓ recipe Mocha Frosting
(page 415)

Roll dough for Coconut Circles ¼ inch thick; cut in finger lengths 3 x 1 inches. Place on greased cooky sheet. Bake in moderate oven (350°) 10 to 12 minutes. Cool and spread a strip of raspberry jam down the center. Force Mocha Frosting through a pastry tube to make a border around jam strip. Sprinkle a few finely chopped almonds over raspberry jam.

Mocha fingers are an English variety of tea cake. They are attractive on a tray of tea cookies, with their nice contrast in size, shape, and texture.

OREILLES DE COCHON
About 5 dozen

2 cups sifted flour
½ teaspoon salt
1 egg, well beaten
1 tablespoon melted butter

½ cup water
1 teaspoon vinegar
Confectioners' sugar

Sift together dry ingredients. Combine beaten egg and melted fat and stir into dry ingredients. Add water and vinegar and mix to a fairly stiff dough. Turn out on floured board and roll ⅛ inch thick. Cut into circles with a 3-inch cutter. Insert fork in center of circle and twist to form oreilles (ears). Fry in deep hot fat (375°) 10 to 12 minutes or until nicely browned. Drain on absorbent paper. Sprinkle with confectioners' sugar.

These crisp oreilles de cochon, or "pig ears" to us, are a French concoction. Heap lightly on a pottery plate and serve with coffee or chocolate.

PECAN BARS
About 3 dozen

½ cup butter
⅓ cup honey
1 egg, well beaten
1 tablespoon cream
1¼ cups sifted cake flour

½ teaspoon baking powder
¼ teaspoon salt
½ teaspoon lemon extract
¾ cup finely chopped pecans

Cream butter; add honey slowly and continue creaming until light and fluffy. Blend beaten egg and cream into honey mixture. Sift flour, baking powder, and salt together; add to creamed mixture and mix thoroughly. Add lemon extract. Turn batter into greased 9-inch square pan. Sprinkle chopped pecans on top. Bake in moderate oven (350°) 8 to 10 minutes or until golden brown. Remove from oven and cut into 1½-inch squares while still warm. Allow to cool in pan.

PECAN FUDGE SQUARES
3 dozen small
or
1½ dozen large

2 eggs
1 cup sugar
½ cup melted butter
2 ounces (2 squares) **unsweetened**
    chocolate, melted
¾ cup sifted flour

½ teaspoon salt
¾ cup coarsely chopped pecans
1 teaspoon vanilla
½ recipe Chocolate Butter Frosting
    (page 412)

Beat eggs slightly; add sugar gradually and mix until well blended. Add melted butter and chocolate. Combine flour, salt, and pecans, and stir into sugar mixture. Blend in vanilla. Mix well. Pour into greased 9-inch square pan. Bake in slow oven (325°) 30 to 35 minutes. Cool. Frost with Chocolate Butter Frosting. Cut into 1½-inch squares.

These pecan fudge squares are just the thing for the high school or college crowd. They are more moist and sweet than most fudge squares and have a crisp, crusty top. They keep well and are fine to tuck into that laundry case when it's sent back to the son or daughter away from home. The fudge squares won't keep long after they arrive at their destination, however. They'll be gone in no time at all.

rich Swedish delicacies . . .

Spritz, page 384.

when church bells ring . . .

Individual Bridal Cakes, page 400.

PEPPARKAKOR
Swedish Gingersnaps
About 6 dozen

1 cup white sugar	1 teaspoon vinegar
½ cup light molasses	2 eggs
1 cup shortening	1 teaspoon soda
1 teaspoon cinnamon	1 tablespoon water
1 teaspoon cloves	5 cups sifted flour
1 teaspoon nutmeg	

Mix sugar, molasses, shortening, and spices in a saucepan, and bring to boil. Cool and add vinegar, then eggs, one at a time. Beat after each addition. Mix soda in the water. Combine flour and soda and water with sugar mixture. Roll out ¼ inch thick. Cut with 3-inch cooky cutter; sprinkle with sugar. Place on greased cooky sheet. Bake in moderate oven (375°) 10 to 12 minutes.

PETITS FOURS

Petits Fours are small fancy cakes of varying shapes. The tops and sides are covered with a thin coating of glossy white or pastel-colored fondant icing, and the tops are decorated with a simple flower or symmetrical designs. They are served at teas or receptions.

CAKE

Use the White Cake recipe (page 411) for Petits Fours. The cake should be about 1¼ inches thick when baked. If baked the day before cutting, there is less tendency for it to be crumbly. Gently brush off any crumbs on the top or bottom.

CUTTING THE CAKE

The sheet of cake may be cut into one or more shapes for dipping. Cut the cake so that the edges are well defined. Square, rectangular, triangular, or diamond shapes may be cut easily and quickly with a sharp pointed knife. When cut in this manner, the entire cake may be utilized as there are no trimmings left over.

If more variety in design is desired, a very small biscuit cutter may be used for a round cake or a large biscuit cutter may be used and then the cake cut in half to form a half circle. A sharp cooky cutter in small heart, crescent, or other simple design may also be used.

DIPPING ICING

Fondant (page 414) for dipping or coating the cut pieces of cake should be made several days in advance and stored in a tightly covered container in the refrigerator. A small amount of simple syrup is added to make it of the consistency for dipping. It should be thick enough to cover the cake so that edges do not show. It may be used without coloring or tinted a pastel shade. Occasionally, melted chocolate is added to make a chocolate dip.

DECORATIVE FROSTING

Sift the confectioners' sugar used for making the frosting because it must be creamy and smooth. Butter Frosting (page 412) may be used to make a decorative frosting. After the flavoring has been added, portions of the frosting may be tinted to suit the color scheme desired.

DIPPING OR COATING

Place the piece of cake to be coated on the blade of a short spatula. Then hold it over a small bowl containing the prepared dipping frosting. Spoon the frosting over the cake. Enough of the frosting should stick to the cake to form a good coating. Let the excess frosting run off the cake and back into the bowl. If the cake is crumbly, the crumbs will fall in the frosting, and it will not make a smooth coating. As soon as each side of the cake is coated with frosting carefully transfer it to a wire cooling rack to dry. After the cakes are dry, trim excess frosting off bottom of cakes. Arrange them in even rows on a tray to facilitate decorating. If frosting is too thin the first time, spoon on a second coating.

DECORATING

Keep the design simple. A small flower or design in the center is usually sufficient decoration. Practice making the design on a sheet of waxed paper before applying the design to the cake.

A small canvas pastry bag or a cake decorating tube may be used. A variety of tips are available, but only the plain, star (rosette), and leaf tips are necessary to make flowers, symmetrical designs, borders, continuous lines, and leaves. The difference in making these lies in the way the decorator is held and the speed of the frosting supply.

USE OF A DECORATING TUBE

1. Make the decorative frosting smooth and stiff enough to hold its shape.
2. Fill tube only ⅔ full and allow no air spaces to remain in decorator.
3. Hold decorator up straight for a symmetrical design; slant it for a border, a continuous line, or for writing.
4. Work close to the cake.
5. Cut off supply of frosting sharply to end a symmetrical design; release pressure gradually for a pointed finish such as a leaf.

SUGGESTIONS FOR DECORATING WITH A TUBE

Frost a sheet cake with Fluffy White Frosting (page 414). Cut cake into strips about 1½ inches by 1¾ inches.

1. Slice a maraschino cherry for center flower and make green leaves with decorating tube (leaf tip).
2. Pipe rose and two leaves in the center of each strip.
3. Use three silver balls and two piped-on leaves in the center of each strip.

SUGGESTIONS FOR DECORATING WITHOUT A TUBE

Frost top of small Tea Cakes (page 387) with Fluffy White Frosting (page 414).

1. Sprinkle chocolate shot or candy confetti on sides of cakes before frosting hardens.
2. Sprinkle chopped almonds on sides of cakes before frosting hardens, and center a whole almond on top.
3. Cut small slice of red gumdrop for flower and slices of green gumdrop for leaves.
4. Christmas Cakes. Cut holly leaves from angelica and use tiny red candies for holly berries.
5. Coconut Balls. Cut sheet cake with a 1-inch round cutter. Cover with frosting and roll in shredded coconut. Coconut may be tinted with cake coloring.

QUICK TEA DAINTIES
About 5 dozen

½ recipe Plain Pastry (page 433)
2 3-ounce packages cream cheese
2 tablespoons cream

1 cup confectioners' sugar
½ cup walnut halves
¼ cup maraschino cherries

Combine pastry, cream cheese, and cream. Divide in half. Roll each half ⅛ inch thick on cloth-covered board sprinkled with confectioners' sugar, ½ cup for each half of pastry. Cut in oblongs, 1 x 3 inches. Place ¼ of a walnut and ½ of a cherry on one end of each oblong and roll up. Place, folded-side-down on greased cooky sheet. Bake in hot oven (425°) 10 to 12 minutes or until golden brown.

RICHMOND MAIDS OF HONOR
English Tea Cakes
3½ dozen

Pastry:

¾ cup softened butter
⅓ cup sugar

3 egg yolks, beaten
2 cups sifted flour

Cream butter and add sugar; mix well. Add beaten egg yolks and blend. Then add flour one half at a time and mix well after each addition. Let pastry stand in refrigerator for 30 minutes, at least. It handles more easily after it has been chilled.

Filling:

3 egg whites
¾ cup finely ground blanched
   almonds

1¼ cups sifted confectioners' sugar
¾ cup raspberry jam

Beat egg whites to soft peak stage, fold in ground almonds and confectioners' sugar. To make Richmond maids of honor: Roll pastry ⅛ inch thick and cut into circles 3 inches in diameter. Use a fluted cooky cutter, if you have one. Fit circles of pastry into small muffin pans 2 inches in diameter. Put ½ teaspoon raspberry jam in pastry shell and then about a teaspoon of the almond filling on top of the raspberry jam. Put two tiny cross strips (X) of pastry on each tart. Bake in slow oven (325°) about 20 minutes or until pastry is done. Remove from muffin pans and place on cooling rack. Serve as afternoon tea cakes.

Each part of these English tea cakes is distinctive — from the rich pastry to the delicate raspberry-flavored jam to the almond-filled meringue. The whole is combined into an ambrosial bit of flavor unexcelled on any tea table. Allow your imagination a free hand in making minia-ture pastry designs for the top of these little "pies." And, of course, you can use your own favorite jelly or jam in them.

ROLLED WAFERS
3 dozen

½ cup shortening
½ cup light corn syrup
½ cup sugar

1 cup sifted flour
¼ teaspoon salt
1 teaspoon ground ginger

Put shortening, syrup, and sugar into a small pan and heat until warm. Stir in sifted dry ingredients. Drop from teaspoon 6 inches apart on back of greased pan. Bake in moderate oven (350°) 10 to 12 minutes. These rolled wafers should be han-dled in the same way as English Rolled Wafers (page 364).

ROLLED PECAN NUT WAFERS
About 2½ dozen

⅓ cup shortening
1 cup light brown sugar
2 eggs, well beaten
¼ cup sifted flour

¼ teaspoon salt
½ cup finely chopped pecans
½ teaspoon vanilla

Cream shortening; add brown sugar and beat until light. Blend in the beaten eggs. Sift flour and salt together and add to creamed mixture. Add pecans and vanilla and mix thor-oughly. Drop from teaspoon on the bottom of inverted oblong pans, 13 x 9½ inches, that have been greased lightly. Put only 3 on pan at a time, so as to leave plenty of space between the wafers; they spread very thin in baking. Bake in slow oven (325°) 5 to 8 minutes. Allow to stand a few minutes before rolling. Roll over handle of wooden spoon while still warm. You will have to work quickly before wafer becomes too crisp to roll.

Though these rolled pecan nut wafers take a little time to make, they are worth the effort. They are crisp and delicate and have an unusually good flavor. They make an attractive addition to a tray of tea cookies.

ROSETTES
4 dozen

2 eggs
1 egg yolk
⅔ cup heavy cream

1 cup sifted flour
⅓ cup sugar

Beat eggs and egg yolk until light, then add cream. Stir in flour and sugar; beat until smooth. This will be a very thin batter. Let stand 2 hours.

Heat rosette iron in deep hot fat two to three minutes; drain and dip into batter to within three-fourths inch of top. Return at once to hot fat (375°) and fry rosette until golden brown and crisp. Remove iron from fat and slip rosette carefully from iron and drain on absorbent paper. Heat iron again and repeat. Sprinkle rosettes with powdered sugar and serve for afternoon coffee.

For dessert, fill with whipped cream and top with fresh strawberries.

NOTE: If batter slips off, iron is too cold; if batter sticks, iron is too hot.

RYE DROP CAKES
18 small cakes

1 cup sifted rye flour
¾ cup sifted flour
3 teaspoons baking powder
½ teaspoon salt

½ cup milk
3 tablespoons molasses
2 eggs, well beaten

Mix and sift dry ingredients together. Combine milk, molasses, and beaten eggs. Add to dry ingredients and blend just enough to dampen. Drop from teaspoon into hot deep fat (360°). Cook 3 to 4 minutes or until nicely browned. Drain on absorbent paper. Serve with butter and maple syrup or molasses.

These rye drop cakes are well liked by New Englanders. They may be used as a bread or served as a dessert with maple syrup or molasses.

SAND BAKKELS
About 2½ dozen

1 cup butter
1 cup sugar
1 egg

2 cups sifted flour
¼ teaspoon salt
½ teaspoon almond extract

Cream butter; add sugar and continue creaming until light. Add egg and blend thoroughly. Stir in flour and salt. Add almond extract and mix well. Chill. Press into ungreased sand bakkel tins — round fluted pans about 1 inch deep and 3 inches in diameter. Bake in hot oven (325°) 8 to 10 minutes or until very light brown. Remove carefully from tins.

These fragile cakes may be served plain with tea, coffee, or ice cream, or they may be served with custard filling.

SAND BARS
About 3 dozen

¾ cup butter
3 tablespoons sugar
½ teaspoon vanilla
2¼ cups sifted flour

½ teaspoon salt
1 cup coarsely chopped pecans
3 cups sifted confectioners' sugar

Cream the butter until light and fluffy. Add granulated sugar, and mix. Add vanilla. Sift flour and salt together. Add flour to creamed mixture and then add chopped nuts. Shape with hands into bars about 2 inches long and ½ inch thick. This is a crumbly mixture and if it will not stick together add a little melted butter. Place on lightly greased cooky sheet, 15½ x 12 inches. Bake in moderate oven (350°) 20 minutes. Put the confectioners' sugar into a bowl, and as soon as sand bars come from oven toss into sugar a few at a time and roll until entirely covered. Reroll, so sand bars are well coated with sugar.

SCOTCH SHORTBREAD
2 dozen pie-shaped wedges

1 cup softened butter 2½ cups sifted flour
½ cup granulated sugar

Cream the butter; add sugar and mix until light and fluffy. Add flour gradually, mixing well after each addition. Turn out on lightly floured board; roll or pat mixture into circle, about ⅓ inch thick. Cut into 3 circles 6 inches in diameter (a salad plate will do). Flute edges as you do for pie crust.

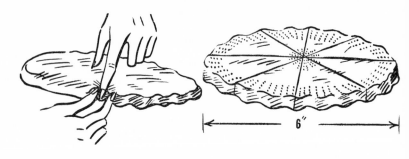

Prick circles in center and around edge several times with a fork. Lift with spatula onto ungreased cooky sheet. Cut each circle into 8 pie-shaped wedges. Do not separate. Bake in slow oven (300°) 30 to 35 minutes. Shortbread should not be allowed to brown, but should be cream colored.

SPRITZ
Rich Swedish Cookies
About 5 dozen

1 cup butter 1 teaspoon almond extract
½ cup sugar ¼ teaspoon salt
1 egg yolk, beaten 2 cups sifted flour

Cream butter and sugar until light and fluffy. Add egg yolk, almond extract, and sifted dry ingredients, and mix thoroughly. Force through cooky press onto ungreased cooky sheet. Bake in moderate oven (375°) 10 to 12 minutes.

CHRISTMAS SPRITZ

Divide Spritz dough (page 384) in 2 parts. Drop a few drops of red coloring into one half. Stir slightly. Drop a few drops of green coloring into the other half of dough. Put both colors into the cooky press and shape. Other colors may be added in the same manner.

NUT SPRITZ

Roll small pieces of Spritz dough (page 384) in balls, dip in egg white, then in chopped nuts, place on cooky sheet and press center with thumb. Bake as Spritz. When baked the center may be decorated with frosting from a pastry tube.

Don't let the pastry tube discourage you. An amateur can easily form these rich, delicate-flavored cookies. You don't have to stick to one shape, either, because the nice-textured dough lends itself to bows, circles, ribbons, S shapes, or any holiday shape. Like most rich doughs, it requires a moderate oven to prevent burning.

SUGAR COOKIES
About 3 dozen

½ cup butter	2½ cups sifted flour
1 cup sugar	2 teaspoons baking powder
2 eggs, beaten	½ teaspoon salt
1 tablespoon milk	1 teaspoon vanilla

Cream butter; add sugar gradually, creaming until light and fluffy. Add beaten eggs and milk and blend into creamed mixture. Sift flour, baking powder, and salt together. Add to other mixture; mix well. Add vanilla. Chill 2 hours. Roll out ⅛ inch thick on lightly floured board. Cut with floured cooky cutter. Place on lightly greased cooky sheet, 15½ x 12 inches. Bake in hot oven (400°) 10 to 12 minutes. Remove and cool on wire racks.

CHRISTMAS COOKIES

Roll Sugar Cooky dough as directed. Cut with star, Christmas tree, bell, or reindeer-shaped cooky cutters. Place on cooky sheet and sprinkle with red or green colored sugar, silver shot, or sugar confetti. Bake as directed.

SWEDISH CREAM LILIES
3 dozen

1 cup egg yolks
1 cup sugar
1 cup sifted pastry flour

¼ teaspoon salt
½ cup heavy cream, whipped

Beat yolks until light and lemon colored. Add sugar gradually, beating constantly. Fold in flour and salt. Spread in small rounds on greased cooky sheets. Bake in slow oven (325°) 10 to 12 minutes. While still hot, remove from cooky sheet with thin spatula. Roll into cone shape. When cold, fill with whipped cream.

SWEDISH NUT COOKIES
About 2½ dozen

¼ cup shortening
¾ cup sugar
1 egg, well beaten
2 tablespoons milk
1½ cups sifted flour

1 teaspoon baking powder
½ teaspoon salt
1 teaspoon vanilla
⅓ cup chopped nuts

Cream shortening; add sugar gradually and continue creaming until light. Combine egg and milk; add to creamed mixture. Mix well. Sift dry ingredients together; add to creamed mixture and blend thoroughly. Add vanilla. Spread evenly on bottom of inverted oblong pan, 13 x 9½ inches, that has been lightly greased. Sprinkle with chopped nuts. Mark in strips 1 inch wide and mark through center of pan. Bake in slow oven (325°) 12 to 15 minutes. Cut in strips and place over rolling pin. Press down so cooky will conform to shape of rolling pin. Work quickly before cookies become crisp. Place strips the length of rolling pin and let remain until they hold a semi-circular shape. Remove carefully from rolling pin.

NOTE: Don't try to shape the cookies after they are cold because they are brittle. However, it's simple to reheat them in the oven, and then they will behave beautifully for you.

For a very chewy cooky with an unusual shape, these Swedish nut cookies are just the thing.

TEA CAKES
6 to 7 dozen

1 cup butter	4 teaspoons baking powder
2½ cups sugar	1 teaspoon salt
5 eggs	1⅔ cups milk
4¼ cups sifted cake flour	2 teaspoons vanilla

Cream butter. Add sugar gradually and cream until light and fluffy. Beat eggs until light and blend into creamed mixture. Sift flour, baking powder, and salt together; add alternately with milk to creamed mixture. Add vanilla and blend well. Drop from teaspoon into well-greased 2-inch muffin pans. Bake in moderate oven (350°) 12 to 15 minutes. Remove from pans and let cool. Frost with Fluffy White Frosting (page 414) and decorate.

The cake may be baked in larger muffin pans, frosted and decorated, and served as dessert.

BUTTERFLY TEA CAKES

Cut off top of cup cake; cut top in half. Fill center with whipped cream, and insert the two tiny pieces of cake at an angle to look like wings.

WALNUT SLICES
2½ dozen

1 cup butter
½ cup brown sugar
2 cups sifted flour
2 eggs
2 tablespoons flour
½ teaspoon baking powder

¾ cup shredded coconut
1½ cups brown sugar
½ teaspoon salt
½ teaspoon vanilla
½ cup chopped walnuts

Cream butter and brown sugar; add flour and mix thoroughly. Spread into two ungreased 9-inch square pans and pat down. Bake in moderate oven (350°) 12 to 15 minutes. Do not let brown. Beat eggs and add the 2 tablespoons flour, baking powder, coconut, sugar, salt, vanilla, and nuts. Mix together and spread over baked crust. Bake in moderate oven (350°) 20 to 25 minutes. Spread with Orange Frosting.

Orange Frosting:

2 teaspoons grated orange peel
1 teaspoon lemon juice
1 tablespoon orange juice

2 egg yolks
1 cup confectioners' sugar

Add peel to juices and let stand 15 minutes. Add gradually to egg yolks. Stir in confectioners' sugar until of right consistency to spread on cookies.

Cakes and Frostings

CAKES

Angel Food
Applesauce
Baked Alaska
Butter
California Cheese Cake
   Zwieback Crust
Cherry
Chocolate
Chocolate Logs
Cocoa Roll
Danish Cake with Lemon
   Sauce
Danish Cake with Fruit
   Topping
English Raspberry Sandwich
Heart Cake for Engagement
   Party
Hollandsche Appel Koek
Individual Bridal Cakes
Jelly Roll

Lincoln Log
Marble
Palm Beach Poinciana
Party Roll
Pineapple Upside-Down
Poppy-Seed
Pound
Red Devil's Food
Refrigerator Cheese Cake
   Graham Cracker Crust
Royal Spice
Scotch Cherry Christmas
Simnel
Sponge
White
   Coconut Layer
   Lady Baltimore
   Pineapple Cashew
   With Lemon Filling
White Cake for Petits Fours

FROSTINGS

Butter
Chocolate Butter
Chocolate Fudge
Confectioners'
   Cinnamon Confectioners'
Easy-To-Make Fudge

Fluffy White
   Feather
Fondant
Lemon Confectioners'
Mocha
Orange Confectioners'
Strawberry Parfait Topping

M ANY A COOK's reputation is based on a beautiful cake, high, light, and tender, with an elegant frosting, gently swirled. It's an American custom for a good hostess to serve delicious cake.

But you don't have to depend on luck or have a special knack for baking to excel in cake-making. Today's recipes are skillfully balanced and carefully written. If you measure ingredients accurately and follow the mixing and baking procedures thoroughly, success is yours — every time.

Cake deserves a luscious frosting. A frosting not only adds good eating, but glamour as well. Your choice may be a rich fudge, a fluffy white, a creamy confectioners' sugar-butter, or a marvelous orange- or lemon-flavored frosting.

First impressions are important, so be sure to decorate your cake. You don't have to go to a lot of extra bother. Gala swirls, a sprinkle of colored coconut, shaved chocolate, chopped nuts, or tiny candies will turn a plain cake into a beauty.

The combination or double-acting type of baking powder has been used in these recipes. About one-third of the leavening gas is released in the mixing, the remainder when heated. To adjust the baking powder to another type, follow the manufacturer's directions.

ANGEL FOOD CAKE

1 cup sifted cake flour
½ cup sifted sugar
1¼ cups egg whites (10 to 12)
½ teaspoon salt

1¼ teaspoons cream of tartar
1 cup sifted sugar
1 teaspoon vanilla
¼ teaspoon almond extract

Add ½ cup sifted sugar to flour. Sift together 4 times. Add salt to egg whites and beat with flat wire whisk or rotary egg beater until foamy. Sprinkle cream of tartar over eggs and continue beating to soft peak stage. Add the remaining cup of sugar by sprinkling ¼ cup at a time over egg whites and blending carefully into the whites, about 20 strokes each time. Fold in flavoring. Sift flour-sugar mixture over egg whites about ¼ at a time and fold in lightly, about 10 strokes each time. Pour into ungreased round 10-inch tube pan. Bake in moderate oven (350°) 35 to 45 minutes. Remove from oven and invert pan on cooling rack. Let stand until cool. Remove from pan. Frost with your favorite frosting or Strawberry Parfait Topping (page 416).

APPLESAUCE CAKE

½ cup shortening
1 cup sugar
1 egg, beaten
2½ cups sifted cake flour
1 teaspoon baking powder
⅓ teaspoon salt
½ teaspoon cloves

1 teaspoon cinnamon
¼ teaspoon nutmeg
1 teaspoon soda
1 tablespoon warm water
1½ cups applesauce
¾ cup chopped raisins
¾ cup chopped nuts

Cream shortening; add sugar gradually and continue creaming until light and fluffy. Add egg. Sift together flour, baking powder, salt, and spices. Dissolve soda in 1 tablespoon warm water and add to applesauce. Add flour mixture alternately with applesauce to creamed mixture. Stir in raisins and nuts. Pour into 3 greased 8-inch layer cake pans. Bake in moderate oven (350°) 25 to 30 minutes. Spread layers with Fluffy White Frosting (page 414) and cover top and sides of cake with the same frosting. Sprinkle chopped nuts on top of cake.

Mrs. Vera Swearingen is our right-hand man in the Institution Tea Room Kitchen. She is always on hand to answer questions and to help make the Tea Room run smoothly. Anything she makes has an artistic touch. Mrs. Swearingen is generous in sharing some of her fine recipes, and this applesauce cake is one of them.

with feather frosting . . .

Marble Cake, page 401.

personalized servings . . .

Party Roll, page 402.

BAKED ALASKA

Layer of Sponge Cake (page 409)   **1 quart brick vanilla ice cream**
   2 inches thick   **Meringue (page 430)**

Cut sponge cake in half, reserving one half for a second Baked Alaska or other dessert. Place cake on bread board covered with heavy paper. With sharp knife make cut about ½ inch deep around sponge cake, one inch from edge, and remove some of cake. Place brick of ice cream in hollowed-out center of cake. Cover cake and ice cream completely with Meringue. Brown meringue in very hot oven (450°). Board, paper, cake, and meringue are poor conductors of heat and prevent ice cream from melting. Slip from paper onto an oblong platter. Decorate base with flowers and leaves. Serve at once, before ice cream has a chance to melt.

NOTE: For variety use several kinds of ice cream, as vanilla, chocolate, and mint, and shape into mound on sponge cake.

Meringue:

6 egg whites   **3 tablespoons lemon juice**
½ teaspoon salt   **½ teaspoon vanilla**
¾ cup sugar

Add salt to egg whites and beat until frothy. Add sugar gradually, beating constantly until soft peak stage is reached. Add lemon juice and vanilla.

The trickiest dessert of all, also the most awe-inspiring to guests. The secret of success is to have all of your utensils organized on one table and then make it just seconds from the ice cream package to the hot oven where the frothy meringue acquires a faint even brown. It's really not hard when you know the trick.

BUTTER CAKE

½ cup butter
1 cup sugar
2 eggs, beaten
1 teaspoon vanilla

2 cups sifted cake flour
3 teaspoons baking powder
½ teaspoon salt
⅔ cup milk

Cream shortening; add sugar gradually and continue creaming until light and fluffy. Blend in beaten eggs and vanilla. Sift flour, baking powder, and salt together. Add alternately with milk to creamed mixture. Mix until well blended. Pour into 2 greased 9-inch layer cake pans. Bake in moderate oven (350°) 25 to 30 minutes. Let cool in pans for 5 minutes, then remove from pans and cool on cake rack before frosting.

CALIFORNIA CHEESE CAKE
10 servings

12 ounces cream cheese
2 egg yolks
2 tablespoons lemon juice
1 teaspoon vanilla
2 tablespoons sugar
2 tablespoons flour

¼ teaspoon salt
½ cup heavy cream
2 egg whites
1 tablespoon sugar
¼ teaspoon lemon juice

Topping:

1 cup sour cream
1 tablespoon sugar

1 teaspoon vanilla

Using mixer, beat cheese until creamy. Add egg yolks, one at a time, beating well after each addition. Add lemon juice and vanilla; blend well. Add sugar, flour, salt, and cream; blend. Beat egg whites until frothy, and add sugar and lemon juice; beat to soft peak stage. Fold into cheese mixture. Pour mixture over baked crust. Place in slow oven (300°), and bake 60 to 65 minutes or until firm. Remove from oven, and spread with topping. Return to oven for an additional 10 minutes. Cool and refrigerate 24 hours before serving.

Zwieback Crust:

¾ cup zwieback crumbs
2 tablespoons confectioners' sugar

⅛ teaspoon cinnamon
2 tablespoons melted butter

Mix dry ingredients together. Add melted butter; mix well. Press into 9-inch spring form or cake pan. Bake in slow oven (300°) about 5 minutes. Cool.

CHERRY CAKE

½ cup shortening
1 cup sugar
2 eggs, unbeaten
2 cups sifted flour
½ teaspoon salt

1 teaspoon soda
2 teaspoons cinnamon
1 cup canned sour red pitted
    cherries and juice

Cream together shortening and sugar until light and fluffy. Add eggs one at a time, beating well after each addition. Sift together flour, salt, soda, and cinnamon, and add to creamed mixture. Add cherries and juice; stir until well mixed. Pour into 2 greased 8-inch layer cake pans. Bake in moderate oven (350°) 25 to 30 minutes. Cool 5 minutes; turn out on cake rack. Put together with Fluffy White Frosting (page 414), substituting cherry juice for part of the water.

CHOCOLATE CAKE

1¼ cups shortening
2¼ cups sugar
1 teaspoon vanilla
4 eggs, beaten
4 ounces (4 squares) unsweetened
    chocolate, melted

3 cups sifted cake flour
3 teaspoons baking powder
1 teaspoon salt
1 cup milk

Cream shortening; add sugar gradually and continue creaming until light and fluffy. Blend in vanilla. Add beaten eggs and mix thoroughly. Blend melted chocolate into creamed mixture. Sift dry ingredients together and add alternately with milk. Mix well. Pour batter into 3 greased 9-inch layer cake pans. Bake in moderate oven (375°) 25 to 30 minutes. Let cool in pans for 5 minutes, then remove from pans and cool on cake rack before frosting.

CHOCOLATE LOGS
44 logs

3 ounces (3 squares) unsweetened chocolate	½ teaspoon salt
⅔ cup sugar	⅓ cup shortening
⅓ cup buttermilk	½ cup sugar
1⅔ cups sifted cake flour	2 eggs, beaten
1 teaspoon baking powder	⅔ cup buttermilk
½ teaspoon soda	1 teaspoon vanilla

Melt chocolate in double boiler; add ⅔ cup sugar and the ⅓ cup of buttermilk and stir over boiling water until sugar is dissolved. Sift flour, baking powder, soda, and salt together twice. Cream shortening and add the ½ cup of sugar and beaten eggs; mix well. Add about ¼ of the flour, mix thoroughly; add chocolate mixture and blend. Add remaining flour alternately with the ⅔ cup buttermilk, a small amount at a time, beating very thoroughly after each addition. Add vanilla and mix well. Fill 2 well-greased plain iron breadstick pans, 15 x 7½ inches, ¾ full of cake batter. Bake in moderate oven (350°) 20 to 25 minutes. Let stand about 5 minutes before removing from pans. When cakes have cooled, remove

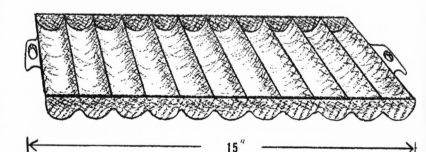

← ——————— 15″ ——————— →

carefully from pans. Cut each strip into halves, cutting diagonally. Frost with Fondant Frosting (page 414) to which melted chocolate has been added. Decorate with Butter Frosting (page 412) in tiny roses, lily of the valley, or other floral designs.

To make a hit with anyone from eight to eighty serve these frosting-coated, log-shaped cakes. The cake is more compact than most and serves as a wonderful base for decoration. So get out your pastry tube and practice your fanciest designs. Miss Carolyn Cason of the Institution Management Staff brought this recipe for chocolate cake with her from Texas.

COCOA ROLL

5 egg yolks	¼ teaspoon salt
3 tablespoons sugar	3 tablespoons sugar
½ teaspoon vanilla	1 cup heavy cream, whipped
2 tablespoons sifted flour	2 tablespoons confectioners' sugar
2 tablespoons cocoa	½ teaspoon vanilla
5 egg whites	

Beat egg yolks, add the 3 tablespoons of sugar gradually and continue beating until light and lemon colored. Blend in vanilla. Sift flour and cocoa together and blend into egg yolks. Add salt to egg whites, beat until frothy; gradually add the other 3 tablespoons sugar and beat to soft peak stage. Fold the whites carefully into the yolk mixture, blending so that the color is uniform. Line a shallow oblong pan, 13 x 9½ x 2 inches, with waxed paper. Turn cocoa mixture into the pan. Bake in slow oven (325°) 15 to 20 minutes or until springy to the touch. Turn out on a cloth that has been sprinkled liberally with confectioners' sugar. Peel off paper. Roll cake as if it were a jelly roll and wrap in cloth. Cool. When cool, unroll and spread with whipped cream to which the confectioners' sugar and vanilla have been added. Roll up. Cut in 1½-inch slices.

DANISH CAKE WITH LEMON SAUCE

2 medium potatoes	3 tablespoons almond paste
½ cup butter	¼ teaspoon almond extract
2 cups confectioners' sugar	½ teaspoon salt
4 egg yolks, well beaten	4 egg whites
1 cup ground blanched almonds	¼ cup fine bread crumbs

Cook potatoes, put through ricer. Measure ¾ cup of riced potatoes. Cream butter; add sugar and beat until light and fluffy. Add the egg yolks and riced potatoes and mix thoroughly. Blend in the ground almonds, almond paste, and almond extract. Add salt to egg whites and beat to soft peak stage. Fold into cake mixture. Pour into greased 9-inch square pan. Sprinkle with bread crumbs. Bake in slow oven (300°) 35 to 45 minutes. Let stand about 15 minutes before turning out of pan. Cut cake in squares and serve with Lemon Sauce.

Lemon Sauce:

1 cup sugar	¼ cup lemon juice
¼ teaspoon salt	6 egg yolks
½ cup pineapple juice	1 teaspoon grated lemon peel
½ cup water	

Mix sugar, salt, pineapple juice, water, and lemon juice together. Beat egg yolks and add mixed juices. Cook in double boiler, stirring constantly until thick. Remove from heat. Stir sauce as it cools. Add grated lemon peel. Serve a generous tablespoon of sauce over cake.

DANISH CAKE WITH FRUIT TOPPING
20 to 24 servings

1 recipe Sponge Cake (page 409)	1 No. 2½ can sliced pineapple
1 recipe Lemon Meringue Pie	1 No. 2 can apricot halves
Filling (page 430)	8 maraschino cherries
1 No. 2½ can pear halves	1½ cups heavy cream

Bake Sponge Cake in oblong pan, 13 x 9½ x 2 inches, or in three 9-inch layer cake pans. Split oblong cake or layers and spread with lemon filling. Drain fruit. Arrange well-drained fruits on top of cake in an attractive pattern. Place maraschino cherries in centers of pineapple rings. Completely cover top of cake with fruit. Spoon Glaze over fruit to keep it moist and give a shiny appearance. Place cake on lace paper doilies on serving dish or tray. Force whipped cream through pastry tube to decorate sides of cake and decorate top with whipped cream roses to fill in where fruit does not cover cake. Cut round cake into wedges and oblong one into squares to serve.

Glaze:

1 cup fruit juice (pear and pine- apple)	¼ cup sugar ¼ cup water
1½ tablespoons cornstarch	1 tablespoon lemon juice

Heat fruit juice. Mix cornstarch, sugar, and water; add to fruit juice. Cook until clear and thickened slightly. Add lemon juice. Spoon over cake to glaze fruit.

To give variety in color the pears can be tinted a delicate green or pink by adding a few drops of red or green food coloring to pear juice and letting pears stand in juice 10 to 15 minutes. Drain well on absorbent paper before placing on cake.

This handsome dessert was introduced to us by Joan Smith of Manchester, England. She had sampled it in Denmark where it is served with afternoon coffee. It makes a spectacular dessert for a buffet party with the gleaming fruit on golden sponge cake all fancied up with flutings of whipped cream.

ENGLISH RASPBERRY SANDWICH

Make Sponge Cake (page 409), about two inches thick. Cut in two and spread with raspberry jam. Replace top layer and sprinkle with confectioners' sugar. Cut into slices, 1 x 3 inches, and serve for afternoon tea.

HEART CAKE FOR ENGAGEMENT PARTY

Bake White Cake (page 409) in heart-shaped mold. Frost with Fluffy White Frosting (page 414). Decorate with tiny hearts placed around edge of cake. Place hearts on wooden picks and stick into cake to give border effect. Hearts may be made in the following manner:

1½ cups sifted confectioners' sugar	¼ teaspoon vanilla
½ cup melted shortening	Red food coloring
¼ teaspoon salt	

Add confectioners' sugar to melted shortening. Add salt and vanilla, and blend well. Add a few drops of red food coloring to give a delicate pink color. Turn mixture out on board. Roll ⅛ inch thick. Make heart cutouts with tiny heart-shaped cutter. Use to decorate cake.

HOLLANDSCHE APPEL KOEK
Dutch Apple Cake

2 cups sifted flour	¾ cup milk
2 teaspoons baking powder	2 cups thinly sliced, pared apples
½ teaspoon salt	⅓ cup sugar
¼ cup butter	1 teaspoon cinnamon
1 egg, beaten	

Sift flour, baking powder, and salt together. Cut butter into flour mixture. Combine beaten egg and milk and pour into flour mixture. Stir to make a soft dough. Turn apples into greased 9-inch square cake pan. Mix sugar and cinnamon and sprinkle over apples. Roll dough to fit pan and place over the apples. Bake in moderate oven (350°) 30 to 40 minutes. Cut cake into squares and serve warm, fruit side up. Serve with Hard Sauce (page 342), Lemon Sauce (page 343), or whipped cream.

This is an inexpensive, easy-to-make dessert. Try it in the wintertime when the family appreciates a hearty dessert.

INDIVIDUAL BRIDAL CAKES
About 16 individual cakes

3 cups sifted flour	1 cup milk
4 teaspoons baking powder	¼ teaspoon vanilla
1 teaspoon salt	¼ teaspoon lemon extract
¾ cup shortening	¼ teaspoon almond extract
1½ cups sugar	5 egg whites, stiffly beaten

Sift together flour, baking powder, and salt. Cream shortening and sugar until light and fluffy. Add flour to creamed mixture alternately with milk. Add flavoring and blend well. Fold in egg whites. Pour part of the batter into greased 3-inch muffin pans to depth of ½ inch, and the remaining batter into very small greased muffin pans, or the batter may be baked in shallow cake pans, and cut into two sizes with cooky cutters. Bake in moderate oven (375°) 20 minutes. When cooled, frost each cake with Fluffy White Frosting (page 414), placing a small cake on top of the larger. If the layers need building out, this may be done with the frosting. Decorate the edges of each tier with tiny silver balls, and top with a white dove.

JELLY ROLL
10 to 12 servings

3 eggs
1 cup sugar
1 teaspoon vanilla
1 cup sifted cake flour
1 teaspoon baking powder

¼ teaspoon salt
5 tablespoons water
4 tablespoons butter
Jam or jelly

Beat eggs until light. Add sugar gradually and continue beating until thick and lemon colored. Add vanilla. Sift flour, baking powder, and salt together. Fold the dry ingredients and water alternately into the egg mixture. Melt butter and add. Line jelly-roll pan, 15½ x 10½ x 1 inches, with greased waxed paper and pour batter into pan. Bake in moderate oven (350°) 15 to 20 minutes. Turn jelly roll out on cloth sprinkled with powdered sugar. Remove paper. Spread with jam, jelly, or Lemon Meringue Pie Filling (page 430), and roll up. Wrap in towel until ready to serve. Cut in 1-inch slices.

LINCOLN LOG

Make Jelly Roll (above). Spread with whipped cream or chocolate filling; roll up. Use rose tube in pastry bag; fill with Chocolate Butter Frosting (page 412). Force frosting onto roll lengthwise to completely cover roll so it looks like bark on a tree. Cover ends with frosting.

This chocolate log may be used for a Lincoln's Day party.

For decorative effect, make mushrooms out of meringue and place on log.

MARBLE CAKE

1 recipe Butter Cake
   (page 394)

2 ounces (2 squares) unsweetened
   chocolate, melted

Make Butter Cake. Divide batter in half. Stir melted chocolate into ½ of batter. Put chocolate and white batter by tablespoons alternately into greased 9-inch square pan. Bake in moderate oven (350°) 35 to 45 minutes or until done. Let stand in pan 5 to 10 minutes; turn out on cooling rack. Frost with Feather Frosting (page 414).

PALM BEACH POINCIANA CAKE
2 loaves

1 pound butter (2 cups)
1 pound sugar (2 cups)
8 egg yolks, well beaten
4 tablespoons lemon juice
2 teaspoons grated lemon peel
1 pound sifted flour (4 cups)
1½ cups chopped blanched almonds

½ pound citron, chopped fine
½ pound white raisins, chopped fine
1 cup glacé cherries, cut into fourths
8 egg whites

Cream butter and add sugar gradually; continue creaming until light and fluffy. Add well-beaten egg yolks and blend thoroughly. Add the lemon juice and grated peel. Combine flour, nuts, and fruit. Add to creamed mixture in fourths, blending well after each addition. Beat egg whites to soft peak stage. Fold into cake mixture. Turn into 2 greased loaf pans, 9½ x 5¼ x 2¾ inches, lined with waxed paper. Bake in slow oven (325°) 45 minutes to 1 hour or until done. Remove to cake rack to cool. Remove from pans and allow to stand 24 hours before cutting. Slice thin and serve for afternoon tea.

This fine, even-textured, rich cake may be made at Christmastime and served as white fruit cake. It may be kept for several weeks if stored in an airtight container in a cool place.

PARTY ROLL

Make Jelly Roll (page 401); fill with jelly, whipped cream, Chocolate Cream Pie Filling (page 424), or any other desired filling. Roll up. Put Chocolate Butter Frosting (page 412) in pastry bag and, using tube with round end, write names on jelly roll.

The party roll can be brought to the table and sliced so that each person gets the slice with his name on it. This is especially attractive for a children's party.

PINEAPPLE UPSIDE-DOWN CAKE
9 servings

Topping:

¼ cup butter	9 slices pineapple (1 No. 2 can)
¾ cup brown sugar	9 maraschino cherries

Melt butter in 9-inch square pan and sprinkle brown sugar over it. Place slices of pineapple in pan and put a cherry in center of each slice.

Cake:

½ cup butter	3 teaspoons baking powder
1 cup sugar	¼ teaspoon salt
2 eggs, beaten until light	⅔ cup milk
2 cups cake flour	1 teaspoon vanilla

Cream butter and sugar until light and fluffy. Add eggs and beat well. Add sifted dry ingredients alternately with milk and mix well. Add vanilla. Pour cake batter over fruit. Bake in moderate oven (350°) 30 to 35 minutes. Turn onto large plate and cut cake so there is a whole slice of pineapple for each serving. Garnish with whipped cream and a maraschino cherry.

POPPY-SEED CAKE

Cake:

⅓ cup poppy seeds
¾ cup milk
¾ cup shortening
1¼ cups sugar
1 teaspoon vanilla

⅛ teaspoon almond extract
2 cups sifted cake flour
2 teaspoons baking powder
½ teaspoon salt
4 egg whites

Soak poppy seeds in milk for about two hours. Cream shortening; add sugar and continue creaming until light and fluffy. Add extracts. Sift flour, baking powder, and salt together. Add alternately with the milk and poppy seeds to the creamed fat and sugar mixture. Beat egg whites to soft peak stage and fold into batter. Pour batter into 2 greased 9-inch layer cake pans. Bake in moderate oven (350°) 30 to 35 minutes. When cool, spread filling between layers. Powdered sugar or whipped cream may be used as topping.

Filling:

2 cups milk
1 cup sugar
1½ tablespoons cornstarch

¼ teaspoon salt
4 egg yolks
¾ cup chopped nuts

Scald milk in double boiler. Mix sugar, cornstarch, and salt together. Add to scalded milk, stirring constantly until thick. Beat egg yolks; add some of cooked mixture to egg yolks, then combine both mixtures and cook for 2 to 3 minutes longer. Cool. Add chopped nuts.

I had been looking for some time for a good poppy-seed cake recipe, but could not seem to find one. One of my students in Catering Class, Mary Ellen Cottrell from Omaha, Nebraska, heard me bemoaning the lack of a good recipe and said she'd be glad to write for her mother's recipe. So we're sharing with you a poppy-seed cake recipe that is the real thing! If you really like poppy seeds you can increase the amount in the cake.

POUND CAKE
2 loaves

1½ cups butter
1 pound (2 cups) sugar
1 teaspoon vanilla
½ teaspoon almond extract
8 eggs

4½ cups sifted cake flour
1 teaspoon baking powder
½ cup milk
2 teaspoons grated lemon peel

Cream butter; add sugar gradually and continue creaming until light and fluffy. Blend in flavoring. Add eggs one at a time; beat well after each addition. Sift flour and baking powder together. Add to creamed mixture alternately with milk; mix until smooth. Stir in lemon peel. Pour into 2 well-greased wax-paper-lined loaf pans, 9½ x 5¼ x 2¾ inches. Bake in slow oven (325°) 35 to 40 minutes or until done.

RED DEVIL'S FOOD CAKE

½ cup shortening
1¼ cups sugar
1 teaspoon vanilla
2 eggs, beaten
2 ounces (2 squares) chocolate,
    melted

1 tablespoon lemon juice
1 cup milk
1 teaspoon red food coloring
1¾ cups sifted flour
½ teaspoon salt
1 teaspoon soda

Cream shortening; add sugar and continue creaming until light and fluffy. Blend in vanilla. Stir in eggs and melted chocolate and blend well. Combine lemon juice and milk, allow to stand a few minutes; add red coloring. Add salt to flour; add with milk alternately to the creamed mixture. Stir soda into last addition of flour. Mix well. Pour batter into 2 greased 9-inch layer cake pans. Bake in moderate oven (350°) 25 to 30 minutes. Cool 5 minutes. Put layers together with Chocolate Butter Frosting (page 412) and frost cake with same frosting.

REFRIGERATOR CHEESE CAKE*

2 12-ounce packages cottage cheese
1 tablespoon vanilla
2 tablespoons lemon juice
¼ teaspoon salt
2 tablespoons (2 envelopes)
    unflavored gelatin
½ cup cold water
3 egg yolks, slightly beaten
2 tablespoons milk
1 cup sugar
2 cups heavy cream
3 egg whites

Rub cottage cheese through a wire sieve. Add vanilla, lemon juice, and salt, and blend well. Soften gelatin in cold water. Combine egg yolks, milk, and sugar, and cook in double boiler until thick, stirring constantly. Add softened gelatin and stir until dissolved. Remove from heat; cool slightly, and stir in cheese mixture. Whip cream and fold into cheese. Beat egg whites to soft peak stage and fold in. Turn into a 9-inch spring form pan (or angel food cake pan) lined with graham cracker crust. Chill for at least 8 hours. This makes a large cheese cake and will easily serve 16.

Graham Cracker Crust:

1½ cups graham cracker crumbs
½ cup confectioners' sugar
½ cup melted butter

Mix graham cracker crumbs and confectioners' sugar together. Stir in melted butter and blend thoroughly. Line pan with mixture by pressing it firmly to the bottom and sides. Chill well before adding cottage cheese mixture. If desired, ¼ cup of crumb mixture may be reserved to sprinkle on top of cake.

This cheese cake was demonstrated on a television program in New York. Before the program was over there were so many calls for the recipe that the telephone lines to that station were jammed. So here it is — cheese cake that is easy to make, has a smooth creamy texture, and tastes as good as it looks.

----

* Courtesy of The Homemakers Exchange, a Harvey and Howe CBS television production.

ROYAL SPICE CAKE

½ cup shortening
1¼ cups sugar
2 eggs, beaten
2½ cups sifted cake flour
4 teaspoons baking powder
1 teaspoon nutmeg

1 teaspoon cinnamon
¼ teaspoon salt
1 cup milk
1 tablespoon cocoa
1 tablespoon boiling water
⅓ cup chopped nuts

Cream shortening; add sugar gradually and continue creaming until light and fluffy. Add beaten eggs and mix well. Sift flour, baking powder, spices, and salt together. Add to creamed mixture alternately with the milk. Pour ⅔ of the batter into 2 greased 9-inch layer cake pans. Mix cocoa and boiling water together, and add to remaining ⅓ of batter. Pour into greased 9-inch layer cake pan. Bake in moderate oven (350°) 25 to 30 minutes. Cool 5 minutes. Put layers together with Mocha Frosting (page 415) and frost top and sides of cake with same frosting. Sprinkle chopped nuts over top of cake.

SCOTCH CHERRY CHRISTMAS CAKE
2 loaves

1 cup shortening
1 cup sugar
4 eggs
½ cup flour
2½ cups currants
⅓ cup glacé cherries, cut in quarters
½ cup mixed fruit peel, finely cut

1½ cups sifted flour
½ teaspoon salt
¼ teaspoon nutmeg
½ cup chopped blanched almonds
1 tablespoon lemon juice
1 teaspoon vanilla
½ teaspoon almond extract

Cream shortening; add sugar and continue creaming until light. Add eggs, one at a time; beat well after each addition. Add ½ cup of flour to the fruits and peel. Sift remaining 1½ cups flour, salt, and nutmeg together. Add fruits, peel, and nuts to creamed mixture and mix well. Stir in lemon juice, vanilla, and almond extract. Pour into 2 waxed-paper-lined loaf pans, 9½ x 5¼ x 2¾ inches. Bake in slow oven (300°) about 2 hours. The crust should be a delicate golden color, not brown. This cake should be kept in a closed container a week or 10 days to ripen. Use as fruit cake.

NOTE: To prevent cake from becoming too brown, cover top with heavy paper for the last hour the cake is in the oven.

SIMNEL CAKE

½ cup shortening
⅓ cup sugar
3 eggs, beaten
1 cup sifted flour
½ teaspoon baking powder
½ teaspoon salt
½ teaspoon nutmeg
¼ teaspoon cinnamon

½ cup raisins
½ cup currants
2 teaspoons grated lemon peel
¼ cup mixed fruit peel
1 tablespoon molasses
1 tablespoon pineapple juice
1 pound almond paste

Cream shortening; add sugar gradually and continue creaming. Blend in beaten eggs. Sift flour, baking powder, salt, and spices together. Add fruits and peel to flour mixture. Combine with creamed mixture; add molasses and pineapple juice, and mix well. Turn ½ of the mixture into round cake pan, 6 inches in diameter and 3 inches deep, that has been lined with heavy brown paper and greased well. Pat ½ of almond paste into a round the size of the cake and place on cake mixture in pan. Cover with remainder of cake mixture. Bake in slow oven (325°) 1 to 1½ hours. Shape remainder of almond paste into balls, and about 15 minutes before cake is done place circle of almond balls around edge of cake, leaving space in center. Before serving, fill center of cake with frosting and garnish with glacé cherries, if desired.

Dorothy Spicer's charming book From an English Oven (*Woman's Press, New York, 1948*) *tells of the legend that long ago in Shrewsbury a man and his wife had a serious dispute about whether to boil or bake a certain pastry. The couple compromised and decided the pastry could be both boiled and baked. Since the man's name was Simon and the woman's Nell, the remaining product was named "sim-nel."*

According to Joan Smith of Manchester, England, the simnel cake is the traditional cake for Mothering Sunday, the mid-Sunday of Lent. In England children living away from home come back and visit their mothers on this day, and the simnel cake is the special cake for the mother on this occasion.

SPONGE CAKE

1 cup sifted cake flour
1 teaspoon baking powder
¼ teaspoon salt
1 cup sugar
4 egg yolks

1 tablespoon lemon juice
1 teaspoon grated lemon peel
2 tablespoons water
4 egg whites

Sift flour, baking powder, and salt together 3 times. Beat egg yolks and add ½ cup of the sugar gradually, beating until light and lemon colored. Add lemon juice, grated peel, and water. Beat well. Sift flour a little at a time over yolk mixture and fold in carefully. Beat egg whites to frothy stage; gradually add other ½ cup of sugar and beat to soft peak stage. Fold into yolk mixture just enough to combine both mixtures. Bake in ungreased 10-inch tube pan in slow oven (325°) 45 to 50 minutes or until spring to touch. Invert pan to cool.

NOTE: For Baked Alaska (page 393), bake sponge cake in oblong pan, 13 x 9½ x 2 inches.

WHITE CAKE

½ cup butter
1 cup sugar
¾ teaspoon vanilla
¼ teaspoon almond extract
2 cups sifted cake flour

3 teaspoons baking powder
¼ teaspoon salt
⅔ cup milk
4 egg whites
⅓ cup sugar

Cream butter; add 1 cup of the sugar gradually and continue creaming until light and fluffy. Blend in flavoring. Sift together flour, baking powder, and salt. Add to creamed mixture alternately with milk. Beat egg whites until foamy, add remaining ⅓ cup of sugar, and beat to soft peak stage. Fold carefully into cake batter. Pour into 2 greased 9-inch layer cake pans. Bake in moderate oven (350°) 25 to 30 minutes. Cool on cake rack in pans about 5 minutes, then turn out of pans and let cool on rack before frosting. If desired, spread Lemon Filling (page 411) between layers and frost with Fluffy White Frosting (page 414).

COCONUT LAYER CAKE

1 recipe White Cake (page 409)
1 recipe Fluffy White Frosting
  (page 414)

1½ cups shredded coconut or
  fresh grated coconut

Bake White Cake. Put layers together with Fluffy White Frosting and spread top and sides of cake with same frosting. Sprinkle coconut over frosting.

LADY BALTIMORE CAKE

1 recipe White Cake (page 409)

1 recipe Fluffy White Frosting
  (page 414)

Bake White Cake batter in layers. Put layers together with Lady Baltimore filling. Frost cake with remainder of frosting.

LADY BALTIMORE FILLING:

To ⅓ of Fluffy White Frosting add ¼ cup glacé cherries, cut in fourths, ¼ cup chopped seedless raisins, ½ cup chopped figs, and ¼ cup chopped pecans.

PINEAPPLE CASHEW CAKE

1 recipe White Cake (page 409)
¾ cup chopped cashew nuts
¼ cup coconut

1½ cups well-drained crushed
  pineapple

To White Cake batter add cashew nuts. Pour into 2 well-greased 9-inch layer cake pans. Bake in moderate oven (350°) 25 to 30 minutes. When cake has cooled, cover top with pineapple mixed with coconut. Cover with Meringue (page 430) and brown in moderate oven (350°). Cool. Cut into wedges.

WHITE CAKE WITH LEMON FILLING

1 recipe White Cake (page 409)

LEMON FILLING:

¾ cup sugar
2½ tablespoons cornstarch
¾ cup water
2 egg yolks, slightly beaten

1 recipe Fluffy White Frosting (page 414)

4 tablespoons lemon juice
1½ teaspoons grated lemon peel
¼ teaspoon salt
1 tablespoon butter

Combine sugar and cornstarch; add water; cook over moderate heat until thick. Then put in double boiler and cook 10 to 12 minutes, stirring occasionally. Add some of mixture to beaten egg yolks, then combine both mixtures and cook 4 to 5 minutes longer. Remove from heat, add lemon juice, grated peel, salt, and butter. Cool. Spread between layers of White Cake. Spread top and sides of cake with Fluffy White Frosting.

WHITE CAKE FOR PETITS FOURS

½ cup shortening
1½ cups sugar
3 cups sifted flour
2½ teaspoons baking powder

¼ teaspoon salt
1 cup water
4 egg whites
1 teaspoon vanilla

Cream shortening; add sugar, and continue creaming until light and fluffy. Sift flour, baking powder, and salt together. Add alternately with water to creamed mixture. Beat egg whites to soft peak stage and fold into cake mixture. Blend in vanilla. Pour batter into greased oblong pan, 13 x 9½ x 2 inches. Bake in moderate oven (350°) 25 to 30 minutes. Cut in small circles, squares, diamonds, or any desired shapes for Petits Fours (page 377). Cover with Fondant Frosting (page 414) and decorate. *NOTE:* This is rather a compact cake that does not crumble when covered with frosting.

Frostings

Make enough frosting to cover the cake evenly. A recipe with 2 cups of sugar will frost two 8-inch layers, a 13 x 9½-inch oblong cake, or 2 dozen cupcakes.

BUTTER FROSTING
For three 8-inch layers

½ cup butter, softened
¼ cup shortening
2 cups confectioners' sugar
2 egg whites, unbeaten

⅛ teaspoon salt
2 cups confectioners' sugar
½ teaspoon vanilla

Cream butter and shortening. Add 2 cups of the confectioners' sugar and mix thoroughly. Add unbeaten egg whites and blend in. Stir in salt and remaining confectioners' sugar and mix until frosting is smooth and of spreading consistency. Add vanilla. If too stiff, a little warm water may be added and blended in.

This frosting may be used to decorate Chocolate Logs (page 396), Petits Fours (page 377), etc.

CHOCOLATE BUTTER FROSTING
For two 8-inch layers

½ cup butter
2 ounces (2 squares) unsweetened
   chocolate, melted
2½ cups sifted confectioners'
   sugar

1 egg, beaten
1 teaspoon vanilla
1 teaspoon lemon juice
⅛ teaspoon salt
1 cup chopped nuts

Cream butter and add melted chocolate, confectioners' sugar, beaten egg, flavoring, and salt. Mix well. This frosting is improved if made on an electric mixer, which makes it light and fluffy. Spread frosting on cake and sprinkle with chopped nuts. Add a tablespoon or two of cream if frosting is too stiff.

CHOCOLATE FUDGE FROSTING
For two 8-inch layers

2 cups sugar
¼ teaspoon salt
1 cup milk
2 tablespoons light corn syrup

2 ounces (2 squares) unsweetened
   chocolate
2 tablespoons butter
1 teaspoon vanilla

Combine sugar, salt, milk, corn syrup, and chocolate. Cook over low heat, stirring constantly until sugar dissolves. Cover saucepan 2 to 3 minutes to dissolve sugar crystals on sides of pan. Uncover and continue cooking to soft ball stage (234°). Remove from heat; add butter and cool to lukewarm. Add vanilla. Beat until of spreading consistency. If frosting becomes too stiff, add a small amount of hot water.

CONFECTIONERS' FROSTING
About 1 cup

2 cups confectioners' sugar
4 tablespoons water

1 teaspoon vanilla

Stir sugar gradually into water. Add vanilla.
NOTE: Fruit juice or strong coffee may be used instead of **water**.

CINNAMON CONFECTIONERS' FROSTING

Add ½ teaspoon cinnamon to Confectioners' Frosting.

EASY-TO-MAKE FUDGE FROSTING
For two 8-inch layers

1 cup sugar
½ teaspoon salt
2 ounces (2 squares) unsweetened
   chocolate

⅓ cup milk
1 tablespoon butter
1 teaspoon vanilla
2 cups confectioners' sugar

Combine sugar, salt, chocolate, and milk. Bring to a rolling boil. Remove from heat and add butter and vanilla. Stir in confectioners' sugar quickly and spread on cake while frosting is still warm. If it becomes too hard to spread, add a little cream and blend into frosting.

FLUFFY WHITE FROSTING
For three 8-inch layers

1 cup granulated sugar
½ cup boiling water
3 egg whites

1 cup confectioners' sugar
1 teaspoon vanilla

Boil granulated sugar and water together rapidly until the syrup forms a soft ball (238°). Whip egg whites, adding gradually ⅓ cup of the confectioners' sugar and beating until the consistency of a meringue. Add syrup gradually, beating constantly. Beat until mixture is thick and creamy. Add remaining ⅔ cup of confectioners' sugar or until frosting will hold its shape when spread. Add vanilla. This frosting can be kept in a covered container in the refrigerator for several days. Then, before using, add a small amount of hot water to make a smooth mixture.

FEATHER FROSTING

1 recipe Fluffy White Frosting   3 squares chocolate

Frost cake with Fluffy White Frosting. Melt chocolate and pour in strips across cake. Draw a wooden pick through frosting at intervals to give feather effect.

FONDANT FROSTING
For Petits Fours

Fondant Base:

2 cups sugar
1 cup water

2 tablespoons light corn syrup

Put sugar, water, and corn syrup into saucepan and place over medium flame. Cook slowly until sugar dissolves and then rapidly until thread stage (234°). Cover pan 2 or 3 minutes during cooking so that sugar crystals will wash down from sides of pan. Remove from heat and pour into buttered platter or shallow dish. When syrup has cooled to 110° beat until creamy, then knead until smooth. Store in covered glass jar. Place in refrigerator and let ripen 24 hours. This is the base for Fondant Frosting for Petits Fours.

Fondant may be kept in refrigerator and used as needed.

Simple Syrup:

1 cup sugar
1 cup water

Cook sugar and water together for 10 minutes. Cool. To make fondant frosting add ¼ cup of simple syrup to 1 cup Fondant Base and mix until smooth. Place cake on spatula and pour frosting generously over cake. Let excess frosting drip back into bowl. Dry cake on cake rack. It is important to have frosting thick enough to cover cake so edges do not show through.

LEMON CONFECTIONERS' FROSTING
About 1 cup

2 cups confectioners' sugar
2 teaspoons grated lemon peel
⅛ teaspoon salt

3 tablespoons lemon juice
¼ cup milk

Combine confectioners' sugar, lemon peel, and salt. Add lemon juice and milk, and mix until smooth and of spreading consistency. This is a thin mixture, to be used on rolls and cookies.

MOCHA FROSTING
For two 8-inch layers

⅓ cup butter, softened
⅛ teaspoon salt
3 cups confectioners' sugar

2 tablespoons cocoa
⅓ cup hot coffee
1 teaspoon vanilla

Cream butter; add salt and blend in 1 cup of the confectioners' sugar. Add cocoa to remaining sugar and add alternately with coffee until frosting is of spreading consistency. Beat well and add vanilla.

ORANGE CONFECTIONERS' FROSTING
For three 8-inch layers

¼ cup orange juice
1 teaspoon lemon juice
2 teaspoons grated orange peel
1 teaspoon grated lemon peel

3 tablespoons butter, softened
3 cups confectioners' sugar
1 egg yolk, unbeaten
⅛ teaspoon salt

Combine orange and lemon juice and peel. Cream butter; add 1 cup confectioners' sugar and blend thoroughly. Add egg yolk and beat well. Add remaining 2 cups of confectioners' sugar, salt, and juices; mix until smooth and of spreading consistency.

This frosting may be used on White Cake (page 409) or on sweet rolls.

STRAWBERRY PARFAIT TOPPING
For Angel Food Cake

2 cups fresh strawberries
2 egg whites
¼ teaspoon salt

¼ teaspoon cream of tartar
½ cup sugar

Mash 1 cup of the berries and force through a coarse sieve. Beat egg whites slightly. Add salt and cream of tartar and beat until frothy. Add sugar gradually and continue to beat until mixture is very stiff. Fold in strawberry pulp gradually. Spread on top and sides of Angel Food Cake (page 392). Garnish with the remaining cup of fresh berries.

NOTE: This dessert should be served as soon as possible after the topping has been put on cake, because topping thins out on standing.

Pies and Tarts

PIES

Apple
Black Bottom
Cheese Custard
Chess
Chocolate Chiffon
Coconut Cream

CREAM PIE FILLING

Banana
Chocolate
Coconut
Strawberry Tarts

De luxe Chocolate Peppermint
  Cream
Dutch Apple
Eggnog

Flaky Puff Pastry
  Patty Shells
  Small Tea Patty Shells
Fried Pies or Half Moons
Ice Cream Apple

Jeff Davis
Lemon Chiffon
Lemon Meringue
  Meringue
Lime Chiffon
  Chocolate Wafer Crust
New England Cranberry
  Individual Cranberry
New England Deep Dish Apple
Orange Chiffon
Pecan
Plain Pastry
Pumpkin
Pumpkin Chiffon
Quick Puff Pastry
Schnitz
Shoo Fly
Smettanick
Strawberry
Strawberry Chiffon
Strawberry Ice Cream

TARTS

Ambrosia
Baklava
Currant Jelly
Empanadas with Cream
  Filling

English Cake
Hawaiian Coconut Turnovers
Lemon Honey
Pear Tarts à la Française

I F MEN ARE coming to your party, you won't go wrong with pie for dessert. And your feminine guests will be just as enthusiastic about the last course.

Why not serve at the table? Your pie is your masterpiece and it deserves the center of the stage. All eyes will be on you as you cut through the crust — tender, flaky, perfectly crimped and browned — into the luscious filling. The suspense of waiting and watching tempts appetites.

Pie for dessert is as American as the Stars and Stripes. Serve it alone, or choose traditional companions to flatter it — big scoops of vanilla ice cream, slices of nippy cheese, or spoonfuls of fluffy whipped cream. You'll have a delightful climax to your meal.

$\mathcal{P}$*ies*

APPLE PIE
6 servings

6 tart apples
⅔ cup sugar
2 tablespoons flour
⅛ teaspoon salt
¼ teaspoon nutmeg

¼ teaspoon cinnamon
1 recipe Plain Pastry (page 433)
2 teaspoons lemon juice
2 tablespoons butter

Pare apples; cut in quarters and slice thin. Mix sugar, flour, salt, and spices. Divide pastry in half; roll one half to fit 9-inch pie pan. Fill with apples; add lemon juice and sprinkle with sugar mixture. Dot with butter. Roll other half of pastry. Cut slits in crust and place over apples. Trim ½ inch larger than pan; seal and flute crust. Bake in hot oven (450°) 10 minutes, then in moderate oven (350°) about 40 to 45 minutes or until apples are done.

BLACK BOTTOM PIE
9-inch pie, 6 to 8 servings

Crust:

14 crisp gingersnaps   5 tablespoons melted butter

Roll gingersnaps to make crumbs. Add melted butter and mix well. Press firmly into a 9-inch pie pan. Bake in slow oven (300°) 5 minutes. Cool.

Filling:

1 tablespoon (1 package)
    unflavored gelatin
4 tablespoons cold water
2 cups milk
½ cup sugar
1 tablespoon cornstarch

¼ teaspoon salt
4 egg yolks, beaten
2 ounces (2 squares) unsweetened
    chocolate, melted
1 teaspoon vanilla

Soften gelatin in cold water. Scald milk in double boiler. Mix sugar, cornstarch, and salt together, and stir slowly into milk.

Cook until thick. Add gradually to beaten egg yolks. Return to double boiler and cook 3 minutes longer. Stir in gelatin to dissolve. Divide in half; add melted chocolate and vanilla to one half of the mixture to make chocolate layer. Pour carefully into gingersnap crust.

Cream Layer:

4 egg whites
⅛ teaspoon cream of tartar
½ cup sugar
1 tablespoon rum flavoring or 1 teaspoon vanilla

¼ teaspoon almond extract
¾ cup heavy cream
1 tablespoon grated unsweetened chocolate

Let remaining half of custard cool. Beat egg whites until frothy; add cream of tartar and gradually add sugar. Beat meringue to soft peak stage. Fold meringue into cooled custard; add flavoring. Pour carefully over chocolate layer. Chill in refrigerator until set. When ready to serve, whip cream. Spread on top of pie and sprinkle with grated chocolate.

This is a very rich dessert — a small piece will suffice.

CHEESE CUSTARD PIE
6 servings

2 3-ounce packages cream cheese
2 tablespoons heavy cream
2 tablespoons butter, softened
½ teaspoon salt
¾ cup sugar
2 tablespoons flour

1 cup milk
1 egg, well beaten
2 tablespoons lemon juice
1 teaspoon grated lemon peel
½ recipe Plain Pastry (page 433)

Combine cream cheese, cream, and softened butter. Mix salt, sugar, and flour together, and add to cream cheese mixture. Blend in remaining ingredients. Beat well. Pour into pastry-lined 9-inch pie pan. Bake in hot oven (425°) 5 to 6 minutes; then finish baking in slow oven (325°) 45 to 50 minutes or until custard is set.

This cheese custard pie with its delicate lemon flavor is a nice change from plain custard pie.

CHESS PIES
6 individual pies

½ cup butter
1 cup sugar
4 eggs
½ cup chopped walnuts
1 cup chopped raisins

1 tablespoon lemon juice
½ recipe Plain Pastry (page 433)
for 6 individual baked pie
shells

Cream butter; add sugar and mix until light and fluffy. Beat the yolks of 2 eggs and two whole eggs together and add to the creamed sugar mixture. Add nuts and raisins to egg and sugar mixture. Add lemon juice and cook in double boiler until thick and rich dark brown in color. Cool. Pour into baked shells and top with meringue. Pies should be served cold.

Meringue:

Beat until foamy the 2 egg whites left from pie filling and then add 4 tablespoons sugar gradually and continue beating until meringue stands in soft peaks. Add ½ teaspoon vanilla. Brown in moderate oven (350°) 12 to 15 minutes.

These very rich chess pies are highly regarded around the Philadelphia area. Fern Gleiser brought us this recipe when she came from Drexel Institute in Philadelphia.

CHOCOLATE CHIFFON PIE
6 to 8 servings

1 tablespoon (1 envelope)
    unflavored gelatin
¼ cup cold water
½ cup boiling water
2 ounces (2 squares) unsweetened
    chocolate
½ cup sugar
¼ teaspoon salt
3 egg yolks

1 teaspoon vanilla
3 egg whites
½ cup sugar
1 9-inch baked Pie Shell (page 433)
1 cup heavy cream
2 tablespoons confectioners'
    sugar
4 sticks peppermint candy

Soften gelatin in the cold water. Combine the boiling water, chocolate, sugar, and salt in double boiler, and heat until chocolate is melted. Beat egg yolks slightly. Pour chocolate mixture over the egg yolks and blend thoroughly. Return mixture to double boiler and cook over low heat 2 to 3 minutes longer. Add the gelatin and stir until gelatin has melted. Cool. Add the vanilla. Beat egg whites to foamy stage and add remaining sugar gradually, beating constantly. Fold into cooled chocolate mixture. Turn into baked pie shell and chill. Whip cream and add confectioners' sugar. Crush rather coarsely the peppermint stick candy. Spread ½ of whipped cream on top of pie and sprinkle with crushed peppermint candy. Put remainder of cream in pastry bag. Cut pie into 6 or 8 pieces; place on serving plates and flute whipped cream around edge of each wedge.

This light, airy chocolate chiffon pie with its fluted whipped cream border and crunchy peppermint candy topping is an ideal dessert for your next luncheon or bridge party.

COCONUT CREAM PIE
6 to 8 servings

1¼ cups milk
½ cup sugar
½ teaspoon salt
3 tablespoons flour
2 tablespoons cornstarch
1 egg, slightly beaten
1 egg yolk, slightly beaten
½ cup milk
1 tablespoon butter
½ teaspoon vanilla

¼ teaspoon almond extract
2 egg whites
¼ cup sugar
1 9-inch baked Pie Shell
   (page 433)
1 cup heavy cream
1 teaspoon vanilla
½ cup grated fresh coconut
   or moist shredded coconut

Scald the 1¼ cups of milk in a double boiler. Add the ½ cup of sugar and the ½ teaspoon salt. Bring to a light rolling boil over direct heat. Mix flour and cornstarch and add gradually to the slightly beaten egg and egg yolk. Beat until smooth. Stir remaining ½ cup of the milk into egg mixture and blend until smooth. Add some of hot milk to egg mixture, then combine both mixtures and return to double boiler, stirring constantly until thick. It may appear lumpy but vigorous beating will smooth it. Cook 30 minutes in double boiler. Remove from heat. Add butter and flavoring and mix thoroughly. Beat egg whites until frothy; gradually add remaining ¼ cup of the sugar and beat to the soft peak stage. Fold the hot custard carefully into the meringue. Pour into baked pie shell. Cool. Whip cream and add vanilla. Spread on pie. Top with fresh coconut.

NOTE: If fresh coconut is not available, moist shredded coconut may be used instead. If preferred, it may be folded into the cream filling instead of being used on top of the pie.

This fresh coconut cream pie is one of the desserts for which Gertrude Allison's Little Tea House in Washington, D. C., is famous.

CREAM PIE FILLING

1 cup milk
½ cup sugar
¼ teaspoon salt
3 tablespoons flour
½ cup milk
2 eggs

1 tablespoon butter
½ teaspoon vanilla
1 9-inch baked Pie Shell
    (page 433)
1 cup heavy cream, whipped

Scald the 1 cup of milk in double boiler. Mix dry ingredients. Add the remaining ½ cup of milk to the dry ingredients and mix to a smooth paste. Pour into hot milk; stir slowly until thick and there is no starchy flavor. Beat eggs; add some of hot mixture slowly to beaten eggs and return to double boiler, cooking 3 to 5 minutes longer. Add butter and vanilla. Cool. Pour into baked pastry shell. Spread whipped cream on pie. If desired, meringue may be used instead of whipped cream.

BANANA

Use four ripe bananas. Fill pastry shell with alternate layers of sliced bananas and cooled Cream Pie Filling.

CHOCOLATE

Add 2 ounces melted chocolate and ¼ cup sugar before adding hot mixture to egg in Cream Pie Filling.

COCONUT

Stir 1 cup shredded coconut into cooled Cream Pie Filling.

STRAWBERRY TARTS

Mash fresh berries; add a little sugar. Fill individual tart shells with Cream Pie Filling and top with a tablespoon of crushed strawberries. Garnish with whipped cream.

DE LUXE CHOCOLATE PEPPERMINT CREAM PIE
6 to 8 servings

⅔ cup butter
1 cup sugar
3 eggs, beaten until light
2 ounces (2 squares) unsweetened
    chocolate
2 ounces semi-sweet chocolate

¼ teaspoon peppermint extract
1 9-inch Graham Cracker Crust
    (page 406)
1 cup heavy cream, whipped
2 tablespoons confectioners' sugar
4 sticks peppermint candy, crushed

Cream butter. Add sugar gradually; continue creaming until mixture is light and fluffy. Add eggs and blend into creamed mixture. Melt chocolate. Cool and add to creamed mixture.

Add peppermint extract. Turn mixture into graham cracker pie shell. Chill 3 to 4 hours. Spread with whipped cream to which confectioners' sugar has been added. Sprinkle crushed peppermint candy on top of whipped cream.

This super-duper, smooth-as-cream dessert will make your friends sit up and take notice. Julianna Austin of Minneapolis introduced it to the Catering Class, and the students pronounced it tops in desserts. But watch out for your waist line!

DUTCH APPLE PIE
6 servings

½ recipe Plain Pastry (page 433)
6 apples, pared and sliced thin
½ cup flour
1½ cups sugar
½ teaspoon cinnamon
¼ teaspoon nutmeg
½ cup sour cream
1 tablespoon butter

Line a 9-inch pie pan with pastry; add the apples. Combine the flour, sugar, and spices, and sprinkle mixture over apples. Pour the sour cream over all and dot with butter. Bake in moderate oven (350°) 50 to 60 minutes, or until the apples are soft. Cover the pie with an inverted pie pan for the last half of the baking time. The apples cook down and just fill the pie pan.

EGGNOG PIE
6 to 8 servings

4 eggs, separated
½ cup sugar
½ teaspoon salt
½ cup hot water
1 tablespoon (1 envelope) unflavored gelatin
¼ cup cold water
½ cup sugar
⅛ teaspoon nutmeg
1 tablespoon rum flavoring or ½ teaspoon vanilla
⅛ teaspoon almond extract
1 cup heavy cream, whipped
1 9-inch baked Pie Shell (page 433)
½ cup chopped toasted almonds

Beat egg yolks slightly; add ½ cup of sugar, the salt, and hot water. Cook in double boiler until thick. Soften gelatin in cold water; add to hot custard and stir until dissolved. Cool. Beat egg whites until foamy; add the remaining ½ cup of sugar gradually and beat to soft peak stage. Add nutmeg and flavoring. Fold meringue mixture into cooled cooked mixture. Turn into baked pie shell. Chill. Spread whipped cream over pie. Top with toasted almonds.

Try this eggnog pie at the Christmas season. It's a nice change from the usual mincemeat pie.

FLAKY PUFF PASTRY
Makes 12 large shells
or
96 small tea patty shells

3 cups sifted flour
1 teaspoon salt
1 cup hydrogenated shortening

1 cup butter
1 cup cold water

Shortening and butter should be soft enough to spread easily, but not soft enough to be runny.

PREPARING THE DOUGH

Combine flour and salt and sift into mixing bowl. Divide shortening into 3 equal portions, ⅓ cup each. Cut ⅓ of shortening into flour with pastry blender until mixture resembles coarse corn meal. Add water gradually, mixing lightly with a fork. As the ingredients are moistened, push to one side. Continue adding water to unmoistened ingredients until all of the flour has been dampened. This will be a rather soft dough.

Turn out on a well-floured board and shape into a ball, then into a level rectangle about 2 inches high with square corners. The long side should be toward you. Flatten the dough to one inch high by pressing lightly with the rolling pin lengthwise on the middle of the rectangle, then once on either side. Repeat in crosswise direction.

ROLLING THE PASTRY

Rolling from the center away from you, then toward you, then out to each side, roll dough into rectangle 15 x 18 inches and ⅛ inch thick. The 18-inch side should be toward you. The rectangle should have as square corners as possible, even sides, and be of even thickness throughout.

Spread ⅓ of shortening on middle 6 inches of rectangle, leaving 6 inches on either side. Fold right side of pastry completely over the shortening. Seal the edge with heel of hand. Spread remaining ⅓ of shortening on doubled portion of pastry, being careful not to cut through the dough. Fold the left ⅓ of rectangle over the shortening on doubled portion; seal edge with heel of hand.

Turn pastry so long side is toward you. Roll again into a 15 x 18-inch rectangle, ⅛ inch thick, with straight edges, square corners, and even thickness. The 18-inch side is again toward you. Divide butter in 2 equal portions, ½ cup each. Spread ½ cup of the butter on center third of rectangle and fold right ⅓ of rectangle over butter. Seal edge. Spread remaining ½ cup of butter on double portion of rectangle and fold left portion of rectangle over butter. Seal the edge. Turn folded pastry. Roll into rectangle 15 x 18 inches.

Fold pastry in thirds as before, omitting the addition of more fat. Roll. Repeat the folding and rolling three times after the butter has been rolled in. After the third rolling, fold the pastry as before, wrap in wax paper, and place in the refrigerator to chill for at least 2 hours. The pastry may be kept in the refrigerator for several days, but must not be frozen or it will not puff properly when baked. When ready to use, remove from the refrigerator, roll to desired thickness, and cut according to directions for the product desired.

Flaky puff pastry may be used for patty shells, small tea patty shells, napoleons, cream horns, or turnovers.

PATTY SHELLS — Makes 12 large shells

Roll Flaky Puff Pastry into a rectangle 10 x 13 inches and ½ inch thick. The pastry must be of uniform thickness to make level patty shells. Cut with a 3-inch cutter. With a 2-inch cutter cut each patty shell in the center ¾ of the way down. Do not remove the center but leave in patty shell. When cutting puff pastry be sure to have sharp cutters and cut straight down in order to get straight sides on the finished product. Place patty shells on cooky sheets covered with brown paper. Chill or let rest for 10 minutes. Bake in very hot oven (450°) 10 minutes; then in moderate oven (350°) 20 to 25 minutes longer. Allow patty shells to cool 15 minutes on a rack. Cut around center circles and take out any doughy portion. Fill patty shells as desired. Place center circles on top of filling. Serve hot.

SMALL TEA PATTY SHELLS — Makes 96 tiny shells

Roll Flaky Puff Pastry into a rectangle 12 x 20 inches. Cut with a 1½-inch cutter. With a 1-inch cutter cut each patty shell in the center ¾ of the way down, following directions for cutting and baking Patty Shells.

FRIED PIES OR HALF MOONS
About 1 dozen

1 recipe Plain Pastry (page 433)
1½ cups stewed dried apricots,
    mashed and sweetened to taste

Roll pastry ⅛ inch thick. Cut into circles about 5 inches in diameter. On each circle place 1½ tablespoons of apricot mixture. Moisten edges with cold water, fold to make semicircles, and press edges tightly together with fork; prick top several times. Fry in deep hot fat (375°) until light brown, about 2 to 3 minutes. Sprinkle with confectioners' sugar.

Everyone knows about pie but few have enjoyed the novelty of fried pies or half moons. The tangy apricot flavor contrasts nicely with the flaky crisp crust, but almost any fruit can be used. Variety in shapes is another way to add interest, too. In the South these delicately browned fried pies are served hot or cold, and are a welcome dessert, especially for lunch in the wintertime.

ICE CREAM APPLE PIE
6 to 8 servings

1 small sponge cake   1 quart vanilla ice cream
½ cup finely diced pared apples

Slice sponge cake ⅓ inch thick. Mix apples with ice cream. Put in freezer if ice cream becomes soft. Line a 9-inch pie pan with slices of sponge cake. Turn ice cream into cake-lined pie pan.

Meringue:

3 egg whites   6 tablespoons sugar
¼ teaspoon salt

Beat egg whites until foamy and add salt. Add sugar gradually, beating constantly until soft peak stage is reached. Completely cover ice cream with meringue. Place pie pan on board. Put in hot oven (425°) 4 to 5 minutes to brown meringue quickly. Serve at once before ice cream melts.

An unexpected flavor treat — this combination of crisp apples and ice cream in a sponge cake crust. The same idea as a Baked Alaska.

JEFF DAVIS PIE
6 to 8 servings

¾ cup butter
1½ cups sugar
1½ tablespoons flour
5 egg yolks, well beaten

¾ cup soda cracker crumbs
¾ cup sour cream
1 teaspoon vanilla
½ recipe Plain Pastry (page 433)

Cream butter. Combine sugar and flour, and add gradually to butter; mix until light and fluffy. Stir in beaten egg yolks and mix well. Add cracker crumbs, sour cream, and vanilla, and blend. Line 9-inch pie pan with pastry. Pour in pie filling. Bake in very hot oven (450°) 10 minutes, then in moderate oven (350°) 35 to 40 minutes or until done. Top with meringue and brown in moderate oven (350°) 10 to 12 minutes or until delicate brown. Cool.

Meringue:

3 egg whites
¼ teaspoon salt

6 tablespoons sugar

Beat egg whites until foamy and add salt. Add sugar gradually, beating constantly until soft peak stage is reached.

This very old recipe for Jeff Davis pie came from Leola Burford. She became acquainted with this southern delicacy at Lindenwood College in Missouri, where it was served on very special occasions. As far as Miss Burford has been able to discover the Jeff Davis pie is a combination of the old southern Chess Pie and President Tyler's Puddin' Pie. Southern Chess Pie has no cream in it and President Tyler's Puddin' Pie does, so we have Jeff Davis pie rich with butter, eggs, and sour cream. You will want to reserve this famous dessert for extra special occasions and then serve only a small piece.

LEMON CHIFFON PIE
6 to 8 servings

1 tablespoon (1 envelope)
   unflavored gelatin
¼ cup cold water
4 egg yolks
½ cup sugar
½ teaspoon salt

½ cup lemon juice
1½ teaspoons grated lemon peel
4 egg whites
½ cup sugar
1 9-inch baked Pie Shell
   (page 433)

Soften gelatin in cold water. Beat egg yolks slightly; add ½ cup of sugar, the salt, and lemon juice. Cook in double boiler until thickened. Remove from heat. Add lemon peel. Add gelatin to cooked mixture and stir until gelatin dissolves. Cool until thick and jelly-like in consistency. Beat egg whites until foamy; add remaining ½ cup of sugar gradually, beating constantly until soft peak stage is reached. Fold meringue into lemon mixture. Turn into baked pie shell. Spread with sweetened whipped cream, if desired.

LEMON MERINGUE PIE
6 servings

1½ cups sugar
6 tablespoons cornstarch
¼ teaspoon salt
1½ cups hot water
3 egg yolks, beaten

2 tablespoons butter
6 tablespoons lemon juice
2 teaspoons grated lemon peel
1 9-inch baked Pie Shell
   (page 433)

Sift sugar, cornstarch, and salt together. Add hot water. Cook over moderate heat until mixture thickens and boils. Put in double boiler and cook 10 to 12 minutes longer, stirring occasionally. Add some of cooked mixture to beaten egg yolks, combine both mixtures, and cook about 4 to 5 minutes longer. Remove from heat. Blend in butter, lemon juice and peel. Cool. Pour into baked pie shell. Top with meringue.

MERINGUE

3 egg whites
¼ teaspoon salt

6 tablespoons sugar

Beat egg whites until frothy; add salt and gradually add sugar, beating constantly to soft peak stage. Spread on pie. Brown in moderate oven (350°) 12 to 15 minutes.

LIME CHIFFON PIE
6 servings

1 4½-ounce can evaporated milk	¼ cup lemon juice
1 3-ounce package lime-flavored gelatin	1½ teaspoons grated lemon peel
	Green food coloring
1 cup hot water	1 cup heavy cream, whipped
½ cup sugar	

Chill evaporated milk and whip until stiff. Dissolve lime gelatin in hot water; add sugar, lemon juice, grated lemon peel, and a little green food coloring. Chill until jelly-like in consistency. Fold into whipped evaporated milk.

Chocolate Wafer Crust:

1¼ cups crushed chocolate wafers   ¼ cup melted butter
1 tablespoon confectioners' sugar

Combine chocolate wafer crumbs, sugar, and melted butter. Pat firmly into a 9-inch pie pan. Pour filling into crust. Chill in refrigerator. Top with whipped cream.

NEW ENGLAND CRANBERRY PIE
6 to 8 servings

2 tablespoons cornstarch	1 cup seedless raisins
1¼ cups sugar	2 cups cranberries
¼ teaspoon salt	1 tablespoon butter
1¼ cups water	1 recipe Plain Pastry (page 433)

Blend cornstarch with sugar and salt. Add water slowly and cook until mixture thickens, stirring constantly. Add the raisins, cranberries, and butter, and cook 5 minutes. Line a 9-inch pie pan with pastry and brush with melted butter. Add filling, and cover top with ½-inch strips of pastry, criss-crossed. Bake in hot oven (450°) 20 minutes.

INDIVIDUAL CRANBERRY PIE

Fill individual pastry shells and bake for 15 minutes in hot oven.

NEW ENGLAND DEEP DISH APPLE PIE
8 to 10 servings

1 quart pared, sliced apples	⅛ teaspoon cinnamon
¼ teaspoon salt	¼ cup butter
½ cup brown sugar	½ recipe Plain Pastry (page 433)
½ teaspoon nutmeg	

Place apples in a 1½-quart casserole; combine salt, sugar, and spices, and sprinkle over apples. Dot with butter. Roll pastry ⅛ inch thick. Make 2 slits in crust for escape of steam. Place crust over apples, trim and flute edges, and press to edge of casserole. Bake in hot oven (400°) 25 minutes; reduce to slow oven (325°) and bake 20 to 25 minutes longer or until apples are done. Serve warm with ice cream or cream to which a little nutmeg has been added.

ORANGE CHIFFON PIE
6 to 8 servings

1 tablespoon (1 envelope) unflavored gelatin	1 tablespoon grated orange peel
¼ cup cold water	1 teaspoon grated lemon peel
4 egg yolks, beaten	4 egg whites
½ cup sugar	½ cup sugar
¼ teaspoon salt	1 9-inch baked Pie Shell (page 433)
1 tablespoon lemon juice	1 cup heavy cream, whipped
½ cup orange juice	2 tablespoons confectioners' sugar

Soften gelatin in cold water. Beat egg yolks until light; add ½ cup of sugar, the salt, lemon juice, and orange juice. Cook in double boiler, stirring constantly until thick. Add grated orange and lemon peel. Add gelatin and stir until dissolved. Cool. Beat egg whites until frothy, and add other ½ cup of sugar slowly, beating until soft peak stage is reached. Fold into cooled mixture. Turn into baked pie shell. Top with whipped cream to which the confectioners' sugar has been added. Sprinkle with chopped pecans, if desired.

PECAN PIE
6 to 8 servings

3 eggs	1 cup pecan halves
¾ cup brown sugar	1 teaspoon vanilla
¼ teaspoon salt	½ recipe Plain Pastry (below)
1 cup light corn syrup	

Beat eggs. Add sugar and salt, and mix well; add corn syrup, pecans, and vanilla. Line a 9-inch pie pan with pastry. Pour in pecan mixture. Bake in hot oven (425°) 8 to 10 minutes; then finish baking in slow oven (325°) 45 to 50 minutes or until set.

PLAIN PASTRY
Crust for two 9-inch pie shells
or
10 to 12 individual shells

2 cups sifted flour	⅔ cup shortening
1 teaspoon salt	4 to 6 tablespoons cold water

Sift flour and salt together. Add shortening and cut in with pastry blender until about the size of small peas. Sprinkle water slowly over mixture and stir with a fork until flour and fat mixture is moist enough to hold together. Turn out on lightly floured board and knead just enough to form a smooth compact ball. Wrap in waxed paper and chill until needed.

To bake one pie shell, use ½ of pastry dough. Roll to ⅛ inch thickness, and about 1 inch larger than pie pan. Fit pastry into pan. Flute edge. Prick bottom and sides of crust carefully. Bake in hot oven (425°) for about 10 to 12 minutes or until a delicate brown.

PUMPKIN PIE
6 to 8 servings

2 cups pumpkin, cooked or canned	½ teaspoon ginger
1 cup milk	¼ teaspoon nutmeg
3 egg yolks	3 egg whites
¾ cup sugar	½ recipe **Plain Pastry** (above)
½ teaspoon salt	1 cup heavy cream
1 teaspoon cinnamon	⅓ cup chopped nuts

Combine pumpkin and milk. Beat egg yolks until light, and blend into pumpkin mixture. Combine sugar, salt, and spices, and add to pumpkin mixture. Beat egg whites to soft peak stage and fold in. Line a 9-inch pie pan with pastry. Turn pumpkin mixture into pie pan. Bake in hot oven (450°) 10 minutes, then in slow oven (325°) about 45 to 50 minutes or until done. Top with whipped cream and sprinkle with nuts.

PUMPKIN CHIFFON PIE
6 to 8 servings

1 tablespoon (1 envelope)
  unflavored gelatin
¼ cup cold water
3 egg yolks, beaten
½ cup sugar
1¼ cups canned pumpkin
½ cup milk
½ teaspoon salt
½ teaspoon ginger

½ teaspoon cinnamon
½ teaspoon nutmeg
3 egg whites
½ cup sugar
1 9-inch baked Pie Shell
  (page 433)
¼ cup coarsely chopped nuts
1 cup heavy cream, whipped

Soften gelatin in cold water. Combine egg yolks, ½ cup of sugar, the pumpkin, milk, salt, and spices, and cook in double boiler until thick. Add gelatin to hot pumpkin mixture and stir until dissolved. Cool. Beat egg whites until frothy and add remaining ½ cup of sugar gradually, beating constantly to soft peak stage. Fold meringue into cooled pumpkin mixture. Pour into baked pie shell. Chill. Top with whipped cream and sprinkle with chopped nuts.

Try this light, airy pumpkin chiffon pie instead of the traditional pumpkin custard for your next Thanksgiving dinner.

QUICK PUFF PASTRY
About 2 dozen individual tarts

1½ cups shortening
4 cups sifted flour
1 teaspoon salt

1 tablespoon lemon juice
Cold water to mix (approximately
  ⅔ cup)

Chill shortening and cut into pieces the size of a walnut. Sift flour and salt together. Add shortening to flour mixture and mix together lightly until mixture is the size of large peas. Combine lemon juice and water. Add a little at a time, stirring in with a fork until dough is of proper consistency to roll. Turn out on lightly floured board; knead 10 to 12 times. Roll into rectangle, 9 x 15 inches. Fold into thirds and then turn and roll again. Repeat 3 times. If possible, let the pastry stand 20 minutes in the refrigerator between rollings.

Make into Josephines and Napoleons (page 371), or Eccles Cakes (page 363).

SCHNITZ PIE
6 to 8 servings

½ pound dried sour schnitz (dried apples)
2 cups cold water
¼ cup orange juice
2 teaspoons grated orange peel

1 tablespoon cinnamon
⅛ teaspoon salt
1 cup sugar
1 recipe Plain Pastry (page 433)

Add water to schnitz. Cook to soft pulp. Add orange juice and peel, cinnamon, salt, and sugar, and mix well together. Cool. Line a 9-inch pie pan with pastry, fill with schnitz mixture and cover top with pastry. Cut several slits in crust to allow for escape of steam. Bake in hot oven (450°) 10 minutes. Reduce heat to moderate (350°) and continue baking 30 minutes longer.

SHOO FLY PIE
6 servings

⅔ cup brown sugar
⅔ cup shortening
2 cups sifted flour
⅔ cup water

½ teaspoon soda
⅔ cup dark molasses
½ recipe Plain Pastry (page 433)

Mix brown sugar and shortening. Blend in flour to make crumbs. Mix water and soda, and add to the molasses. Place layer of crumbs in the unbaked pastry shell, then cover with the molasses mixture, and next a layer of crumbs. Continue until all are used. Bake in hot oven (450°) 10 minutes. Reduce temperature to moderate (350°) and bake 35 to 40 minutes.

Here is a dessert that well deserves its fabulous reputation, for all molasses lovers enjoy this unforgettable, rich gingerbread baked in a plain pie crust. Work rapidly with the molasses mixture so you don't lose the leavening power of the soda before it's in the oven.

SMETTANICK

Czecho-Slovakian Jam and Sour Cream Pie
6 to 8 servings

1½ cups blanched almonds
¼ cup milk
¼ cup cherry jam
¼ cup raspberry jam

¼ cup sour cream
1 egg, beaten
⅛ teaspoon cinnamon
½ recipe Plain Pastry (page 433)

Pound the almonds to make a paste. Mix together the almond
paste, milk, jam, sour cream, egg, and cinnamon. Line a 9-inch
pie pan with the pastry. Pour almond and jam mixture into
pie shell. Bake in hot oven (450°) 8 to 10 minutes to brown
crust; finish baking in moderate oven (350°) 20 to 25 minutes
longer or until set.

STRAWBERRY PIE OR TARTS

6 to 8 servings

1 quart fresh strawberries
1 cup sugar
¼ teaspoon salt
4 tablespoons cornstarch
1 cup water

Red food coloring
1 9-inch baked Pie Shell
  (page 433)
1 cup heavy cream, whipped
2 tablespoons confectioners' sugar

Pick over the berries. Crush ½ of the berries and combine with
the sugar. Add salt, cornstarch, and water; cook over low heat
until thick and clear, stirring constantly. Add a small amount
of red food coloring to intensify red color. Cut the remainder
of the berries in half and put into the baked pie shell. Pour
cooked mixture over the berries. Chill. Spread with whipped
cream to which confectioners' sugar has been added. Garnish
with additional berries if desired.

Instead of using one large pie shell, you can use six individual ones and fill in same manner.

*You get the fresh strawberry flavor when the pie is prepared in this
way. A wonderful dessert for a spring luncheon party.*

STRAWBERRY CHIFFON PIE
6 to 8 servings

1 tablespoon (1 envelope)
  unflavored gelatin
¼ cup cold water
3 egg yolks
½ cup sugar
½ teaspoon salt
2 teaspoons lemon juice

1½ cups fresh strawberries,
  crushed
3 egg whites
½ cup sugar
1 9-inch baked Pie Shell
  (page 433)
1 cup heavy cream, whipped

Soften gelatin in cold water. Beat egg yolks until light, and add ½ cup of sugar, the salt, and lemon juice. Cook in double boiler until thick, stirring constantly. Add gelatin to cooked mixture and stir until dissolved. Remove from heat and add strawberries. Chill until mixture begins to thicken. Beat egg whites until frothy and add remaining ½ cup sugar, beating constantly to soft peak stage. Fold meringue into cooled strawberry mixture. Pile lightly into baked pastry shell; chill until firm. Top with whipped cream and garnish with a few whole strawberries, if desired.

STRAWBERRY ICE CREAM PIE
6 to 8 servings

1 cup strawberries, fresh or frozen
12 marshmallows
¼ teaspoon salt
2 egg whites
¼ cup sugar

Red food coloring
1 quart vanilla ice cream
1 9-inch baked Pie Shell
  (page 433)

If fresh berries are used, crush slightly and add a little sugar to sweeten. Heat marshmallows in double boiler, slowly folding over and over until marshmallows are half melted. Remove from heat and continue folding until mixture is smooth and fluffy. Cool. Add salt to egg whites and beat until foamy. Add sugar slowly, beating constantly until soft peak stage is reached. Blend lightly with marshmallow mixture. Tint a delicate pink. Put ice cream in cold baked pastry shell, cover with the cup of strawberries, and top with fluffy marshmallow meringue, swirled attractively. Brown quickly in broiler or hot oven (425°) 1 minute or until nicely browned. Remove pie from oven and serve immediately, before ice cream has time to melt,

Tarts

AMBROSIA TARTS
6 servings

¾ cup sugar
4 tablespoons cornstarch
¼ teaspoon salt
1¼ cups water
½ cup orange juice
2 tablespoons lemon juice

1 tablespoon grated orange peel
½ teaspoon grated lemon peel
2 egg yolks, slightly beaten
½ recipe Plain Pastry (page 433)
    for 6 individual baked tart
    shells

Combine sugar, cornstarch, and salt; gradually add water. Cook slowly in double boiler until clear, about 8 to 10 minutes. Add fruit juice and fruit peel; cook 2 minutes longer. Slowly add cooked mixture to egg yolks. Return to double boiler and cook until thick. Cool. Pour into cooled baked tart shells. Top with coconut meringue.

Coconut Meringue:

2 egg whites
½ cup sugar
⅛ teaspoon salt

2 tablespoons water
Shredded coconut

Combine unbeaten egg whites with sugar, salt, and water, in double boiler. Beat with rotary beater until thoroughly blended. Cook 1 minute over boiling water, beating constantly. Remove from hot water; beat 2 minutes longer or until mixture stands in peaks. Pile lightly on filled tarts. Sprinkle with coconut.

BAKLAVA
Greek Pastry
9 to 12 servings

Pastry:

2 cups sifted flour
1 teaspoon salt
½ cup shortening

2 eggs, slightly beaten
2 tablespoons water

Combine flour and salt. Cut shortening into flour until consistency of coarse corn meal. Blend egg and water and add to dry ingredients, mixing until thoroughly dampened. Turn onto waxed paper. Knead lightly 6 to 8 times to make a smooth ball of pastry. Let rest ½ hour.

Filling:

1½ cups finely slivered blanched
    almonds
½ cup brown sugar, firmly packed

1 cup melted butter
1 teaspoon cinnamon
½ teaspoon nutmeg

Mix all ingredients together for filling. Divide into fourths.

Syrup:

1 cup water
1 cup sugar

1 tablespoon grated orange peel
1 tablespoon grated lemon peel

Blend ingredients and boil for 5 minutes to make syrup.

To Make Baklava:

Divide pastry into 5 portions. Roll each portion of pastry very thin on lightly floured pastry cloth, into square 8 x 8 inches. Place one square in bottom of 8-inch square pan. Spread ¼ of filling over pastry. Place second layer of pastry on top of filling. Spread with another ¼ of filling. Continue making layers of pastry and filling until 4 portions of pastry and filling have been used. Place 5th portion of pastry on top.

Cut baklava into 8 serving portions. Pour 3 tablespoons of syrup over baklava. Bake in moderate oven (350°) 35 to 40 minutes. Serve remaining sauce, cooled, over hot baklava.

CURRANT JELLY TARTS
2 dozen small tarts

½ cup butter
1 3-ounce package cream cheese
1 cup sifted flour
¼ teaspoon salt

¼ cup currant jelly
1 egg yolk, beaten
2 tablespoons milk
¼ cup chopped nuts

Cream butter and cheese until well blended and fluffy. Add flour and salt; mix to a smooth dough. Wrap and chill for several hours. Roll dough ⅛ inch thick. Cut into 2-inch circles. Place ¼ teaspon jelly on each circle. Fold over, completely covering jelly. Press down to seal. Brush with beaten egg yolk mixed with the milk. Sprinkle brushed surface with nuts. Place on greased cooky sheets, 15½ x 12 inches. Bake in hot oven (400°) 12 to 15 minutes.

EMPANADAS WITH CREAM FILLING
12 to 15, small

Cream Filling:

½ cup milk
¼ teaspoon salt
2 tablespoons sugar
2 teaspoons butter

2 teaspoons cold water
2 teaspoons cornstarch
1 egg yolk, beaten
½ teaspoon vanilla

Heat milk, salt, sugar, and butter in double boiler. Add water to cornstarch; mix to smooth paste and stir into mixture in double boiler; cook until thick. Add to egg yolk. Cook 3 minutes longer. Add vanilla. Cool.

Crust:

1 cup sifted flour
2 tablespoons butter
1 egg yolk

3 tablespoons hot milk
¼ teaspoon salt
Fat for deep frying

Put flour in bowl, add fat and cut in until consistency of corn meal. Combine yolk of egg and hot milk; add salt and pour into flour. Mix to a smooth dough. Divide into portions and roll out very thin. Cut into 2-inch rounds. When ready to fry pies, put 1 teaspoonful of filling on each round; moisten edges, fold over dough, and pinch edges together. Fry in deep hot fat (360°) until golden brown.

These little empanadas or fried pies are a welcome addition to a tea tray of assorted cookies or cakes.

a tangy apricot flavor . . .

Fried Pies (Half Moons) , page 428.

to suit individual tastes . . .

Pies and Tarts, pages 420–442.

ENGLISH CAKE TARTS
About 3½ dozen

3 tablespoons butter
6 tablespoons sugar
¼ teaspoon vanilla
1 egg yolk, beaten
½ cup sifted flour
¾ teaspoon baking powder
Dash of salt

¼ cup milk
1 egg white
1 recipe Plain Pastry (page 433)
1 cup raspberry or apricot jam
Confectioners' Frosting (page 413)
4 glacé cherries

Cream butter; add sugar, and continue creaming until light and fluffy. Add vanilla and beaten egg yolk; mix well. Sift flour, baking powder, and salt together. Add alternately with milk to creamed mixture. Beat egg white to soft peak stage and fold into cake mixture.

Roll pastry ⅛ inch thick. Cut pastry into 3-inch rounds with fluted cutter, if you have one. Press pastry into 2-inch muffin pans. Prick pastry and bake in hot oven (400°) 8 to 10 minutes. Remove from oven and put ½ teaspoon jam into baked shells; cover jam with a scant teaspoon of cake batter. Bake cake in moderate oven (350°) 10 to 12 minutes. It is a good idea to place the muffin pans on a tray when put in the oven a second time, so pastry will not get any browner on the bottom. When cake is baked, run spatula around tart to loosen from sides of pan and remove carefully. Cool and frost with Confectioners' Frosting. Decorate with a bit of glacé cherry.

HAWAIIAN COCONUT TURNOVERS
About 4½ dozen

1 recipe Plain Pastry (page 433)
3 tablespoons butter
¾ cup sugar

2¼ cups fresh grated or shredded
    coconut
¼ cup milk

Roll pastry ⅛ inch thick. Cut into 2-inch circles. Cream butter and sugar together until fluffy. Add coconut and mix well. Place a teaspoon of coconut mixture on each round of pastry. Moisten edges with water and fold over to make a half-moon shape. Prick top. Brush with milk. Bake in hot oven (425°) 10 to 12 minutes or until a delicate golden brown in color.

Serve as afternoon tea pastry.

LEMON HONEY TARTS
About 2½ dozen

½ cup sugar
2 tablespoons butter
4 tablespoons lemon juice

1½ teaspoons grated peel
1 egg, beaten

Mix ingredients together. Cook in double boiler until thick. Fill small 2-inch tarts with lemon mixture.

PEAR TARTS À LA FRANÇAISE
About 2 dozen

1 recipe Quick Puff Pastry
   (page 434)
Thick applesauce

Halves of pears, fresh or canned
Lemon juice
Powdered sugar

Line individual tart pans with a thin layer of pastry. Fill tart shell just less than half full of applesauce. Bake in hot oven (450°) 10 to 12 minutes. Remove from oven and place half of pear in tart shell. Sprinkle with a little lemon juice and powdered sugar and bake again until light brown in color.

Serve with chocolate sauce when you want a deluxe touch.

Confections and Nuts

Apple Crystals
Candied Orange or Grapefruit
 Peel
Decorated Mints
Eye of the Mother-in-law
Glacé Apricots
Iced Cranberry Sweets
Little Boats

Marzipan Potatoes
Marzipan Strawberries
Mexican Panocha
Mexican Spiced Pecans
Old English Toffee
Orange Sugared Walnuts
Salted Nuts
Texas Pralines

To GIVE that extra, mouth-watering touch to your tea party add a plate of tea confections. Use your prettiest crystal dish. Arrange an assortment of vari-colored candied fruit, nuts, and decorated mints to please the eye and delight your guests.

APPLE CRYSTALS

4 apples	**Green food coloring**
3 cups sugar	**¼ teaspoon mint extract**
1½ cups water	**1 cup sugar, to roll apple crystals**
Red food coloring	

Pare apples and cut into circles about ¼ inch thick. Cut each circle into 4 pieces. Combine sugar and water, and boil 10 minutes. Add a few drops of red food coloring to one half of syrup and green food coloring and mint extract to other half. Drop apple pieces into syrup and cook slowly until transparent; remove to rack to drain. When excess syrup has been removed, roll apple slices in sugar. Let stand overnight to dry and roll in sugar again to give crystallized effect. Then reroll in sugar.

CANDIED ORANGE PEEL

4 oranges	**1 cup water**
2 cups sugar	

With sharp knife, score peel of each orange into quarters. Remove peel. Cover with cold water and cook slowly until tender, about 35 to 45 minutes. Cut with scissors into ⅓-inch strips. Combine sugar and water, and boil 5 minutes. Add orange peel to syrup and cook over low heat 20 to 25 minutes. Let stand in syrup overnight. Remove peel from syrup and place on cooling rack to drain. Roll each strip in sugar; place on rack to dry, and reroll in sugar. Let stand until dry.

CANDIED GRAPEFRUIT PEEL

Grapefruit peel may be used instead of orange peel and prepared in the same way. However, in order to remove bitter taste, the grapefruit peel should be boiled 4 or 5 times, and cooking water discarded each time.

DECORATED MINTS
40 to 50 mints

1 pound party mints
(assorted colors)
½ recipe Butter Frosting
(page 412)

Red, yellow, and green food
coloring

Place mints on waxed paper, smooth side up. Divide Butter Frosting into 3 parts and put in small bowls or custard cups. Add a few drops of food coloring to each to give a delicate tint to frosting. Use small rose tube to make tiny pink and yellow roses in center of each mint. Use leaf tube with green frosting to make leaves on roses.

EYE OF THE MOTHER-IN-LAW
Stuffed Prunes

24 large prunes, pitted
2 egg yolks
1 cup confectioners' sugar

2 egg whites
½ teaspoon vanilla
1 cup confectioners' sugar

Beat egg yolks with 1 cup of the confectioners' sugar. Mold into small balls for "eye" pupils. Add vanilla to egg whites and mix with remaining cup of confectioners' sugar to mold into almond shapes for white of "eye." Then mold the complete "eyes" and insert into the prunes.

GLACE APRICOTS

2 cups dried apricots
4 cups water
2 cups sugar
1 cup water

1 teaspoon cream of tartar
⅔ cup pecans
1 cup sugar, to roll apricots

Wash the dried apricots and cook in the quart of water about 20 minutes. Pour into colander to drain. Combine sugar, the remaining cup of water, and cream of tartar; boil mixture 3 minutes. Add the apricots and cook until soft, but not mushy. Take each apricot out of the syrup separately and place on a rack to drain. When apricots have cooled enough to handle, place pecans in center of apricots and fold over to enclose pecans. Roll in sugar and place on rack to dry. After apricots have dried, reroll in sugar.

ICED CRANBERRY SWEETS

1 egg white, unbeaten   2 cups cranberries
1 cup confectioners' sugar

Combine egg white and confectioners' sugar and beat until smooth. Dip cranberries in mixture so that they are completely coated. Place cranberries on cooky sheet. Put in very slow oven (250°) 5 to 8 minutes or until frosting is dry.

LITTLE BOATS
About 3 dozen

1 cup sifted confectioners' sugar   ½ teaspoon lemon extract
1 egg yolk

Mix together confectioners' sugar, egg yolk, and lemon extract. Beat until smooth. Put into cake decorator and force through tube into long shapes like little boats. Allow to dry overnight. These little boats are attractive to use on a tray of sweets for afternoon tea. They are a soft yellow color and have an intriguing flavor and texture.

This is a Czechoslovakian confection and derived its name from the shape obtained by pouring the mixture onto pleated waxed paper. When dry the paper is pulled out and the confection comes out in narrow triangular strips that look like small boats. However, it's easier to put them through the cake decorator, and they taste just as good.

Mrs. Vera Swearingen of our Institution Management Staff makes these colorful confections for our tea parties.

MARZIPAN POTATOES
About 3 dozen

6 ounces finely ground almonds   ¼ teaspoon almond extract
1¼ cups granulated sugar   1 egg, beaten
1 cup confectioners' sugar   1 tablespoon cocoa

Mix almonds, granulated sugar, confectioners' sugar, and almond extract. Combine with the beaten egg, blending to a smooth paste. Shape into small ovals and roll in cocoa. Make a few holes in either end to imitate the eyes of the potato. Allow to dry. Serve with assorted candies at tea.

MARZIPAN STRAWBERRIES

2¼ cups blanched almonds
1 egg white, unbeaten
1¾ cups confectioners' sugar
1 teaspoon almond extract

½ teaspoon vanilla
¼ teaspoon salt
Red food coloring

Grind almonds with fine knife of food chopper. Combine ground almonds and unbeaten egg white; mix well. Add remaining ingredients and mix. Add enough red food coloring, drop by drop, to tint mixture a strawberry color; blend so mixture will have an even color. Shape like strawberries; poke holes with wooden pick to give effect of seeds. Use a tiny mint leaf for stem on each one.

These marzipan strawberries look like the real thing and are a colorful addition to a sweetmeat tray at teatime.

MEXICAN PANOCHA
About 2 dozen squares

½ ounce (½ square) unsweetened chocolate
3 cups dark brown sugar
1 cup milk

1 tablespoon butter
1 teaspoon vanilla
1½ cups chopped nuts

Combine chocolate with sugar and milk and bring to boil. Add butter and stir occasionally until candy reaches soft ball stage (238°). Remove from heat. Add vanilla and nuts, mixing in thoroughly and beating until candy begins to harden. Turn into buttered 9-inch square pan. Cut into squares.

The Mexicans make this delicious variation of panocha with vanilla beans, but a teaspoon of vanilla extract works as well and is much simpler. Pecans are excellent but other kinds of nuts are also good.

MEXICAN SPICED PECANS
2 cups

3 cups confectioners' sugar
¼ cup cornstarch
1 teaspoon salt
2 teaspoons cinnamon
½ teaspoon cloves

½ teaspoon allspice
½ teaspoon chili powder
2 egg whites
4 tablespoons cold water
2 cups pecans

Sift dry ingredients together. Beat egg whites slightly; add cold water. Dip pecans in egg white; drain on absorbent paper. Roll in sugar mixture. Spread on cooky sheet so they do not touch. Put in very slow oven (250°) until dry, about 30 to 35 minutes.

OLD ENGLISH TOFFEE

4 cups blanched almonds
¼ pound butter
3 cups sugar
1 pound butter

½ cup water
1 8-ounce package semi-sweet
    chocolate, melted

Brown almonds lightly in the ¼ pound of butter. Drain on absorbent paper and chop fine. Cook sugar with the pound of butter and ½ cup water to the soft crack stage (280°). Add 2 cups of the almonds and boil to hard crack (305°). Pour into buttered 9-inch square pan. When cold, spread with 4 ounces of the melted chocolate and sprinkle with 1 cup of the almonds. When the chocolate has set, turn candy over and spread with remaining 4 ounces chocolate and the remaining cup of almonds.

ORANGE SUGARED WALNUTS

3 cups sugar
½ cup water
½ cup orange juice

1 teaspoon grated orange peel
1 pound shelled walnuts

Cook sugar, water, and orange juice together to soft ball stage (238°). Remove from heat, add orange peel and walnuts; stir until syrup begins to look cloudy. Before mixture hardens drop from spoon onto waxed paper or greased surface. Separate into smaller pieces. Serve at afternoon tea.

SALTED NUTS

TO BLANCH ALMONDS:
Blanch almonds by covering with boiling water. When skins are loosened and puffy, pour hot water off and remove skins. Slip off skin of almond by pressing at large end and forcing kernel out at pointed end. Dry blanched nuts thoroughly.

TO SALT NUTS ON RANGE:
Heat ½ cup butter or salad oil in skillet; add 1 cup nuts at a time. Cook over low heat, stirring constantly until browned. Spread on absorbent paper to drain. Sprinkle with salt.

TO SALT NUTS IN OVEN:
Dry blanched nuts thoroughly. Spread in shallow pan. Dot with 1 tablespoon butter for each cup of nuts. Brown in hot oven (400°), stirring every 5 minutes. Do not overcook — nuts darken as they cool. (Remove pecans from oven as soon as the butter sizzles.)

TEXAS PRALINES
About 2 dozen

3 cups brown sugar
1 cup cream
⅓ cup butter

1 teaspoon vanilla
1 cup pecans or black walnuts

Combine sugar, cream, and butter. Boil slowly to soft ball stage (240°). Stir occasionally to prevent scorching. Cool, without stirring, to lukewarm. Add vanilla, then beat until mixture changes color and thickens. Pour quickly into buttered 9-inch square pan. Cut into squares and roll into balls. Flatten into patties and press 3 or 4 pecans or walnuts into each.

New Orleans is especially known for rich sugary pralines, but this recipe happens to be of the Texas variety, which is more chewy. The sugar and pecan flavor of pralines is distinctive from all other kinds of candy.

How did the "praline" get its name? The story is told that back in the early days of this young country when news and fashions took many months to travel from Paris to New Orleans, there lived in Paris a French marshal and diplomat, César du Plessis Praslin (pronounced pralin). Marshal Praslin had a sweet tooth, and his chef, in an effort to please him, coated almonds with sugar and called the new concoction, Praline, after the Marshal. When our Southern gentlemen made trips to Paris they brought back some of these delicious pralines. The southern cook, not to be outdone, prepared a confection of pecans and brown sugar but instead of one nut she used a handful to a "patty" for good measure. And so the praline has come down to us in its various versions.

Menus

FOREIGN

Buffet Featuring Foods of
  India
Chinese Filipino Dinner
English High Tea
French Dinner
Guatemalan Dinner
Hawaiian Dinner
Hungarian Dinner
International Dinner
Italian Dinner
Mexican Dinner
Panamanian Dinner
Pan-American Buffet Supper
Russian Dinner
Smörgåsbord

REGIONAL

Iowa Dinner
Old-Fashioned New England
  Supper
Pennsylvania Dutch Dinner
Southern Dinners

HOLIDAY AND SEASONAL

New Year's Eve Buffet
New Year's Eve Watch Party
St. Patrick's Day Party
Easter Dinner
Fourth-of-July Dinner
Thanksgiving Dinner
Spring Dinner
Summer Dinner
Fall Dinner
Winter Dinner

SPECIAL

After-the-Football-Game
Barbecue Picnic
Sunday Morning Brunch
Sunday Morning Coffees
Luncheon Menus
Informal Teas
Formal Receptions
Sportsman's Dinner
Stag Dinner
Teen-Age Snack Party
Teen-Age Supper Party
Theatre Dinner

THE SUCCESS of a party depends largely on working out the details in advance. Then your service can be casual, your hospitality gracious. And you can relax and have as much fun as your guests.

Once you've decided on the guest list, you turn the spotlight on the menu. It's the blueprint of your party.

You don't have to fume over what you'll serve. Leaf through these pages and pick the menu that fits your guests, kitchen, and pocketbook. You'll find that part of the foods in each menu can be prepared in advance. There's abundant good eating and a sprinkling of color and glamour through all. These meals will start your guests talking about what a wonderful hostess you are. That's the true test of a party.

Foreign Menus

BUFFET FEATURING FOODS OF INDIA

Chicken Curry [1]

Coconut Rice [2]
(*Rice cooked in Coconut Milk*)

Beans Fugarth [3]
(*Green Beans with Coconut and Onions*)

Pooris [4]
(*Puffed Bread Balls*)

Potatoes for Pooris [5]
(*Seasoned Potatoes with Peas*)

Potato Cutlets [6]

Potato Puffs [7]

Fried Cauliflower [8]

Tomato, Onion, and Cucumber Salad [9]

Fruit Cup with Mint Sherbet

Kulkuls [10]
(*Christmas Sweet*)

Jeelobis [11]
(*Syrup-Coated Cookies*)

Coconut Pancakes [12]

Plantain Fritters [13]

Shrikand [14]
(*Creamy Dessert*)

Coffee

[1] P. 126	[4] P. 183	[7] P. 189	[10] P. 373	[13] P. 328
[2] P. 181	[5] P. 183	[9] P. 174	[11] P. 370	[14] P. 339
[3] P. 164	[5] P. 188	[9] P. 240	[12] P. 307	

CHINESE FILIPINO DINNER

Won Ton Noodle Soup [1]

Arroz à la Valenciana [2]
(*Rice with Meat and Chicken*)

Bola-Bola Special [3] with Sweet-Sour Sauce [4]
(*Fried Pork, Shrimp, and Chestnut Balls*)

Lumpia Macao [5]
(*Steamed Pork and Shrimp in Wrapper*)

Pincit Frito [6]
(*Crisp Pork and Shrimp in Wrapper*)

Fried Fish [7] with Chinese Meat Sauce [8]

Crisp Fried Won Ton [9]

Hard Rolls

Fresh Fruit

Chinese Almond Cookies [10]

Green Tea

[1] P. 44	[3] P. 103	[5] P. 109	[7] P. 147	[9] P. 104
[2] P. 124	[4] P. 214	[6] P. 110	[8] P. 208	[10] P. 357

ENGLISH HIGH TEA

**Tomato, Cucumber, and Egg Salad
on Curly Endive** [1]

Pork Pie [2]   **Sausage Rolls** [3]

Assorted Sandwiches

Currant Scones [4]   **Bread and Butter**

Strawberry Jam   **Lemon Curd** [5]

Tea Cakes [6] **and Cookies**

English Trifle [7]

Tea

[1] P. 239	[3] P. 112	[5] P. 289	[7] P. 310
[2] P. 106	[4] P. 54	[6] P. 387	

FRENCH DINNER

French Pork Chops with Capers [1]

Pommes de Terre Parisienne [2]
(Potato Balls with Parsley)

Salade d'Endive   **Pain au Beurre**
(Tossed Green Salad)[3]   *(Garlic Bread and Butter)* [4]

Pear Tarts à la Française [5]

Café
(Coffee)

[1] P. 107	[3] P. 240	[5] P. 442
[2] P. 190	[4] P. 68	

GUATEMALAN DINNER

Chile con Queso [1]
(Peppery Cheese)

Pollo con Salsa de Almendras [2]
(Chicken with Almond Sauce)

Chiles Rellenos [3]   **Sopa de Arroz** [4]
(Stuffed Green Peppers)   *(Rice Soup)*

Ejotes Estofados
(Stewed String Beans)

Ensalada de Tomate y Aguacate
(Tomato and Avocado Salad)

Tortillas [5]

Calabaza Confitera
(Candied Pumpkin)

Café
(Coffee)

[1] P. 7	[3] P. 182	[5] P. 83
[2] P. 134	[4] P. 40	

HAWAIIAN DINNER

Green Onion Soup [1]

Sweet Potato Chips [2]

Pincit Frito [3]

Chicken Curry [4] on Rice

Salted Peanuts   Pineapple Chutney [5]   Grated Coconut

Finely Chopped Egg Yolk and White

Candied Sweet Potatoes [6]

Asparagus with Lemon Butter [7]

Hot Baking Powder Biscuits [8]

Fruit Salad [9] in Coconut Shells

Avocado Orange Sherbet [10]

Chinese Almond Cookies [11]

Coffee

[1] P. 38	[4] P. 126	[7] P. 207	[10] P. 314
[2] P. 191	[5] P. 219	[8] P. 53	[11] P. 357
[3] P. 110	[6] P. 191	[9] P. 228	

HUNGARIAN DINNER

Burgonyaleves [1]
(Potato Soup)

Csirke Paprikas [2]
(Chicken Paprika)

Karfiol [3]
(Cauliflower with Cheese Sauce)

Rantott Sargarepa [4]
(Sweet-Sour Carrots)

Kolacky [5]
(Fruit-Filled Buns)

Zitney Chleb [6]
(Rye Bread)

Hungarian Nut Torte [7]
(Chocolate-Nut Torte)

Kávé
(Coffee)

[1] P. 33	[3] P. 175	[5] P. 72	[7] P. 310
[2] P. 131	[4] P. 173	[6] P. 85	

INTERNATIONAL DINNER

Barszcz [1]
(Polish Beet Soup)

Empanadas Argentina [2]
(Argentine Tarts)

Veau Roulu [3]
(French Veal Rolls)

Kartoffel Knödel [4]
(German Potato Balls)

Broccoli à la Fiorentina [5]
(Italian Broccoli)

India Nut Salad [6]

Swedish Rye Bread [7]   **Corn Sticks** [8]

Danish Cake with Lemon Sauce [9]

Café
(Coffee)

[1] P. 32	[4] P. 186	[7] P. 74
[2] P. 17	[5] P. 169	[8] P. 63
[3] P. 120	[6] P. 234	[9] P. 398

ITALIAN DINNER

Antipasto

Tortellini en Brodo di Pollo [1]
(Filled Dough in Chicken Broth)

Spaghetti con Polpetti
(Spaghetti and Meat Balls) [2]

Ravioli [3]   **Broccoli à la Fiorentina** [4]
(Meat-Filled Dough Squares)   *(Garlic-Flavored Broccoli)*

Insalata Verde
(Tossed Green Salad) [5]

Pane Bastone [6]
(Bread Sticks)

Biscuit Tortoni [7]
(Italian Ice Cream)

Pizza Figliati [8]
(Pastry with Honey and Nuts)

Caffè
(Coffee)

[1] P. 42	[3] P. 116	[5] P. 240	[7] P. 314
[2] P. 94	[4] P. 169	[6] P. 76	[8] P. 328

MEXICAN DINNER

Mexican Canapés [1]
(Savory Fish Appetizers)

Chicken Tamale Pie [2]

Tacos [3]   **Spanish Green Beans** [4]
(Meat-Filled Pancakes)   *(Green Beans with Tomato Sauce)*

Frijoles Refritos [5]
(Mexican Pork and Beans)

Toasted Garlic-Buttered Bread [6]

Mexican Salad [7]

Guacamole [8]
(Peppery Avocado Spread)

Almendrada [9]
(Molded Fruit Gelatin)

Mexican Chocolate [10]
(Coffee-Flavored Hot Chocolate)

[1] P. 10   [3] P. 99   [5] P. 166   [7] P. 233   [9] P. 329
[2] P. 129   [4] P. 167   [6] P. 68   [8] P. 229   [10] P. 298

PANAMANIAN DINNER

Arroz con Pollo [1]
(Rice with Chicken)

Fried Green Bananas

Spanish Green Beans [2]
(Green Beans with Tomato Sauce)

Avocado and Grapefruit Salad [3] with

Lemon French Dressing [4]

Garlic-Buttered French Bread [5]

Lemon Chiffon Pie [6]

Coffee

[1] P. 124   [3] P. 225   [5] P. 68
[2] P. 167   [4] P. 250   [6] P. 430

PAN-AMERICAN BUFFET SUPPER

Chicken Broth

Empanadas Panama [1]
(Fried Pies)

Tostadas [2] with Guacamole [3]
(Fried Tortillas with Peppery Avocado Spread)

Arroz con Pollo [4]
(Rice with Chicken)

Mexican Stuffed Eggs [5]

Spanish Green Beans [6]   Broccoli

Tossed Green Salad [7]

Garlic-Buttered Bread [8]   Corn Sticks [9]

Pudín de Laranjas [10]
(Orange Pudding)

Mexican Spiced Pecans [11]
(Cinnamon-Sugared Pecans)

Eye of the Mother-in-Law [12]
(Stuffed Prunes)

Coffee

[1] P. 18	[4] P. 124	[7] P. 240	[10] P. 338
[2] P. 84	[5] P. 260	[8] P. 68	[11] P. 448
[3] P. 229	[6] P. 167	[9] P. 63	[12] P. 446

RUSSIAN DINNER

Borsch [1]
(Beet Soup)

Caucasian Shashlik [2] with Rice
(Broiled Lamb with Rice)

Buttered Peas

Zitny Chleb [3]
(Rye Bread)

Tossed Green Salad [4]

Goureff Kacha [5]
(Farina Fruit Pudding)

Coffee

[1] P. 32	[3] P. 85	[5] P. 334
[2] P. 100	[4] P. 240	

SMORGASBORD

Inlagd Sill   **Sillsallad**
(Pickled Herring)   *(Herring Salad)*[1]

Hummersallad i Mayonnaise   **Fisk Färs**
(Lobster Salad with Mayonnaise) *(Fish Mousse)*

Rökt Shinka   **Sylta**[3]   **Potatis Korf**[4]   **Rökt Medwurst**
(Baked Ham)[2] *(Pressed Veal)* *(Potato Sausage)* *(Summer Sausage)*

Kål Sallad   **Potatis Sallad**   **Röd Betor**   **Frukt Sallad**
(Cabbage Salad)[5] *(Potato Salad)*[6] *(Red Beets)* *(Fruit Salad)*[7]

Köttbullar[8]   **Potatis i Persiljesmör**   **Bruna Bönor**
(Meat Balls)   *(Potatoes with Parsley)*[9]   *(Brown Beans)*[10]

Råg Bröd   **Limpa**[11]   **Jule Kage**[12]
(Rye Bread) *(Swedish Rye Bread)* *(Christmas Bread)*

Bond Ost   **Kummin Ost**
(Cheese)   *(Cheese)*

Ostkaka[13]   **Smorbakelser i Berlinerkransar**[14]   **Frukt Soppa**
(Pudding)   *(Swedish Cookies)*   *(Fruit Soup)*[15]

Jul-öl   **Kaffe**
(Root Beer)   *(Coffee)*

[1] P. 238   [4] P. 111   [7] P. 228   [10] P. 168   [13] P. 336
[2] P. 112   [5] P. 225   [8] P. 95   [11] P. 74   [14] P. 353
[3] P. 117   [6] P. 235   [9] P. 187   [12] P. 70   [15] P. 42

Regional Menus

IOWA DINNER

Fried Chicken [1]   Mashed Potatoes [2]

Giblet Gravy

Corn on the Cob   Buttered Green Beans

Tomato Salad   French Dressing [3]

Coleslaw [4]

Parker House Rolls [5]   Jam and Jelly

Fresh Peach Ice Cream

Chocolate Cake [6]   Angel Food Cake [7]

Coffee

[1] P. 131   [3] P. 249   [5] P. 79   [7] P. 392
[2] P. 186   [4] P. 171   [6] P. 395

OLD-FASHIONED NEW ENGLAND SUPPER

(Use old glass and Early American decorations)

Codfish Balls [1]   Corned Beef Hash [2]

Boston Baked Beans [3]   Boston Brown Bread [4]

Anadama Bread [5]

Fried Potatoes

Cabbage Salad [6]

Pickled Beets [7]

Green Tomato Pickles [8]

Peach-Plum Jelly   Blackberry Jam

Baked Indian Pudding [9] with Ice Cream

Coconut Layer Cake [10]

Pumpkin Pie [11]

Coffee

[1] P. 149   [4] P. 58   [7] P. 218   [10] P. 410
[2] P. 263   [5] P. 52   [8] P. 219   [11] P. 433
[3] P. 165   [6] P. 225   [9] P. 330

PENNSYLVANIA DUTCH DINNER

Sauerbraten with Gingersnap Gravy [1]

Boofers [2]

Savory Red Cabbage [3]

Cucumbers in Vinegar

Dill Pickles   Sweet Pickles

Cinnamon Rolls [4]   Butterhorn Rolls [5]

Shoo Fly Pie [6]

Coffee

[1] P. 98	[3] P. 172	[5] P. 60
[2] P. 184	[4] P. 55	[6] P. 435

SOUTHERN DINNER

Chicken Rice Soup [1]

Roast Turkey [2] with Cornbread Stuffing [3]

Candied Yams [4]

Turkey Gravy [5]

Black-Eyed Peas [6]   Corn Custard [7]

Cranberry Jelly [8]

Avocado and Grapefruit Salad [9]

French Dressing [10]

Ambrosia [11]

Palm Beach Poinciana Cake [12]

Coffee

Texas Pralines [13]

[1] P. 34	[4] P. 191	[7] P. 175	[10] P. 249	[12] P. 402
[2] P. 137	[5] P. 138	[8] P. 218	[11] P. 322	[13] P. 450
[3] P. 140	[6] P. 180	[9] P. 225		

SOUTHERN DINNER
Plantation Style Ham Slice [1]
Fried Peaches [2]   **Rice**
Buttered Spinach
Tomato Aspic Salad with Avocado and Celery [2]
Baking Powder Biscuits [4]   **Corn Sticks** [5]
Jeff Davis Pie [6]
Coffee

[1] P. 113
[2] P. 326
[3] P. 239
[4] P. 53
[5] P. 63
[6] P. 429

Holiday and Seasonal Menus

NEW YEAR'S EVE BUFFET
Individual Baked Ham Loaves [1]
Mustard Sauce [2]
Candied Sweet Potatoes [3]
Onions Baked with Mustard Sauce [4]
Watermelon Pickles   **Celery Hearts**
Carrot Curls   **Olives**
Apple Dumplings [5]
Coffee

[1] P. 112
[2] P. 211
[3] P. 191
[4] P. 178
[5] P. 322

NEW YEAR'S EVE WATCH PARTY

Pizza [1]   Canapé Lorenzo [2]

Tomato and Anchovy Canapés [3]

Delectable Cheese Spread [4]   Potato Chips

Assorted Relishes

Hot Tomato Juice

[1] P. 77   [3] P. 13
[2] P. 6   [4] P. 9

ST. PATRICK'S DAY PARTY

Grapefruit-Mint Cocktail [1]

Mock Almonds   Parsley Crescents [2]

Fillet of Sole with Almonds [3]

O'Brien Potatoes [4]

Green Beans with Mushrooms [5]

Cloverleaf Rolls

Lime Chiffon Pie [6]

Coffee

[1] P. 22   [3] P. 146   [5] P. 166
[2] P. 48   [4] P. 187   [6] P. 431

EASTER DINNER

Shrimp Cocktail [1]

Cheese Straws [2]   Parsley Crescents [3]

Baked Ham [4]   Mustard Sauce

Creamed New Potatoes [5]

Buttered Broccoli

Sesame-Seed Rolls [6]

Jelly

Spring Salad [7]

Orange Chiffon Pie [8]

Coffee

[1] P. 26   [3] P. 48   [5] P. 184   [7] P. 237
[2] P. 16   [4] P. 112   [6] P. 78   [8] P. 432

FOURTH OF JULY DINNER

Fried Chicken [1]   Chicken Gravy [2]

New Peas in Cream   Buttered New Potatoes

Garden Radishes   Green Onions

Cucumbers in Vinegar

Parker House Rolls [3]

Angel Food Cake [4] with

Strawberry Parfait Topping [5]

Grenadine Punch [6]

[1] P. 131   [3] P. 79   [5] P. 416
[2] P. 131   [4] P. 392   [6] P. 298

THANKSGIVING DINNER

Mulled Cider [1]

Cheese Straws [2]

Roast Turkey [3]

Celery and Chestnut Stuffing [4]   Cranberry Sauce [5]

Candied Yams [6]

Lyonnaise Green Beans [7]

Fruit Salad [8]

Parker House Rolls [9]   Anadama Bread [10]

Plum Pudding [11]

Hard Sauce [12]

Coffee

Salted Nuts [13]   Mints

[1] P. 24   [4] P. 140   [7] P. 167   [10] P. 52   [12] P. 342
[2] P. 16   [5] P. 219   [8] P. 228   [11] P. 338   [13] P. 449
[3] P. 137   [6] P. 191   [9] P. 79

SPRING DINNER

Fruit Cocktail [1]

Crisp Wafers   Cheese Twists [2]

Barbecued Lamb [3] with Mint Sauce [4]

Duchess Potatoes [5]

Peas à la Française [6]

Crescents [7]   Relishes

Spring Salad [8]

Orange Almond Mousse [9]   Sugar Cookies [10]

Coffee

[1] P. 27	[3] P. 100	[5] P. 185	[7] P. 60	[9] P. 317
[2] P. 16	[4] P. 210	[6] P. 181	[8] P. 237	[10] P. 385

SUMMER DINNER

Buffet Melon Bowl [1]

Crisp Wafers   Cheese Straws [2]

Baked Ham [3]   Orange Sauce [4]

Lyonnaise Green Beans [5]   Sweet Potato Soufflé [6]

Layer Rolls [7]   Tiny Parker House Rolls [8]

Finger Rolls [9]

Crisp Green Salad   Roquefort Dressing [10]

Ann's Meringues [11] with
Vanilla Ice Cream
and
Fresh Raspberries

Coffee

[1] P. 21	[4] P. 212	[7] P. 78	[10] P. 253
[2] P. 16	[5] P. 167	[8] P. 79	[11] P. 350
[3] P. 112	[6] P. 192	[9] P. 78	

FALL DINNER

Shrimp Cocktail [1]

Crisp Crackers

Baked Chicken with Mushrooms [2]

Rice

Buttered Frozen Peas

Molded Grapefruit-Almond Salad [3]

Butterhorn Rolls [4]

Marron Bombe [5]

Almond Fingers [6]

Coffee

[1] P. 26	[3] P. 234	[5] P. 316
[2] P. 124	[4] P. 60	[6] P. 349

WINTER DINNER

Consommé à la Royale [1]

Parsley Crescents [2]   Deviled Crackers [3]

Roast Turkey [4] with Savory Stuffing [5]

Mashed Potatoes [6]   Giblet Gravy [7]

Brussels Sprouts with Chestnuts [8]

Parker House Rolls [9]   Relishes

Avocado and Grapefruit Salad [10]

French Dressing [11]

Vanilla Ice Cream   Oriental Sauce [12]

Spritz Cookies [13]

Coffee

[1] P. 35	[4] P. 137	[7] P. 139	[10] P. 225	[12] P. 344
[2] P. 48	[5] P. 140	[8] P. 170	[11] P. 249	[13] P. 384
[3] P. 47	[6] P. 186	[9] P. 79		

Special Menus

AFTER-THE-FOOTBALL-GAME

Carne con Chile [1]
Bread Sticks [2]   **Crackers**
Carrot Curls
Dill Pickles
Celery Sticks
Pumpkin Pie [3] **with Whipped Cream Topping**
Coffee

[1] P. 92
[2] P. 76
[3] P. 433

BARBECUE PICNIC

Barbecued Hamburgers on Buns [1]
Mustard   Pickles   Relish
Potato Salad [2]
Pickles   Olives
Radishes   Celery Curls
Vanilla Ice Cream
Chocolate Cake [3]
Coffee

[1] P. 90
[2] P. 235
[3] P. 395

SUNDAY MORNING BRUNCH

Chilled Pineapple Juice
Waffles [1]   **Creamed Chicken** [2]
Fried Apples
Coffee

[1] P. 84
[2] P. 132

SUNDAY MORNING COFFEES

Large Fruit Hors d'Oeuvre Plate [1]

Tiny Cinnamon Pecan Rolls [2]   Cinnamon Toast Squares [3]

Chicken Biscuit Fingers [4]

Stuffed Olives wrapped in Broiled Bacon [5]

Salted Nuts [6]

Coffee   Cocoa

[1] P. 28   [3] P. 62   [5] P. 12
[2] P. 56   [4] P. 17   [6] P. 449

Fruit Hors d'Oeuvre Plate [1]

Brioche [2]   Baba Cakes [3]

Spanish Coffee Cake Puffs [4]

Orange Bowknot Rolls [5]

Mints

Coffee

[1] P. 28   [3] P. 53   [5] P. 57
[2] P. 59   [4] P. 80

LUNCHEON MENUS

Orange Cocktail [1]

Crisp Wafers

Chicken Loaf [2]

Almond Mushroom Sauce [3]

Buttered Asparagus   Tomato Slices

Assorted Relishes

Butterhorn Rolls [4]

Vanilla Ice Cream in Meringue Shells [5] with

Fresh Strawberries

Coffee

[1] P. 24   [3] P. 203   [5] P. 350
[2] P. 127   [4] P. 60

Grapefruit-Mint Cocktail [1]

Cheese Straws [2]

Maryland Deviled Crab [3]

Parsley Buttered Potatoes [4]

Broiled Tomato Halves [5]

Poppy Seed Rolls [6]

Olives   Jelly

Hearts of Lettuce Salad   Roquefort Dressing [7]

Chocolate Chiffon Pie [8] with Whipped Cream and

Crushed Peppermint Candy

Coffee

[1] P. 22   [3] P. 152   [5] P. 196   [7] P. 253
[2] P. 16   [4] P. 187   [6] P. 78   [8] P. 422

Chicken Salad [1]

Peas à la Française [2]

Potato Chips   Ripe Olives

Hot Biscuits [3]   Jelly

Orange Almond Mousse [4]

Coffee

[1] P. 226   [3] P. 53
[2] P. 181   [4] P. 317

LUNCHEON MENUS

Cheese Soufflé [1]   Cheese Sauce [2]
Buttered Fresh Asparagus
Celery and Carrot Curls   Gherkins
Cantaloupe Ring with Melon Balls [3]
Lime-Honey Salad Dressing [4]
Rum Rolls [5]
Chocolate Ice Cream
Butterscotch Pecan Squares [6]
Coffee

[1] P. 258   [3] P. 226   [5] P. 57
[2] P. 215   [4] P. 251   [6] P. 354

Crabmeat Snug Harbor [1]
Peas à la Française [2]
Broiled Tomato Halves
Sesame-Seed Finger Rolls [3]
Grapefruit Jellied Salad [4]
Honey Salad Dressing [5]
California Cheese Cake [6]
Coffee

[1] P. 153   [3] P. 78   [5] P. 251
[2] P. 181   [4] P. 229   [6] P. 394

Essence of Tomato Soup [1]
Parmesan Cheese Sticks [2]
Breast of Chicken Supreme [3]
Brussels Sprouts with Chestnuts [4]
French Fried Cauliflower [5]
Hearts of Celery   Ripe and Green Olives
Orange Bowknot Rolls [6]
Strawberry Parfait Amour [7]
Coffee

[1] P. 37   [3] P. 125   [5] P. 174   [7] P. 320
[2] P. 48   [4] P. 170   [6] P. 57

LUNCHEON MENUS

Canadian Cheese Soup [1]
French Fried Tuna Salad Sandwich [2]
Celery Hearts   Olives   Pickles
Manhattan Ice Cream [3]
Chocolate Mint Wafers [4]
Tea

[1] P. 34   [3] P. 316
[2] P. 293   [4] P. 358

Orange Jellied Soup [1]
Cheese Straws [2]
Chicken Croquettes [3]
Almond Mushroom Sauce [4]
Hungarian Carrots [5]   Lyonnaise Green Beans [6]
Hearts of Lettuce   Green Goddess Salad Dressing [7]
Radishes   Celery Curls   Stuffed Olives
Butterhorn Rolls [8]
Lady Baltimore Cake [9]
Coffee

[1] P. 25   [4] P. 203   [7] P. 250
[2] P. 16   [5] P. 173   [8] P. 60
[3] P. 126   [6] P. 167   [9] P. 410

Southern Luncheon

Jambalayah [1]
Turnip Greens [2]   Black-Eyed Peas [3]
Coleslaw [4]
Fruit Salad [5]
Hot Baking Powder Biscuits [6]
Strawberry Jam
Crème Brûlée [7]
Almond Macaroons [8]
Coffee

[1] P. 266   [3] P. 180   [5] P. 228   [7] P. 309
[2] P. 197   [4] P. 171   [6] P. 53   [8] P. 350

a contrast to the everyday . . .

Fig Square, page 66.

the cap is "streusel topping" . . .

Coffee Ring, page 62.

Southern Luncheon

Sweetbreads and Broiled Ham [1]

Beets in Orange Sauce [2]
Green Beans with Mushrooms [3]

Coconut Twists [4]

Celery Curls   Green Olives

Fruit Salad [5]

Black Bottom Pie [6]

Coffee

[1] P. 115   [3] P. 166   [5] P. 228
[2] P. 169   [4] P. 54   [6] P. 420

INFORMAL TEAS

Tiny Hot Cinnamon Rolls [1]

Cheese Mushrooms [2]   Walnut Cheese Pastries [3]

Assorted Cookies

Candied Grapefruit Peel [4]

Tea   Lemon   Sugar

[1] P. 55   [3] P. 20
[2] P. 15   [4] P. 445

———

Assorted Sandwiches
Tiny Cream Puffs [1] with Chicken Salad [2]
Scotch Shortbread [3]   Chocolate Mint Wafers [4]

Cherry Pecan Balls [5]

Candies

Tea   Lemon   Sugar

[1] P. 308   [3] P. 384   [5] P. 356
[2] P. 226   [4] P. 358

FORMAL RECEPTIONS

Assorted Tea Sandwiches [1]

Cheese Straws [2]

Chocolate Logs [3]   Petits Fours [4]

Richmond Maids of Honor [5]

Butterkuchen [6]

Mocha Fingers [7]   Coconut Circles [8]

Lime, Orange, and Pineapple Sherbet in
Individual Fluted Cups

Salted Nuts [9]   Decorated Mints [10]

Coffee   Reception Chocolate [11]

[1] P. 284	[4] P. 377	[7] P. 375	[10] P. 446
[2] P. 16	[5] P. 380	[8] P. 360	[11] P. 299
[3] P. 396	[6] P. 354	[9] P. 449	

Tiny Cream Puffs [1] with Tuna Salad Filling

Empanadas Argentina [2]   Cheese Twists [3]

Cheese Straws [4]   Walnut Cheese Pastries [5]

English Cake Tarts [6]   Petits Fours [7]

Scotch Shortbread [8]

Orange Sugared Walnuts [9]   Toasted Almonds

Apple Crystals [10]   Glacé Apricots [11]

Pineapple Punch [12] with Lime Sherbet

Coffee   Reception Chocolate [13]

[1] P. 308	[4] P. 16	[7] P. 377	[10] P. 445	[12] P. 299
[2] P. 17	[5] P. 20	[8] P. 384	[11] P. 446	[13] P. 299
[3] P. 16	[6] P. 441	[9] P. 449		

SPORTSMAN'S DINNER

(For room decorations use duck decoys, guns, leather jackets, and other hunting paraphernalia. Use fall flowers on the table.)

Red Caps with Plumes (*Tomato Bouillon*) [1]

Turkey Talk (*Roast Turkey,* [2] *Cornbread Stuffing* [3])

Sauce for the Goose (*Mashed Potatoes,* [4] *Turkey Gravy* [5])

Green Covey (*Green Peas with Mushrooms*)

Birds of a Feather (*Relish Plate*)

Special Decoy (*Cranberry Sherbet* [6])

Hunter's Horns (*Butterhorn Rolls* [7])

Hunter's Delight (*Burnt Almond Sponge* [8])

Tally Ho (*Coffee*)

[1] P. 47
[2] P. 137
[3] P. 140
[4] P. 186
[5] P. 138
[6] P. 314
[7] P. 60
[8] P. 332

STAG DINNER

Planked Porterhouse Steak [1]

Duchess Potatoes [2]   **Buttered Peas**

Broiled Tomato Halves [3]

Celery Hearts   Green Olives

Parker House Rolls [4]

Frozen Lemon Pudding [5]

Coffee

[1] P. 96
[2] P. 185
[3] P. 196
[4] P. 79
[5] P. 334

TEEN-AGE SNACK PARTY

Popcorn   Apples
Filled Cookies [1]   Drop Doughnuts [2]
Mulled Cider [3]

[1] P. 365   [2] P. 65   [8] P. 24

TEEN-AGE SUPPER PARTY

Chicken Velvet Soup [1]
Cheese and Ham Rolls [2]   Egg Salad Sandwiches
Assorted Relishes
Gingerbread [3]   Whipped Cream
Milk

[1] P. 34   [2] P. 291   [3] P. 69

THEATRE DINNER

Cranberry-Ginger Ale Cocktail [1]
Parsley Crescents [2]   Parmesan Cheese Sticks [3]
Rolled Rib Roast of Beef [4]   Brown Sauce with Mushrooms [5]
Franconia Potatoes [6]   Broccoli with Lemon Butter [7]
Hearts of Lettuce Salad
Thousand Island Dressing [8]
Layer Rolls [9]
Apple Pie [10] à la Mode
Coffee

[1] P. 22   [3] P. 48   [5] P. 206   [7] P. 207   [9] P. 78
[3] P. 48   [4] P. 96   [6] P. 185   [8] P. 254   [10] P. 420

Special Helps

INGREDIENTS AND METHODS USED

BAKING POWDER. The combination or double-acting type of baking powder has been used in these recipes. About one-third of the leavening gas is released in the mixing, the remainder when heated. To adjust the baking powder to another type, follow the manufacturer's directions.

CREAM

CREAM. Coffee cream or light cream.

HEAVY CREAM. Cream sufficiently heavy to whip.

EGGS

SLIGHTLY BEATEN EGGS. Whole eggs beaten until whites and yolks just mix. This is the amount of beating that is best for custards and when eggs are used as coating with crumbs for deep-fat frying.

BEATEN EGGS. Whole eggs beaten until the whites and yolks are well blended. This amount of beating is best for eggs used in batters and doughs and as an emulsifier in salad dressings.

WELL-BEATEN EGGS. Whole eggs beaten until whites and yolks are well blended and become light and fluffy. This is the amount of beating necessary to give a fine texture, as for pound cake.

WELL-BEATEN EGG YOLKS. Yolks beaten until light and lemon colored. This is the amount of beating best for egg yolks used in sponge cakes.

WHITES BEATEN TO FROTHY OR FOAMY STAGE. Whites beaten until foamy. This is the stage at which to begin to add sugar.

WHITES BEATEN TO SOFT PEAK STAGE. Whites beaten until they hold a soft peak that barely stands alone when the beater is pulled out of the bowl. If egg whites are under-beaten they do not hold enough air, but if beaten too stiff the air that has been incorporated is lost when the whites are folded into other ingredients.

FATS

BUTTER. Designated for cakes, cookies, and sauces, or for flavoring vegetables where flavor is important. Margarine may be used, if desired.

FAT. Designated for frying or sautéing and may be oil, lard, hydrogenated vegetable fat, or margarine.

SHORTENING. Designated for pastry and some baked products and may be hydrogenated vegetable fat, lard, or margarine.

FLOUR

FLOUR. All-purpose flour.

CAKE FLOUR. Flour milled from soft wheat and designated for use in cakes and some cookies.

GELATIN

GELATIN. Unflavored gelatin that is softened in a cold liquid and dissolved over hot water or in a hot liquid. One envelope is equivalent to one tablespoon.

FLAVORED GELATIN. Gelatin in which both sugar and flavoring are included. It is dissolved in hot liquid.

SUGAR

SUGAR. White granulated sugar. It is used wherever sugar is specified.

BROWN SUGAR. Specified when a light brown sugar is to be used. It is packed firmly into the cup to measure.

CONFECTIONERS' SUGAR. Powdered sugar XXXX, consisting of very fine particles. It is used chiefly in meringues and uncooked frostings.

YEAST

COMPRESSED YEAST CAKES are designated in these recipes, but the dry granular yeast may be used if preferred, by following directions on package.

MEASUREMENT GUIDE
(Level Measures)

3 teaspoons	= 1 tablespoon
½ fluid ounce	= 1 tablespoon
16 tablespoons	= 1 cup
2 gills	= 1 cup
½ liquid pint	= 1 cup
8 fluid ounces	= 1 cup
1 liquid pint	= 2 cups
16 fluid ounces	= 2 cups

2 cups = 1 lb

OVEN TEMPERATURE GUIDE*

Oven	Degrees F.
Very slow	250 to 275
Slow	300 to 325
Moderate	350 to 375
Hot	400 to 425
Very hot	450 to 475
Extremely hot	500 to 525

* From "Handbook of Food Preparation," American Home Economics Association, 1950.

CUP MEASURES
(Approximate)

1 cup granulated sugar	= ½ pound
1 cup butter	= ½ pound
1 cup lard	= ½ pound
1 cup flour	= ¼ pound
1 cup rice	= ½ pound
1 cup corn meal	= 5 ounces
1 cup raisins (stemmed)	= 6 ounces
1 cup bread crumbs (stale)	= 2 ounces
1 cup chopped meat	= ½ pound

TEMPERATURES AND TESTS USED FOR CANDIES AND FROSTINGS*

Test in Degrees F.	Range in Degrees F.	Description of Test
Soft Ball—238	234 to 240	Syrup, when dropped into very cold water, forms a soft ball which flattens on removal
Firm Ball—246	244 to 248	Syrup, when dropped into very cold water, forms a firm ball which does not flatten on removal
Hard Ball—260	250 to 266	Syrup, when dropped into very cold water, forms a ball which is hard enough to hold its shape, yet remain plastic
Soft Crack—280	270 to 290	Syrup, when dropped into very cold water, separates into threads which are hard but not brittle
Hard Crack—305	300 to 310	Syrup, when dropped into very cold water, separates into threads which are hard and brittle

* From "Handbook of Food Preparation," American Home Economics Association, 1950.

TEMPERATURE GUIDE FOR DEEP-FAT FRYING*

Degrees F. on Frying Thermometer	Seconds to Brown 1" Cube Day-Old Bread	Food
360 to 375	50 to 60	Doughnuts; fritters; shellfish coated with batter or egg-and-crumbs
375 to 385	30 to 40	Croquettes; fish balls; other cooked mixtures
385 to 395	20 to 30	French fried potatoes, onions, and other vegetables; potato chips

* From "Handbook of Food Preparation," American Home Economics Association, 1950.

AMOUNTS TO ORDER FOR A GROUP

	FOR 1 PERSON	FOR 24 PERSONS
Beans, baked	½ cup	1 No. 10 can
Beverages		
Cocoa	1 cup	1½ gallons
Coffee, ground		½ to ¾ pound
Coffee, liquid	1 cup	1½ gallons
Cream, for coffee	2 tablespoons	1 pint
Punch	1 sherbet cup	1 to 1½ gallons
Tea, iced	1 glass	1½ gallons
Butter	⅓ ounce	½ pound
Candies, small	1 teaspoon	½ to ¾ pound
Mints	2	1 pound (50 to 60 per pound)
Cocktail, fruit and vegetable, diced	⅓ cup	2 quarts
Cream, heavy, for topping desserts	2 tablespoons	1 pint
Fish	¼ pound	6 pounds
Fruit, canned	½ cup	1 No. 10 can
Grapefruit, size 64	Depends on use	6 to 8 for salad
Ice cream		
Brick	1 slice	4 quarts (6 per quart)
Bulk	⅙ quart	4 quarts
Jelly	2 tablespoons	3 8-ounce glasses
Meat and Poultry		
Bacon	2 slices	2 to 2½ pounds
Beef, ground	¼ to ⅓ pound	6 to 8 pounds
Beef, veal, or pork, for roast	⅓ to ½ pound	9 to 12 pounds
Chicken, creamed	⅓ pound	8 to 10 pounds
Chicken, fricasseed	½ pound	12 pounds
Chicken, roasted	½ to ¾ pound	12 to 18 pounds
Ham, precooked	¼ pound	8 to 10 pounds
Ham, tenderized	⅓ pound	10 to 12 pounds
Swiss steak	¼ to ⅓ pound	6 to 8 pounds
Turkey, roasted	¾ to 1 pound	18 to 24 pounds

Nuts, salted ....1 teaspoon		½ to ¾ pound
Potatoes		
Cream sauce ....2 to 3 tablespoons		3 to 4 cups
Creamed ....¼ pound		6 pounds
Mashed ....⅓ pound		7 to 8 pounds
Salad ....¼ pound		6 pounds
Scalloped ....¼ pound		6 pounds
Puddings ....½ cup		3 quarts
Rolls ....1½ to 2		3 to 4 dozen
Salads		
Bulk ....½ cup		3 quarts (8 per quart)
Lettuce		
(salad cup) ...1 lettuce cup		2 to 3 heads
Lettuce, wedges ....⅙ to ¼ head		4 to 6 heads
Salad Dressing		
French ....1 tablespoon		1½ cups (16 per cup)
Mayonnaise ....1 rounded tablespoon		2 cups (12 per cup)
Soup ....¾ to 1 cup		1 to 1½ gallons
Strawberries, for		
sundae, crushed ..2 tablespoons		1½ to 2 quarts (1 quart crushed averages about 2 cups)
Sugar, loaf ....2 cubes		½ pound
Vegetables, canned ..½ cup		1 No. 10 can
Vegetables, fresh		
Asparagus ....⅓ to ½ pound		8 to 12 pounds
Beans, green ....⅙ to ¼ pound		4 to 6 pounds
Beets ....¼ to ⅓ pound		6 to 8 pounds
Broccoli ....⅓ to ½ pound		6 to 8 pounds
Brussels sprouts ....⅙ to ¼ pound		4 to 6 pounds
Cabbage ....⅙ to ¼ pound		4 to 6 pounds
Carrots ....¼ pound		6 pounds or 6 to 8 bunches
Cauliflower ....⅙ to ¼ head		4 to 6 heads
Parsnips ....¼ pound		6 pounds
Spinach ....¼ to ⅓ pound		6 to 8 pounds
Tomatoes, sliced ...¼ pound		6 pounds
Vegetables, frozen ...½ cup		2 40-ounce packages

PRONUNCIATIONS AND DEFINITIONS

A

À la (ah-lah) — After the style of; in the fashion of. (French)

À la carte (ah-lah-cart') — Food prepared to order; each dish priced separately. (French)

À la Créole (ah-lah-kray-ohl') — In the manner of Louisiana; usually with onions and tomatoes. (French)

À la king (ah-lah-king') — Cooked diced chicken in a cream sauce with mushrooms, pimento, and green pepper added. (French)

À la mode (ah-lah-mohd') — 1. With beef, designating a pot roast larded and braised, and simmered with vegetables in a sauce. 2. With desserts, topped with ice cream. (French)

À la Newburg (ah-lah-noo'-burg) — With sauce of wine, egg yolks, butter, and cream. (French)

Allemande, sauce (ahl-mahnd') — Velouté sauce with cream, yolk of egg, and lemon juice added. (French)

Anchovy (an-choh'-vi; an'choh-vi) — Small fish of the herring family, salted or pickled, rolled or flat. Used as an appetizer.

Anise (an'is) — A plant which produces aniseed. Licorice-flavored seeds used for flavoring salads and confections.

Antipasto (ahn-tee-pahs'toe) — 1. Mixture of smoked or pickled fish, mushrooms, and pimentos. 2. Name for hors d'oeuvre. (Italian)

Arroz (arr-roz') — Rice. (Spanish)

Arroz con Pollo (arr-roz' kon poy'ah) — A dish of chicken, pimentos, saffron-yellow rice. (Spanish)

Aspic (ass'-pik) — A clear savory meat or poultry jelly in which meat, fish, or vegetables are set. (French)

Au gratin (oh grah-tan') — Browned covering of bread crumbs often mixed with butter or cheese. (French)

Au jus (oh-zhu') — Served with natural juices or gravy. (French)

Avocado (ah-vo-kah'doh) — The pulpy green or purple edible pear-shape fruit of certain tropical American trees. Has soft yellow meat and large pit. Used in salads.

B

Baba (bah-bah') — A light cake made with yeast, often flavored with rum, fruit or fruit juices. (French)

Barszcz (barsh) — A Polish soup containing sieved vegetables, with beets in predominance.

Beans Fugarth (foo-garth') — Green beans to which freshly grated coconut has been added. A favorite method of vegetable preparation in India.

Béarnaise, sauce (bay-ar-nayz') — A yellow sauce of egg yolks, vinegar, butter, onion, and spices. (French)

Béchamel, sauce (bay-sha-mel') — A white sauce of butter, flour, chicken stock, cream, and mushrooms. (French)

Biscuit tortoni (bee-skwee-tor-toh'-ni) — Frozen cream and crumb dessert. (Italian)

Bisque (bisk) — 1. A rich soup of shellfish or game; also a rich cream soup thickened into a purée, as of tomato. 2. A rich ice cream containing nuts or macaroons. (French)

Boeuf (buff) — Beef. (French)

Bombe (bawm) — A frozen dessert of one or more ice cream mixtures in a bomb-shaped mold. (French)

Bordelaise, sauce (bawr-d'layz') — A brown sauce of meat stock, butter, onion, carrot, bay leaf, and other seasonings. (French)

Borsch (borsh) — A Russian soup containing a variety of vegetables, beets in predominance. Usually served with thick sour cream. (Russian)

Bouillabaisse (bou-yah-bes') — Five or six varieties of fish in a fish stew or chowder. Popular in the south of France and in New Orleans. (French)

Bouillon (boo-ee-yon) — Clear beef soup. (French)

Bouquet-Garni (boo-kay-garnee') — A tied bunch of herbs used in soups or sauces. (French)

Bourgeoise, à la (boor-jwahz') — Family style. (French)

Braise (brayz) — To brown meat or vegetables in a little fat, then cook, covered, in a small amount of liquid. (French)

Brioche (bree-ohsh') — A light, feathery yeast roll, popular in France as a breakfast roll. (French)

Brochette, à la (bro-shet') — Broiled on a skewer. (French)

Brûlé (bru-lay') — A molded pudding of cream, egg yolks, and flavoring.

C

Chicory (chik'-aw-ri) — A salad green of the endive family. The leaves used for a salad; the roots roasted, ground, and added as an adulterant to coffee.

Chiffonade (shee'-fahn-ahd) — With finely shredded vegetables. French dressing with onions, egg, parsley, and pimento.

Chiles Rellenos (chee'-lais-ray-yay'-nos) — Peeled green peppers stuffed with a meat and raisin mixture; dipped in batter and fried in deep fat. (Spanish)

Chive (chyv) — A perennial plant related to the onion. Its slender leaves are finely chopped and used for flavoring.

Chutney (chut'ni) — A relish usually of fruits, such as mango, pineapple, or apple with spices, vinegar, and sugar.

Compote (kom'-poht) — Fruit stewed in syrup. (French)

Consommé (kon-so-may') — Clear broth made from white stock. (French)

Crème (kraim) — Cream. (French)

Cuisine (kwee-zeen') — Art of cookery. (French)

D

Daube (dohb) — A stew. (French)

Demi-tasse (deh-mee-tahss') — A small cup of black coffee, literally half a cup. (French)

Drawn butter. Melted butter.

Drawn butter sauce. Melted butter, flour, seasoning, and hot water. Used as a sauce for fish or vegetables.

Duchess potatoes. Mashed potatoes with eggs added, forced through a pastry tube to make rosettes, potato borders for planks, etc.

E

Éclair (ay-klair') — A light, finger-shaped pastry shell filled with whipped cream or custard and brushed with a chocolate glaze. (French)

Enchilada (en-chee-lah'-dah) — Tortillas dipped in hot fat, then in a hot sauce, then sprinkled with onion, lettuce, and cheese. Served rolled up, topped with sauce, or made into stacks of three with filling between and topped with a fried egg. (Mexican)

Escarole (es-ka-rohl') — The broad-leaved type of endive used for salad.

Escoffier (ays'-koh-fee-ay) — Famous French chef.

Espagnole, sauce (es-pah-nyohl') — A brown sauce. (French)

F

Farina (fa-ree'-na) — A fine meal made from cereal grains. Used for puddings and breakfast cereal.

Filet mignon (fee-lay'mi-nyon') — Tenderloin of beef. (French)

Fillet (fee-lay') — A strip of lean meat or fish without bone. (French)

Flannel cake. A thin, tender griddle cake.

Fondue (fahn-du') — A cheese dish. (French)

Francaise, à la (frahn-sayz') — In the French manner. (French)

Franconia potatoes. Raw potatoes pared and browned with a roast.

Frappé (fra-pay') — A fruit juice mixture frozen to a mush.

French ice cream. A rich dessert of frozen cream and cooked custard.

Frenched green beans. Beans cut in two strips lengthwise, then each strip cut in two narrow strips.

Frijoles (free-hol'ayz) — Mexican beans cooked with fat and seasoning. (Mexican)

Frijoles refritos (re-free'tos) — Refried kidney beans. (Mexican)

G

Gâteau (gah'toh) — Cake. (French)

Gherkin (gir'kin) — A small, spiny fruit of the cucumber family used as a pickle.

Glacé (glah-say') — Cooked in, or coated with, a thin sugar syrup as with fruits or nuts; iced, frozen. (French)

Gorgonzola (gor'-gon-zo'la) — A kind of Italian pressed milk cheese resembling Roquefort. (Italian)

Grenadine (gren'a-deen) — Pomegranate syrup used for beverages.

Gruyère (gru-yair') — Swiss type of cheese made in France and Switzerland. (French)

Guava (gwah'va) — A tropical fruit, apple- or pear-shaped. Used for making jelly, jam, and guava paste.
Gumbo (soup) — Thick chicken soup containing okra, onion, green peppers, and tomatoes.

H

Haricots (hah-ree-coh') — String beans. (French)
Hollandaise, sauce (hol'ahn-dayz) — A yellow sauce of butter, vinegar or lemon juice, egg yolks, and seasonings. (French)
Hors d'oeuvre (ohr-doe'vr) — Small relishes or appetizers served before a meal or as the first course of a meal. (French)

I

Italienne, sauce à l' (ee-tah-lee-en') — A rich brown sauce with mushrooms, truffles, ham, tomatoes, and seasoning. (French)

J

Jambon (sham-bohn') — Ham. (French)
Jeelobi (jĕ-lay'-bee) —A deep-fat fried sweet of India.
Julienne (shu-lee-en') — Referring to vegetables cut in matchlike strips. (French)

K

Knäckebröd (khnah-kah-broed) — Whole rye, flat, hard, Scandinavian bread.
Kolacky (ko-lahch'-kee) — Bohemian fruit-filled buns.
Kuchen (koo-ken) — A cake, often coffee cake. (German)
Kulkuls (kul-kuls) — A deep-fat fried Christmas sweet of India.

L

Lard. To insert strips of salt pork into lean meat to add flavor.
Leek. A small, onion-like plant, used for seasoning.
Liaison (lee-ay-zawn') — Mixture of egg and cream used for thickening sauces and soups. (French)
Lyonnaise (lee'-oh-nayz) — Sautéed with slices of onion. (French)

M

Macédoine (mah-say-dwan') — Different fruits or vegetables, cut in uniform pieces. (French)
Maître d'Hôtel, sauce à la (mai-tre-doh-tel') —A yellow sauce of butter, lemon juice, parsley, salt, and pepper. (French)

Mango (mang-goh) — A small sweet melon or pickle.
Maraschino cherries (mar-a-skee'-noh) — Royal Anne cherries preserved in maraschino syrup.
Marinade (mah-ree-nahd') — Mixture of vinegar, wine, oil, and herbs in which meat or fish is soaked to make it tender and full of flavor. (French)
Marinate. To let stand in the marinade.
Marjoram (mahr'-joh-ram) — Flavoring and seasoning herb.
Marron (mah'rohn) — A large sweet chestnut.
Marzipan (mahr'zi-pan) — Almond and sugar-paste confection in small fruit and vegetable shapes.
Meunière, à la (meh-nyair') — Fish dipped in flour, sautéed in butter, served with butter sauce and lemon, sprinkled with parsley. (French)
Minestrone (mee-ne-stroh'nay) — A soup of vegetables and herbs in a meat broth. (Italian)
Mocha (moh'ka) — Flavor of coffee or coffee and chocolate.
Mornay, sauce (mohr-nay') — Sauce of thick cream, eggs, cheese, and seasoning. (French)
Mousse (Mooss) — Frozen dessert of whipped cream, flavoring, and sweetening; frozen without stirring. (French)
Mousseline, sauce (moo-se-leen') — Sauce similar to Hollandaise, with heavy cream. (French)
Mulligatawny (mul-i-ga-taw'ni) —An East Indian curry soup with chicken and spices.

N

Neopolitan ice cream. Ice cream made of different colors and flavors, frozen in layers.
Newburg sauce. A yellow sauce of eggs, cream, and sherry, for fish or shellfish.

O

Okra (oh'kra) — A vegetable pod used in soups, or as a vegetable.
Orégano (oh-ray'-gah-noh) —A Mediterranean herb. (Spanish)

P

Pain (pan) — Bread. (French)
Panocha (pah-noh'chah) — A candy made of brown sugar, milk, butter, and nuts. (Mexican)

Paprika (pa-pree′ka) — The dried ground fruit of a mild red pepper, used for color and flavor.

Parboil. To boil until partly cooked.

Parfait (pahr-fay′) — A rich dessert of syrup, egg, or whipped cream, and flavoring; frozen without stirring. Also refers to ice cream in a parfait glass. (French)

Parmesan (par-me-zan′) — A hard, dry Italian cheese made from skim milk. (Italian)

Pâté (pah-tay′) — Pie, pastry, or paste. (French)

Pâté de foie gras (pah-tay-d′fwah grah′) — A paste of fat goose livers, used to make canapés. (French)

Pêche (pesh) — A peach. (French)

Peppercorn. A berry of the black pepper plant.

Petite marmite (pe-teet-mahr-meet′) — A meat broth with meat and vegetables. (French)

Petits fours (pe-tee-foor′) — Small cakes, frosted and decorated. (French)

Pièce de résistance (pee-es de resee-stahns′) — The main course or dish of the meal. (French)

Pilaf (pih-lahf′) — An Oriental dish of rice boiled with meat, fowl, or fish and spices.

Piquante, sauce (pee-kahnt′) — Sharp, highly seasoned sauce. (French)

Pistachio (pis-tash′i-oh) — The edible kernel from the nut of the pistachio tree.

Pizza (peet′-sa) — A pastry of raised dough covered with a tomato and cheese sauce, garnished with bits of anchovy. (Italian)

Polenta. A thick corn-meal mush formed into cakes. (Italian)

Pooris (poor-ees) — Deep-fat fried flat cakes made of wheat flour, without any leavening. (India)

Pot-au-feu (poh-toh-fu′) — A dish of broth, meat, and vegetables boiled together. (French)

Praline (prah′-leen) — A flat cake of sugar candy with pecans. (French)

Purée (pu-ray′) — Cooked, sieved fruits or vegetables. (French)

Q

Quahog (kwah′-hawg) — Atlantic Coast round clam.

R

Ravioli (rah-vee-oh′-lee) — A mixture of chopped meat, cheese, and spinach cooked in small pieces of noodle dough and served with a seasoned sauce. (Italian)

Romaine. A long, narrow, crisp-leaved lettuce.

Roulade (roo-lahd′) — A thin slice of meat rolled around minced meat and cooked. (French)

Roux (roo) — Equal parts of butter and flour used for thickening sauces and soups. (French)

S

Saffron. Deep orange, dried stigmas of the saffron plant used to color breads, cakes, or other food.

Sally Lunn. Quick bread of eggs, milk, butter, and sugar, used as a tea cake. These cakes are named for Sally Lunn, a woman of Bath, England, who originally made them and sold them in the streets.

Saratoga chips. Potato chips.

Sauerbraten (sour′brah-ten) — A German pot roast of beef marinated in spiced vinegar, cooked and served with a gingersnap gravy. (German)

Sauté (soh-tay′) — Cooked quickly in a small amount of fat. (French)

Schnitz (snitz) — Dried apples. (German)

Scone. Scotch quick bread containing currants.

Shallot (sha-lot′) — A type of onion used for seasoning. (French)

Shashlik Caucasian. Cubes of lamb marinated and broiled on a skewer. (Russian)

Shoyu or soy sauce. A Japanese or Chinese liquid made from fermented soy beans.

Shrikand (shree′-kand) — A rich creamy dessert made of sour cream curd to which sugar and cardamom have been added. (India)

Smörgåsbord (smur-gahs-bohrd′) — Tidbits or appetizers usually arranged on a long table. (Swedish)

Soubise (soo′bees) — A thick onion sauce. (French)

Soufflé (soo-flay′) — A fluffy baked dish into which beaten egg whites are folded; sweet or savory. (French)

Soufflé potatoes. Potato slices puffed up like little pillows. (French)

Spoon bread. A type of southern corn bread baked in a casserole and served with a spoon.

Spumoni (spoo-moh'-nee) — Fancy Italian ice cream. (Italian)

Strudel (stroo'dl) — Pastry of paper-thin dough with fruit rolled inside. (German)

T

Tabasco (tah-bas'-koh) — Red pepper sauce. (Mexican)

Table d'Hôte (tabl-doht') — Fixed-price meal. (French)

Tacos (tah'cos) — Tortillas filled with meat, lettuce, onion, and hot sauce. The Mexican sandwich.

Tamale (ta-mah'lee) — Mexican dish of minced meat and corn meal, highly seasoned; wrapped in corn husks and steamed. American version is baked in a casserole.

Tarragon. An herb used to flavor vinegar.

Tartare sauce (tar'-tar) —Mayonnaise to which chopped green onions, chives, and sour pickles are added.

Tarte (tart) — Small pie or pastry. (French)

Thyme (time) — A pungent aromatic herb used in seasoning and soup.

Timbale (tim'bal) — A mixture of eggs, meat, or vegetables cooked in a cup-shaped mold; or a shell or case of fried batter in which creamy desserts are served. (French)

Tortilla (tohr-tee'yah) — A thin un-leavened pancake prepared from coarse corn meal and baked on a hot sheet or slab of stone. (Mexican)

Trifle (try'fl) — A dessert of sponge cake soaked in fruit juice with wine; covered with almonds, jam, custard, and whipped cream. (English)

Truffle (truf'l) — Fungus-like mushrooms grown underground. Used as a seasoning and garnish.

V

Velouté, sauce (ve-loo-tay') —A white sauce made with veal or chicken stock. (French)

Vermicelli (vr-mi-sel'i) — A wheat paste formed into long slender threads thinner than spaghetti. (Italian)

Vol-au-vent (vol-loh-vahn') — Puffed pastry filled with delicately flavored meat or chicken. (French)

W

Wiener Schnitzel (wee'ner-shnit-sel) Breaded veal cutlet served with slice of lemon. (German)

Won ton. Stuffed dumplings cooked in chicken broth. (Chinese)

Z

Zucchini (zoo-kee'nee) —Italian summer squash; long, green, and slender.

Zwieback (tsvee'-bahk) — Toast made from specially baked bread; twice-toasted. (German)

Index

Index

A

The Author

Lenore Sullivan is a connoisseur of fine foods. She thoroughly enjoys the art of cookery, and has taken great pleasure in teaching the secrets of successful cooking to home economics students. As Professor of Institution Management at Iowa State College, she has had the opportunity of discovering and testing thousands of recipes. To this collection she has added many regional and national favorites gathered in her travels through the United States, Mexico, Hawaii, and Europe.

Prior to joining the Home Economics staff at Iowa State College, Miss Sullivan taught at Montana State College and at the University of Washington. She received her bachelor of science degree at Montana State College, served her dietetic internship at the Mayo Clinic, Rochester, Minnesota, and received her master of science degree at Iowa State College.

Miss Sullivan is also the author of the *Quantity Recipe File,* which contains time-tested favorites standardized to serve fifty. Among her other activities are membership in the American Dietetic Association, American Home Economics Association, Phi Upsilon Omicron, and the American Association of University Women.

Composed in Linotype Baskerville and Century Bold by The Iowa State College Press.

Headings in Ludlow Coronet.

Engravings by Tru-Art Engravers, Cedar Rapids, Iowa.

Paper stock: 60-pound Warren's Olde Style Antique.

Cover cloth: Bancroft's Arrestox No. 4550.